D1475044

Gift of the Estate of
Robert (1938-2013)
and Gay Zieger (1938-2013)
October 2013

Heritage University Library
3240 Fort Road
Toppenish, WA 98948

THE WORKING CLASS IN AMERICAN HISTORY

Editorial Advisors

David Brody
Alice Kessler-Harris
David Montgomery
Sean Wilentz

A list of books in the series appears at the end of this volume.

Workers, Managers,
and Welfare Capitalism

Workers, Managers, and Welfare Capitalism

The Shoeworkers and Tanners of Endicott Johnson, 1890–1950

GERALD ZAHAVI

University of Illinois Press

URBANA AND CHICAGO

*Publication of this work was supported in part by grants
from the Andrew W. Mellon Foundation
and the State University of New York at Albany.*

© 1988 by the Board of Trustees of the University of Illinois
Manufactured in the United States of America
C 5 4 3 2 1

Material that appeared earlier in Gerald Zahavi, "Negotiated Loyalty:
Welfare Capitalism and the Shoeworkers of Endicott Johnson, 1920–
1940," *Journal of American History* 71 (Dec. 1983): 602–20, is used by
permission of the Organization of American Historians.

This book is printed on acid-free paper.

Library of Congress Cataloging-in-Publication Data

Zahavi, Gerald, 1951–
    Workers, managers, and welfare capitalism.

    (The Working class in American history)
    Bibliography: p.
    Includes index.
    1. Endicott Johnson (Firm)—Personnel management—
History.   2. Endicott Johnson (Firm)—Employees—
History.   3. Welfare work in industry—United States—
History—Case studies.   4. Paternalism—United States—
History—Case studies.   I. Title.   II. Series.
HD9787.U6E654   1988   331.2′0475′0973   87-6035
ISBN 0-252-01444-8 (alk. paper)

Contents

Introduction

Letters of appreciation poured into the office of George F. Johnson, newly elected president of the Endicott Johnson Corporation, after the first distribution of bonus checks had been received by the workers in February 1920. A note from the Fire Prevention Department included this vow: "As to the future, may we pledge to you, OUR HEARTY SUPPORT, and BEST EFFORTS, in endeavoring to extend the GOOD WILL feeling to our co-workers, and in living up to the SQUARE DEAL POLICY in ALL OUR LABORS."[1] From the Upper Leather Basement of the New Scout Factory came the following missive:

> Resolved: We the undersigned workers of the Upper Leather Basement . . . wish to extend our thanks to our friend, fellow worker and benefactor of the community, Geo. F. Johnson, for his kindness and our share of the surplus earnings.
>
> Resolved: That we show our appreciation by trying each day to improve our work by being loyal to the Square Deal policy.[2]

From other factories came similar resolutions, as well as long petitions thanking Johnson for his generosity and congratulating him upon his election to the presidency of the firm. But it was a note from the oldest factory of the Endicott Johnson complex that suggested most poignantly the broader implications of Johnson's benevolence. A committee of workers from the treeing room of the old Pioneer Factory, where Johnson had begun his career as a foreman many years earlier, wrote the following:

> The men longest in your employ in the department, that served under your foremanship, inform us, of a later day, that the policies you are exemplifying on a larger scale, were encouraged and exemplified then. We accept them as a heritage that has been handed down to us, and shall strive to perpetuate them in the future as a token of our regards for the Corporation with which we are proud to be associated, and for our mutual interest.[3]

Indeed, with the introduction of the profit-sharing plan, the new president of the shoe manufacturing firm had put into place the major elements of a corporate welfare system. Building on paternalistic practices that dated back to the 1890s, the corporation had established an extensive medical department that would soon furnish surgical, dental, and a wide variety of relief services. It had initiated recreational and athletic programs, begun the construction of attractive, low-cost homes for sale to its employees, and provided countless other services for its workers and for the surrounding communities of Endicott, Johnson City, and Binghamton, New York. But more important, as the popular press and numerous highly impressed visitors continually pointed out, Johnson and his fellow corporate officers had created a unique solidarity between workers and managers, a solidarity that was perpetuated by good works, intense propaganda, and a powerful communal ideology that was at once both tolerant and paternalistic. The origins, development, limits, and ultimate demise of that solidarity is the subject of this work.

In many ways the major argument of this book parallels themes developed in recent studies of chattel slavery, most particularly in the work of Eugene D. Genovese. Although equating twentieth-century industrial paternalism with nineteenth-century plantation paternalism would be a gross distortion of reality, as Genovese was careful to point out, it is nonetheless apparent to me that certain meaningful similarities do exist. In particular, I have come to see in the two regimes a common dialectical struggle for control over the definition of paternalistic obligations and rights. The contradictions that Genovese recognized in southern paternalism were also present in industrial paternalism. As a mode of labor control, paternalism in general undermined the "solidarity of the oppressed by linking them as individuals to their oppressors." But in both the context of slavery and industrial capitalism, paternalism also represented a "moral victory" of the exploited. Just as slaves found "an opportunity to translate paternalism into a doctrine different from that understood by their masters and to forge it into a weapon of resistance," so, too, were Endicott Johnson workers able to transfigure the paternalistic system of labor control within which they operated.[4]

In focusing on the workers and managers of Endicott Johnson, I have sought to broaden traditional conceptions of the American working class and notions of labor power and struggle. That worker struggle occurs both within and without the umbrella of formal labor organizations is one of the themes of this study; that it occurs in the most unlikely setting of a liberal and relatively benevolent industrial order is another. The latter point might make even the most sanguine celebrators of America's triumph over class and class consciousness take pause to reconsider their assumptions.

This study is neither pure labor history nor pure business history, but a hybrid. It reflects my strong belief that there cannot be a history of labor without a history of capital. Thus, I have focused on workers *and* managers, viewing the entity of the industrial firm as an arena of struggle in which the two groups shape the terms of their coexistence. Since Endicott Johnson's brand of corporate paternalism encompassed community paternalism, and had an extensive community impact, I was naturally tempted to cast a wide net, placing the company in the broad social and cultural context of a community study. But it was within the realm of work that welfare capitalism sought most avidly to achieve its ends, and it was within that realm that the struggle for control was most explicitly expressed, with all its contradictions and ironies. Thus, I have chosen to keep the shop floor at center stage. The wider field of Endicott Johnson's paternalistic policies is not neglected, but it is relegated to the background and introduced where it becomes most relevant to the central issues I treat.

Because, as countless historians have pointed out, workers rarely left as extensive a record of their feelings and thoughts as managers, oral history plays a large part in this study. Whatever objections one might make to the reliability of oral history, and historians have offered many, the clear and obvious logic of tapping such a rich source on working people's consciousness and behavior seems to me hardly contestable. Luckily, both corporate and union records existed to at least partly corroborate (as well as stimulate) the recollections of interviewees. Where written records did not exist, I tried to cross-check particular oral accounts with those of other workers who witnessed or participated in common events. The utilization of both oral and written sources resulted in an enrichment of one by the other and allowed me to trace the relationship between managers and workers through each group's perspective. I should emphasize that oral history was "mined" for both its objective and subjective content. Not only did workers provide me with numerous vivid descriptions of shop floor behavior, strikes, committee actions, and so on, but the tone and language of their recollections, as well as what they remembered, misremembered, or forgot, also offered me important insights into the psychological legacy of corporate paternalism. How else, except through oral history, can such information be obtained?

This study owes its existence not merely to my own efforts but also to the many institutions and individuals who offered me material, psychological, and editorial assistance. Syracuse University, the Lincoln Educational Foundation, and the Snow Foundation provided me with greatly needed and much appreciated financial support. To my wife, Deborah D. Maxwell, I owe an immense debt. Her assistance on many of the interviews cited within and in editing numerous versions of my chapters has been invaluable. I am especially grateful that she became as enthusiastic about this project as I was. My thanks also go out to Jared Namenson, an old and dear friend, who took the time to read and edit early drafts of this work. David Brody and Melvyn Dubofsky offered valuable advice that has considerably improved the manuscript. Aaron Appelstein, of the University of Illinois Press, helped purge it of several minor and major errors. Three former teachers, David H. Bennett, Sally Gregory Kohlstedt, and William C. Stinchcombe, were especially helpful in nurturing this study in its original form. Bill Stinchcombe continued to offer his much-valued advice well beyond the dissertation stage of my work. To the other faculty members and numerous Syracuse University graduate students who took the time to read and comment on various chapters, I would also like to express my thanks. Whatever chaff remains in the finished work, of course, is my responsibility.

Individuals from Binghamton and environs have also provided me with a great deal of aid. First and foremost on this list are the dozens of former Endicott Johnson workers who graciously welcomed me into their homes and offered me glimpses into their past working lives. Nancy Grey Osterud and David Nielson, both formerly of the State University of New York at Binghamton, shared with me some of the fruit of their research, including oral interviews, and pointed me in the direction of important sources. To them I am particularly grateful.

Several institutions and individuals have helped me in yet other ways. The State University of New York at Albany, and my new colleagues there, provided me with an ideal environment in which to complete the revision of my manuscript. Ross McGuire, former head of the Broome County Historical Society in Binghamton, greeted me with open arms and made available to me the resources of the society. Michele Morrisson was equally generous with the interviews collected by the Broome County Immigration History Project. Professor Luciano Iorizzo of the State University of New York at Oswego loaned me over thirty-five linear feet of Endicott Johnson employee files that he had salvaged from the company in the late 1960s. He later donated the collection to the George Arents Research Library, where they now reside and complement other corporation records.

To the staff of Bird Library and the George Arents Research Library, of Syracuse University, with whom I shared my labors for more than three years, I would like to pass along special words of praise. It has been a real pleasure to work with such dedicated and responsive professionals; I hope they realize how much they have been and are appreciated. I also want to thank the staff of the following libraries for their help: Baker Library, Harvard Graduate School of Business Administration, Boston; Goldfarb Library, Brandeis University; State Historical Society of Wisconsin Library; Binghamton Public Library; Your Home Library, Johnson City; George F. Johnson Memorial Library, Endicott; New York Public Library; Broome County Historian's Library, Binghamton; New York State Library, Albany; S.U.N.Y. at Albany Library; United States Department of Labor Library; Labor-Management Documentation Center, New York State School of Industrial and Labor Relations, Cornell University.

Finally, to my father, Jakob, who did not live to see the product of my labors, and my mother, Judith, I dedicate this book.

NOTES

1. E-J Fire Prevention Dept. to George F. Johnson, Mar. 1, 1920, "Employee Correspondence" folder, box 18, George F. Johnson Papers, George Arents Research Library for Special Collections, Syracuse University, Syracuse, N.Y.
2. Workers Committee, Upper Leather Basement of the New Scout Factory to George F. Johnson, Mar. 1, 1920, "Employee Correspondence" folder, box 18, George F. Johnson Papers.
3. Corliss Ave. [Factory] Treeing Department to George F. Johnson, Mar. 2, 1920, "Employee Correspondence" folder, box 18, George F. Johnson Papers.
4. Eugene D. Genovese, *Roll, Jordan, Roll: The World the Slaves Made* (New York, 1974), 6–7, 689n.

1

The Emergence
of Corporate Paternalism

It is manifest that relations between labor and capital are seriously
strained. Even when these relations are not marked by an occasional
outbreak, there is still a sort of passive antagonism between the employer
and the employe; the force that operates upon them mutually is a re-
pellent one, and this is due in great measure to the fact that conditions
have conspired to array their respective sympathies in opposite sides of
the great questions that concern them individually and unitedly. This is
particularly noticeable in the case of corporations and their employes.[1]

In such terms the editor of a local Binghamton newspaper summarized the
status of labor-management relations in the 1890s. The rapid rise of a huge
and impersonal industrial order in the late nineteenth and early twentieth
centuries and the often violent reactions that it engendered had begun to
challenge Americans' facile adherence to laissez-faire doctrines. Social mobility ideologies, which replaced the traditional Jeffersonian ideals of land,
independence, and the free yeoman farmer, strained against the sour realities
of late nineteenth-century capitalism.[2] Increasingly, the Sumnerian version of
capitalism practiced by many industrialists came to be questioned by a growing number of social critics, theologians, and enlightened businessmen who
feared the destruction of America's social fabric.

This was not the first time that custodians of social morality had questioned
a capitalism devoid of social responsibility. Nor was it the first time that
business expediency, class anxieties, and social control combined to produce
industrial paternalism. From the 1790s, when Samuel Slater first established
his mill in Pawtucket, Rhode Island, American industrialists had adopted
various paternalistic schemes to make their mills and factories more palatable
to both hesitant laborers and social critics. Hence, Samuel Slater operated a
Sunday school and hired a teacher in order to recruit young workers to his
Rhode Island mill. The Merrimack Manufacturing Company built a school, a
church, and a hospital to attract young women into its mills in Lowell,
Massachusetts. Inexpensive housing was provided for operatives by numerous

1

New England industrialists confronted with problems of labor recruitment, retention, and "moral supervision." During a period characterized by concern over the preservation of America's fragile agrarian, republican heritage, the demonic products of industrial growth—proletarianization and class conflict—could only be avoided by humanizing industry.[3]

When, in the latter decades of the nineteenth century, a similar concern over the uncontrollable forces of industry arose, it was not kindled by the initial birth pangs of industrialization but by its coming of age. The strike wave of 1877 and the ensuing labor struggles of the next two decades led many industrialists such as George Pullman, Harold McCormick, John H. Patterson, William Cooper Procter, Frederick R. Hazard, and Henry John Heinz to question prevailing labor-management practices. They began experimenting with industrial reforms aimed at alleviating labor conflict, improving worker morale, and cultivating employee loyalty. They raised wages, instituted profit sharing, adopted medical and relief programs, built homes and recreation facilities for their workers; and thus they initiated a reorientation of industrial capitalism, one destined to lead to welfare capitalism.[4]

Among the early industrial pioneers who ventured into corporate paternalism were the founding officers of the Endicott Johnson Corporation. The early history of the firm mirrored the experiences of hundreds of manufacturers who confronted a work force slow to yield to industrial discipline. Management's adoption of various paternalistic solutions, at first cynically and halfheartedly, suggests a variety of motives—personal, structural, pragmatic, and defensive. But underlying them all was the fear of class conflict. The emergence of corporate paternalism was ultimately a product of conflict, at once a result of and a response to the struggle for control of the means and fruits of industrial capitalism.

I

In 1888 G. Harry Lester, Binghamton's most prominent shoe manufacturer, decided to build a new factory two miles west of the city. Most likely, his decision to relocate outside the small Broome County metropolis was based on such financial considerations as avoidance of burdensome city taxes and the hope of profiting from land sales of inflated property—inflated by the mere presence of his factory. But labor relations also played a part in Lester's calculations, for he intended to construct more than a factory; he aimed to build an industrial village. The Binghamton press, in both descriptive reports and promotional advertisements, praised the civic and moral qualities inherent in Lester's planned community. Here would be a modest population of workers, living in a community controlled by a well-respected capitalist determined to provide the benefits and guidance of a middle-class life to his operatives. It would be "Real Philanthropy," one newspaper headline suggested, a community from which the harsher elements of modern urban and industrial life would be eliminated. No liquor would be sold. A library, reading room, and public hall were to be provided for the workers. Low-cost housing, food, and fuel would also be made available.[5]

Themes of paternalism, security, civility and safety, and a disdain for the worst qualities of urban living and the harsh realities of a market economy tended to characterize newspaper descriptions of Lester's planned town. These were common themes in the latter part of the nineteenth century in the writings of social critics and moralists and reflect considerable anxiety over the social costs of a rapidly expanding industrial order. Not surprisingly, such concerns provoked interest in models of alternative industrial communities, which sometimes took the shape of "ideal" villages, like Pullman's famed town. In practice, however, what emerged from these experiments with utopia were factory towns—small, gray, lifeless communities, created and dominated by visions of wealth, power, or misguided patriarchy.[6]

Lester's community, although seemingly striving for utopian ideals, in practice came to resemble the typical factory town. His much-publicized "philanthropy" came to naught; there would be no amenities for his workers. In 1888 Lester had an agent buy several parcels of land in the vicinity of his planned community, while he himself acquired additional acreage. He quickly had the tract surveyed, parceled, and laid out as a village, and he began construction of a spacious home for himself. Lester also arranged for a number of well-publicized land auctions, directed at both workers and "investors."[7] To attract merchants and professionals, and the well-to-do middle class in general, it was necessary to convince Binghamton's finest that the new village of Lester-Shire would not go the way of many boom towns, with their rough and undisciplined working class. These fears were addressed in advertisements that stressed the "steady," "industrious," and "intelligent" qualities of the shoe firm's labor force.[8] To attract the still-hesitant investors, Lester used other methods that soon put the lie to any idealistic features his schemes might have had:

> About the first thing that Harry Lester undertook to do, when he came to Lester-Shire and built the factory and wanted to sell lots, was to promise work to those who would come and buy lots of his real estate agent. He then undertook to compel working people to patronize stores and hire houses which had been built by those people who were induced to come there, under the promise that they would be protected in that way.[9]

Indeed, the authoritarian aspects of Lester's community were soon demonstrated. In September 1891 a number of men employed by the Lester-Shire Factory were discharged. Local papers reported their number at anywhere from thirty-five to a hundred and noted that the men asserted they were "discharged because they do not own property in Lester-Shire." Here, as in other exploited industrial communities, coercion linked work and community.[10]

Lester's further quest for quick profits and the immense expense of his project soon led him to seek additional capital and ultimately culminated in the transformation of what had been a family business into a stock company. In March 1890 local papers announced that the shoe firm, including land and factory, would be purchased by a syndicate and would be reorganized as the Lester-Shire Boot and Shoe Company. Lester and Company, however, retained control of the factory's jobbing trade, and Lester himself remained at the helm of the newly organized manufacturing firm.[11]

But a safe investment was not to be had in Lester-Shire. Almost immediately, the syndicate's fortunes were imperiled. The Lester-Shire Boot and Shoe Company had looked forward to a period of rapid expansion. Instead, it confronted the depression of 1893, which came early to the shoe town. The anticipation of continuing rapid growth, one that the firm had grown accustomed to through the eighties, was not fulfilled. Orders decreased, and the work force, which had swelled from 95 in 1880 to a high of about 475 in 1890, began to decline.[12] In the winter of 1891–92 the firm, under severe financial pressure, was forced into a second reorganization. On January 11, 1892, the Lestershire Manufacturing Company, the new name of the firm, assumed control of the jobbing trade, real estate, and factory of the two former firms. Financed by large western shoe jobbers as well as by several Boston businessmen, the company was able to weather temporarily very lean times. Yet that summer it faced still another financial crisis. This time the business was on the verge of total collapse.[13] Only the hasty salvage operation of Henry B. Endicott of Boston, a major stockholder and head of the Commonwealth Shoe and Leather Company, was able to save it. Once again the firm was reorganized, with Endicott as treasurer. George F. Johnson, who had been the factory's assistant superintendent since 1887 and who had recently been chosen by Lester to replace his unsuccessful general manager, was retained by Endicott and was left to manage the firm.[14] Endicott and Johnson, destined soon to become partners, thus began three decades of collaboration.

II

While organizational changes were transforming the financial and managerial leadership of the firm, even more radical changes were taking place within the factory. When Lester removed his manufacturing enterprise to what became Lester-Shire, he did more than merely transplant production from one building to another. He added a considerable amount of new technology, vastly increased the size of the factory, and structured it in ways that streamlined and rationalized production. Such transformations of the workplace had a profound impact on the firm's employees and introduced new challenges to managerial control.

Four hundred feet long, fifty feet wide, and three stories in height, the new factory cast a wide shadow over the valley in which it stood. Its long and narrow design provided for maximum entry of sunlight into the various workshops. Although it was built of wood, brick partitions divided it into three sections. A large 225 horsepower Corliss engine provided power for the factory's extensive and varied collection of machinery, and a smaller 50 horsepower generator furnished power for its 600 incandescent lights. No longer would workers need to furnish their own oil lamps, as they had at the Binghamton factory. A contemporary description of the new factory and its various departments captures the physical and functional integration of workshops and offers us a glimpse into the working world of late nineteenth-century shoeworkers.

On the top floor in the west section of the building is the cutting room, where everything in the line of uppers is cut into the forms desired. In this department . . . there are twenty eight cutting stalls, in which employes are kept busy from morn til night. After leaving the cutters' hands, the pieces are sorted into grades and cases. In the southwest corner of this room is the big freight elevator running from the top of the building down to the cellar and on which the heavy rolls of leather and the cases ready for shipment are hoisted and lowered. The middle section of this floor is devoted to the crimping department where the uppers for boots are crimped into shape and which requires the services of fifty employes. In the east section is the stitching department where a large number of men and women are constantly engaged at numerous Singer and National sewing machines and all the Thompson riveting machines. The pasting and trimming of the different parts of the boots and shoes is also done in the center of this room.

In the east section of the middle floor is the finishing room where the manufactured goods are brought for the finishing touches. In the middle section is the treeing department where the uppers are finished and in the west section is the packing and shipping department. . . . On the first floor is the sole leather department where the soles for the boots and shoes are cut into shape by two Parsons, two Pease and three Hawkins machines. About 7,000 pounds of leather are cut into shape every day. After being cut into form the soles are sorted into grades and sizes and properly labeled. . . . Here also the heels for the boots and shoes are made up. After being cut into shape by machines and by hand they are put through a compressing machine which exerts a compression of a seventy-five ton weight. In this department there are also machines for nailing and pegging the heels which are marvelous specimens of mechanical arts.

The lasting department occupies the middle section of the first floor. In this there are twenty lasting machines and a large force of workmen is busily employed. In the east section is the bottoming department. . . . Here the work is facilitated by three New Era machines, seventeen

Varney pegging machines and four Rapid heelers. These complicated machines perform their work with lightning rapidity. . . .[15]

This "veritable bee hive of industry," as the *Binghamton Republican* referred to it, functioned as a human magnet, drawing workers from surrounding rural counties and from the coal-mining regions of Pennsylvania. The general decline of Northeastern agriculture in the latter decades of the century, manifested locally by the abandonment of upland farms along the Susquehanna and Chenango valleys, greatly contributed to the influx of laborers.[16] A long strike or slack work in the coal mines also sent forth a stream of outmigrants, and the Lester-Shire Factory was one of their many destinations.

When the factory opened in the winter of 1889–90, hundreds of workers crowded into the village, all vying for work. Grant Chambers was one of them. He came to the community from Livingston County, a rural, central New York county lying just to the south of Rochester, a region typified by small farming communities. Along with him came his brother and sister and five of his neighbors, young men and women, all of them attracted by the opening of the new shoe factory. Chambers later recalled the arrival of these eight rural migrants: "We reported to the factory office on Dec. 2 [1889], ready for work, but were told that there were 1,500 applications ahead of us and that we would have to take our turn. . . . The shoe company had advertised for 3,000 men and women to learn to be shoemakers, when they needed not more than 300. The result was that the community was filled with . . . young people looking for a job."[17]

A large number of workers who entered the Lester-Shire Factory in the 1890s probably resembled Chambers and his band: young, recently arrived, from a rural background. Data from the 1892 New York State census, from the 1900 federal census, and from city directories confirm this. Of the 153 shoeworkers counted in the 1892 New York census in the township of Union (most of whom resided in Lester-Shire), 60 percent were twenty-nine or younger.[18] Furthermore, reflecting their recent arrival, a substantial number of Binghamton and Lester-Shire shoeworkers lived in transitory accommodations. Of the 216 shoe- and bootmakers listed in the 1892 Binghamton directory (which also included Lester-Shire), 44 percent were boarders, up from 12 percent in 1880.[19] While most of the workers were drawn from within the state in the 1890s, a growing number were coming in from Pennsylvania, which lay only seven miles to the south of the village. Occasional county-of-birth entries in the 1900 federal manuscript census suggest their rural background. Toward the latter part of the 1890s, immigrants from Italy, Hungary, Austria, and Russia began trickling into the factory. Their numbers, however, would not significantly swell the factory labor force until the first and second decades of the new century.[20]

Among the new workers flocking into the factory were many young women. While employment of women had been increasing in the 1880s, it was the opening of the new factory that led to a dramatic rise in their numbers. Between 1889 and 1890, when the new factory opened, female employment more than doubled, increasing from 50 to 125 (from 12 percent to 26 percent of the work force). Improvements in productivity in various departments of the shoe factory created a need for additional stitching-machine operatives. But the growing importance of women workers also represented an expansion of the sexual division of labor within the factory. Indeed, women took over many of the unskilled, monotonous, and low-paying jobs, working not only as stitching-machine operators (a traditionally female domain) but also as lining makers, heel blackers and graders, and finishing room workers. Once entrenched, women continued to figure prominently in the labor force.[21]

Most of the recently arrived Lester-Shire workers were not skilled and probably had little experience either in shoemaking or in general factory work. When they entered the new plant, they confronted an unfamiliar landscape. Their integration into a factory environment involved a radical re-education, a transformation of their perceptions and habits of work. The physical reconstruction of work, expressed concretely in the rational design and mechanical enhancements of the new factory, required the psychological reconstruction of workers. The casual pace of traditional and rural laboring habits would be transformed into the disciplined rhythm of hundreds of men and women whose labors were increasingly becoming mechanically dependent on one another's timing and efficiency. Such a process, as Herbert Gutman has detailed, did not occur overnight.[22] Nor was the internalization of "industrial time" and the adjustment to factory regimentation ever entirely accomplished. New workers brought with them old ideas about work and time; old workers manipulated "industrial time" to their own needs. Even while workers learned the rules of mass-production labor in the Lester-Shire Factory, they had opportunities to bend these rules to their own whims. A shoeworker later recalled such an instance:

> When the first real spring days came "Dory" would mount the bench and shout, "All in favor of laying off today say Aye." . . . The proposition was always carried and the men would lay off for the balance of the day. . . . This "laying off" was no great loss for "full time" was not known and the length of the "run" determined by the amount of orders, and as there always was a dull period in the summer, laying off occasionally in the spring simply prolonged the working season.[23]

While such demonstrations of autonomy strained heavily against the dictates of efficiency and gradually faded into oblivion, they were replaced by other, more modern forms of industrial resistance.

The increasing numbers of young, female, and relatively new workers, as well as changes taking place within the factory, signaled the emergence of a fully developed factory system, one becoming ever less dependent on the artisanal order of the past. In the 1880s the nature of work in the Lester Factory had been a mixture of skilled or semiskilled, partially mechanized hand labor and relatively unskilled, heavily mechanized labor.[24] The process of mechanization rapidly progressed once the firm moved to Lester-Shire. But when the first crimping machines were introduced into the new factory, management did face some obstacles. One worker recalled how he hesitated to go on the machine "because in those days the workers rather looked upon machinery as an experiment, and also as taking their places."[25] Jobs that had formerly required substantial skills were continually segmented into relatively unskilled operations.[26] Of course, there remained artisanal bastions that were relatively untouched by mechanization or that retained important components of skill in spite of technological changes. This was true of cutters, lasters, outsole stitchers, treers, and various other skilled workers. They developed work cultures that remained quite strong through the first four decades of the twentieth century. It was among such workers that resistance to managerial prerogatives would become most pronounced.

III

Symptomatic of the new industrial order emerging in Lester-Shire was a growing distance between operatives and managers. The sheer size of the enterprise, the impersonal quality of factory relations, and the proletarianization of rural workers widened the gap. Nor did Lester's exploitation of his workers foster good labor-management relations. All these factors, further exacerbated by a depressed economy and the seasonal unemployment that was part and parcel of the shoe industry, meant a precarious existence for the firm's employees. Hiring and firing were entirely in the hands of foremen in those years, subject to their whims and not open to appeal. No payroll office existed. The pace of work varied with the season. An influx of orders during the busy seasons, particularly in the early spring, might mean as many as fifteen to eighteen hours of work a day. But when orders declined, the hours of work were cut drastically—and, of course, so was income. Not surprisingly, under such conditions some of the firm's employees became receptive to unionizing.[27]

Early organizing efforts among the shoeworkers began in the summer of 1890, in the wake of a major Binghamton cigarworkers' strike. Two thousand cigarworkers had left their benches, demanding the recision of wage reductions introduced in the previous year. These 2,000 workers, most not unionized, amounted to one-fifth of Binghamton's entire labor force. The four-month strike was the longest and most serious labor protest in Binghamton's history, stimulating intense and bitter animosities within the community. And the militancy of the city's cigarworkers was contagious.[28]

In early August 1890, while the strike was still raging in Binghamton, a delegation of striking workers, invited to Lester-Shire by sympathetic shoe-workers, arrived in the village to solicit strike funds and petition signatures. They stood at the factory gates during the noon hour accosting departing workers. A foreman confronted the delegation and ordered them to leave the village "or they would be arrested." The company's control over the village, by virtue of almost total ownership of the land, gave force to his threat.[29] The firm's hostility to the delegation was motivated not only by a feeling of solidarity with Binghamton's cigar manufacturers but also by anxiety over the possible spread of worker activism to its own workers. With good reason: on August 2, in a report on the progress of the strike, the *Democratic Daily Leader* noted that "the pulse of the organization has already begun to thrill through the body of labor in this city. Quite a successful attempt is being made to organize the shoemakers, whose condition it is well known is even worse in the way of wages and obnoxious rules than those of the cigar makers."[30]

The cigarmakers' strike was a catalyst for labor organizing, although the defeat of the strike in the late summer of 1890 demoralized the strikers and their comrades and slowed progress in unionizing the shoeworkers. Yet the class feelings and activist spirit that it ignited did have an impact on disgruntled shoemakers, for in September 1891, on Labor Day, about sixty shoeworkers participated in the annual Labor Day parade, marching along with the organized trades of the city.[31] Slow but persistent organizing efforts finally culminated in the formation of a small union local in Binghamton in 1893, with officers drawn from the Lester-Shire Factory.

Unfortunately, few union records survive to give us the inside story of Local 120's arrival and organizing attempts in Binghamton and Lester-Shire.[32] The local belonged to the Boot and Shoe Workers International Union, the latter recently formed as a result of a major battle waged within the Knights of Labor over the issue of organizational strategies and structures. Advocates of mixed trade assemblies found themselves opposed by trade unionists seeking the formation of national trade assemblies. The trade union faction lost, thus leading to the fracturing of the Knights of Labor. The battle over organizational strategies had major ideological implications for the labor movement as a whole. It was a central element in the division between the American Federation of Labor (AFL) and the Knights.[33]

Tensions between advocates of mixed locals and proponents of trade unions finally came to a head in 1888, when Henry J. Skeffington, leader of the trade union faction, called upon shoeworkers who were members of District Assembly 216, which had been a de facto national trade union, to surrender their Knights of Labor charters and to form their own separate union. The first convention of what came to be known as the Boot and Shoe Workers International Union (BSWIU) was held in Boston in 1889. A later amalgamation with two other shoeworkers' unions led to the formation of the Boot and Shoe

Workers' Union (BSWU) in 1895. Both the BSWIU and the BSWU became members of the AFL.[34]

The formal organization of Local 120 (later changed to Local 42 after the formation of the BSWU) was soon followed by the initiation of major wage and managerial reforms by George F. Johnson, the Lestershire Manufacturing Company's new superintendent. He introduced a piece wage system to a factory that had employed mostly day or hourly wages. Piece rates had been applied in only a select number of jobs, generally skilled handwork. In extending it to both machine and handwork, Johnson believed that productivity would be greatly increased as a result of the built-in incentive.[35] Johnson also began to cut costs by eliminating middlemen wherever he could and by undertaking a more aggressive selling strategy. Wage reforms, drastic cost-cutting measures, and aggressive selling paid off, successfully turning around the financial condition of the factory and helping it weather a national depression.[36] Indeed, job opportunities even expanded as the firm began an early recovery from the depression.[37]

Initially, Johnson's new wage and factory policies were well received by the workers. Johnson had surely anticipated this when he initiated his reforms. Wages (and productivity) increased dramatically.[38] Even officials of Local 120 acknowledged the improved employment conditions when they reported to state officials on the status of the workers in 1894: "At the time the union was formed the boot and shoe workers were employed by the day, and the wages ranged from $6 to $12 a week. It is all piece-work now, and the weekly earnings run from $7 to $18. We average 11 months' work in a year."[39]

Unfortunately, whatever satisfaction the union or the firm's workers obtained from the new superintendent's factory reforms was short-lived. Johnson came to realize that he had opened up a Pandora's box with his introduction of piecework. Wages had risen far faster and far higher than he had anticipated. He was placed in a typical managerial predicament: "Whenever piece work was introduced and workers began to receive significantly higher pay than they had under the day wage system, the manufacturer was tempted to cut the rate so the wage earners, though producing more, would earn approximately what they had under day work."[40] Johnson began to lower wages selectively. Ironically, the very piece rate system that had led to wage increases also served to decrease the workers' power to defend their gains. Piece rates functioned both as incentives for increased production and as divisive forces within the factory. They emphasized the divisions between fast workers and slow, experienced workers and inexperienced, older craft workers and "green hands." The union would find it difficult to unite workers who equated just remuneration with individual effort.[41]

Johnson, engrossed in his drive to streamline production and increase worker efficiency, soon came into conflict with some of the company's skilled workers who were attempting to defend both wage gains and the traditional work practices that his reforms were challenging. Near the end of February 1894, the general manager, claiming a need to economize during the slack season, fired an employee who delivered lasts to lasters. This action forced the men to fetch their own lasts, which resulted in an effective reduction of their piece rates by one or two cents a case. Failing to convince Johnson to rehire the man, several dozen lasters went out on strike. Johnson explained his version of the events to a reporter from the *Binghamton Republican* who went out to Lester-Shire to investigate the matter.

> We have always employed a man, whom the lasters call a waiter, to bring lasts, and have paid him two cents a case. On Monday we laid him off. This was done to avoid cutting down the wages of those employed as nearly all other concerns are doing. Business is very dull and this is sample season, and owing to the hard times we have found it necessary to economize in every possible way. This cannot be construed into a cut of two cents a case, as it is a very common occurrence to see lasters sitting idle waiting for the waiter to bring lasts, when they might just as well have got up and fetched their lasts themselves.[42]

As soon as the lasters walked off their jobs, union organizers quickly stepped in with their support and encouraged other workers to join the strike. The fitters, peggers, and treers, as well as the screw, heeling, and trimming machine operators, walked off their jobs in support of the lasters, demonstrating a worker solidarity that transcended craft lines. But other workers, in particular the stitchers and cutters, did not. The strike was initially effective. It brought to a near standstill the entire factory work force. Only three lasting machines remained in operation. To maintain production the firm began recruiting workers in Binghamton to replace striking workers. In response allies among Binghamton's organized trades held a meeting on the evening of March 1 in Cigarmaker's Hall and issued resolutions of sympathy with the lasters: "Resolved, that we are in hearty sympathy with the employes of the Lester-Shire Boot and Shoe Company, who are now resisting an unnecessary reduction of 50 cents per man a day; that we pledge ourselves to aid them in their struggle to the best of our ability and call upon organized labor of this city to join us in such support."[43]

Resolutions of sympathy, however, were powerless against the determination of management; the lasters' strike was short-lived. Mention of the strike disappeared just as suddenly as it had appeared. Strikers soon began returning to work, and there seems to have been plenty of eager workers around, victims of the 1893 depression, who were desperate for jobs. There was probably more than a little truth in Johnson's version of the end of the strike: "They have now been out two days and several of them are applying for their old places again. The fact that these men went out makes no difference with the other employes, who do not sympathize with them. Over fifty persons applied to-day for the places of the men who are out."[44]

Johnson continued making adjustments in piece rates through the rest of the 1890s, provoking repeated resistance from his workers. In late winter of 1895, price reductions went into effect throughout the factory. Workers complained that the reductions cost them anywhere between twenty-five and seventy cents on a day's work. Furthermore, they accused the company of maintaining an arbitrary fining system for damaged work, with fines as high as twenty-five to fifty cents deducted from workers' pay. Workers claimed that they had "known of cases where an employe[e] had been charged 25 cents and 50 cents for putting a buckle on a shoe wrong, and the shoe has been put in the case and sent with the rest of the case, showing that it was no damage to the firm at all."[45] For a worker making only four dollars a week, as some were, such fines constituted a heavy burden.

Management tried to convince workers that slack business made price reductions necessary. The usual strategy of the firm was not to make general rate cuts, which would be collectively felt and perhaps collectively resisted. Instead, Johnson selectively reduced rates when he felt he could do so without provoking rebellion. Such reductions tended to hit hardest at the skilled workers, particularly the cutters and lasters whose work was the least mechanized. Cutting was still entirely a hand operation, and, while lasting machines were being introduced in the 1890s, it nonetheless required a considerable amount of skill and judgment to operate them without damaging the uppers.[46] Since their wages constituted a high percentage of the cost of a shoe, cutters and lasters were prime targets for price cuts.

In 1897, when a reduction in wage scales reached the cutting room, a number of men rebelled and left their cutting stalls. Their rates had been reduced from fifteen to twelve dollars per week. When interviewed by a local reporter, superintendent Johnson explained his version of what had occurred.

We have made one or two changes in the scale of prices, due to the introduction of machinery. In fact we are constantly raising or lowering prices as conditions change. There was no dissention [*sic*] until the cutting room was reached. We decided that some of the men were getting more pay than they earned, the men being paid by the day in that department. We cut them and the men left work. This made the men think that the cut was general, and until they had the matter explained to them they talked strike.[47]

Johnson's selective reduction prevented collective action. Once the "cutters learned . . . that only the men notified were affected by the reduction they went to work as usual." Meanwhile, one of the striking workers sent an advertisement to Boston papers notifying cutters there to stay away from Lestershire, an act that surely aroused the anger of Johnson, as it put "the Lestershire factory in a bad light among shoe jobbers and the trade in general." Perhaps his departure for Boston two days later, on August 4, was motivated by his determination to set things right with Boston merchants.[48]

Although Johnson continually faced price rebellions from his workers, by 1897 he was no longer threatened by a union. He had taken care of that two years earlier. In 1895 Local 120 officers admitted to New York State labor investigators that "our union is not powerful enough to control this place at present," although they did express the conviction that their "best work will be done in 1896."[49] There was little reason for their optimism. The general increase of wages in the factory, the persistence of depression conditions outside Lestershire, and the effective use of divisive managerial strategies all contributed to the union's failure to obtain strong support among Lestershire shoeworkers.

Partly due to its weakness, the local came to place emphasis on a union label campaign, which amounted to an economic boycott of the firm. In 1895, with the full cooperation of the Trades and Labor Assembly of Binghamton, it began such a boycott in the city.[50] Johnson did not react well to such tactics. Nearly two weeks later a committee of workers from the Lestershire Factory published an open letter in the Binghamton papers protesting against several of the pricing and fining policies of the firm, noted earlier. They objected most strongly, however, to the recent firing of several workers who they claimed were union men and concluded that "it is evidently their determination to destroy the union."[51]

Johnson was indeed determined to destroy the union, and he was successful. No subsequent record remains of the union's presence in the community. By 1896 it was absent from both press mention and from the city directory. The report of the second convention of the BSWU, held in the summer of 1896, noted that the local had disbanded but had not yet returned its charter.[52] Years later the *Shoe Workers' Journal* recalled that "in the year 1895 there was a local union of shoe workers in . . . Binghamton, N.Y. which local union was forced out of existence by the discharge and disbandment route."[53]

Johnson attempted to reach an accommodation with as many of the union men as he could. Activists like Fred Haycock, the local's delegate to the 1895 convention, were probably fired (he disappeared from the city directory).[54] H. W. Parsons, the local's vice president, also lost his job with the firm. Others, like the union's president, James P. Connerton, adapted to Johnson's regime. Connerton had been with the firm since 1885 and was to stay with it well into the 1920s, working his way up to the superintendency of the Pioneer Factory, the original Lestershire plant. He died in retirement in 1932, receiving the tribute of company officers for his many years of loyal service.[55]

Johnson would not suffer a union that either challenged his authority in the factory or threatened to destroy the firm's reputation. He believed, as he later would endlessly repeat, that the "employer is the natural labor leader." Johnson sought a direct relationship with his workers, one that harked back to the ideal of guild production. Having been a benchworker and having experienced the reactions of his workers to his factory reforms, particularly workers whom he respected, he came to reconsider the responsibilities of management to its employees. He grew responsive to the voices of reform that advocated humanizing industrial institutions. He came to believe that the relationship between factory and community should be a more benevolent one. These realizations were the product of two decades of national and local conflicts between workers and capitalists, realizations that were increasingly shared by other industrialists. But they also marked an attempt by a worker-turned-capitalist to resolve within his own conscience the dilemmas and contradictions inherent in industrial capitalism.

IV

In later life George Francis Johnson would come to portray himself as a "changed man," a man who had tasted of riches and privileges, only to find them hollow; a man not altogether atypical of the progressive business community at the turn of the century, who found that true success implied responsibilities. Andrew Carnegie, who declared that the wealthy man was a "mere agent and trustee for his poorer brethren, bringing to their service his superior wisdom, experience, and ability to administer," was a highly visible model for Johnson and for progressive industrialists everywhere. Johnson never credited Carnegie for any of his ideas; but by the time Johnson came into control of the firm's management, the "Gospel of Wealth," as well as numerous versions of the social gospel, were widely heralded in the popular press. Entrepreneurs like Carnegie had come to recognize that the major problem of their age was "the proper administration of wealth, so that the ties of brotherhood may still bind together the rich and poor in harmonious relationship."[56] Johnson would come to a similar recognition, derived in some measure from the reformist ideologies of churchmen and progressive entrepreneurs but rooted also in the world of his youth and young adulthood. Not unlike Carnegie, who carried with him from his native Scotland the seeds of a radical social ideology derived from British Chartism, an ideology that shaped and mediated his later ideas, Johnson brought with him from Massachusetts equally radical ideas, destined to influence similarly his own emotional and intellectual development.[57]

George Francis Johnson was born on October 14, 1857, in Milford, Massachusetts. He grew up in a family where husband, wife, and children all contributed to the family economy. His father was a boot-treer, tavern-keeper, and honored Civil War captain, a man of "tremendous energy." His mother was a devout Methodist, whose kindly deeds for neighbors were often recalled by her son in later years. They were hardly as poor as Johnson would later come to portray them, his father owning "considerable property." Parents and children alike subscribed to the value, honor, and necessity of hard work: "We were poor—very poor—but always managed to get a good living. Father worked in the shop and the boys worked in the shop. There were three or four of us. Mother was a great manager. Took care of a family of children, and generally had anywhere from ten to twenty-five boarders to take care of, besides. As a rule, she did her own work."[58]

As a youth Johnson grew restless working in his father's shop and soon left. At the age of thirteen he took his first job in a local shoe factory in Ashland. Following the trade of his father, he soon became an expert treer, a worker whose skill lay in the finishing of boots and shoes. Johnson did not stay long at his first job, nor for that matter in the next one, but spent the next ten years of his life as an itinerant shoeworker in eastern Massachusetts, as his father had been.[59] Perhaps he inherited his father's restlessness, but Johnson's mobility also reflected the realities of the Massachusetts shoe industry. Seasonal production, frequent factory closings, and an abundance of shoe manufacturing enterprises led to periodic moves by shoeworkers from one community to another. Since hundreds of factories lay within forty miles of Boston, however, the search for employment opportunities rarely involved long-distance relocation.

Through the shoe towns of Massachusetts—Holliston, Natick, Hopkinton, Ashland, Milford, Worcester, Plymouth—the young Johnson traveled, seeking employment for a season or a year. The drabness of life in the harsh factory towns, where employers showed more "hate than good will," was partially allayed by the companionship of fellow workers who indulged themselves in drink and baseball.[60] Yet even while he sought out the camaraderie of fellow workers, Johnson's energy and ambitions were driving him away from them. At the age of twenty-one, he became a foreman of a treeing room at a Plymouth factory, a position that marked his growing distance from his former comrades. It also marked the erosion of ideas and ideals he had absorbed in his travels.

In later recollections of his Massachusetts years, Johnson described himself as a young man with natural leadership proclivities, one who loved team sports, and one who had tasted the fruit of New England radicalism. He confessed, without detail, that he had been "something of a socialist and radical" in his youth.[61] It was not a surprising admission. Radicalism pervaded the shoeworkers of Massachusetts and the towns of Milford, Plymouth, Holliston, and Haverhill, all towns Johnson had worked in. The founder of the Knights of St. Crispin, one of the largest and most aggressive of nineteenth-century American trade unions, came from Milford, Johnson's birthplace.[62] Massachusetts shoeworkers were a militant group. They had formed radical unions in the 1860s and afterward and were to find socialist doctrines relevant to their industrial experience. In the labor theory of value, they recognized a central controlling idea that sustained their pride in their work and themselves in an era of technological displacement.[63]

Whatever radical or socialist ideas Johnson absorbed in his wanderings through the shoe towns of eastern Massachusetts, they had been diluted by the time he arrived in Binghamton in 1881. By his own admission he had taken a job as treeing room foreman at the Lester Factory in order to direct "a bigger crew of workers" and to make more money.[64] In many respects, during the 1880s and 1890s, Johnson seemed little different from the driving foreman whom he had encountered as a worker in Massachusetts. Yet it was also during these years that he began to moderate his ambitions. As he recalled:

> I had at that time no particularly definite ideas upon the subject of man management. I had been brought up in the old, hard school in which the worker was considered somebody that the employer had to have just as he had to have leather. I imagined that the best way to get work out of men was to keep them going as hard as they would go and especially to see piece rates were low enough to force a man to do a good day's work in order to gain a living. . . . We prospered and made money. I had always been anxious to have money, but as I began to get more and more of it, I discovered that really it did not amount to much—that there were few things that one might buy that were really worth while. I began to wonder if it would not be better to give more attention to the human side—that workers had hearts as well as hands and that a leader of industry shouldered certain responsibilities beyond pocketing the profits. Out of that thought grew our present plan of organization.[65]

Johnson did not experience a personal transformation, so much as he rediscovered former values. He had always possessed a dual personality, one side pulling toward acquisitive capitalism, the other toward collectivist and somewhat socialistic ideals.

Johnson was doomed to inhabit two worlds, neither comfortably. He was a bold manager, a natural entrepreneur, destined to build an empire on such an unlikely product as shoes. He would come to associate with governors, senators, presidents, and the top corporate leaders of the nation. But in his own mind he remained a worker. He yearned for the simplicity of his youth, for the company of his former comrades. His constant ambivalence was exhibited in numerous ways. In his correspondence the most genuine sentiments appear in letters to his old worker buddies. In his dealings with employees as a foreman under Lester, he evinced a firm yet flexible style that hardly changed over the years. A worker who had been employed in the treeing room in the 1880s, under Johnson, recalled him in these terms:

> I guess George F. had been there a couple of years when I began to work in the treeing room. . . . I was seventeen then. He started me on one dozen pairs of boots a day, and added more when I could handle them. He was one of the finest men I ever worked for. When he wanted a thing

done, it had to be done right or you'd hear from him. He was easy-going, but you had to be up to the mark.[66]

It is a telling testament that a worker should remember Johnson as both a driving foreman and "one of the finest men" for whom he had ever worked.

Johnson also exhibited a duality of mind in the factory reforms he initiated in the 1890s. Although he instituted a policy of fines and pushed through numerous piece rate reductions, he nonetheless increased the average wages of his workers substantially, and he did it during a period of business depression. The competing forces that tugged and pulled at Johnson are even more poignantly captured in a passage written by his official biographer:

> Within a year after he was made superintendent of Pioneer [the factory], he moved to a house some miles down Riverside Drive. He bought a horse, buggy, harness, laprobe and whip for eighty dollars, so he could drive to work. He had to save every possible minute to devote to the needs of the business—but he felt so embarrassed by his eighty dollars' worth of luxury while his comrades had to walk to work that he never drove up to the factory door. Instead, he stopped the horse between a haystack and a little knoll, out of sight of the factory, and walked to the door. After the six o'clock whistle, he walked to the haystack, where his wife was waiting to drive him home.[67]

This description, narrated by William Inglis to illustrate Johnson's consideration for the sensibilities of his workers, suggests a great deal about the dilemma that plagued him. Brought up in a modest home, having risen from the ranks of the workers into his present class, Johnson was never able to hold power and wealth without pangs of conscience. The industrial world that he helped forge was one plagued by an identical dilemma. To be both capitalist and laborer, to exploit labor and yet to call it comrade, to nurture while manipulating: how would he merge such inconsistent goals?

They were combined, first of all, in a pragmatic paternalism designed to assuage both the problems of an expanding company and village as well as the psyche of an emerging worker-turned-capitalist. In the context of active challenges to his authority and growing social problems associated with the physical expansion of the firm, Johnson began to respond with increasingly paternalistic solutions. As he rose within the firm and his control of labor policies increased, as he accumulated more and more company stock and his successful management came to be appreciated by Endicott, he was able to steer the firm's labor policies in a new direction, one destined to lead to welfare capitalism.

V

In early 1900 Johnson became Endicott's partner by buying the real estate interests of the Lestershire Manufacturing Company along with a substantial amount of stock. He had begun to buy into the firm in 1894 and by 1899 had over $80,000 invested in the company. But most of the $222,000 that he paid for his half-interest in the business was, in fact, loaned to him by Endicott, who was confident that Johnson would make good on the loan.[68] Soon after becoming a partner, Johnson began to formulate plans for a dramatic expansion of the firm. About the middle of February 1901, the Lestershire Manufacturing Company announced its intentions of opening another factory several miles to the west of Lestershire. Johnson and Endicott concluded a deal with local land developers and purchased several hundred acres of land along the Susquehanna River.[69]

Plans for expansion of the company into what land developers had tactfully named "Endicott" reflected the general growth of the manufacturing enterprise, a growth that was bringing with it serious human problems. At the turn of the century, the firm's labor force hovered at 2,000 workers, a considerable increase from the 450 employees of a decade earlier. The Lestershire Factory was, at this time, among the largest in the country. It continued to draw in workers from Pennsylvania and surrounding New York counties, and it was attracting an ever-growing number of Eastern European immigrants. To both Binghamton and the village of Lestershire, the factory was a mixed blessing, a source of pride, awe, hostility, and ruin. Neighboring rural folk were especially wary of the behemoth. They hesitated to sell their land to developers whom they believed would in turn sell it to the company. Overcrowded housing and filthy tenements, products of the rapid growth of the shoe factory and the large influx of new workers, offered evidence to critics that factories brought liabilities as well as benefits. A reporter from the *New York Herald,* touring various upstate cities, described conditions in western Binghamton as follows: "The big shoe factory in Lestershire employs many hundred foreigners, who reside along the railroad tracks in the western part of the city, and here conditions are also bad. The long, low tenements are crowded with persons who never knew what it was like to live in clean quarters."[70]

While the factory had delivered prosperity to the community, it also brought individual ruin. The experiences of a young orphan who heard that "Lestershire was a good town for a young man" and came to get a job in the factory, only to be fired for careless work, reflected the underlying insecurity of industrial life.

> The poor boy now became worse off than ever, and what he should do was more than he could understand. His friends were gone—work had been denied him, and not having had any experience in outdoor life he became utterly helpless. After his few dollars had been spent he was turned out of his boarding house and compelled to roam the streets at all hours of the night. Once or twice tender hearted citizens who happened to meet him and after hearing his pitiful story took him to their homes where food and shelter were given him.[71]

A far greater violation of public sensibilities than poverty and destitution was the rise of prostitution that accompanied industrial growth. "The Downward Path" of a young woman, drawn to the factory by its promise of "fortune and friends," was traced by the local *Lestershire Record,* with all the rich descriptive language of a sentimental novel of the period. "Fresh from the green hills of Union Center," Rose Cornell, "an innocent looking little maid of less than twenty summers," came to "Shoeville." "She had heard her brothers speak of the big shoe factory where 2,500 honest toilers seek to earn a livelihood, and often wondered how it would be to be a worker among them." The community, however, did not meet her expectations. The paper went on to describe her transformation from innocent rural maid to "fallen woman":

> Unable to get immediate employment in the factories she hired out to a family to do general house work, and here her downfall commenced. The head of the house was an unscrupulous fellow whose brute nature forced him to take advantage of this young girl. After accomplishing his desire he became tired of his new acquaintance and cast her out in the world, penniless and without a person whom she could command as friend. Drifting from one corner to another under the shadow of the electric lights, she soon became tired and despondent, and was willing to do most anything in order to secure shelter and rest. In her half crazed, half starved mood she proved an easy mark for a number of young men of the town. . . .[72]

The plight of young women workers in the shoe town, dependent on the factory for employment, remained somewhat precarious throughout the latter years of the nineteenth and early decades of the twentieth century. Reports of the conversion of young female shoeworkers into prostitutes periodically appeared in the local press.[73] Streams of repentant and not-so-repentant prostitutes, as well as numerous pregnant young women cast off by their seducers, made their way into the local House for Fallen Women and Binghamton's YWCA.[74]

Johnson and other company officers recognized that they had to address the growing problems that accompanied industrial expansion, both inside and outside the factory. They began by trying to bridge the psychological and social distance between operatives and managers. In his early years as a factory superintendent, faced with growing conflicts with employees, Johnson had instituted a policy of workers' direct and personal access to upper management. Grant Chambers, the young Livingston County transplant introduced earlier, recalled how soon after Johnson took charge of the Lestershire Factory he had put up notices in each department stating that "any one in our employ can get an audience with me at any time. If you are not satisfied, come in and see me."[75] It was an offer destined to become a central element in later labor policy.

This policy of accessibility was further developed in another practice designed to strengthen the bonds between workers and managers. It was expected of junior members of the firm that they would take menial positions in the company and "work their way up" to managerial posts. George F. Johnson's son and younger brother both began work in factory jobs, the former in the firm's shipping department, the latter in the packing room of the Lestershire Factory. Of course, there was no question in their minds or in the minds of their fellow workers that they were headed for eventual promotions. Nevertheless, this gesture made a positive impression on both the community and the workers.[76] When Wendell Endicott, H. B. Endicott's son, took a job in the packing room of the Lestershire Factory, the local press characterized it as "Truly Democratic."

> One of the most noteworthy features about the young man is that he does not feel himself too good to live in the village of Lestershire and eat the food that keeps common shoemakers alive. He rooms with a respectable family on Main St. and takes his meals at one of our hotels. He is a favorite with the boys, who feel that when he shall take his father's place at the head of our great industry, they will have a loyal friend who knows what it is to labor in a shoe factory.[77]

Other members of the company's management also took it upon themselves to commingle with "common shoemakers." Joseph E. Tilt, a prominent shoe manufacturer from Chicago, became involved with the new venture in Endicott in 1901, after a decade of extensive financial dealings with the firm.[78] The Lestershire paper publicized Tilt's intentions to move to Endicott and occupy a small farmhouse as "Thoroughly Democratic," in light of his leaving behind a Chicago lakefront mansion.[79] Taking a position as general manager of the Goodyear shoe department of the new factory, the Chicago industrialist brought with him an elaborate scheme for shaping the community of Endicott into what the *New York Herald* referred to as an industrial "Utopia," complete with "fine homes" for workers, recreation centers, a beneficiary insurance system, and assorted other corporate labor reforms. Tilt was more modest. To those who celebrated his "democratic" spirit in taking up residence among lowly shoeworkers, he replied: "I do not want to pose as a philanthropist . . . for I am not one. I am closing up my house here and going to Endicott to live in a cottage like the ones in which the men live for effect. . . . It is pure business; nothing more." Tilt's plans for Endicott were equally pragmatic in motivation. As he confessed, the dual object of his proposal was to "make our payroll a permanant one" and to "obviate all necessity" for labor unions.[80]

While the Lestershire Manufacturing Company did not immediately adopt many of the ideas that Tilt advocated, it did continue to steer its own course toward corporate paternalism. Indeed, even before the arrival of Tilt and his plans for "utopia," the firm had come to be regarded as a model of industrial virtue. A Binghamton historian, writing in 1900, commented on the exceptional relations between capital and labor that existed within the firm:

> The company pays larger proportionate wages than any other manufacturing concern in this region, while privileges and kindnesses are freely extended to the employees by the superintendent and his assistant that generally are unheard of in large establishments. Indeed, this company never allows any of its faithful employees to suffer through want or distress, neither does it allow the property of any of its men to be sold under process of law. Between employer and employees there exists a bond of warm friendship, and the interests of master and servant are identical. Herein lies the secret of the success which has rewarded the efforts of the managing officers of the Lestershire Manufacturing Company.[81]

The "success" that "rewarded the efforts" of management was dramatic indeed. The rising profits of the firm were reinvested in capital expansion and improvements in the new village of Endicott. Along with plant construction, management also entered the real estate business, duplicating Lester's earlier speculative endeavors.[82] The years between 1900 and the coming of World War I were characterized by constant growth and diversification of the company, interrupted only by the depression of 1907–8. New factories were built, and new partners were taken in. The firm expanded, both vertically and horizontally, constructing four tanneries in Endicott and over a dozen factories and annexes in both Endicott and Lestershire. It also entered the lucrative retail sales trade, opening more than a dozen store outlets in various upstate New York communities. It expanded its manufacturing departments; entered into production of tanning oils, cartons, counters, linings, and assorted findings; and broadened its lines of footwear. Following the repayment of Johnson's debt to Endicott, in 1902, the company ceased to be known as the Lestershire Manufacturing Company and became the Endicott Johnson Company. In 1909, two years after admitting several additional partners, the firm became known as Endicott, Johnson and Company.[83] Strengthened by its diversification into dress shoes, as well as women's and children's footwear, by its expansion into tanning and the manufacture of shoe components, and by its entry into retail sales, the firm became one of the largest and most structurally integrated shoe manufacturing firms in the nation.

Paralleling the growth of the physical plant, the size of the company's labor force increased significantly in the pre–World War I years, most dramatically after 1910, when the expansion of the firm was at its peak.[84] The thousands of workers who streamed into the factories placed additional pressure on the firm's informal paternalistic practices. But the pace of labor reforms in the prewar years was slow, suggesting that the personal proclivities of management for corporate paternalism were moderated by labor market considerations. Recruitment of workers was relatively easy in those years: immigrants, women, ex-farmers, and farm laborers provided the firm with a steady flow of new personnel. Only rudimentary gestures were required to attract and retain them as employees of the firm. Even the growing housing shortage experienced by both Lestershire and the newly founded village of Endicott was capable of igniting only a modest (and hardly generous) effort of relief on the part of management. Seventy-five homes costing between $3,000 and $3,500 were built in Endicott in 1904.[85]

The slow pace of corporate reform is particularly evident in the realm of health and sick-relief services. Early in 1896 the firm had first demonstrated a recognition of this need when it organized a mutual benefit society for its workers. The bylaws of the organization stated that members would receive sick benefits from the second to the eighth week of an illness, amounting to $5 a week. Ten cents a week was deducted from members' wages to fund the society. The company, for its part, contributed $3 every week to the benefit fund. The organization was fundamentally flawed from the start. The foreman of each room was responsible for determining whether a worker was truly ill and eligible for relief—a practice open to serious abuse.[86] Furthermore, the company's monetary contribution was miniscule; it would not be until 1916 that the firm would increase its financial commitment. The businesslike, intrusive, and capricious qualities of the plan led to a somewhat hostile response from workers. Few joined.[87]

In the prewar years the firm's concern for the health of its employees was expressed, for the most part, through the personal involvement of the Johnsons. Insuring medical attention for injured employees became part of the direct responsibility of top management. It was typical, for example, for George F. Johnson, or one of the other Johnsons, to directly attend to and fetch injured workers to a doctor.[88] Yet such personal attention disguised the reality that the firm's medical services in the first decade of the century remained limited, highly arbitrary, and designed more to deal with the threat of lawsuits than with the health of workers. In 1903 the New York State Department of Labor, in a survey of "Employers' Welfare Institutions," described the extent of the company's medical and health commitment to its operatives:

> Provision for prompt aid in case of the accidental injury of any employee is made in a hospital room in the factory, which is kept always ready for occupancy, and in all accidents the company pays for the first attendance of a physician. . . . No formal system of benefits is maintained, but in each case of sickness the firm makes careful inquiry into the circumstances of the employee who is incapacitated from work and frequently wages are paid during this period of disability. Voluntary expenditures of this sort which the company has been in the habit of making have amounted to between $2,000 and $2,600 a year.[89]

Considering the size of the labor force in 1903 — close to 3,000 — an expenditure of $2,000 or $3,000 a year on disability was hardly adequate.

While the firm provided various other services to its employees in the prewar years, these, too, were modest in scope and impelled by mixed motives. A savings plan, through which workers could deposit savings with the firm and receive a 6 percent yearly return on their money, was instituted to encourage thrift, as well as to provide cheap capital for the firm's expansion. The many women who entered the firm required special treatment that both conscience and public prejudice sanctioned. By 1900 over 400 women worked in the Lestershire Factory, their numbers having increased dramatically in the latter part of the 1890s.[90] The large representation of women amidst a far larger male population led management to consider providing factory amenities for female employees. In July 1901 local papers announced that George F. Johnson planned to establish space for a "Rest Club" for women workers at the Lestershire Factory. A dining room for lunches, coffee, and tea was to be provided, along with a rest lounge with a "fine line of good literature."[91] After the expansion of the fine shoe departments of the company in 1901 and the construction of the Endicott Fine Welt Factory, more and more young women were sought to take over stitching jobs. Local papers periodically reported that "young women from here have found employment in the Endicott shoe factory."[92] Recognizing that by humanizing the factory environment the firm would have a better chance of attracting and retaining female workers, management soon came to provide the same sort of amenities for its female Endicott employees as it had for their Lestershire counterparts. One former Endicott stitcher could still recall, in later years, the loft in the Fine Welt Factory where two or three cots were available for tired women workers to rest upon during their lunch break.[93]

VI

The bonds of "warm friendship" between managers and workers, as the Binghamton historian writing in 1900 had referred to it, were cultivated not merely within the confines of factory walls; for George F. Johnson believed that "it is not entirely what happens inside the factory, as what happens outside, that affects working conditions." What happened outside was a careful cultivation of an identity of interests between capitalist and worker: "Those who control, live with, work with, and play with the working people. The families, outside the factory, meet on an equal basis; the children play together."[94]

From the late 1890s through the early years of World War I, the firm's corporate paternalism was community oriented and was generally manifested informally in the personal acts of its managers and their families. Johnson had brought his two brothers into the firm earlier—the oldest, C. Fred Johnson, in 1884, and the younger, Harry L. Johnson, in 1895. In a blend of philanthropy and self-interest, they cultivated the good will of their workers and the community. They became involved in all varieties of civic affairs. George F. Johnson's second wife, for example, who had been a forelady in the Lestershire Factory's stitching room, took local girls into her home and taught them sewing and other domestic skills, a precursor of her more extensive Americanization projects during World War I.[95] As early as 1897 local papers took notice of the community spirit exhibited by the Lestershire Manufacturing Company: "They are more than ordinarily interested in the town outside of their industry. The different members of the firm are active in all of the public enterprises of the town, and subscribe liberally to help along every project which is of benefit to the village." Contributions to local charities and churches, as well as for local civic improvements such as parks and road construction, came continually from the Johnson family, particularly from George F. Johnson. In 1897 he donated $1,000 for a local park. A year later, mainly through Johnson's influence, the Lestershire Manufacturing Company offered to pay close to half of the cost of a central fire station and recreation center for the village of Lestershire. In contributing extensively to community charities, civic projects, and local recreation, the Johnsons solidified their influence over local public life. For them, this was not only good business but also a reflection of their loyalty to the community. George F. Johnson and his brothers believed that a manufacturing enterprise should be rooted in its surrounding community, and they emphasized the mutuality of interests that necessarily existed between firm and village. The contribution of a new fire truck or of funds for the macadamizing of roads represented expenditures valuable to both the company and Lestershire.[96]

The wedding of community paternalism and business expediency was particularly exemplified in the Johnsons' involvement in local civic organizations. Both C. Fred Johnson and George F. Johnson were active in Lestershire's Board of Trade, with C. Fred Johnson serving as president in 1897.[97] George F. Johnson became a trustee of the local Businessman's Club, whose motto was "Lestershire's Interest is Our Interest."[98] In the 1890s C. Fred Johnson was periodically elected chief fire engineer of Lestershire and later became fire commissioner.[99] In 1904, when all of the fire companies of Lestershire were united into one organization, George F. Johnson was chosen president. The Johnsons recognized the important social and economic function of the volunteer fire companies. Not only were they necessary to protect the property of the firm, but they also represented an arena where workers and capitalists met on a somewhat equal ground and thus functioned to erode class tensions.[100]

Through politics, too, the Johnsons tried to merge community and company interests, although in this realm their obvious selfish motives undermined their effectiveness. In 1908 Harry L. Johnson, George F. Johnson's younger brother, ran for and won the presidency of the recently incorporated village of Endicott.[101] C. Fred Johnson became president of the village of Lestershire in 1909, amidst a great deal of controversy. It was charged that he was seeking too much influence over the village board of trustees. He wanted full authority to make all appointments; as a result, four of the village's six trustees resigned.[102] Politics for the Johnsons obviously involved controversy. But the selection of key municipal officials was crucial to ensure the secure operation of their factory. The appointment of a "friendly" water commissioner would prevent the sort of inconvenience that occurred in 1904, when water was ordered shut off to the firm's factories until water meters had been installed in each one. Although a local justice issued an injunction preventing the shutoff, such events highlighted the importance of appointing and maintaining sympathetic local officials in municipal posts.[103] This was particularly true with respect to taxes, since the power to set tax rates or assess property valuation of company factories placed an understandable temptation on village officers and tax assessors. It is hardly surprising to learn that C. Fred Johnson, as president of Lestershire, had managed to reduce property taxes in 1909 from $13 to $10 per $1,000 of assessed valuation.[104] As the Johnsons amassed community allies, it became less necessary and, in fact, counterproductive for management to involve itself directly in local politics. George F. Johnson, by the late 1910s, had made it the firm's policy that company officers could no longer serve in local government posts.

Far more conducive to the cultivation of cordial community relations was the participation of the Johnsons in local battles over the annexation of Lestershire by Binghamton, a move they sought to prevent, and over sabbatical recreation, which they supported. In both community controversies George F. Johnson took a particularly active role. He became the president of the local Anti-Annexation League and lobbied heavily in the state legislature against attempts by Binghamton and Lestershire businessmen to annex Lestershire. His lobbying paid off. The antiannexationists triumphed when the state assembly committee failed to report the annexation bill to the floor.[105]

As he had become the champion of Lestershire in his victory over the annexationists, so too did Johnson become a champion in his advocacy of community athletics. He had always loved athletics as a worker. Now, as a capitalist, he recognized its other virtues. In 1900 Johnson donated land to the newly formed Lestershire Athletic Association. His support of the association was rooted not merely in his boyhood love of baseball and sports in general but also in a recognition that the organization had a more important social function in muting class consciousness. A local Lestershire paper acknowledged such a function in praising the egalitarian structure in which workers and capitalists commingled in the association: "It certainly is a rare pleasure for a poor man, for such nearly all the citizens of Lestershire are, to reside in a village where everybody seems to feel like brothers and have the blessed privilege of associating with men who possess an abundant [*sic*] of the world's goods that do not feel out of place because of such, who work together for the interests and prosperity of the community without any selfish motive whatever."[106]

The unity of interests between capitalist and working-class promoters of athletics was particularly evident during community battles over Sunday baseball, disputes that periodically surfaced in the first few decades of the century and that were mirrored in similar controversies over Sunday movies and other forms of sabbatical recreation.[107] The debates over Sunday baseball, from the start, were translated from a cultural controversy into a class conflict, but with a twist. Middle- and upper-class professionals and businessmen who backed Sunday baseball defined the issue along class lines, thus creating a bogus cultural class enemy that helped to diffuse more volatile economic and industrial conflicts.

The controversy over Sunday baseball that surfaced in 1913 is an excellent example of the way in which the issue could ally worker and capitalist interests. George F. Johnson had been extremely active in promoting local baseball and in initiating Sunday ball games. The previous year he had purchased the Binghamton state league club and franchise, and only recently he had completed the construction of a new baseball stadium in Lestershire.[108] Although he donated proceeds from Sunday ball games to local charities, Johnson still came under fire from the local custodial middle class, particularly Protestant ministers and lodges. A pitched battle between supporters and detractors ensued, one carefully followed by local papers. One particular letter in the *Binghamton Press*, responding to the controversy, demonstrated the transformation of Sunday baseball into a class issue when the writer argued that

> it is rather inconsistent for those who ride Sunday afternoons in their automobiles or drive their horses and carriages or go boating on our beautiful Susquehanna river or have a number of other pleasant but harmless recreations to say that it is wrong for others who are not as fortunate as themselves to go to a Sunday baseball game. To my mind we are reaching a very important and serious problem on the labor question and Binghamton and vicinity with its largely increasing foreign population is a different place than the city of twenty years ago. . . . The rabid order known as the International [*sic*] Workers of the World have created havoc in other places by the inciting of the non-thinking workers against manufacturers, and such things may be repeated also right in this beautiful city with the argument appealing to them that the classes are against them. A great deal of bitterness has sprung up between the people who are interested on each side of this Sunday baseball proposition which is not going to help the success of this city.[109]

Such sentiments were by no means unique to Binghamton or Lestershire. In a conference of mayors held in Auburn, New York, in June 1913, the mayor of that city made very similar points:

> If you say to the laboring man you can have no recreation on Sunday as your rich friend has, you are laying the foundation for future anarchy. But if while he is sweating in his shop his employer is doing his part in contributing for parks, playgrounds and breathing places for the working man, his wife and children, he realizes his employer is doing his share. If you tell him that on Sunday when he goes to church in the morning the city is going to allow the baseball club to play a game of ball in the afternoon, it makes for contentment.[110]

By becoming a champion of the "working classes" in supporting a policy opposed by many of the local, middle-class Protestant clergy, Johnson established himself as an ally of his own workers. Thus, ironically, the politicization of recreation and its translation into class terms served to dampen class consciousness. Indeed, petitions were circulated in the community and factories in support of Johnson's position. A worker suggested the prevailing sentiment in a letter appearing in the *Binghamton Press:* "Sunday baseball is a great help to the masses of people who have only Sunday afternoon in which to enjoy this harmless recreation. Now, why should these people who labor six days in the week be coaxed to keep away from this enjoyable pastime? . . . George F. Johnson, a man who has started this clean recreation, should be given loyal support."[111]

For decades afterward Johnson's battle for Sunday baseball remained lodged in workers' minds. In fact, it became part of the collective memory of the community and an important part of the Johnson legacy. As late as the 1970s and 1980s, older, retired workers fondly recalled Johnson's renegade role in these early community battles: "He had a philosophy that he would do everything for the worker. You know they wouldn't let them have Sunday baseball years ago. . . . They wouldn't let them charge admission to them. He'd take and give everybody tickets to go to that game. He'd give me tickets there in Derby's Drugstore. You could meet him there and he'd give you tickets to go, you and your family. I've been to ball games and he'd sit right along side of me, my Mrs. and him."[112]

The employee benefits offered by the firm, the civic paternalism practiced by management, and the cross-class collaboration fostered by George F. Johnson and his kin tended to, in the words of a sympathetic local newspaper editor, "draw the working people closer and closer" to the company.[113] That was, after all, the Johnsons' goal. By promoting a solidarity not only between managers and workers but also between firm and village, the company hoped to create a community of loyal and stable workers.

Yet, as we have also seen, the firm's practices, in these early years of the century, remained inchoate and limited in scope. An ever-growing work force and a structurally and geographically expanding business strained its modest efforts; so, too, did the new social and labor conditions that accompanied the First World War. They constituted a challenge to managers committed to a paternalistic labor course and were important factors in transforming an informal and capricious paternalism into a far more coherent and structured labor policy—in short, into a corporate welfare system.

NOTES

1. *Binghamton Daily Leader,* Dec. 6, 1894.
2. This is not to say that the influence of such ideologies waned. On their importance in mid- and late nineteenth-century America, see Stephan Thernstrom, *Poverty and Progress: Social Mobility in a Nineteenth Century City* (Cambridge, Mass., 1964); Herbert G. Gutman, "The Reality of the Rags-to-Riches 'Myth,'" in Gutman, *Work, Culture & Society in Industrializing America* (New York, 1976); Irvin G. Wyllie, *The Self-Made Man in America: The Myth of Rags to Riches* (New York, 1954).
3. Stuart D. Brandes, *American Welfare Capitalism, 1880–1940* (Chicago, 1976), 10–11; John F. Kasson, *Civilizing the Machine: Technology and Republican Values in America, 1776–1900* (New York, 1976), chap. 2; Leo Marx, *The Machine in the Garden: Technology and the Pastoral Ideal in America* (New York, 1964); Morrell Heald, *The Social Responsibilities of Business: Company and Community, 1900–1960* (Cleveland, 1970), chap. 1.
4. Edward Berkowitz and Kim McQuaid, *Creating the Welfare State: The Political Economy of Twentieth-Century Reform* (New York, 1980), chap. 1; Brandes, *American Welfare Capitalism,* chap. 2; Heald, *The Social Responsibilities of Business,* chap. 1.
5. *Binghamton Daily Republican,* Nov. 23, 1888. On the early history of Lester's firm, the predecessor to the Endicott Johnson Corporation, see my dissertation, "Workers, Managers, and Welfare Capitalism: The Shoeworkers and Tanners of Endicott Johnson, 1880–1950" (Ph.D. diss., Syracuse University, 1983), chap. 1.
6. An excellent sociopsychological study of paternalism and the Pullman community can be found in Richard Sennett, *Authority* (New York, 1980). See also Almont Lindsey, *The Pullman Strike: The Story of a Unique Experiment and of a Great Labor Upheaval* (Chicago, 1942); and Stanley Buder, *Pullman: An Experiment in Industrial Order and Community Planning, 1880–1930* (New York, 1967). John F. Kasson's *Civilizing the Machine* is a fine treatment of American anxieties over the growth of industrialization.
7. William S. Lawyer, ed., *Binghamton: Its Settlement, Growth and Development and the Factors in Its History, 1800–1900* (Binghamton, N.Y., 1900), 650–51; *Binghamton Press,* Apr. 11, 1914; *Binghamton Daily Republican,* Jan. 14, June 3, June 11, 1890, Aug. 31, 1891.
8. *Binghamton Daily Republican,* June 4, 1890.

9. *E-J Workers Magazine* 4 (Sept. 1925). This is George F. Johnson's recollection of Lester's activities.

10. *Binghamton Evening Herald,* Sept. 23, 1891; *Democratic Weekly Leader,* Sept. 25, 1891.

11. Among the new firm's major stockholders were ex-secretary of the Navy William Collins Whitney, whose sons married into the Vanderbilt and Hay families; Ohio senator Henry B. Payne, who had extensive connections with the Standard Oil Company and whose son Oliver H. Payne was the treasurer of Standard Oil; and Daniel Scott Lamont, private secretary and close confidant of Grover Cleveland, destined to serve as secretary of war during Cleveland's second presidential term. On the board of directors of the new firm was Charles S. Fairchild, ex-secretary of the Treasury and president of the New York Trust Company. *Democratic Daily Leader,* Mar. 15, 1890; *Democratic Weekly Leader,* Mar. 21, Apr. 11, 1890; Dumas Malone, ed., *Dictionary of American Biography* (New York, 1933), 20:165–66, 14:325–26, 10:563–64, 6:251–52.

12. The average size of the work force shrank to 425 in 1891. In 1892 it remained at that figure, and in 1893 it dipped to 400. These statistics do not tell the whole story. At one point the factory shut down entirely. New York State, *Report of the Factory Inspector,* 5th through 8th annual reports (Albany, 1891–94).

13. *Democratic Weekly Leader,* Dec. 25, 1891, July 22, 1892; *Lestershire Record,* Mar. 26, 1897.

14. Endicott's reorganization of 1892–93 created two companies, the Lestershire Manufacturing Company, which retained its predecessor's name, and the Lestershire Boot and Shoe Company. The latter corporation held ownership of the factory buildings and land, while the former took over the manufacturing end of the business. George F. Johnson to G. Harry Lester, Mar. 12, 1928, box 9, George F. Johnson Papers, George Arents Research Library for Special Collections, Syracuse University, Syracuse, N.Y.; *Biographical Review* (Binghamton) (Boston, 1894), 91–92; *Binghamton Sun,* Nov. 29, 1948; *Binghamton Republican,* Mar. 17, 1897; *Binghamton Evening Herald,* Mar. 17, 1897.

15. *Binghamton Republican,* Jan. 27, 1890. For another description of the factory, see *Lester-Shire News,* Apr. 11, 1891.

16. G. Ralph Smith, "Aspects of Economic Development of Broome County, New York, 1900–1951" (Ph.D. diss., Syracuse University, 1954), 35.

17. *Binghamton Press,* July 6, 1952.

18. New York State, Department of Labor, *Eleventh Annual Report of the Bureau of Statistics of Labor* (Albany, 1894), 1:644–45. Binghamton workers tended to be older, reflecting the city's more established shoeworker population. See ibid., 502–3.

19. The 1892 directory underrepresented the actual number of transients (and shoe-workers) in the community, since it was biased toward stable residents. Furthermore, the hundred-or-so shoeworkers of Binghamton's small shoe factories and custom shops also bias the estimate of temporary Lester-Shire Factory employees downward. The proportion of boarding shoeworkers in 1880 is based on analysis of the 1880 federal manuscript population census for Binghamton, a source that should have "captured" *more* boarders than the city directory. Binghamton, *City Directory* (1892); New York State, Department of Labor, *Tenth*

Annual Report of the Bureau of Statistics of Labor (Albany, 1893), 1:139; idem, *Eleventh Annual Report of the Bureau of Statistics of Labor* 1:502–3, 644–45; U.S. Bureau of the Census, "Population of the United States in 1880," for Broome County, N.Y.

20. U.S. Bureau of the Census, "Population of the United States in 1900," for Broome County, N.Y.; Imrich Mazar, ed., *Dejiny binghamtonských slovákov za dobu štyridsat' rokov, 1879–1919* [Forty years of the history of Binghamton Slovaks, 1879–1919] (Binghamton, N.Y., 1919), 7, 61. More will be said on the immigrants in chap. 3.

21. New York State, *Report of the Factory Inspector,* 4th through 15th annual reports (Albany, 1890–1901). The proportion of women workers fluctuated from a low of 20 percent to a high of 31 percent through the 1890s.

22. Gutman, *Work, Culture and Society in Industrializing America,* chap. 1.

23. *E.-J. Workers' Review* 1 (Apr. 1919): 28.

24. See the recollections of a worker in ibid. (May 1919): 25.

25. Ibid. (June 1919): 53.

26. This transformation is reflected in an increase in occupational categories employed by some federal census enumerators. See the federal manuscript schedules of 1880 and 1900 for Broome County. Not all enumerators, however, distinguished between occupational groups among the shoeworkers. Most simply wrote "shoeworker."

27. Subsequent events should also be viewed in the context of the broader currents of worker militancy of the 1880s and 1890s. See Philip S. Foner, *History of the Labor Movement in the United States,* vol. 2, *From the Founding of the A.F. of L. to the Emergence of American Imperialism* (New York, 1975); Jeremy Brecher, *Strike!* (San Francisco, 1972), chap. 3; Chester McArthur Destler, *American Radicalism, 1865–1901* (Chicago, 1966). On the rise of agrarian militancy and the Populist movement, see Lawrence Goodwyn, *The Democratic Promise: The Populist Moment in America* (Oxford, 1976).

28. For a more detailed treatment of the cigarworkers' strike, see my dissertation, "Workers, Managers, and Welfare Capitalism," 52–59; and Nancy Grey Osterud's "Mechanics, Operatives and Laborers," in Ross McGuire and Nancy Grey Osterud, *Working Lives: Broome County, New York, 1800–1930, a Social History of People at Work in Our Region* (Binghamton, N.Y., 1980), 55–61.

29. *Democratic Weekly Leader,* Aug. 8, 1890. See also *Democratic Daily Leader,* Aug. 2, Aug. 4, 1890.

30. *Democratic Daily Leader,* Aug. 2, 1890.

31. *Democratic Weekly Leader,* Sept. 11, 1891. This had not taken place in previous years.

32. In Sept. 1893 Local 120 members proudly participated with fellow unionists from other trades in the annual Labor Day parade. By the following year the local and its officers were listed in the city directory. *Democratic Weekly Leader,* Sept. 8, 1893; Binghamton, *City Directory* (1894), 72; New York State, Department of Labor, *Twelfth Annual Report of the Bureau of Statistics of Labor* (Albany, 1895), 36.

33. Gerald N. Grob, *Workers and Utopia: A Study of Ideological Conflict in the*

American Labor Movement, 1865–1900 (New York, 1969), 117, 119–24.

34. Augusta E. Galster, *The Labor Movement in the Shoe Industry, with Special Reference to Philadelphia* (New York, 1934), 57–64, 74–79; *The Shoe Workers' Journal* 11 (July 1910): 5–14; (Aug. 1910): 5–11.

35. In fact, hourly pay remained in force in many departments through the next three decades. The process of conversion to piecework was not an overnight affair. Johnson merely initiated the process during this period. A photograph of old Lester-Shire Factory time-book pages clearly shows both hourly and piece wage-workers in the factory's lasting and bottoming rooms in 1895 and 1897. See *E.-J. Workers' Review* 1 (Feb. 1920): 67. Employment records from the late 1910s and early 1920s also document a mix of hourly and piece wages in many factory departments. According to one student of the shoe industry, overall, fully one-third of the nation's shoe factory work force remained on timework as late as the early 1920s. Frederick J. Allen, *The Shoe Industry* (New York, 1922), 273.

36. William Inglis, *George F. Johnson and His Industrial Democracy* (New York, 1935), 33–36.

37. New York State, *Twelfth Annual Report of the Bureau of Statistics of Labor,* 288.

38. Average yearly wages of the workers rose from a low of about $200 in 1892 to $490 in 1895. New York State, Department of Labor, *Fourteenth Annual Report of the Bureau of Statistics of Labor* (Albany, 1897), 28–29. According to the official historian of the firm, daily production increased from 1,000 to 18,000 pairs of shoes and boots in "a little more than two years." Inglis, *George F. Johnson,* 39.

39. New York State, *Twelfth Annual Report of the Bureau of Statistics of Labor,* 87. Previously the workers had averaged only about ten months of work a year. The union exaggerated the extent of piecework. It was *not* "all piece-work."

40. Daniel Nelson, *Managers and Workers: Origins of the New Factory System in the United States, 1880–1920* (Madison, Wis., 1975), 45.

41. For a particularly good, although overstated, discussion of the divisive impact of piece rates on the firm's workers, see Osterud, "Mechanics, Operatives and Laborers," 73–74. For an equally fine discussion of the rise of various wage-incentive schemes in the steel industry and their impact on workers, see Katherine Stone, "The Origins of Job Structures in the Steel Industry," *Review of Radical Political Economics* 6 (Summer 1974): 128–32.

42. *Binghamton Republican,* Mar. 1, 1894. "Sample season" referred to the slack period before the influx of heavy orders, when the firm produced shoe samples to be shown to buyers.

43. *Binghamton Daily Leader,* Feb. 28, Mar. 2, 1894. For more on the incident, see *Binghamton Republican,* Mar. 1, Mar. 2, 1894; *Binghamton Evening Herald,* Feb. 28, Mar. 1, Mar. 2, 1894.

44. *Binghamton Republican,* Mar. 1, 1894.

45. *Democratic Daily Leader,* Mar. 13, 1895.

46. Irwin Yellowitz, "Skilled Workers and Mechanization: The Lasters in the 1890s," *Labor History* 18 (Spring 1977): 197–213. Cutting or "clicking" machines were not introduced until 1908. The new machines, however, did not

diminish the skill required of a cutter. See the *Shoe Workers' Journal* 9 (May 1908): 9.

47. *Binghamton Evening Herald,* Aug. 2, 1897. See also *Democratic Weekly Leader,* Aug. 6, 1897.

48. *Binghamton Evening Herald,* Aug. 2, 1897. It was common practice for skilled shoeworkers, like cutters, to "tramp" from one factory town to another, hence the notification of cutters to stay away from Lestershire. [Note that by the mid-1890s "Lester-Shire" had become "Lestershire."]

49. New York State, Department of Labor, *Thirteenth Annual Report of the Bureau of Statistics of Labor* (Albany, 1896), 412.

50. *Binghamton Evening Herald,* Mar. 2, 1895.

51. *Democratic Daily Leader,* Mar. 13, 1895.

52. Boot and Shoe Workers' Union [BSWU], *Report of Proceedings of the Second Convention of the Boot and Shoe Workers' Union* (Boston, 1896), 20. Per capita dues from Local 42 continued to come into the national union office after Apr. 1895, suggesting that the union struggled to hold on. See ibid., 28.

53. *Shoe Workers' Journal* 20 (Nov. 1919): 15.

54. BSWU, *Report of Proceedings of the Joint Convention of Boot and Shoe Workers* (Boston, 1895), 9. Haycock had resided in Lestershire. He returned in 1916 and was reemployed by the firm. *E.-J. Workers' Review* 1 (Jan. 1920): 21.

55. *E.-J. Workers' Review* 1 (Aug. 1919): 50; *Binghamton Sun,* Feb. 6, 1932. Connerton, either during the time he was serving in the union or soon afterward, may have been utilized by Johnson as a company spy. See Charles F. Johnson, Jr., to George F. Johnson, Jan. 31, 1939, box 32, ser. 1, Charles F. Johnson, Jr., Papers, George Arents Research Library for Special Collections, Syracuse University, Syracuse, N.Y.

56. Andrew Carnegie, "Wealth," *North American Review* 148 (June 1889): 657–62; cited in Edward Chase Kirkland, *Dream and Thought in the Business Community, 1860–1900* (Chicago, 1964), 146–47. See also Joseph Frazier Wall, *Andrew Carnegie* (New York, 1970), chap. 21. On the social gospel movement of the period, see Sidney Fine, *Laissez Faire and the General-Welfare State: A Study of Conflict in American Thought, 1865–1901* (Ann Arbor, Mich., 1956), chap. 6; and Charles Howard Hopkins, *The Rise of the Social Gospel in American Protestantism, 1865–1915* (New Haven, Conn., 1940).

57. On the impact of Carnegie's early encounter with Chartism on his later life, see Wall, *Andrew Carnegie.*

58. George F. Johnson to Mrs. Nina G. K. Heft, Jan. 18, 1927, box 8, George F. Johnson Papers; *Biographical Review* (Binghamton), 91; Inglis, *George F. Johnson,* chap. 1.

59. George F. Johnson to William Johnson, Aug. 27, 1929, box 10; George F. Johnson to Lewis Alberine, Nov. 2, 1926, box 8, George F. Johnson Papers; Inglis, *George F. Johnson,* chap. 2.

60. Mike Fahey to George F. Johnson, Oct. 25, 1921, box 4, George F. Johnson Papers; Inglis, *George F. Johnson,* chap. 2. Johnson would later name the Lestershire Factory after his old baseball team, the Pioneers.

61. George F. Johnson, "30 Years without a Strike," *System* 37 (Jan. 1920): 46.

62. Don D. Lescohier, *The Knights of St. Crispin, 1864–1874,* Bulletin of the University of Wisconsin, no. 355 (Madison, Wis., 1910), 5.

63. On the militancy and socialist sympathies of Massachusetts shoeworkers, see Alan Dawley, *Class and Community: The Industrial Revolution in Lynn* (Cambridge, Mass., 1976); Henry F. Bedford, *Socialism and the Workers in Massachusetts, 1886–1912* (Amherst, Mass., 1966); Mary H. Blewett, "The Union of Sex and Craft in the Haverhill Shoe Strike of 1895," *Labor History* 20 (Summer 1979): 352–75; and John H. M. Laslett, *Labor and the Left: A Study of Socialist and Radical Influences in the American Labor Movement, 1881–1924* (New York, 1970), chap. 3.

64. Inglis, *George F. Johnson,* 21.

65. Johnson, "30 Years without a Strike," 46–47. See also George F. Johnson to Harold and Lena Chamberlain, Apr. 25, 1933, box 12, George F. Johnson Papers, for a similar version of his "transformation."

66. Inglis, *George F. Johnson,* 42.

67. Ibid., 37.

68. H. B. Endicott to George F. Johnson, Feb. 10, 1900, box 2; "Cancelled Checks" folder, box 20, George F. Johnson Papers. Inglis, *George F. Johnson,* 40–41; *Democratic Weekly Leader,* Apr. 9, 1901. By the time Johnson bought into the firm, Endicott had pretty much gained control over all of the real estate and property of both the Lestershire Manufacturing Company and the Lestershire Boot and Shoe Company. See *Lestershire Record,* Mar. 26, 1897; *Binghamton Republican,* Mar. 17, 1897; *Democratic Weekly Leader,* Mar. 19, 1897.

69. *Democratic Weekly Leader,* Feb. 21, 1901; *Binghamton Evening Herald,* Feb. 21, 1901. On the early development of Endicott, see Jeffrey Pines, "Endicott, New York: Industry, Immigrants & Paternalism" (Honors thesis, Dept. of History, S.U.N.Y. at Binghamton, 1982), chap. 1.

70. *Democratic Weekly Leader,* May 24, 1900. The *Leader* was quoting from the Sunday *New York Herald,* May 19, 1900.

71. *Lestershire Record,* Dec. 13, 1901.

72. Ibid., Aug. 16, 1901.

73. See, for example, *Binghamton Press,* Mar. 18, 1910.

74. On local, middle-class women's efforts to combat prostitution and sexual vice, see Alice Miller, "Binghamton's Good Women — 1890 to 1917" (Research paper, S.U.N.Y. at Binghamton, 1980), 38–42 and passim. The House for Fallen Women was established in 1895 by the local chapter of the Women's Christian Temperance Union. Late in the 1890s control was transferred to the Binghamton Ministerial Association, and in the early years of the twentieth century, it became closely affiliated with the Broome County Humane Society. Information on the House for Fallen Women, also known as the Refuge for Unwed Mothers, can be found in vol. 38, Putnam Document Collection, Binghamton Public Library; the *Binghamton Press,* Apr. 11, 1914; and in Miller's paper. I would like to thank Professor Sarah Elbert of S.U.N.Y. at Binghamton for making Alice Miller's paper available to me.

75. *Binghamton Press,* July 6, 1952.

76. Biographical material on Harry L. Johnson (George F. Johnson's younger

brother) and George Willis Johnson (George F. Johnson's son) can be found in Rev. William MacAlpine's memorial biography of Harry L. Johnson, *A Brief Memoir of Harry Leonard Johnson* (Johnson City, N.Y., [1922]), in box 2, ser. 2, of the George W. Johnson Papers, George Arents Research Library for Special Collections, Syracuse University, Syracuse, N.Y. For further information, see box 1, ser. 1, in this same collection.

77. *Lestershire Record,* Mar. 8, 1901.
78. General ledger for 1892–1914, box 20, George F. Johnson Papers.
79. *Lestershire Record,* June 21, 1901.
80. *New York Herald,* June 30, 1901. This article was partially reprinted in the *Lestershire Record,* July 5, 1901. In late Oct. 1901 Tilt left the employ of the firm. See the following for more information on him: *Lestershire Record,* Nov. 1, 1901; *Democratic Weekly Record,* Nov. 7, 1901; *Union Boot and Shoe Worker* 2 (Nov. 1901): 11, 14; *Binghamton Sunday Press* [magazine], Oct. 1, 1978, Mar. 25, 1979.
81. Lawyer, ed., *Binghamton,* 664.
82. See the firm's appeals to investors in the *Lestershire Record,* June 7, June 28, Aug. 16, 1901.
83. G. Ralph Smith, *The Endicott Johnson Corporation* (New Orleans, 1956), 7. The firm continued to take in partners through 1919, when it was incorporated. Just previous to incorporation, eleven partners made up the firm: H. B. Endicott, George F. Johnson, H. L. Johnson, Eliot Spalding, George W. Johnson, Chester B. Lord, H. W. Endicott, J. A. R. Bowes, George W. Holyoke, C. F. Johnson, Jr., and C. Fred Johnson. Henry B. Endicott and George F. Johnson held the largest shares of the business. In June 1907 $10,000 of capital stock was sold to five junior partners by Johnson and Endicott. The original five partners were H. L. Johnson, Eliot Spalding, Chester B. Lord, G. W. Johnson, and H. W. Endicott, all officers in the company. H. L. Johnson was a factory manager. Eliot Spalding had been treasurer of the Lestershire Manufacturing Company and later continued in that position in the companies that succeeded it. Chester B. Lord was in charge of sales, continuing in that role until his resignation in 1927. G. W. Johnson headed the tannery operations of the firm, and H. W. Endicott took charge of the Wholesale Department in Boston. Eliot Spalding to Herbert C. Freeman, Feb. 19, 1919, box 18; Endicott Johnson Corporation Stock Listing Certificates, 1919, box 22; "Statement of Taxes of Partners," box 16, George F. Johnson Papers.
84. Between 1900 and 1910 the firm's labor force grew from 2,000 to 4,000. Yet in the next three years an additional 2,000 workers found employment in the company. *Binghamton Press,* Dec. 24, 1910; "To the Workers" notice, Jan. 13, 1944, box 34, ser. 1, Charles F. Johnson, Jr., Papers.
85. Richard S. Saul, "An American Entrepreneur: George F. Johnson" (D.S.S. diss., Syracuse University, 1966), 16–17. The firm later came to regret its failure to build on a larger scale. See "A Brief Statement of Facts of Interest to Home Owners of West Endicott," June 1, 1923, box 4, ser. 2, George W. Johnson Papers.
86. *Lestershire Record,* Dec. 11, Dec. 18, 1896.
87. Inglis, *George F. Johnson,* 221–22.

88. *Binghamton Press,* Aug. 16, 1910; *Broome Republican,* Dec. 7, 1907; *Democratic Weekly Leader,* Feb. 11, 1904. Recognizing the need for adequate community medical facilities for their workers, the Johnsons took an avid interest in developing such facilities. Both C. Fred Johnson and George F. Johnson served on the board of the Lestershire King's Daughters' Hospital and endowed beds at the facility. *Broome Republican,* June 17, 1905.

89. "Employers' Welfare Institutions," in New York State, Department of Labor, *Third Annual Report of the Commissioner of Labor* (Albany, 1904), 252–53. On the legal, social, and political context within which medical care and compensation were provided by businesses in the early years of the century, see Roy Lubove, "Workmen's Compensation and the Prerogatives of Voluntarism," *Labor History* 8 (Fall 1967); Robert F. Wesser, "Conflict and Compromise: The Workmen's Compensation Movement in New York, 1890s–1913," *Labor History* 12 (Summer 1971); James Weinstein, *The Corporate Ideal in the Liberal State, 1900–1918* (Boston, 1968), chap. 2; National Industrial Conference Board, *The Workmen's Compensation Problem in New York State* (New York, 1927).

90. New York State, *Fifteenth Annual Report of the Factory Inspector* (Albany, 1901), 661.

91. *Democratic Weekly Leader,* July 4, 1901.

92. Ibid., Dec. 5, 1901.

93. Helen Bruno, interview by Gerald Zahavi, with the assistance of Deborah D. Maxwell, July 13, 1981, tape recording (personal possession).

94. Johnson, "30 Years without a Strike," 45, 47.

95. *Democratic Weekly Leader,* Jan. 17, 1901; "Biographical Data" file, box 1, George F. Johnson Papers; Inglis, *George F. Johnson,* 211–12. What, if any, influence Mary A. Johnson had on her husband is uncertain, since he rarely mentioned her in his correspondence.

96. *Lestershire Record,* Mar. 26, Sept. 17, 1897, Nov. 11, 1898; *Democratic Weekly Leader,* Nov. 3, 1901; *Binghamton Republican,* Mar. 17, 1897.

97. *Democratic Weekly Leader,* Feb. 19, 1897.

98. Ibid., Nov. 29, 1900.

99. Ibid., Feb. 5, 1899; *Lestershire Record,* June 7, 1901.

100. *Democratic Weekly Leader,* Feb. 11, 1904. See Paul G. Faler's discussion of the role of fire companies in nineteenth-century Lynn in his *Mechanics and Manufacturers in the Early Industrial Revolution: Lynn, Massachusetts, 1780–1860* (New York, 1981), 202–4 and passim.

101. *Broome Republican,* Mar. 21, 1908.

102. Ibid., Apr. 10, May 1, 1909.

103. The company also utilized the local postal commissioner, William H. Hill (later to achieve prominence as a New York legislator), to circulate cheaply the *Lestershire Record* throughout the country to advertise the firm. This led to charges of postal fraud and the removal of Hill as postmaster. Hill was half-owner of the *Record* at the time and son-in-law of C. Fred Johnson. See *Broome Republican,* Apr. 27, May 11, 1907; *Endicott Bulletin,* Aug. 22, Oct. 31, 1918.

104. *Binghamton Press,* Feb. 3, 1910. This was during a period of contraction of the village's industrial base, a product of the depression of 1907–8.

105. *Democratic Weekly Leader,* Mar. 30, Apr. 6, Apr. 20, 1905; *Binghamton Press,*

Apr. 11, 1914. See also numerous articles appearing in the *Broome Republican* and other local papers in Apr. 1905.

106. *Lestershire Record,* May 24, 1901. The importance of sport in the community was constantly attested to by local and national papers. See *Democratic Weekly Leader,* Apr. 26, 1900, June 25, 1903; *New York Sun,* June 25, 1903.

107. Two particularly bitterly fought battles over Sunday baseball took place in 1904 and 1913. See the *Democratic Weekly Leader,* Apr. 21, Apr. 28, May 5, June 2, July 7, 1904. For the 1913 controversy, see May and June issues of the *Binghamton Press*.

108. *Binghamton Press,* May 7, 1910, May 6, 1913, Apr. 11, 1914.

109. Ibid., May 27, 1913.

110. Ibid., June 5, 1913.

111. Ibid., May 24, May 26, 1913. The petitions were circulated not only in Endicott Johnson factories but also among other industrial firms in the area. For a fascinating and more comprehensive analysis of the politics of working-class recreation, see Roy Rosenzweig, *Eight Hours for What We Will: Workers and Leisure in an Industrial City, 1870–1920* (New York, 1983).

112. D——, interview by David Nielson, June 25, 1974, transcript, 236.

113. *Lestershire Record,* Aug. 9, 1901.

2

The Rise of the "Square Deal"

The same factors that had impelled Endicott, Johnson and Company to venture into industrial paternalism led hundreds of other firms to do likewise, often on a far grander scale. Fear of government regulation, the need for mechanisms to integrate immigrants better into American industrial life, and a recognition of the benefits of good public relations were additional motivations—so, too, were the private quests of businessmen for a legitimating philanthropy, in Thorstein Veblen's words, a search "for some other than an invidious purpose in life."[1]

By the second decade of the new century, the collective efforts of hundreds of employers, in assuming more responsibility for the well-being of their operatives, had given rise to a movement that came to be known as welfare capitalism. Welfare advocates asserted that labor was not a mere commodity but a partner, albeit junior, that deserved fair treatment and consideration from capital. They emphasized that labor and capital shared a common goal—increasing production. Both partners would reap the bountiful harvest produced by cooperation. In translating these ideas into concrete reforms—such as company-provided housing, health care, profit sharing—progressive business leaders hoped to forge a corporate solidarity between workers and managers, one that would pay rich social and economic dividends.[2]

In the years preceding World War I, some forty major American firms had adopted extensive welfare programs. Many more, like Endicott, Johnson and Company, developed less comprehensive welfare policies. By 1917 perhaps as many as 2,000 firms throughout the country had incorporated some element of welfarism into their labor management practices.[3] Additional signs attesting to the growing acceptance and spread of welfare capitalism were visible. Universities, for example, started to offer courses in practical industrial welfare work as early as 1906, when the Chicago Institute of Social Science began to teach the subject. In 1908 Yale University created a course in "Industrial Service Work," and by 1916 over 150 engineering schools were providing such courses.[4] Numerous state and federal government departments studied the welfare practices of industry and published reports on companies employing welfare programs.[5] The administrations of Theodore Roosevelt, William Howard Taft, and Woodrow Wilson supported welfare work under various institutional and practical guises. Veteran welfare worker Gertrude Beeks, for example, was sent down to Panama to supervise welfare work among Panama Canal workers.[6]

Yet, of all the factors that fostered the growth of the industrial welfare movement, none was more powerful than World War I, for it was the war that profoundly affected private industry's receptiveness to welfare capitalism — that made converts of previously hostile or unresponsive businessmen. Reacting to the disruption of the prewar labor market, as well as to the rising tide of labor militancy that followed World War I, industries adopted or expanded welfare programs as a means of holding on to workers in a labor-starved economy and as a hedge against labor unions.[7] It was the war, in fact, that led to the enlargement of Endicott, Johnson and Company's paternalistic practices and that created the "Square Deal."

I

Endicott Johnson was a relative latecomer to welfarism, although in its informal and paternalistic policies it did exemplify many of the sentiments that motivated welfare capitalists, both humanitarian and pragmatic. It only required the additional catalyst of the war to push the firm into more formal welfare programs and policies. The underlying philosophical foundations for an extensive welfare system already existed, a product of nearly two decades of personal cultivation by George F. Johnson and his brothers. Certainly, all of the Johnsons accepted the fundamental idea behind welfarism: that management had "an obligation for the well-being of its employees."[8] It was expressed daily in the firm's community and labor policies in the 1890s and early 1900s. But both the wartime and the postwar economic climate reshaped and enlarged this basic idea and combined it with various notions of business efficiency until welfarism became far more explicitly a mechanism of labor efficiency and control. It is not without significance that the firm came to refer to welfare expenditures as "efficiency expenses."[9]

World War I placed exceptional strains on Endicott Johnson's labor policies. The blockage of immigration and the rising demand for labor made issues of labor attraction and labor retention primary in the mind of management. Between 1914 and 1920 the firm's work force doubled in size, increasing from 6,500 to over 13,000. Like many other firms, Endicott Johnson found that maintaining rapid expansion and high wartime profits necessitated ever-growing attention to its employees.[10] George Willis Johnson, George F. Johnson's son, once explained the context of the firm's expanding services to a fellow official, who later conveyed the information to an officer of the Plymouth Cordage Company, another welfare firm: "You will recall at the beginning of the European War business became brisk and we soon ran into the most unusual times, (so far as Labor was concerned) that we had ever experienced. Wages doubled and trebled and many concerns offered all sorts of inducements, in addition to wage increases, that would tend to keep workers happy and contented. We were among those who did all we could for our workers."[11]

It was in the midst of the war that company managers Harry L. Johnson and George Willis Johnson visited the Ford plants to learn about Ford's personnel practices. Harry L. Johnson's seven-page letter to the senior Johnson, a description and critique of Ford's personnel policies and a comparison with Endicott Johnson practices, offers some superb insights into the state of management thinking during this period of self-evaluation. Although Harry Johnson was awed by the scale and efficiency of Ford's "Educational Department," he nevertheless did have one large and important criticism:

> However, it seemed to me that there was one note lacking, and that was the *personal* note. They have done in a very systematic, thorough, business-like and professional way during the last five years something of what has been done in our business in a *personal* way for the last twenty-five years. They have planted the idea, have cultivated it, nourished it, watered it, and made it blossom—the same kind of an idea which took a *natural root in our business with the advent of your connection with it,* and has grown naturally ever since, until it has *commenced* now to bear fruit. . . .
>
> They are at a *tremendous disadvantage. Their people do not live around the works. Mr. Ford does not live with the people—he goes into the works but seldom—they do not know him personally—it is all handed down to them through the medium of a lot of hired people—devoted* people, good people, hard working people, but, still, hired people.
>
> The problem, it seems to me for our Company is: How can we maintain the personal contact? How can we broaden our community ideas—"working with and for the people who work with and for us", without doing it professionally—mechanically? . . . How can we perpetuate it—because it is going to be harder to perpetuate the personal note than the professional and business note. He can perpetuate his policy because it is a policy. Can we perpetuate ours, which is a *personality?*[12]

In a search for models to emulate, Harry L. Johnson found instead confirmation for his faith in traditional paternalism. Yet he also recognized that there was much to learn from employers such as Ford, who had adopted systematic labor management techniques.[13] And there were other firms to learn from—firms more closely associated with Endicott Johnson. The United Shoe Machinery Company (USMC), for example, with which every shoe manufacturing company in the nation was extremely familiar since it controlled and supplied 90 percent of all shoe machinery for the industry, was a quintessential practitioner of welfare capitalism and an influential propagator of the welfare ethic. Its officers were extremely active in the National Civic Federation, the major advocate of welfarism in the country. In such booklets as *The Story of Three Partners,* the USMC attempted to spread the good word on creating a "perfect sociological symphony," a wedding of the interests of "Capital, Labor and Society."[14] What Endicott, Johnson and Company borrowed from other firms and what it created on its own is difficult to gauge. But between 1916 and 1921 the firm's labor management policies rapidly took shape and established an identity unique to the firm—part system, part personality, part ideology, and part informal practice.

II

A new worker entering the employ of the Endicott Johnson Corporation in the early 1920s (it had incorporated in 1919) received a small booklet, a modest little work entitled "An E-J. Workers First Lesson in the Square Deal." It was one of many instructive manuals that the firm periodically produced to introduce its labor policies to new employees. "You have now joined the Happy Family," the booklet declared, and it proceeded to describe the compact that constituted the essence of the company's "Square Deal" policy. To the worker the firm promised fair treatment and security: "Certain claims of your family are recognized. Medical and Hospital service is yours. Privileges of many kinds are yours." There were, of course, expectations on the part of management: "This company and its Directing Heads, *know their business. . . . Their* business is to see that *you* give *them a 'Square Deal';* which means *fair* return for what you *receive*—an *honest* effort to do the work *well,* and a *fair* and sufficient amount *of* it." It was a very businesslike little pamphlet, no appeals to the heart, no philosophical discourses on the common goals of management and worker, just a tidy little bargain.[15]

In the minds of Endicott Johnson's top management, however, the "Square Deal" meant much more than this rudimentary first lesson. On these simple contractual foundations, and on the tradition of paternalism upon which they rested, the Johnsons built an ideology whose primary goal was the establishment of an industrial community in which the interests of workers and managers would be perceived as inextricably bound. The obligations and responsibilities of both management and workers were extended. George F. Johnson summarized what was expected of management as "'Personal contact.' 'Putting yourself in the other fellow's place.' 'The square deal.' 'Trying to get the other fellow's point of view.' Being reasonable and fair, including fair wages, considerate treatment, a real practice of the 'brotherhood of Man,' and sympathy—created (as sympathy can *only* be created) by personal contact, close observation, living together, playing together."[16] Likewise, the corporation's expectations of the workers were expanded. Fundamental to the development of a corporate community was labor loyalty. Johnson continually expounded on the idea of loyalty in open letters to his workers and in speeches. Company publications constantly repeated the theme. In articles and poems in the *E.-J. Workers' Review,* the employee magazine, the ideal of loyalty was prominently displayed:

> May the E.-J. wheel keep turning
> As long as the world shall stand;
> May each cog prove ever faithful
> Under its guiding hand.[17]

Loyalty meant a personal allegiance to management as well as a commitment to the good of the corporation. Efficiency and teamwork were part of this definition. "Team work applied to shoe making," explained one writer in the *E.-J. Workers' Review,* "means that the workers must do their part well. For every day's wages, they must give an honest day's work."[18] Another article in the magazine lectured, "Every worker should do his best. Let us look for the leaks and avoid all mistakes and waste of material. An interest taken for the E.J. Corporation is an interest for us all."[19]

To cultivate worker loyalty further, Endicott Johnson tried to inculcate in its workers a proprietary attitude toward their company. "I have consistently sought to create a feeling of responsibility in the mind of each worker, plus a feeling of proprietorship—ownership, if you will, in the business. I have sought to make each individual a 'business man' operating his (or her) own business, for their own particular benefit," wrote George F. Johnson in 1928.[20] The company's profit-sharing plan, instituted in 1919, was designed primarily to create "a feeling of responsibility" in the workers by transforming individual material self-interest into a collective interest. It expressed in concrete terms the unity of purpose that Johnson hoped to forge between managers and workers. In early 1920, after the first year of the plan, Johnson sent out a notice to the workers: "Many of you are now *real* 'partners' . . . because *you* have *your* share of the 'surplus profits.' . . ."

> Your own *selfish* interest, *now, demands* that you *protect* this business. You would not stand by and see a burglar break into a house, or a pickpocket in a crowd get in his work. *Certainly not.* Then don't let anyone beat this "old business of ours." . . . I want to see the day when you will all be self-appointed, sworn in, "special policemen," to stop "time killing," and "dead Beats," and the "leeches" which gather around every industry.[21]

The profit-sharing plan was incorporated into the bylaws of the company, apparently in spite of H. B. Endicott's misgivings, when it became a public corporation in 1919.[22] Originally the idea of Waddill Catchings, a prominent

New York financier and an early director in the firm, it functioned quite simply.[23] All profits after common and preferred stock dividends were paid (10 percent and 7 percent respectively) were divided between stockholders and workers on a fifty-fifty basis. The stockholders' share of the excess profits, however, was plowed back into the firm's surplus funds. Workers, including foremen, superintendents, and upper-level managers, received their share in cash at the end of the year. Only those employed for a year (on the payroll at the beginning and the end of the year) were eligible to receive the "bonus." But workers absent for parts of the year received a prorated share for the weeks they were employed. The basis of eligibility was extended to two years in early 1926.[24]

Catchings's basic rationale for the plan, and one that Johnson no doubt used to win over H. B. Endicott, was to maintain labor stability. As Johnson explained to the firm's auditor:

> The great big thought in the Surplus Sharing, is to lessen turn-over. It costs a lot of money to start a new man, or a new worker, in any department of the business. It adds to the cost of making leather and shoes, tremendously. We have a big investment in every worker, and when one worker, for any reason, leaves the Company, and a new one has to take his or her place, there is created a very heavy tax. . . . And so, if you can stabilize the workers, so they stick, and become regular and skillful, and through acquaintance with the policies of the Company, loyal—you have established, I think, one of the biggest assets in Industry, and one hard to estimate as to its value to the Company.[25]

Management's recognition of the linkage between high labor turnover and low productivity was one more legacy of the First World War. Of course, this was not a new insight. Corporate managers had justified paternalistic policies on the pragmatic basis of stabilizing the labor force since as early as 1901. But the war transformed turnover into an acute problem and forced the firm to seek out new mechanisms to achieve labor stability. In choosing profit sharing as a viable solution, it joined hundreds of other companies that had made a similar choice.[26]

Indeed, it appeared that the corporation had come upon an effective policy. A year after the initiation of its profit-sharing plan, a representative of the firm wrote to the National Civic Federation that "it is a noticeable fact that our workers value their positions more highly and are very loath to leave them."[27] The immediate response of the workers to profit sharing must have been especially heartening to management, particularly when expressed in terms such as these:

> Just merely writing a letter seems a very feeble way of expressing our thanks and appreciation relative to the profit-sharing plan. But knowing you as no other workers of no other concern on earth have the privilege of knowing their manager, we feel you will accept this offer of thanksgiving

as you always accept anything that comes from the workers. You can be assured that the workers of our dept. and we dare say the entire concern will show their gratitude by putting forth *all* their energy in the coming year.[28]

This was typical of the letters received by management after the first distribution of surplus profits in early 1920. Johnson expressed delight in receiving "the splendid wires on profit sharing from the workers, not so much because they expressed their thankfulness, but because they expressed their determination to try and earn this—to try and do more and better work [and] be more loyal and faithful." He concluded, "We have made this investment for this very purpose believing, (not without some misgivings, however) that the workers would take exactly this view of it, and it would have exactly this effect."[29] Management's delight undoubtedly was reinforced when, in January 1923, W. F. Dickson, the corporation's auditor, noted the increasing number of workers participating in the profit-sharing plan and concluded that their participation was a testament to a "tremendously small turnover" as well as the "contentment on the part of the workers to remain at their work."[30]

As a further vehicle to involve workers in "their" company, management sought to increase the number of employee stockholders in the firm by promoting the sale of common and preferred stock, selling it both at a discount and on the installment plan. In 1920, 2,205 workers (17 percent of the labor force) owned stock in the firm, amounting to 11,761 shares of common and 6,254 shares of preferred stock.[31] But attempting to interest employees in the business by promoting stock ownership backfired when the depression of 1921–22 hit and stocks declined. Management redeemed stock from workers at par value but ceased doing so when requests for redemption grew too burdensome. In September 1921 Johnson finally notified the workers that "we shall redeem *no more stock*."[32] Soured by the experience, management ceased pushing employee stock ownership and instead encouraged workers to deposit their savings with the company, where they could obtain 6 percent interest on their money.[33]

Sharing profits and encouraging workers to become stockholders were attempts by the company to give a concrete reality to the ideal of labor-capital partnership. There were other aspects of Endicott Johnson's welfarism that also served to achieve this end. The pervasive themes of loyalty and the merging of worker and management interests were subsumed in a more powerful image of mutuality, the metaphor of the family. "A business concern . . . ought to be like a family as much as possible," declared a writer in the *E.-J. Workers' Review*.[34] In company magazines, through the local press, and on bulletin boards and signs posted throughout the factory complex, the firm advertised the corporate bonds that held together the "Happy Family." At the head, of course, was George F. Johnson.

The corporate leader was prominently depicted as the "father" of a vast and loyal family. A typical cover of the company magazine portrayed George F. Johnson helping a young girl roll a ball of yarn. A back cover in another issue displayed a cartoon of a large shoe with a feminized version of George F. Johnson watching a line of workers marching by and a "Father George F. who lived in a shoe" poem below. Johnson would occasionally address letters to his employees "To members of the 'Happy Family.'" An E.J. marching song carried the line "George F.'s the daddy of this family."[35] The image of Johnson as benevolent patriarch pervaded the community. One local clergyman expressed his gratitude to Johnson for contributing to his church by writing the following "poetic" tribute to him:

> In this happy prosperous Valley
> There are things aplenty,
> Which bespeak the generosity
> of Geo. F. its "Daddy."

> "Daddy" Johnson we are grateful,
> Of your kindness ever mindful;
> May God bless you and protect you
> From all that is harmful![36]

George F. Johnson carefully cultivated the image of a "father." He made it a point to drive through the various working-class neighborhoods surrounding the factories, particularly the ethnic enclaves, and to visit each one of the company's factories periodically. Workers recalled him waving from his chauffeur-driven car, calling out greetings to local children, whose names he would often know.[37] He wrote, with pride and a strain of postured weariness: "As I go among my foreign neighbors, I am their "Father"—even some of the older men and women, older than myself. They look to me for everything they lack, or think they need, to make life happy. This is a great reputation . . . except it has its penalties. So I am besieged with requests for relief from every and all sorts of troubles and trials, and real needs."[38] Johnson developed a special relationship with the firm's ethnic workers as a result of persistently championing their interests: he lobbied for additional village services for the immigrant wards of Johnson City and Endicott, he attacked the Ku Klux Klan and its anti-Catholicism, he defended the rights of ethnics to their own culture and political beliefs (including bolshevism) against overzealous Americanizers, and he partially funded most of their churches and lodges.[39]

Johnson's tours through the factories, which interviewed workers recollected with humor and some fondness, were carefully orchestrated. He wrote to an acquaintance in Scotland, after one such tour: "The job will be finished this week, for this year."[40] He viewed such visits as a burden, although a necessary one, and continued making them even after he was struck down by the infirmities of old age. One worker recalled Johnson's visits, suggesting both their mechanical aspects as well as the favorable impression they nonetheless made: "George F. was really the best of them all. He'd come through the factory and they'd round up the crowd. Usually, it would be in the summer time. They'd take us outside, and he would talk and maybe give us a voucher for the time we had lost—so that we wouldn't lose anything in the deal."[41] Other workers remembered more distinctly his speeches and metaphors, as well as his amiable personality.[42]

Johnson's personable style was also evident in his generosity to his workers. His private correspondence is replete with requests for aid from workers. Not all such requests were favorably answered; but when he did agree to help a worker, Johnson did it in a way designed to create a personal bond between worker and manager. One tannery worker, Sam Salvatore, recalled the special treatment he had received when he approached Johnson to request financial help in paying for his mother-in-law's funeral:

> I went down. The secretary knew me. She went in, and she says, "Mr. Johnson, Sam Salvatore is here." "Send him in, send him in. . . ." I went in, and he says, "Sit down." I sit down. "You smoke?" I says, "Yeah." "Light a cigarette," he says. "In the office?" "Yeah," he says. "We're friends, aren't we?" I says, "Yeah." "Help yourself, smoke." Then he told Mary, "Close the door. I'll be busy for the next half hour or so." He says, "I don't want any phone calls, hold them." "What is it that you have to tell me?" And I told him. . . .[43]

The next day Salvatore learned that the funeral director had received a check from Johnson covering the entire cost of the funeral.

There were other studied behaviors that promoted industrial harmony, not the least of which lay in the realm of language. Carefully exercised rhetoric could convey a sense of community and collectivity. Johnson fastidiously avoided the public use of class-tainted vocabulary or words that might in any way alienate his employees. He called foreign-born workers "new Americans"; he referred to foremen and foreladies as "directors"; he used words like "partners" and "family members" in corresponding and conversing with his employees. Yet in private letters and memos to company officers and close friends, he persisted in employing words like "help," "employees," and "foreigners," clearly demonstrating the dramaturgical use he made of language. Nonetheless, that was the side of Johnson never seen by workers. His public self was what counted, and he groomed his public persona clearly and carefully to create an image of an industrial family, with himself as patriarch.

George F. Johnson had been cultivating the role of patriarch for some time.[44] As the major benefactor of community charities, as responsible civic leader, as progressive industrialist, he had achieved a stature second to none in Broome County. In 1915 the community of Lestershire had honored him by changing the name of the village to Johnson City. It was not the last honor he would receive. When H. B. Endicott died in 1920, there was no question as to who should succeed him as president of the corporation. And with Endicott gone and Johnson family members in key managerial positions throughout the corporation, Johnson became truly the patriarch at the helm of the firm. Although the company had become a public corporation, at heart it was, and would be for decades to come, a family firm, preserving a structure of management far more akin to a nineteenth-century enterprise than a twentieth-century one. It was hardly surprising, then, to find that the central organizational ideal behind the firm's labor policies would reflect management itself: family.

The family connoted harmony, security, authority, and stability—all values the corporation sought to develop and exploit. It was a powerful metaphor, both a confining and comforting image, one that promoted the internal resolution of conflict. The transposition of the employer into a father figure was aimed at making industrial protest and rebellion the equivalent of patricide. Seeking actively to cultivate the symbolic merger of family and firm, publications directed at workers were replete with photographs of families, children, babies, homes, and so on.[45]

The company attempted to do more than merely cultivate an image of a corporate family. It also sought to unite the functions of firm and family. The corporation became a partner in providing basic family needs such as medical care, relief, recreation, and housing. Many of the company's welfare policies were specifically designed to attract and hold working-class families to the firm.

The corporation's house-building program is a case in point. The booming war years led to a rapid growth of the firm's work force and a strain on local housing resources. Exploitation by local landlords and deteriorating housing conditions led Harry L. Johnson and other company executives to initiate privately financed home construction for workers. Although the firm had gone into home building in 1904, it was on a small scale and was soon discontinued. Harry L.'s efforts in 1919, however, escalated as the various members of the Johnson clan began to sponsor similar ventures. By 1921–22 home building had become a company policy, and a separate Realty Department was opened. George F. Johnson later placed the events of those years in context: "In the first place, then—because we built many factories and tanneries and employed many people, and did not build many homes, there was created a most unhealthy condition, which made it easy for people who are always looking for a chance to make money by exploiting such conditions, at the expense of both the workers and the business."[46]

Within the corporate ethos, however, home building became much more than a mere response to need. It became a vehicle for fostering labor loyalty, a "staying clause" in the "Square Deal." Inexpensive company-built houses were sold first to workers with large families and last to families with few children, as one description of a company housing tract confirmed: "Endwell

Terrace is a place of Ideal homes, built for Ideal families. In order to become a resident of Endwell Terrace there must be kiddies and plenty of them in the family."[47] Homes were offered on very liberal terms, with flexible payment schedules allowed during periods of slack work, particularly during recessions or depressions. The waiting period for available houses grew quite long, as hundreds of workers applied for them. Employment officers played an important role in the selection of qualified buyers to insure that only "desirable workers" with good employment records would be considered.[48]

The housing program was clearly aimed at cultivating close ties between working-class families and the corporation and in promoting labor peace and stability. Home building, in George F. Johnson's mind, was also the answer to numerous social and industrial ills, not the least of which was bolshevism: "There can be no security—there can be no guarantee of prosperity and Industrial peace—except through homes owned by the plain citizen. I believe myself, that the home is the answer to Bolshevism, Radicalism, Socialism, and all other 'isms.'"[49]

The policies of the firm's Realty Department changed over the years. Early on, the company retained first rights to buy back homes in case a worker left its employ or chose to sell a company-provided home within twenty years of the initial purchase. But the Realty Department soon adopted a two-price system, depending on the inclusion or exclusion of a buy-back clause in the deed. The repurchase provision was maintained to limit "speculation." By the late 1940s and early 1950s, this policy was haphazardly enforced and finally revoked. A five-year employment requirement before consideration for a company home was also flexibly enforced. Qualifications for homeownership changed over time, becoming less tied to family size and more to traits of "loyalty."[50]

The corporation continued to construct houses well into the 1950s and built, over the years, close to 4,500 units for its employees. The firm's policies made it possible for many workers, who would otherwise not have been able to purchase homes, to afford them. It is not surprising that large numbers of Endicott Johnson workers retired as homeowners. By 1955, according to a local newspaper estimate, about 85 percent of retired Endicott Johnson workers owned private dwellings, and one analysis employing data from local city directories disclosed that, between 1920 and 1940, Endicott Johnson employees were more likely to become homeowners than were other workers in the community.[51]

As important as the firm's Realty Department was and would be, it only touched a minority of the labor force. Of greater importance to both workers and management was a division that affected a far broader segment of the firm's employees, the company's Medical and Relief Department. Begun during World War I, it was initiated on a modest scale as a one-room medical office in one of the firm's tanneries. Created to deal with the many accidents that occurred in the tanneries, and with an eye to satisfying workmen's compensation laws, the clinic nonetheless swiftly expanded its functions:

> In 1916 one full-time physician and one nurse was [*sic*] employed. Very soon thereafter, a number of the employees requested general medical service for themselves and their families. They asserted that they could not afford to pay for medical care in the customary way. In 1918, finding difficulty in drawing a line between those workers who could and those who could not afford to pay for medical care, the management decided to extend medical service to all its employees. This new policy was inaugurated during the peak of the industrial boom that accompanied the World War.[52]

Under the influence of Dr. Daniel C. O'Neil, an advocate of industrial medicine, the Johnsons were soon convinced of the many benefits that would come from providing extensive medical care for their employees. By 1928 the Endicott Johnson Workers Medical Service had grown to include eighteen physicians, four dentists, five dental hygienists, two physical therapists, four bacteriologists, four pharmacists, seventeen technicians, sixty-seven nurses, and sixteen clerks and office assistants.[53] Medical centers had been built in Binghamton, Johnson City, and Endicott. Both the Johnson City and Binghamton facilities had maternity divisions and ear, nose, and throat departments. The company also operated smaller clinics for pre- and postnatal care, as well as a convalescent home at a nearby farm and two tubercular asylums in Saranac, New York. The medical services of the corporation were available to workers and dependent members of their families but excluded kin who were employed by other companies.[54] An extensive study of the firm's medical plan, undertaken in 1928, noted that "94 out of 100 eligible individuals made use of the Endicott Johnson Service in whole or in part, or were members of family groups which did so."[55] The Medical Department, indeed, touched the lives of most of the corporation's workers.[56]

But health care was only one of many functions undertaken by the firm's Medical and Relief Department. In addition the department provided workmen's compensation, old age and widows' pensions, sickness relief, burial funds, housekeeping assistance, and food, fuel, and clothing allowances to needy workers.[57] Company welfare workers would visit the ill, the infirm, and the bereaved, evaluating needs and alloting financial or service assistance, as well as investigating the authenticity of ailments.[58] George F. Johnson often involved himself personally in the decisions of the department, interceding on behalf of workers or making a final ruling on a questionable appeal for aid. As a result employees sometimes recalled the work of the department as a direct product of Johnson's beneficence: "I lost my mother when we were all small, and he [Johnson] sent a woman to do the washing and other things. I think it was a couple of hours every day that she'd come over until my older sister got old enough to do these chores. At that time my older sister was about eight or nine. When she got to be around ten or eleven, it [stopped]."[59]

By injecting itself into the private home and health lives of its employees, the company reinforced the bonds between family and firm and further strengthened the collective identity of the corporation. But there were yet other practices that the corporation and its managers engaged in to further foster labor loyalty. The company's Legal Department offered free legal aid to employees. Workers' stores, initiated by the corporation, supplied inexpensive foods. A company bakery provided cheap bread. The Johnson family periodically distributed shoes to local neighborhood children, an act of gift giving benefiting not merely employees. A full inventory of services and gifts would form a long list indeed. Viewed as a whole, the services offered by the corporation were clearly designed to provide maximum benefits to employees with familial responsibilities, just the sort of workers the corporation sought.

Believing that families would aid in labor recruitment, insure a more stable work force, and limit labor militancy, the Johnsons strongly encouraged family employment. They tolerated flexible hiring practices that bypassed the centralized employment office and that aided workers in placing family members in jobs. They urged employees to write relatives about the firm's many virtues.[60] They encouraged workers to send their children into the factories. A photo in the *E.-J. Workers' Review* contained the following typical caption: "We have here a very interesting family which includes four generations. Two of these are members of the 'Happy Family' and no doubt more will join our 'family' as they grow older and are ready to take up their life's work. . . ."[61] A "Future E.-J. Workers Department" regularly appeared in the *E.-J. Workers' Review,* along with numerous articles addressed to working and nonworking mothers—all devoted to advice on raising babies and infants. There, mothers could read about their responsibilities to their children, as well as to the firm: "In a few years from now most of these children will be citizens and shoemakers. If we mothers do our part, the future of Johnson City, the future of the E.-J. Co., and the future of the shoemakers home will become 'Ideal.'"[62] Such attempts at encouraging family employment apparently paid off. Many local families had several members working for the firm, and recruitment of workers often occurred through family networks.[63]

Wives and husbands sometimes worked side by side in the factories, although more typically they were segregated by sex-typed jobs. Partly because of the encouragement of management and the lure of company benefits and partly out of sheer necessity, large numbers of married women sought employment at Endicott Johnson. By 1927–28 married women constituted over 50 percent of the company's 4,000 to 4,500 women. The firm was by far the largest employer of both single and married women in the region. The large number of married women in Endicott Johnson contributed to the inordinately high ratio of married to single working women in the Binghamton area.[64]

Family recruitment stretched far beyond the confines of the immediate community. Native-born workers seeking escape from an impoverished rural existence or the insecurity of work in the Pennsylvania coal mines brought in relatives from surrounding New York and Pennsylvania counties. Polish, Slovak, Russian, and Italian workers who had entered the company in the first two decades of the century wrote to relatives abroad and in neighboring states, telling them of the opportunities available in Endicott Johnson.[65]

The presence of kinfolk in the factories not only helped foster a familial atmosphere, it also helped to maintain work discipline. One worker recalled the time when his son took the afternoon off from his job. The father went out, located him, and brought him back to the factory: "I took him down there, and I took him right into his machine, and I told him, 'Don't you ever leave that machine again as long as there's one shoe to do!'"[66]

The close functional ties between family and firm strengthened the communal identity of the corporation. This identity was further reinforced by rituals that sought to advertise and celebrate the ideal of labor-capital partnership. The company parade, a pageant dating back to 1916 when the firm, along with several other local companies, adopted the eight-hour day and held a communitywide celebration of the event, became a regular ritual in the life of the corporation. Parades were held on such varied occasions as George F. Johnson's birthday, Labor Day, and upon Johnson's return to the community from his winter retreat in Florida. They were carefully planned for the maximum effect. In contemplation of one such celebration, Johnson warned his son that the parade should be "big or not attempted at all."[67] In "Geo. F. Day" and "Workers' Day" celebrations, the firm sought to promote a sense of corporate community.

The parades were one sort of ritual. Sports were another. As they had in previous years, sports figured prominently in the corporation's social life. In this arena the world of work and the world of personal leisure met, further blurring the distinctions between personal time and industrial time.[68] As George F. Johnson's biographer noted: "Nothing strengthens the bonds of fellowship more than mutual devotion to a game."[69]

Although the firm's recreational programs were born in the early 1900s, it was World War I, again, that had the most important role in promoting their expansion. It was "under the stress of producing material for use in the World War," the firm's official historian recounted, that employers such as Endicott Johnson were led to "stimulate their people not only with 'pep' talks at noon but by furnishing baseball outfits and diamonds and many other amusements for off hours, all of which were good for their health and bettered their morale, thereby increasing efficiency."[70] Beginning with the war and continuing well into the 1920s and 1930s, the firm enlarged its athletic and recreational programs and facilities. It constructed softball and hardball diamonds, skating rinks, tennis courts, bowling alleys, swimming pools, parks, picnic grounds, dance pavilions, a horse racetrack, and an eighteen-hole golf course. The Endicott Johnson Athletic Association, as it came to be known, sponsored baseball, bowling, football, boxing, and dozens of other sports.[71] Teams were organized along factory lines, to promote a factory solidarity that was hoped would carry forward into work: the quest for victory on the playing field would ignite an equal desire to "beat" another factory's production rate. As Johnson remarked in observing one softball team: "They have the old fashioned team-work and fighting spirit. That's what counts, out there and in our business."[72] Hence, factory "Daily Production Records" were published in the "Workers Daily Page" right along with the latest company athletic scores.[73]

More than just to sports, Johnson was committed to any form of "healthy and safe" recreation. He believed that providing recreational facilities to his workers would prevent labor problems and increase worker productivity. He wrote to the former owner of his baseball team: "As to cost, it [the "means of amusement and recreation"] represents a pretty big investment, to date, and costs considerable to keep it up. But it is much better than discontented, unhappy Labor, with frequent strikes; and if, with good steady wages and fair treatment, it makes possible for us to have a steady, uniform production, we shall be very well satisfied with the arrangement."[74]

Following the course that was established in the 1890s and early 1900s, the firm continued to provide recreational facilities not merely for its workers but for the community at large. Endicott Johnson did this not only to maintain cordial relations between firm and community but also to allay charges of paternalism and self-interest. Opening the corporation's facilities to the general public, Johnson believed, was "the best plan, because it takes away that uncomfortable feeling of obligation or dependence, and is not subject to the charge of 'Paternalism,' quite as much, if open to the public."[75]

In becoming the "godfather" of sports and recreation of Broome County, a title bestowed upon him by the *Binghamton Press* in 1931, Johnson strengthened his influence over the community and his workers.[76] His former battles over Sunday baseball were replicated again and again in the 1920s, as he fought for Sunday movies and Sunday horse racing, and even that unholiest of all workingman's recreation, alcohol. His positions in all of these battles reinforced his carefully cultivated identity of "Workingman's Advocate." In a letter to an acquaintance, he outlined his belief that the worker was entitled to his pleasure, just as the rich man:

> I do believe that people must be occupied. The working people are no different than you and I and others. We must be occupied, and we will be occupied. If we have an auto, and means which justify its use freely, we are travelling on Sundays, looking for recreation and relaxation and pleasure. Of course we have allowed people of means to enjoy their Seventh Day, or Sabbath, as it pleased them. There has not been any

attempt to govern their actions. And when you come to think of it, most restraining Laws are intended for the poor. Even our present popular Prohibition, is not expected to seriously interfere with the appetites and desires of wealthy people. . . . This Law was made for the poor, and most restraining Laws, which interfere with personal liberties are only intended to restrain and regulate the poor. I mean now the people without representation in Law-making Bodies—who have no newspapers, no public leaders—and the very natural result of this unjust and unfair situation with respect to men and women who labor, is the very natural uprising and discontent throughout the world.[77]

Johnson's commitment to providing recreation and sports facilities for his workers reflected more than merely "good business." After all, he had been a worker himself, an avid baseball player and fan, a lover of golf and boxing. If he used athletics and recreation to transform his workers into competitive, ambitious, and nonmilitant operatives, it was also because he partook equally in their pleasure and believed in the character traits that were fostered by sports and recreation.

The Realty Department, the medical and relief divisions, numerous social and economic services, as well as corporate rituals all functioned outside the workplace to foster a collective identity between managers and workers. But the "Square Deal" was also manifested in the world of work. Upper-management accessibility, a commitment to internal promotions, relatively high wages, and work sharing were central elements in the firm's "Square Deal." The corporation's labor policies revolved around a basic commitment to bridging the gap between operatives and managers. Not only was "accessibility" of workers to managers consistently cultivated as an image—through the employee magazines and the local press, suggestion boxes, personal responses by corporate officers to workers' correspondence, open letters to employees, and so on—but the image gained substance from the constant presence of the Johnsons in the community and in the factories. The Johnsons frequently reminded their workers that their doors were always open for the airing of complaints. Indeed, while there were certainly obstacles in the way—the resentment of foremen and superintendents, the criticism of peers, the fear of being branded a malcontent—this option was always available and was sometimes effective in resolving conflict.[78]

The firm's promise of internal promotions gave "accessibility" a different meaning. "All our better positions filled by promotion. All the best jobs in the Factories and Tanneries filled from the ranks. No good positions filled from the outside, but always from the inside," the firm advertised.[79] Although the company did not always live up to this policy, a large number of Endicott Johnson executives *did* work their way up through the ranks. Foremen and superintendents almost always began their careers as shop workers in one of the firm's factories.[80]

Liberal wages and a commitment to work sharing during lean economic times were the final ingredients in the corporation's labor policies. Although the shoe industry was one of the poorest-paying industries in the nation, Endicott Johnson wages were relatively high in comparison with other shoe firms, as even one strong critic of the firm acknowledged: "For many years this firm continued to maintain an hours-and-wages schedule which compared very favorably with those in the more-or-less unionized centers of Rochester on the one hand and New York City on the other."[81] In its work-sharing policies, the firm further demonstrated its sense of responsibility to employees by providing regular workers with a guarantee of employment even in recessions and depressions.[82]

Welfare capitalism at Endicott Johnson was thus composed of ideology, personality, image, and policy. By a variety of measures it succeeded. Workers *did* partially adopt the ideal of the "Happy Family," the notion of industrial partnership, and the vocabulary and symbols with which the welfare ideology was expressed, as dozens of interviews disclose. Many workers demonstrated close identification with the corporation by participating in company-sponsored social and athletic events and clubs. Insofar as welfarism sought to create a stable work force, it accomplished its goal. Employment stability appears to have been relatively high in the 1920s and through the 1940s. Quit rates, at least from 1930 to 1946, when more systematic data are available, were 40–60 percent of the industry average.[83] Furthermore, strikes were infrequent and of short duration, and perhaps most significant, Endicott Johnson workers continually rejected the unions. Throughout the 1920s and 1930s, union organizers made little headway among the firm's employees.[84]

And yet, if these were some of the indices of the success of the corporation's "Square Deal," there were nonetheless signs of failure. As welfarism at Endicott Johnson had always been Janus-faced, concerned with efficiency and productivity on the one hand and with humanitarian aims on the other, so, too, did the response of workers take on a similarly bifurcated identity. On the one hand was the experience of image, welfare, personality; on the other, work, monotony, foremen, and the authoritarian structure of factory life in general. It is this schizophrenic encounter with the firm that yielded an equally schizophrenic response to welfarism. And to understand it, one needs first to understand the workers in their factory lives.

NOTES

1. Thorstein Veblen, *The Theory of the Leisure Class: An Economic Study of Institutions* (New York, 1953), 220. See also Alan R. Raucher, *Public Relations and Business, 1900–1929* (Baltimore, 1968), 65–69; Stuart D. Brandes, *American Welfare Capitalism, 1880–1940* (Chicago, 1976), chap. 4; and Stephen Meyer III, *The Five Dollar Day: Labor Management and Social Control in the Ford Motor Company, 1908–1921* (Albany, 1981), chap. 7.

2. A number of excellent works on welfare capitalism exist. The most recent and comprehensive study is Brandes's *American Welfare Capitalism*. Other studies include Irving Bernstein, *The Lean Years: A History of the American Worker, 1920–1933* (Boston, 1960), chap. 3; David Brody, "The Rise and Decline of Welfare Capitalism," recently revised and reprinted in Brody's *Workers in Industrial America: Essays on the Twentieth Century Struggle* (New York, 1980); Sanford M. Jacoby, *Employing Bureaucracy: Managers, Unions, and the Transformation of Work in American Industry, 1900–1945* (New York, 1985), chap. 2; Daniel Nelson, *Managers and Workers: Origins of the New Factory System in the United States, 1880–1920* (Madison, Wis., 1975), chap. 6; Morrell Heald, *The Social Responsibilities of Business: Company and Community, 1900–1960* (Cleveland, 1970); and Stephen J. Scheinberg, "The Development of Corporation Labor Policy, 1900–1940" (Ph.D. diss., University of Wisconsin, 1967). On the contribution of welfare capitalism to the formation of the welfare state, see Edward Berkowitz and Kim McQuaid, *Creating the Welfare State: The Political Economy of Twentieth-Century Reform* (New York, 1980). Stephen Meyer III's *Five Dollar Day*, Robert Ozanne's *Century of Labor-Management Relations at McCormick and International Harvester* (Madison, Wis., 1967), and Tamara K. Hareven's *Family Time and Industrial Time: The Relationship between the Family and Work in a New England Industrial Community* (New York, 1982) are excellent case studies of three very different welfare firms.

3. Nelson, *Managers and Workers*, 115–16. Among the list were the following firms: Remington Typewriter, National Cash Register, International Harvester, United Shoe Machinery Company, General Electric, Proctor and Gamble, Goodyear Tire and Rubber, Firestone Tire and Rubber, H. J. Heinz, United States Steel, Solvay Process, and Western Electric.

4. Brandes, *American Welfare Capitalism*, 23. That engineering schools were offering such courses suggests the link between welfarism and scientific management. On this, see David F. Noble, *America by Design: Science, Technology, and the Rise of Corporate Capitalism* (New York, 1979), 265, 287–88; David Montgomery, *Workers' Control in America: Studies in the History of Work, Technology, and Labor Struggles* (New York, 1979), chap. 2 and passim; Henry Eilbert, "The Development of Personnel Management in the United States," *Business History Review* 33 (Autumn 1959): 345–64; Mansel G. Blackford, "Scientific Management and Welfare Work in Early Twentieth Century American Business: The Buckeye Steel Castings Company," *Ohio History* 90 (Summer 1981): 238–58. Welfarism and scientific management, however, were not always so intimately linked. See Daniel Nelson and Stuart Campbell, "Taylorism versus Welfare Work in American Industry: H. L. Gantt and the Bancrofts," *Business History Review* 46 (Spring 1972): 1–16.

5. See U.S. Bureau of Labor Statistics, *The Betterment of Industrial Conditions*, Bulletin, no. 31 (Washington, D.C., 1900); idem, *Employers' Welfare Work*, Bulletin, no. 123 (Washington, D.C., 1913); idem, *Welfare Work for Employees in Industrial Establishments in the United States*, Bulletin, no. 250 (Washington, D.C., 1919); "Employers' Welfare Institutions," in New York State, Department of Labor, *Third Annual Report of the Commissioner of Labor* (Albany, 1904); "Industrial Betterment Institutions in New Jersey Manufacturing Establish-

ments," in New Jersey, Bureau of Statistics of Labor and Industries, *Twenty-seventh Annual Report* (Trenton, 1904).

6. Brandes, *American Welfare Capitalism,* 24–25.

7. Ibid., 26–27.

8. Brody, *Workers in Industrial America,* 61.

9. On the various notions of business efficiency (particularly "scientific management") that were circulating in the early twentieth century, see the following: Samuel Haber, *Efficiency and Uplift: Scientific Management in the Progressive Era, 1890–1920* (Chicago, 1964); Nelson, *Managers and Workers;* Daniel Nelson, *Frederick W. Taylor and the Rise of Scientific Management* (Madison, Wis., 1980); Harry Braverman, *Labor and Monopoly Capital: The Degradation of Work in the Twentieth Century* (New York, 1974); Noble, *America by Design;* Reinhard Bendix, *Work and Authority in Industry: Ideologies of Management in the Course of Industrialization* (New York, 1956), chap. 5.

10. From 1914 to 1917 the firm's profits increased by nearly 250 percent, from $1.9 million to $4.6 million. Extensive factory construction also took place during the war. Box 34, ser. 1, Charles F. Johnson, Jr., Papers, George Arents Research Library for Special Collections, Syracuse University, Syracuse, N.Y. On war profits in the shoe industry, see Horace B. Davis, *Shoes: The Workers and the Industry* (New York, 1940), 83–85.

11. George W. Johnson to Herbert C. Clarke, Apr. 27, 1922, box H-2, IV:D, Plymouth Cordage Collection, Baker Library, Harvard University Graduate School of Business Administration, Boston. Johnson emphasized that the firm's actions were merely a continuation of its traditional labor policy.

12. Harry L. Johnson to George F. Johnson, Feb. 1, 1917, box 3, George F. Johnson Papers, George Arents Research Library for Special Collections, Syracuse University, Syracuse, N.Y. Emphasis in original.

13. See Meyer III, *The Five Dollar Day,* on Ford's labor management policies.

14. United Shoe Machinery Company, *The Story of Three Partners* (Beverly, Mass., [1912]), 7, 9.

15. "An E-J. Workers First Lesson in the Square Deal," pamphlet [1922], box 19, George F. Johnson Papers.

16. *E.-J. Workers' Review* 1 (Sept. 1919): 32-A.

17. *Magazine* 1 (Mar. 1919): 37. Another article declared that "the *loyal* worker is the man who is heart and soul with the organization, because he knows that his welfare is bound up in the success of the business." *E-J Workers Magazine* 2 (July 1924): 10.

18. *E.-J. Workers' Review* 1 (Sept. 1919): 16.

19. Ibid. (Apr. 1919): 62.

20. George F. Johnson to Paul Wynn, Nov. 13, 1928, box 9, George F. Johnson Papers.

21. George F. Johnson, "To the Workers" notice [1920], box 5, George F. Johnson Papers.

22. It seems, according to Johnson, that the Endicott interests tended to oppose many of the progressive reforms of the firm. See George F. Johnson to William H. Hill, Feb. 25, 1920, box 3; and George F. Johnson to D. C. Morgan, Oct. 22, 1927, box 9, George F. Johnson Papers.

23. George F. Johnson to George Willis Johnson, Dec. 18, 1935, box 14, George F.

Johnson Papers. A short overview of Catchings's ideas on labor-management relations can be found in Waddill Catchings, "Our Common Enterprise: A Way Out for Labor and Capital," *Atlantic Monthly* 129 (Feb. 1922): 218–29.

24. *E.-J. Workers' Review* 1 (Apr. 1919): 59; "To the Workers" notice, Jan. 6, 1926, box 8, George F. Johnson Papers. Each worker received the following bonuses under profit sharing between 1919 and 1928: $237.90 (1919), $45.55 (1920), $200.20 (1921), $245.44 (1922), $92.56 (1923), $96.72 (1924), $87.36 (1925), $30.68 (1926), $97.76 (1927), and $23.92 (1928). After 1928 no bonuses were distributed until the late 1940s, with the exception of a holiday bonus in 1936. Average wages during the 1920s were about $25 a week, hence bonus payments amounted to an equivalent of one to ten weeks' wages. The company's board of directors received an unpublicized "Special Bonus" above and beyond the profit-sharing distribution. In 1922 they shared about $400,000. Richard S. Saul, "An American Entrepreneur: George F. Johnson" (D.S.S. diss., Syracuse University, 1966), 35; W. F. Dickson to George F. Johnson, Nov. 22, 1922, box 16, George F. Johnson Papers.

25. George F. Johnson to W. F. Dickson, Feb. 2, 1923, box 7, George F. Johnson Papers.

26. Brandes, *American Welfare Capitalism,* 83–84.

27. National Civic Federation, *Profit Sharing by American Employers* (New York, 1921), 46. The National Civic Federation was surveying the extent of profit sharing in American industry. The work is an excellent summary of contemporary programs.

28. "The Workers of McKay Upper Leather Cutting Room" to George F. Johnson, Mar. 3, 1920, box 18, George F. Johnson Papers.

29. George F. Johnson to Mrs. Julia Bowes, Feb. 24, 1920, box 5, George F. Johnson Papers.

30. W. F. Dickson to George F. Johnson, Jan. 24, 1923, box 16, George F. Johnson Papers. See also W. F. Dickson to George F. Johnson, Feb. 2 and Feb. 9, 1923, in the same box. Between 1922 and 1923 participation in the distribution of profits increased from 10,600 to 12,600 workers.

31. *Endicott Bulletin,* June 6, 1919; W. D. Dickson to George F. Johnson, Feb. 11, 1921, box 16, George F. Johnson Papers.

32. George F. Johnson, "To the Workers" notice, Sept. 26, 1921, box 6, George F. Johnson Papers.

33. The firm issued two-year notes in amounts of five dollars and above. The Workers' Savings Plan was really a revival of an earlier company policy that had been abandoned in the 1910s. *E-J Workers Magazine* 3 (Dec. 1924). By 1929, with a work force of about 15,000, the number of worker stockholders had declined to 682 holders of common stock and 364 holders of preferred stock. By that year employees owned 2.3 percent of the firm's common and 2.4 percent of the firm's preferred stock. "Endicott Johnson Workers Daily Page," *Binghamton Sun,* Nov. 26, 1929.

34. *E.-J. Workers' Review* 2 (July 1920): 17.

35. *Magazine* 1 (Mar. 1919); *E.-J. Workers' Review* 1 (Apr. 1919); ibid. (Nov. 1919): 2; ibid. 2 (May 1920): 23.

36. "St Joseph's Church" file, n.d., box 4, George F. Johnson Papers.

37. Sam Salvatore, interview by Gerald Zahavi, with the assistance of Deborah D. Maxwell, July 7, 1981, tape recording (personal possession); Teresa Schuttack, interview by Gerald Zahavi, with the assistance of Deborah D. Maxwell, Apr. 30, 1982, tape recording (personal possession).

38. George F. Johnson to A. G. Breckinridge, Jan. 5, 1923, box 7, George F. Johnson Papers.

39. On one aspect of this special relationship, see Jay Rubin, "The Ku Klux Klan in Binghamton, New York, 1923–1928," *Bulletin of the Broome County Historical Society* 20 (Winter 1973): 26–27 and passim. On Johnson's complex relationship to ethnic socialists and communists, see folders 5–8, box 6, New York State Joint Legislative Committee to Investigate Seditious Activities (Lusk Committee) Papers, Manuscript Division, New York State Library, Albany, N.Y. Johnson felt that as long as radicals did not pose a serious threat, they should be tolerated. Overt expressions of radicalism, he believed, were far easier to deal with than covert conspiracies; hence, he defended the right of radicals to free speech. See George F. Johnson to Edward Barder, Dec. 10, 1919; George F. Johnson to Rev. Wm. McPeak, July 23, 1920, box 5, George F. Johnson Papers.

40. George F. Johnson to J. F. Thompson, June 24, 1935, box 14, George F. Johnson Papers.

41. Stanley L. Moody, interview by Gerald Zahavi, with the assistance of Deborah D. Maxwell, June 1, 1981, tape recording (personal possession).

42. Earl I. Birdsall, interview by Gerald Zahavi, May 5, 1982, tape recording (personal possession); Helen Bruno, interview by Gerald Zahavi, with the assistance of Deborah D. Maxwell, July 13, 1981, tape recording (personal possession).

43. Salvatore, interview.

44. Other members of the Johnson family, in particular, Harry L. Johnson, also cultivated this image. Harry Johnson, manager of the Johnson City factories in the late 1910s, probably had a far stronger commitment to liberal labor policies than the elder Johnson. In fact he was being "groomed" for the presidency of the firm by his older brother. But Harry Johnson died in 1921, after suffering a nervous breakdown. Local oral tradition recalls his breakdown as a response to the cutbacks of wages and benefits instituted by the firm in the wake of the 1921–22 depression. His death, likewise, is remembered as a possible suicide and not as the product of apoplexy, which was the physician's pronouncement. George F. Johnson to G. W. Thompson, Oct. 3, 1921, box 6; George F. Johnson to Frank Montague, Sept. 16, 1921, box 6; George F. Johnson to H. L. Johnson, Dec. 8, 1919, box 5, George F. Johnson Papers; Rev. William MacAlpine, *A Brief Memoir of Harry Leonard Johnson* (Johnson City, N.Y., [1922]); conversation with Rodney K. Ketchum, Dec. 8, 1980 (notes).

45. Any issue of the employee magazine would illustrate this point. The magazine was published between 1919 and 1925, with one short interruption during the 1921–22 depression. Between 1925 and 1928 management utilized posted notices and public letters to communicate to workers. From 1928, and well into the 1960s, the corporation published a "Workers Daily Page" in the *Binghamton Sun*. A casual perusal through these pages will further reinforce my point. An almost complete run of the company magazine and the "Endicott Johnson Workers Daily Page" can be found in the various papers of Johnson family executives held by the George Arents Research Library, Syracuse University, Syracuse, N.Y.

46. George F. Johnson, "A Brief Statement of Facts of Interest to Home Owners of West Endicott" (June 1, 1923), 3, box 4, ser. 2, George W. Johnson Papers, George Arents Research Library for Special Collections, Syracuse University, Syracuse, N.Y. Also see George F. Johnson to W. F. Dickson, Apr. 15, 1924, box 7, George F. Johnson Papers.

47. *Magazine* 1 (Mar. 1919): 36. A headline in the "Endicott Johnson Workers Daily Page" (*Binghamton Sun,* June 22, 1932) declared, "Plenty of Children Encouraged by E.J. Building Program." See also George F. Johnson to Thomas Bidwell, July 15, 1931, box 11, George F. Johnson Papers. The procedure for allotting homes was not free from corruption. Bribes were sometimes given to officials in the realty office by workers eager to obtain a home. Palmer Perkins, interview by Gerald Zahavi, with the assistance of Deborah D. Maxwell, Apr. 30, 1982, tape recording (personal possession); North Endicott Senior Center group, interview by Nancy Grey Osterud, Feb. 16, 1982, summary and partial transcription (Broome County Immigration History Project).

48. H——, interview by David Nielson, June 23, 1973, transcript, 4; H——, interview by David Nielson, July 24, 1974, transcript, 322; George F. Johnson to Champion Fibre Company, May 14, 1936, box 14, George F. Johnson Papers. Because of David Nielson's pledge of anonymity to interviewees, they are not identified.

49. George F. Johnson to D. C. Warner, Aug. 17, 1920, box 5; George F. Johnson to John A. Brown, May 21, 1924, box 7; George F. Johnson to Don Morgan, Sept. 12, 1928, box 9, George F. Johnson Papers. Johnson did not want to "advertise" the pragmatic basis of home building, but he believed it was good business. In fact, home building was one of the firm's longest-lived welfare policies.

50. Johnson, "A Brief Statement of Facts of Interest," 16; Charles F. Johnson, Jr., to Leo Mills, Nov. 23, 1954, box 1, ser. 3; Charles F. Johnson, Jr., memo re: "Company Policy with Respect to Workers' Homes," Jan. 21, 1954, box 2, ser. 3, Frank A. Johnson Papers, George Arents Research Library for Special Collections, Syracuse University, Syracuse, N.Y.; John Kovak [pseud.], interview by Gerald Zahavi, with the assistance of Deborah D. Maxwell, session 1, July 15, 1981, tape recording (personal possession); Lucille Farrar, interview by Gerald Zahavi, with the assistance of Deborah D. Maxwell, July 13, 1981, tape recording (personal possession); George F. Johnson to Burl Nimmons, June 1, 1926, box 8; George F. Johnson to E. H. Ellison, July 19, 1923, box 7; George F. Johnson to John A. Brown, May 12, 1928, box 9, George F. Johnson Papers. Benjamin Seligman to Charles F. Johnson, Jr., June 23, 1950, box 19, ser. 1, Charles F. Johnson, Jr., Papers.

51. *Binghamton Press,* Oct. 10, 1955; William Wilson Shear, "Industrial Relations in the Endicott Johnson Corporation: A Case Study of Welfare Capitalism in the 1920s" (Master's thesis, S.U.N.Y. at Binghamton, 1978), 70–72.

52. Niles Carpenter, *Medical Care for 15,000 Workers and Their Families: A Survey of the Endicott Johnson Workers Medical Service, 1928* (Washington, D.C., 1930), 13–14. It was in May 1917 that the first medical card was issued. By 1919 six doctors and four nurses were employed. *E.-J. Workers' Review* 1 (Apr. 1919): 41. A first-person account of the early development of the E.J. Medical by one of

the first doctors to be employed by the firm can be found in the *Binghamton Press,* Jan. 4, 1959.

53. George F. Johnson to George W. Johnson, Apr. 9, 1931, box 11, George F. Johnson Papers; Daniel C. O'Neil, "The Endicott Johnson Medical Service," *Industrial Doctor* 1 (Oct. 1923): 168; Carpenter, *Medical Care for 15,000 Workers and Their Families,* 9. See also Daniel C. O'Neil, "A Plan of Medical Service for the Industrial Worker and His Family," *Journal of the American Medical Association* 91 (Nov. 17, 1928): 1516–19; and idem, "Where Industrial Service Becomes Community Service," *Nation's Health* 6 (Jan. 15, 1924): 1–3, 60. Endicott Johnson's Medical Department stood out among similar divisions created in other corporations. For an overview of industrial medical facilities and services in the early decades of the twentieth century, see Brandes, *American Welfare Capitalism,* chap. 10. Brandes acknowledged that Endicott Johnson's medical system was "the grandest affair," although he did not identify the firm by name. See p. 100 in Brandes.

54. The company also carefully screened job applicants to insure that incoming workers would not create an immediate medical burden on the firm. Applicants required a doctor's approval in order to be hired. In some cases workers were hired with the stipulation that they could not obtain relief or medical services for a particular ailment. "The Endicott Johnson Workers Medical Service," pamphlet (1928), box 19, George F. Johnson Papers; Endicott Office Files, Endicott Johnson Employee Records, George Arents Research Library for Special Collections, Syracuse University, Syracuse, N.Y.

55. Carpenter, *Medical Care for 15,000 Workers and Their Families,* 22–24. The analysis of extent of use was based on a random sample of 1,358 workers, or about 9 percent of the labor force. In 1928 company physicians made 87,000 house calls and attended to 119,740 office visits. The budget for the year was over $800,000, equivalent to about 22 percent of the firm's net profits for the year. See ibid., 9, 10, 15.

56. Without exception interviewed former workers acknowledged the importance of the firm's health services. See also William Patrick Burns, "A Study of Personnel Policies, Employee Opinion and Labor Turnover (1930–1946) at the Endicott Johnson Corporation" (Master's thesis, New York State School of Industrial and Labor Relations, Cornell University, 1947), 35.

57. The Workers' Relief Association, a mutual benefit society funded by the firm and by workers, was initiated in 1916 and formed the seed of the relief division of the Medical and Relief Department. The association was far more popular and successful than the firm's initial venture of 1896.

58. Kenneth E. Compton, interview by Gerald Zahavi, May 5, 1982, tape recording (personal possession); Paul Coletti [pseud.], interview by Gerald Zahavi, with the assistance of Deborah D. Maxwell, July 13, 1981, tape recording (personal possession). On the extensive services provided by the department, see Carpenter, *Medical Care for 15,000 Workers and Their Families.*

59. Coletti [pseud.], interview.

60. Sylvan P. Battista, interview by Gerald Zahavi, with the assistance of Deborah D. Maxwell, session 1, July 13, 1981, tape recording (personal possession); Mary

Seversky, interview by Gerald Zahavi, with the assistance of Deborah D. Maxwell, July 22, 1982, tape recording (personal possession); Salvatore, interview. One student of the firm's employment practices noted that "it is company policy to give preference in employment to relatives of workers," although he acknowledged that it was traditional rather than formal practice. Burns, "A Study of Personnel Policies," 53.

61. *E.-J. Workers' Review* 1 (Apr. 1919): 27. Another photo contained this caption: "W. L. Smith, father of this interesting group, may be found on the second floor of the New Fibre Board Mill, where he has worked for over four years. He is an enthusiastic booster of E.-J., and we hope that in a few years we will have added the children to our happy family of workers." Ibid. 2 (July 1920): 17. The Johnsons gave newborn "E.J. Babies" a pair of shoes and a savings account with ten dollars in it.

62. Ibid. 1 (Apr. 1919): 45.

63. Owen J. Ryall, interview by Gerald Zahavi, with the assistance of Deborah D. Maxwell, Apr. 30, 1982, tape recording (personal possession); Schuttak, interview; Norman W. Councilman, interview by Gerald Zahavi, with the assistance of Deborah D. Maxwell, June 5, 1981; Battista, interview, session 1. Surviving employee records and the 1925 New York State manuscript census give further evidence of extensive family employment. More information on recruitment of workers will appear in the next chapter. Tamara Hareven found a similar pattern in the Amoskeag Manufacturing Company in Manchester, N.H. See Tamara K. Hareven and Randolph Langenbach, *Amoskeag: Life and Work in an American Factory-City* (New York, 1978); and Hareven's *Family Time and Industrial Time*.

64. Numerical estimates of the female labor force for 1927–28 are extrapolated from percentage figures of the corporation's auditor. Women made up about 35 percent of the labor force in 1927–28. Statistics on female employment should be used with caution since women were far more subject to seasonal unemployment than men due to their concentration in the fashion and seasonal footwear departments of the firm. Yet, whatever the exact figures, Endicott Johnson *did* employ large numbers of married women, a fact that generated some controversy at the time. Apparently, the publication of this fact carried with it the implication that the firm exploited cheap female labor and disrupted traditional family roles. George F. Johnson to *American Shoemaking*, Dec. 20, 1927, box 9, George F. Johnson Papers; "Endicott Johnson Workers Daily Page," *Binghamton Sun*, June 8, Sept. 18, 1928; New York State, Department of Labor, *Special Bulletin: Women in Binghamton Industries* (Mar. 1928).

65. More details on the origins of the labor force follow in the next chapter.

66. Moody, interview.

67. George F. Johnson to George W. Johnson, Apr. 30, 1929, box 10, George F. Johnson Papers. The well-orchestrated parades, however, made it difficult for Johnson to tell when his workers were demonstrating genuine affection or when it was merely contrived. Upon the occasion of one such "tribute," he wrote to a friend that "because it was seemingly spontaneous and natural, and not manufactured, I permitted myself to enjoy it to the fullest." Yet even as he "permitted" himself to enjoy it, Johnson had his doubts, reflected in his use of the

word "seemingly." George F. Johnson to Louis J. Warner, Apr. 13, 1923, box 7, George F. Johnson Papers.

68. On the broad notion of "industrial time," see Hareven, *Family Time and Industrial Time*.

69. William Inglis, *George F. Johnson and His Industrial Democracy* (New York, 1935), 254.

70. Ibid., 277. See Brandes, *American Welfare Capitalism*, chap. 8, for a more extensive discussion of the origins and function of industrial recreation programs.

71. On the firm's athletic and recreational programs, see Inglis, *George F. Johnson*, chap. 15; and William J. Duchaine, "Industrial Recreation Here Embraces the Entire City," *Industrial Sports* [12] (Aug. 15, 1952): 27–28, 31.

72. Quoted in Inglis, *George F. Johnson*, 257.

73. See, for example, "Endicott Johnson Workers Daily Page," *Binghamton Sun*, July 17, Aug. 14, 1928. For a discussion of the replication and reinforcement of work values in baseball, see Steven M. Gelber, "Working at Playing: The Culture of the Workplace and the Rise of Baseball," *Journal of Social History* 16 (Summer 1983): 3–22.

74. George F. Johnson to John C. Calhoun, Aug. 13, 1919, box 5, George F. Johnson Papers.

75. Ibid.

76. *Binghamton Press*, Aug. 26, 1931.

77. George F. Johnson to William A. Dillon, Apr. 18, 1919, box 5, George F. Johnson Papers. On Johnson's positions on Sunday movies and Prohibition, see *Endicott Bulletin*, Jan. 6, 1920; George F. Johnson to Benjamin H. Dittrich, Jan. 29, 1921, box 6; George F. Johnson to Ransom H. Gillett, Mar. 15, 1920, box 5; George F. Johnson to William H. Anderson, Sept. 21, 1922, box 6; George F. Johnson to Ransom H. Gillett, Oct. 13, 1922, box 6, George F. Johnson Papers.

78. Although some letters to the Johnsons and personal interviews suggest that individual workers feared the possible wrath of their foremen and foreladies if they chose to go over their heads, many other workers related instances of successful use of this option.

79. "An E-J. Workers First Lesson in the Square Deal." The firm continually publicized this policy. See also the pamphlets "Endicott Johnson Workers: Tanners and Shoemakers" (1936) and "70 Years of Mutual Respect and Confidence" (1953), in box 19, George F. Johnson Papers.

80. This was true at least until the late 1950s.

81. Davis, *Shoes*, 147. Davis participated in the CIO attempts to organize the firm in the late 1930s and early 1940s.

82. William Patrick Burns, after analyzing Endicott Johnson turnover rates, concluded: "At Endicott Johnson, there were no layoffs between January 1930 and April 1935, with the exception of Dec. 1933, when a layoff rate of .38% is recorded. During the entire prewar [World War II] period, layoffs in the industry amounted on the average to 2.4% per month. In Endicott Johnson they were .1% per month. Roughly, the layoff rates in the industry were twenty four times the size of those in Endicott Johnson." During World War II, layoff rates at Endicott Johnson were one-quarter of the industry average (0.1 percent versus 0.4 percent a month). Burns, "A Study of Personnel Policies," 88–89. The firm did, however,

maintain a category of "temporary" workers to whom no employment or welfare obligations were beholden (see chap. 5). During the Great Depression of the 1930s, they amounted to between 3,000 and 4,000 workers. Whether these workers were included in turnover rates reported to the Bureau of Labor Statistics, the data upon which Burns bases his conclusions, is not specified. Internal company records suggest they were not. Nonetheless, for "regular workers" work sharing was a reality.

83. For the period 1930 to 1941, the average monthly quit rate at Endicott Johnson was 0.6 percent, compared with the industry average of 1.0 percent. For 1942 through 1946 it was 2.0 percent versus 5.0 percent for the whole industry. Endicott Johnson rates are based only on Endicott employment office records, and not the firm as a whole. See Burns, "A Study of Personnel Policies," 88 and 83–103, for a thorough discussion of labor turnover at Endicott Johnson in the 1930s and 1940s. On labor stability in the 1920s, see Shear, "Industrial Relations in the Endicott Johnson Corporation," 54–59; see also Saul, "An American Entrepreneur," 307, for similar conclusions about turnover at Endicott Johnson. For a general discussion of the favorable impact (from a managerial perspective) of progressive employment policies on labor turnover, see Sumner H. Slichter, *The Turnover of Factory Labor* (New York, 1921), chap. 12.

84. Attempts to unionize the firm will be treated in later chapters.

3

Workers and Work

For many workers, employment at Endicott Johnson began in hope—the hope of an immigrant for more money, of an anthracite miner for a safer and more secure life, of an unemployed worker for a job, of a country girl for escape from the closed world of a rural hamlet. Thousands of similar expectations drew workers into the firm in the early decades of the century and continued to do so through the 1920s and 1930s.

I

In the last two decades of the nineteenth century, the company's labor force had been drawn mainly from rural New York counties, from Pennsylvania, and from nearby New England states. Perhaps 15–20 percent of the labor force were immigrants, the majority coming from Ireland and Germany.[1] Beginning in the late 1890s and into the first two decades of the new century, the identity of the company's work force underwent important changes. Native-born workers continued to predominate, with ever-growing numbers coming north from Pennsylvania. Increasingly, however, southern and eastern European immigrants came streaming in, transforming the work force into a highly diverse population composed of Slovaks, Czechs, Italians, Poles, Russians, and Lithuanians, as well as the older ethnic and native groups.

With the extensive construction of tanneries and factories in the second decade of the century and the expansion of employment opportunities in Endicott, Italians and Slavs flocked into the village and took positions in the new plants. Their presence in large numbers in the tanneries provided the firm with a cheap and convenient labor force willing to do work natives avoided. As George F. Johnson acknowledged: "These 'new Americans' have done much to make this community what it is today, through the fact that they have been willing to do the character and kind of work . . . tannery work . . . which the average American has refused to do."[2]

By the early 1920s, when data on the national origins of the company's

TABLE 3-1
Endicott Johnson Workers—by Nationality (1922)

Nationality	Number	Percent of Total Labor Force	Percent of All Foreign Nationalities
American	9,143	67%	—
"Slavish"	1,901	14%	42%
Italian	982	7%	22%
Polish	492	4%	11%
Russian	254	2%	6%
Lithuanian	242	2%	5%
English	103	1%	2%
Greek	87	1%	2%
German	66	1%	1%
Irish	58	1%	1%
Ukrainian	50	1%	1%
Austrian	47	1%	1%
Armenian	46	1%	1%
Other	191	1%	4%
Total	13,665		
Total foreign nationalities	4,522	33%	

NOTE: Employment officers were inconsistent in categorizing "Slavish" immigrants. In some cases they were identified as Ukrainians, Slovaks, Czechs, Poles, Russians; in other cases they were simply listed as Slavs (the more common practice). Note also that due to rounding errors, totals do not add up to 100 percent.

SOURCE: *E-J Workers Magazine* 1 (Nov. 1922).

workers were first compiled and published, foreign-born workers made up one-third of the firm's labor force. (See table 3-1.) The imposition of immigration restrictions in the 1920s and afterward slowed the influx of foreign workers and reduced the overall proportion of foreign-born in the firm. Nevertheless, secondary migrations from such cities as New York, Akron, Utica, Pittsburgh, and Scranton, as well as from numerous smaller communities, continued to bring new immigrants into the firm's factories and tanneries.[3] In addition to this a large, and ever-growing, number of native-born children of immigrant parentage also found employment in the company. By the mid-1930s probably half of the firm's workers were immigrants or second-generation ethnics.[4]

Slavs constituted the largest immigrant ethnic group at Endicott Johnson, making up about 20 percent of the labor force in 1922. Within this diverse group—composed of Poles, Ukrainians, Slovaks, Czechs, and Russians—the Slovaks were the most numerous. Early migrants had come up from Pennsylvania, continuing a chain migration that had as its source the western Slovak province of Nitra. Agricultural villages such as Gbely and Petrovah Ves, as well as various other proximate hamlets in the Nitra province, figured prominently as the roots of the earliest migrations. Gbely itself, by 1919, had contributed about 20 percent of Binghamton's Slovak population, and the Nitra province as a whole was probably responsible for half of the community's Slovak residents.[5] Along with Nitra Slovaks came Moravian Czechs, Galician Poles, Ukrainians, Byelorussians, and numerous other Slavic subgroups, many also coming via chain or family migrations.[6]

Italians first arrived in the community in the 1870s, but their numbers remained insignificant until the first decade of the new century. Like many of their Slav counterparts, Italians followed fellow villagers and kinfolk to new opportunities of employment. Townspeople from small villages like Reggio, in Calabria, or Montaldo, in Piemonte, followed one another to Binghamton and Endicott. Immigrants who arrived in America and found "lucrative" jobs might write to friends or former village neighbors in Italy, as one worker did, that "here you can make your fortune. . . . If you can keep in good health you can make about 1000 *lire* a day, just like nothing."[7]

Family and village networks promoted and eased the migration and settlement of the new immigrants. The majority came indirectly to the firm, first finding employment in various jobs in New York and Pennsylvania—in mines, tanneries, or on railroad gangs. Heads of families, perhaps accompanied by sons or brothers, took jobs at Endicott Johnson for a year or two, went back to their native lands to pay off debts or to relieve a growing homesickness, and then returned for another few years. They generally boarded with kin or fellow countrymen and countrywomen. Many who made the return voyage to the "old country" never came back to America. Others, finding their hopes satisfied by employment in Endicott Johnson, sent for their wives and children and rooted themselves in the community.[8]

Most of the newly arrived European workers settled in the north side of Endicott ("across the railroad tracks") and in the northwest section of Binghamton, in the First Ward. Johnson City, populated mainly by native-born Protestants and some second-generation Irish-Americans, drew only a few new immigrant families in the early decades of the century.[9] But through the late 1910s and early 1920s, with Endicott Johnson managers building homes in Johnson City for workers—homes that were not closed to immigrants by restrictive housing clauses or covenants—a modest but growing Slavic population established itself in the north side of the village and continued to expand through the next decade.[10]

Ethnic prejudice, both reflected in and fueled by the geographic separation of workers into various immigrant and native neighborhoods, led to a great deal of tension among ethnic groups in the early years of the century. Feuds between Irish and Italians, as well as between native-born Protestants and immigrant Catholics, occasionally broke out in Binghamton and Endicott.[11]

The new immigrants' relatively low position in the factory hierarchy and their equally low wages (in comparison with native-born workers) exacerbated these tensions. In one case an Italian worker shot and killed a native after the latter taunted him by yelling out, "The dirty dago, he works for 50 cents a day."[12] In another incident a native leather cutter (it was rare for an Italian or Slav to be a leather cutter in the first decade of the century) and an Italian stitching room employee came into conflict in their haste to punch out on a factory time clock. The incident precipitated a feud between the two men that, partially fueled by ethnic animosities, finally ended in the Italian attacking the American with a knife and hatchet.[13]

In time the worst manifestations of ethnic and religious conflicts disappeared. Neighborhood gangs still clashed in the 1920s and 1930s, and ethnic slurs could still be heard in the community and in the factories, but serious physical violence grew rare. Part of this was due to a growing familiarity that arose naturally between the natives and new ethnics as they mixed in public schools and in work, but part should also be credited to the tempering influence of George F. Johnson, who acted as an effective intermediary between natives and immigrants, and whose progressive, cultural-pluralist viewpoint did much to assuage ethnic tensions in the community and in the factories.[14]

Eastern and southern European immigrants and their native-born children faced not only community prejudice but also employment discrimination. Slavs and Italians were overrepresented in tannery jobs. This was not merely a product of "pull" factors—the rising demand for unskilled labor in the tanneries and the fact that the lowest paying tannery jobs paid better than the lowest paying shoe-factory jobs—but also reflected exclusionary hiring practices in the factories. The best factory jobs—upper leather cutting, Goodyear stitching, bed lasting, edge trimming—generally went to natives.[15] Native-born foremen skipped over Italians or Slavs in making selections for choice positions. As a result, in the factories, immigrants initially were placed in low-skilled, low-paying menial jobs such as rack pushing, stitching, lacing, tack pulling, and general labor. Finding themselves in such jobs and aware that better paying work was available in the tanneries, many elected to transfer. In the tanneries, too, they were usually placed in the least desirable jobs—on "wet work" in the beamhouse or the tanyard—where they came into daily contact with caustic bleaching and tanning agents. Many were satisfied with such work and the relatively good wages that it paid. Others were not. "First I had a good job upstairs," recounted one Italian tannery worker in 1910, "then the boss put me downstairs in the water and I went back to New York."[16] Of course, there were some immigrants who did get good jobs. Most likely they came into the firm with some experience in tanning or shoe manufacturing, which they had obtained in the "old country" or in some other American factory.[17]

Other desirable jobs in the corporation were equally unavailable to recent immigrants. For example, there were few eastern and southern Europeans to be found in the mechanical divisions of the company, which included electricians, plumbers, and powerhouse engineers. A typical power plant staff in the middle of the second decade of the century included two engineers with Anglo-Saxon surnames, three coal handlers and firemen with Slavic surnames, and one coal handler with an Anglo-Saxon surname. A list of nineteen electricians working in the Lestershire (Johnson City) plant contained only Anglo-Saxon surnames.[18]

Promotions to supervisory positions were also generally reserved for natives. In the first four decades of the century, a foreman who was not of Anglo-Saxon, German, or Irish ancestry was extremely rare. A list of foremen in the Pioneer Factory in 1915 disclosed not a single Slavic or Italian surname.[19] In fact, such conditions persisted through the early 1940s. A 1941 list of superintendents and supervisors employed by Endicott Johnson contained relatively few Slavic and Italian surnames. Even in the tanneries, where eastern and southern Europeans were heavily concentrated, the vast majority of the supervisory personnel had Anglo-Saxon, German, or Irish surnames.[20] Considering that Slavs and Italians, both foreign-born and second or third generation, made up about two-fifths of the company's labor force, this certainly suggests that ethnic prejudice limited promotional opportunities at least until the early 1940s. While the company greeted foreign-born workers and their children with open arms, it did not readily promote them.

Eventually, Slavs and Italians did make their way into the more skilled and higher-paying factory and tannery jobs, as well as into supervisory positions, making it easier for those who followed them to do likewise.[21] Entry into skilled work like cutting, edge trimming, and bed lasting came earliest in newly built factories where large numbers of natives had not previously established a firm footing. But by the late 1930s, Italians and Slavs were to be found in most of the choice factory jobs throughout the corporation.[22] Furthermore, as many Anglo-Saxon Protestants (as well as German and Irish ethnics) left relatively good shoe-factory jobs and supervisory positions and entered even better-paying industrial jobs during World War II or flocked into the expanding International Business Machines (IBM) plants that were located in Endicott, they were replaced by Italians and Slavs. As one Italian worker, who had broken into cutting in 1931, summed up: "At first, for the Italians, it was kind of rough to get the good jobs like edge trimming jobs. Now you got a lot of Italians on all jobs. It's altogether different. But us guys were the first ones around."[23]

While immigrant workers significantly added to Endicott Johnson's labor force in the early decades of the century, they were nonetheless still far outnumbered by the native born. By this time the latter included second- and third-generation assimilated German ethnics, Irish-Americans, and a large population of native-born Protestants of Anglo-Saxon ancestry. The corporation drew thousands of its employees from rural farming and mining regions in New York and Pennsylvania, as well as from small industrial towns scattered throughout these two states. In 1916, for example, the "Fourth Annual Reunion of Hillsgrove and Sullivan County, Pennsylvania" was held at Ideal Park in Endicott. The reunion drew 102 of the 200 migrants who had left that northeastern Pennsylvania county (which lay thirty miles to the southwest of Endicott) and who settled in Endicott, Johnson City, or Binghamton. As the local Endicott paper noted, "Nearly all the heads of these families work for the Endicott-Johnson Co."[24]

Hillsgrove was one of many tannery towns nestled in the northern Pennsylvania forests. Like other tannery towns—Elkland, Towanda, Ralston—it sent out a steady stream of dissatisfied or unemployed workers who had heard of the better job opportunities at Endicott Johnson.[25] William Haight's family probably typified the pattern of these migrations. His father was employed by the Hillsgrove tannery and had come up to Endicott to take a job with the company. Haight recalled that the corporation had a good reputation among the Hillsgrove tanners. Other workers who had left the community and obtained jobs in Endicott came back and told former coworkers about the fine conditions and the better wages available up north. The Haight family, convinced by such reports, finally made the move in 1914. Most of the children, as their father had, ultimately entered the tanneries.[26] Another Endicott Johnson worker, from Morris, Pennsylvania, recalled a very similar version of his family's move to Endicott:

> Well, down in Pennsylvania . . . Dad was driving a team down there and hauling bark to the tannery. That was almost petered out. They heard about Endicott here and a couple of others—the Hanly family and a fellow by the name of Flynn—well, the Hanlys had already come up here, and they wrote to this Flynn and told him what opportunities there was, and Dad and Mike Flynn—they came up here in 1902. And so we moved up here. He drove a team for a while . . . then he got a job in the tannery.[27]

More important sources of native-born Endicott Johnson workers were the numerous farming regions that surrounded Binghamton, Johnson City, and Endicott. Thousands of surviving Endicott Johnson employment applications listed farming as the previous occupation of job applicants. Typically, a rural New York or Pennsylvania town was named as the previous community of residence.[28] Like tannery town migrants, rural farm folk learned of the firm from friends or kinfolk who had made their way to Johnson City and Endicott.

> We had folks from our home town [near Carbondale, Pennsylvania] come up there, and when they'd come back for an old home day or something like that you'd get to visiting with them and it sounded good, so when I finished up the job at home, that's the first place I went,

Johnson City. The fellow that came with me, he got his job, we both got jobs, and I got my job over in the South End Factory cutting samples, a pattern cutter, and he went back. But I came at the right time of the year when they washed the streets and everything was so clean and the parks were wide open and everything. I said this is the place for me, I'm going to stay here.[29]

A considerable number of native-born workers came from mining communities. As with many Slavs and Italians who left the mines, they, too, were frustrated by the frequent mine shutdowns, the brutal conditions of work, the hermetic existence, and the limited opportunities available in such towns, and they sought a better life at Endicott Johnson. Hundreds of company job applications listed mine shutdowns or strikes as "reason for leaving last place" of employment. Many more simply noted "dissatisfied."[30]

Migrations from farming communities, mining, and one-industry towns followed a pattern similar to immigrant chain migrations. Often, the male head of the family would come and take a job in one of the tanneries or factories, finding a room in a local hotel or else boarding with a local family. After establishing himself in this way and deciding that the community was to his liking, he would send for his family.[31] Once settled, friends and more distant kin from the former home town might be drawn to the area and to jobs in Endicott Johnson. There was security and comfort in following fellow townspeople to a new community.[32]

The kinship ties that formed important links in both the transatlantic and domestic chains that brought workers to Endicott Johnson were exploited to the fullest degree by both the corporation and the workers. From the company's point of view, such ties helped recruit workers during periods of labor shortage. Generally, Endicott Johnson managers did not have to engage in active recruitment of workers. Encouraging employees to write relatives abroad or elsewhere in the United States sufficed. Occasionally, however, particularly during World War I, the firm needed additional mechanisms to augment its labor force. Company employees were then sent down to New York City, or other cities with substantial immigrant populations, to recruit new workers actively.[33]

From the workers' point of view, family employment preferences shown by shop supervisors and employment officers gave them a "vested interest in employment opportunities" for relatives.[34] Typically, in the early decades of the century, a worker obtained a job through a family member or a close friend. One worker recalled how a "long-away" relative helped him get a job blacking sole edges: "He took me to his foreman, you know, and they give me a job in the next department there, right away."[35] Parents found it especially easy to secure positions for their children. A mother employed in the corporation diner was able to find employment there for most of her children.[36] Mothers, fathers, cousins, aunts, and uncles provided convenient employment conduits for both close and distant kin. As one Italian worker summed up: "That's how they did it in those days, they helped each other out. If you had a cousin working, you'd get a job."[37]

Although depressions and recessions drastically constricted the power of individuals to find jobs for relatives, such periods of limited employment opportunities also *increased* the importance of having family connections. Kinship became the primary vehicle available for obtaining a job in such times. Workers who succeeded in securing employment at Endicott Johnson during the worst years of the Depression generally had fathers, wives, husbands, or other relatives already working in the firm.[38] A worker without such connections found it difficult, if not impossible, to obtain employment with the company:

> I wasn't able to get a job. . . . E.J. had a policy, if your parents worked there, children got first preference as far as getting hired. I remember one time, I was about seventeen years old, it was during the Depression, they were taking applications for work. I remember getting up about two or three o'clock in the morning just to get in line to be able to file an application for work. This was about 1935, 36. It was in the middle of winter. I was there until about ten o'clock in the morning, from two. Just to be able to walk in and put in an application. And that was the end of it; I never heard anything more from them.[39]

Among the thousands of European immigrants, rural transplants, and small-town migrants who were drawn to Endicott Johnson were many women. Since the 1890s women had figured prominently in the firm's labor force. Following the national trend both their numbers and relative representation had risen dramatically in the 1880s and 1890s. In the former decade they had constituted between 5 and 15 percent of the company's work force. By 1900 there were 400 women employed by the firm, representing about 22 percent of the company's workers. Although some of this rise in female employment was due to displacement of male workers and to the expansion of the sexual division of labor in the factories, a far more important factor was the rising demand for stitching room operatives to match gains in productivity made by other departments—gains fostered by the introduction of new machinery.[40]

Between 1900 and 1920 the proportion of women working for the firm experienced minor growth, but their absolute numbers rose considerably. In mid-December 1919, there were 3,962 female employees, approximately 27 percent of the firm's 14,498 workers.[41] A more dramatic increase occurred in the 1920s. Responding to the growing market in seasonal, light-wear, and stylish shoes, Endicott Johnson opened new factories that specialized in such lines. Since women workers were generally employed in the manufacture of lighter-grade footwear, the number of women in the firm's labor force naturally rose. Thus, in the 1920s, with the overall work force fluctuating between

14,500 and 15,500, the relative proportion of female employees increased. By 1927 women made up 35 percent of the labor force.[42]

The vast majority of women shoeworkers worked as stitchers in the stitching rooms. But they also skived and marked in the cutting rooms; they packed and laced shoes in the shipping rooms; they graded sole leather in the sole leather cutting rooms. They were perforators and stampers, cementers and trimmers, lining makers, treers, ironers, repairers, inspectors, and "cripple" (damaged shoe) chasers. Except in some of the better jobs, like skiving, perforating, and fancy stitching, their wages were far lower than men's wages. In 1926, for example, when the average weekly wage at Endicott Johnson was about twenty-five dollars, most women were making between sixteen and twenty dollars.[43]

Women sought employment at Endicott Johnson for a variety of reasons. To young women or girls growing up in rural New York and Pennsylvania, a job in the shoe firm might be viewed as a vehicle for liberation from the constraints of parental authority or the hermetic world of rural farm life. Their desire to become "city girls" or "working girls" was often quite strong:

> I wanted to get away from home! How many times I cried to my mother, I said I wanted to leave, I wanted to leave. She'd be washing clothes by hand . . . and I would be nagging her I wanted to go to work, and she'd take a wet towel and slap me around the face. . . . She didn't even want to listen to me—"you're staying here, you're not going to work." But then one time my father come, and . . . I told him that I wanted to go to work. So when he went back to Endicott, he took me.[44]

Local girls, just out of high school or nearing the legal working age of sixteen, naturally looked to "E.J.s," the community's largest employer, for a job. They sought employment to contribute to the family's income, to save money for secretarial, teaching, or nursing school, and to find romance. Many had begun to work for the firm during summer vacations or had taken part-time jobs in the corporation's diners.[45] Younger girls often lied about their ages to obtain full-time employment with the company. As employment officers were not overly vigilant in such matters, they often got away with their deceptions, although not without paying a price: "I wasn't sixteen when I started to work at E.J.s; they didn't ask for my certificate, and I didn't have it. Every man come along towards me, I thought oh, he's gonna ask me for my certificate, he's coming to take me back to school, but he didn't. After I passed November 14th, well, they're not gonna take me now."[46]

Most of the women who made their way into the Endicott Johnson factories were native born. A 1926 survey of working women in the Triple Cities (Binghamton, Johnson City, and Endicott), undertaken by the New York State Department of Labor, disclosed that 81 percent of local female shoeworkers—most of whom were employed by Endicott Johnson—were born in the United

States. Of the remaining 19 percent, 12 percent were Slavs. Only 1 percent of the surveyed women shoeworkers came from Italy. The relatively low number of Italian women working in local shoe factories reflected cultural values that limited their involvement in work outside the home.[47]

In the mid-1920s about half of Endicott Johnson's women workers were married.[48] For many married women employment at Endicott Johnson meant being able to take advantage of the firm's welfare services. As one woman recalled: "I was determined to get to E.J.s, no matter how, because I could get benefits, and my family. I thought well, if I don't make high wages, so what? I'll get the benefits, and I'll be better off."[49] Such thoughts probably motivated many wives of local farmers, as well as married city women whose husbands worked outside the shoe firm, to seek work at Endicott Johnson.[50]

There was always some ambivalence in management's attitude toward employing married women. In 1923 George F. Johnson wrote to a clergyman that "too many of our families, in order to make a little more money, send their wives into the factories. I don't approve of this except in cases of extreme necessity. The place of the housewife, it seems to me, is in the home."[51] Indeed, in some ways the firm made things difficult for married women. It was inflexible in part-time hiring, claiming that such a policy was "not practical."[52] Foremen and superintendents did, however, occasionally permit married women to engage in evening and home work, which allowed them to care for infants and young children while adding to the family economy.[53] Although George F. Johnson had personally donated money to a Binghamton day-care center, as corporation president he was never willing to provide day-care services to his employees.[54] Yet for many women the extensive welfare benefits that the firm offered partially made up for the lack of child-care facilities. Most married women simply left children with older brothers or sisters, with grandparents, or with other kin. The widespread kinship ties in the community fostered such informal solutions.

> My mother, she took care of my two nephews and a niece when my two sisters went to work—not at the same time. . . . She [my sister] would bring her children—her first one—here, and he would stay here all week and he'd go home just weekends. But they'd come everyday to see him after work. And we could hardly wait for Sunday noon. . . . We could hardly wait for him to come back. There were eleven of us, and we made room for him too. Then she had a girl. . . . It was the same way with her when she was little.[55]

Women who were not able to take advantage of kin to care for their children were forced to seek out less desirable arrangements, often paying neighbors to care for their infants.

Although Johnson was initially cool to the idea of married women being "sent" into the factories, he soon changed his opinion when faced with public controversy over the firm's high percentage of working wives. In 1927 and

1928, after a New York State Department of Labor report on women in Binghamton industries had made note of this fact and the results of the study had been released and widely publicized in the national and trade press, George F. Johnson felt compelled to defend the firm's policy with respect to employment of married women.[56] He wrote to *American Shoemaking:* "Women seek employment in our factories, because of the good wages they earn, and the easy work and pleasant factory conditions. If women continue work after marriage, it is because they want the money they earn; and who questions their perfect right?"[57] To his workers Johnson put his case even more forcefully, communicating sentiments diametrically opposed to those he had expressed in 1923. He wrote in the "Endicott Johnson Workers Daily Page" that

> for my part, I admire a young man and woman who start out in life, both working together to get a start in the world. Such a plan is more apt to lead to independence, than the plan which contemplates that there shall be only one wage earner in the family. In these days of conveniences, light housekeeping, short hours of work, and much easier and better methods, a young woman who is willing to help her young husband, looks better to me than those who feel that because they are married they ought *not to do any more work,* or try to earn any money to help out.[58]

Not all workers agreed with Johnson. For many a male shoeworker, a nonworking wife was a sign that he had "made it," that he could provide for his family—in short, that he was truly "head" of his household. Some went out of their way to prevent their wives from obtaining jobs in the firm. One foreman, for example, when faced with a wife who adamantly insisted on returning to work in the factory, called up the employment office and told them to destroy her application, which apparently they did obligingly. Furthermore, many married male shoeworkers strongly believed that their children's proper upbringing required the constant supervision of their wives.[59]

The large number of married women in the Endicott Johnson work force was also a source of contention between women employees, particularly during periods of slack work. One such period, in the summer of 1928, precipitated the following letter from a worker, published in the "Endicott Johnson Workers Daily Page":

> Why is it that the work is taken from the girl, who has no home and has to keep up and the widows who have children to feed and educate? But it is given to those who have husbands and homes, and the men have to have their pleasure, such as fishing and hunting trips, when they are in season. Lest we forget, there is the lovely golf links for pastime if wifie will consent to buying the clubs for hubbie.[60]

When the Depression arrived in full force, the question of working mothers and wives became even more controversial and finally exploded into a public debate, aired in the "Workers Daily Page." It was begun by an anonymous "E.J. Worker":

If they [married women] were relieved of their duties, there would be steady employment for others. I am not unmindful of the fact that machines have changed much of our manner of working; one machine in many cases doing the work which three or four men formerly did. But what about the woman who works so that she may enjoy luxury? This is not considering the social side of the question—the matter of divorce, children roaming the streets, locked out of their homes while their mother is engaged in gainful occupation. It is no wonder that our youth are responsible for so much crime today. The lack of adequate home life has caused much of the crime among our young people.

But I was only going to consider this problem from an economic standpoint. If the wife and mother were not working, the head of the house would of necessity have more steady work, and better pay. On the other hand, it has been my observation after years in an E.J. factory, that the man who has a wife working does not do his best. Why should he?[61]

The letter touched upon almost every conceivable prejudice relating to married women working.[62] It was, in a working-class community with a large number of employed mothers and wives, "not a popular subject," as the letter writer conceded in closing. It was also, predictably, soon followed by a slew of letters both critical and supportive. The first came from Al Very (actually Alice Very), an outspoken worker who was active in various relief committees in the firm and who came to be highly respected by management, particularly George F. Johnson. She argued forcefully that "the married woman worker is usually the fast, dependable, experienced worker, on whom the directors depend to 'produce their production.' They are older, steadier, have an aim in life—to own a home, to educate their children, to care for dependent relatives, perhaps a few luxuries also. Why not if you've gumption and ambition to earn them."

Why should we cling to the eighteenth century idea, that woman's place is in the home—dragging and nagging her husband for necessities and luxuries. On the small apartments of today the upkeep is small and light—the homekeeper in many cases (not all) has many idle hours on her hands.

How many shoe workers—men—do you know who are able to support their families in ease, comfort and a few luxuries—unassisted.

How many of the young unmarried help stay that way? To keep up to your law of unmarried the company would be continually employing "green labor" which is a mighty costly proposition. . . .

As to the married woman whose children are locked out and run the street—if she's that type of motherhood, they would run the street even if she were [not] employed. A lot of them do, don't they?

The right kind of an employed mother leaves her children in someone's care while she earns the where-with-all to provide them with clothes, schooling and spending money.

There is still another side to this married woman worker. She works hard on the machine all day, yet has to return home, do her housework, cook for the family, and somewhere in between get what little social diversion she can find time for.

The married woman's life isn't all luxuries.

As to the man's lack of ambition, when the woman works. Darned if I don't think you are right, in cases too numerous to be pleasant. But if he's that unambitious, no doubt life would be fully as hard for the married woman if she didn't work, with its lack of luxuries and necessities, for the many positions filled by married women—most men couldn't do, or would scorn to do—for fear of loss of dignity. . . .[63]

Responses continued to stream into the "Workers Daily Page." Two employees wrote in to deny that married women worked for luxuries. They argued that single women did not have the responsibilities that married women had. Turning the original luxury argument on its head, they replied with an *ad feminam* by charging the original writer with being "selfish" and wanting "to have more money to dress and go to shows and parties."[64] Another woman wrote in to signal her agreement with Alice Very's views, that few men "could make a go without the wife's help someway."[65] A nonworking wife disagreed:

In nine cases out of ten, it is not necessity that compels the married woman to work. It is the desire for luxuries and also the idea she can not stay in. Her sense of freedom and her own pay envelope. Ask any woman that has once worked to give it up and see what she says. Why I know of several instances where the man alone is working, drawing ten and twelve dollars each week all Summer and trying to support a family of six and eight, while scores of families of two or three have fifty and sixty dollars at their disposal each week. Does that seem fair? Why not make an inventory of the factories and investigate these things. Lay off these married women and give the single ones a chance. . . . It certainly does not appear to me to be lack of pride and gumption when a woman is willing to sacrifice luxuries to make a home happy and if more women felt that way, there would be less race suicide among American people today.[66]

Generally, those who took a position against the employment of married women argued that "every woman's place is in the home, taking care of her family, and if she has none, taking care of her house work." A working wife violated their conception of a woman's proper sphere. "Another thing if there's a war or anything like that why don't they put some of these smart married women in it instead of the boys that they won't give work to now, huh?" was one woman's response to the whole issue.[67] George F. Johnson's public position, supporting and even encouraging the idea of working wives, caused some workers particular concern: "I see Geo. F. decides with Al [Alice

Very] and still he says have more babies. Have the babies, let them run the streets, and the mothers go to work. Well I tell you that hurts me for I think Geo. F. is one wonderful man."[68]

The debate did not let up. Into early November letters continued to pour into the "Workers Daily Page" editor's office. Again and again the same points were emphasized; the same lines of division surfaced. And once more Alice Very contributed to the controversy:

> I s'pose all you intensely "home loving" women could hold down a factory job—could force yourself to work on your nerve all day—turn out acceptable work—then go home, get a meal, straighten out your house, cook and mend—and when the season rolls around squeeze in time to do your house cleaning. Perhaps its easier to do without the "luxuries" for yourself, children and man and be "home-loving." Easier to let the man bear the brunt of earning and bills—easier to get your work done in the daylight—to feel free to attend P.D. meetings, serving circles, bridge parties of an afternoon—to be out in the fresh air, in your own home away from supervision of bosses, striving to keep up production. The path to the "luxuries" for married women isn't "soft" or "fun" or all "luxuries."[69]

A male critic quickly replied to Very with a long harangue on the proper place of women and the injury they do to men, themselves, and their infants in entering the industrial sphere:

> Women are being "emancipated!" They are usurping the places and privileges of the male! Shall they also assume the responsibilities of man? Will they adopt the chivalrous, protective attitude towards their mates heretofore displayed by those same mates towards them?
>
> If women completely eliminate man from the industrial field, which appears highly probable, will they, the women, be willing to provide for their mates, to put it bluntly, keep them? There is nothing in their present attitude to imply this. . . .
>
> In their lust for what they consider the better things in life, many women of today not only do not hesitate to destroy the very best things with which life can endow them, but even risk their own lives. In their efforts to defeat nature's supreme purpose, so that there may be no decrease in their pay checks, they abjure the life of their unborn babes.[70]

This highly emotional and seemingly interminable debate was abruptly brought to a close by the editor, but not before George F. Johnson published a letter on the matter in which he summed up both his and the corporation's position: "It *is a pity* that all can not find work who desire it, either married or single. *That is the great pity of it all.* Any person who is willing to work *ought to be able to find work.* But inasmuch as they can not, it certainly is *most unfair* to consider discharging a woman just because she is 'married.' It would be just as unfair to discharge a woman because she was *not married.*"[71]

And so the public debate died, just as suddenly as it had come to life. No doubt, in the community and in the factories, workers continued to voice their opinions on the subject. There is little evidence that many changed their minds. Married women continued to work for the firm, and the firm continued to employ them.[72] They took their maternity leaves or dropped out of the work force for a few years to have and raise their babies and then returned to work when their children were old enough to be left on their own or with other family members.[73]

II

These, then, were Endicott Johnson's workers—married and single, men and women, immigrants and native born. They came from a variety of backgrounds and brought with them equally varied expectations. What united them was that they had all become "E.J. Workers." But this was a superficial unity indeed. In the factories, first and foremost, workers identified themselves as "stitchers," "cutters," "skivers," "lasters," "cripple chasers," "edge trimmers," "welt beaters," or any number of other job titles that placed them in the chain of production that constituted the twentieth-century shoe factory—a chain that, at Endicott Johnson, began in the tanneries and ended in the shipping rooms. Their work identities were derived from the functions they performed in the highly specialized and segmented world of the factories and tanneries. Although they shared the title of "E.J. Worker," their work experiences varied considerably.

For tannery employees the experience of work generally took place in wide, open workrooms filled with curing, drying, soaking, or hanging hides and leather. In these workrooms the manufacture of shoes began, for it was here that hides from South America and the American Midwest were received and processed into leather. Calf skins, sheep skins, steer hides, elk skins, and numerous less common varieties of animal hides were stacked, re-cured, and stored under controlled temperature conditions in the Hidehouse. After storage, and as needed, the hides were sent to the beamhouses of the various tanneries, where they were run through fleshing machines that removed remnants of animal flesh clinging to the hide. Next, they went to the "wash wheels," where they were loaded into huge rotating drums that washed and purged the hides of the residual curing agent, salt. The washing of the hides prepared them for immersion in lime vats, where the hides were soaked for a week or so to soften the hair. The skins were then removed from the vats, washed again, and put through "unhairing" machines. Hand beamers finished off the process of removing the hair. Once more, the hides were washed and then sent off to the tanyard to be transformed into leather.

The tanyard housed dozens of ground-floor pools containing various concentrations of tanning agents. In these pools the cleaned hides were immersed for several weeks to absorb the tanning fluids that purged their pores of all animal oils and coagulated all of the albuminous material. Following this immersion the hides were bleached to remove the tanning agents and then prepared for the oiling process. They were wrung and fed into huge "oil wheels," which turned like washing machines, mixing and forcing the oil into the hides. Once tanned, the leather went up to the drying loft to hang for several weeks, although upper leather, which was usually dyed, went through "coloring wheels" before being sent to dry. After drying, the leather was moistened with water before going to the hand and machine setters, who removed the wrinkles from the skins, and, in the case of sole leather, to the rollers—the most skillful and best paid of the tannery workers—who smoothed and polished the leather by operating huge one-armed steel rollers. The finished leather was finally sorted and sent off to the various factories or to outside buyers.[74]

Of the jobs in the company, tannery work was among the toughest. "Wet work" involved coming into contact with any number of caustic chemicals, heaving piles of heavy hides over wooden "horses," bending and scraping flesh and hair, often still infested with the remains of worms or other parasites:

> That's where the bull work was, and I mean that was bull work. It was unbelievable how hard you had to work. . . . The stench was terrible . . . the conditions were terrible. You were wet most of the time. You were full of lime. It would splash on you. You would wear a blue denim shirt . . . you'd probably wear it, at most, a month. It would be all starched. You would wind up with sores and stuff like that from the burns.[75]

"Dry work"—sorting, hanging, buffing, or rolling the dry leather—was a bit more pleasant but by no means easy. It often meant breathing large amounts of leather dust. Some jobs, like rolling, were extremely dangerous, and many a roller had suffered the unpleasant experience of watching and feeling a finger crushed beneath the shiny, metal roller that swung back and forth across the leather. Rolling required a great deal of skill, not necessarily to learn the task but to learn to do it well and safely. Expertise conferred considerable status.[76]

Other jobs such as loading the coloring wheels or the wash wheels required little skill but a great deal of muscle. In fact, the handling of the hides, wet or dry, required great physical strength. Tannery work in general was considered a masculine occupation, and very few women were to be found in the tanneries. In mid-December 1919, of 1,835 workers employed in the company's tanneries, only 70 were women. More than twenty years later, their numbers had hardly increased.[77] Female tannery workers generally worked in the Calfskin, Sheepskin, or Upper Leather tanneries, where hides were smaller, thinner, and much lighter than sole leather hides. Furthermore, even in these tanneries women were assigned to relatively light work, although it should be emphasized that *no* work in the tannery was light. They might be found trimming hides or unloading the dryers. They were conspicuously absent from the beamhouses, Hidehouse, and from wet work in general.[78] In being channeled into the "less arduous" positions in the tanneries, women were excluded from the higher-paying jobs. It was thus not surprising to find that they were the lowest paid of the tannery workers. Even when they were able to get on a "man's" job, they had to assert their right to a "man's" wage. "You gonna pay my day like the man today," one Slovak woman tanner demanded of her foreman after being allowed temporarily to perform heavier, normally "male," work.[79]

Most female tanners were either Italian or Slavic.[80] Few native Anglo-Saxon women sought tannery work. It was, after all, not "respectable" employment. Yet this did not prevent them from viewing women tanners with awe. From the perspective of all women factory workers, the female tanners were a special group indeed. That they had invaded a male domain made them stand out. "There was some women in the tanneries," one former factory stitcher recollected in a reverential tone. "There was some females that done men's jobs."[81] Male tannery workers also seemed to share in this awe. "They were strong as horses," a male tanner recalled.[82]

It was no wonder that women tanners were viewed with such marvel. They worked alongside men known for their strength, stamina, and machismo. "They were bigger, stronger men down there. It was heavier work, and some of them liked to fight," recalled one former shoeworker.[83] Another worker asserted: "You had to be a man to work up in the tanneries. Some of those Polish fellows up there . . . them guys would work hard all day long. . . . The average worker in the shoe factory couldn't take it. They weren't that much of a man."[84]

The organization of work in the tanneries differed radically from that of the shoe factories, where most workers labored individually and were paid by the piece. In the tanneries workers often functioned in teams on particular operations. Many were paid by the hour, particularly in the beamhouse. Those who were paid by production, however, generally knew in advance how many sides or hides they would complete on a given day. Production quotas established by the superintendents in consultation with the sales department and factory managers generally set the pace of work in the tanneries. Unlike in the factories, where individual productivity was open-ended, in the tanneries there were limits. These were set not only by market demands, which determined how much leather would be needed for sale to other firms and how much would be required for the corporation's own footwear, but also by the very process of tanning, where manufacturing procedures required several weeks to complete. When the requirements of the factories and of outside buyers were high, the pace of work in the tannery hastened; production quotas rose, and workers labored through their full eight-hour shifts. But when quotas were low, as they often were in the late 1920s and 1930s, extended periods of short-time occurred, allowing workers to leave their jobs early and to take up outside employment.[85]

The nature of production and teamwork had important social implications. Generally speaking, tannery employees demonstrated a greater cooperative spirit than that found in most of the factory workrooms, where piecework and competition for "good jobs" sometimes divided workers. A retired tannery crane operator who had worked for decades in the Sole Leather Tannery recalled the sense of fellowship he found at work:

> In the tanneries you're more like a family. You work around that way for years and the same people would do different things. If a fellow'd get behind or something, you'd jump in and help him. . . . It's dog-eat-dog in the shoe factories. What I mean . . . if this guy gets behind maybe he'll do this guy's work, but he isn't gonna do it to help him. He's gonna do it for what he makes out of it. Where in the tanneries, they don't expect to get anything for helping the fellow out.[86]

Other tanners recalled a very similar sense of collectivity. A Calfskin tanner remembered that spirit in this way:

> In the tannery it used to be production . . . we used to get so many pieces of leather apiece to do. Some guys were a little slower than the others. Well, we finished first. The guy maybe had twenty-five, thirty pieces left. He should have worked another hour extra. Well, we jump over. I take three pieces, you take three pieces, he takes three pieces, and we all finish the same time. . . . The next day it might happen to me. Maybe I got a little behind, I don't feel too good, or something, or I come in a little late. . . . The guys—we used to help each other like that. We used to go hunting together, fishing together. We used to socialize together. . . .[87]

The physical layout of the tanneries, vast open spaces with work areas both visible and easily accessible to one another, made for a work geography that fostered cooperation. With production quotas allowing workers to pace themselves as they wished, as long as they finished the quota by the end of their shifts, it was not uncommon to find men casually socializing or perhaps even gambling in some corner of the tannery, away from the watchful eyes of the foreman. Some took advantage of their "free time" opportunities to learn new jobs:

> When I was running this jitney, I used to stop and talk with guys, and once in a while I would help them out with their machine, whatever it was they were doing. So I got pretty well acquainted with what they call feeding the color machine. That's where you put color on the hides when they were all processed and ready to color. So I used to talk with this one

fellow a lot, and then he used to let me, when he would go to the toilet, he'd say, "Stick a couple of 'em in through the machine." So I done that off and on for a while. Time passed on, and one day my boss come to me, and he says, "How'd you like a job on there, feeding the color machine?"[88]

Occasionally, it is true, arguments or fights might break out between tanners or between the members of a team. Perhaps one was going too fast, or too slow. Here ethnic prejudices might surface, generally in name-calling. Although such altercations could degenerate into fisticuffs, more often than not they constituted opportunities to blow off steam—to relieve tensions, not to exacerbate them. Ethnic animosities between Pennsylvania-born Protestants, who constituted the bulk of the native tanners, and Italians and Slavs infrequently caused work disruptions by the late 1920s and 1930s. Job and skill divisions were no longer as well defined along ethnic lines as they had been earlier in the century, and while the various ethnic groups may not have mixed much outside of work, in their daily work lives they learned, at least, to live and let live, and often to cooperate.

Like the tanneries, the Rubber Mill and Rubber Reclaim plants of the corporation, in Johnson City, also fostered a cooperative work culture. A male domain, hard and dirty work, teamwork units: all functioned to create a unique community of workers. At the Reclaim Plant, salvaged automobile tires and other waste rubber products were processed and prepared for mixing with crude rubber. Huge machines that pulverized, devulcanized, masticated, and partially refined the scrap rubber required stamina and muscle to feed and operate. In the Rubber Mill, or the Paracord as it was otherwise known, the process of manufacturing the rubber was completed; and finished sheets were made into heels, soles, and rubberized cloth.[89] Here, heat presses, molding machines, and rollers required equal stamina. The sole and heel pressrooms were two of the more unpleasant areas of work. In these rooms the men operated in teams of two, pacing themselves to the presses, pulling out trays of hot molds, pushing cool ones in. "The temperature in the summertime was almost unbearable. A lot of these men came down with pneumonia."[90] It was not surprising to find that millwork, at least until World War II, was considered "no job for a woman."[91]

This male world of hot and taxing labor produced a fellowship among the workers. It was a place "where everybody used to have a nickname . . . like Singer, Wormy, Popeye, Wimpy. The language was pretty colorful, too." Employees who worked in the Paracord established a reputation very similar to that of the tannery workers.

The boys in the old Paracord were always thought of as the rough and ready boys of EJ. They were a tight-knit group, but they were a rough-tough group, too. It used to be a practice in the old days that one guy would ring everybody in and out. . . . If somebody was in the habit of getting to work at 6:45, he'd grab all the cards for his department and ring everybody in. Some of these guys would come in at all hours, and occasionally they never showed up. If somebody was going to work overtime, half of the department worked overtime because one guy rang everybody's card out when he left, whether they put in overtime or not. . . .[92]

Although the environment was unpleasant, the work in the Paracord did pay well. Best paying were the sole cutting jobs, where workers operated four-foot beam machines, much like sole leather cutting machines, which cut out the soles from sheets of rubber. The worker would place a tall steel die over rubber sheets while operating a foot lever that dropped a heavy block against the die to cut out the pattern. Like the sole leather cutter in the factory, the rubber sole cutter might lose a finger or two in the course of his career from flipped-over dies. Machine changes in later years alleviated such hazards, but through the 1920s and 1930s the loss of a finger was an ever-present danger, as well as a badge of honor.[93]

In stark opposition to the male-dominated worlds of the tanneries, the Reclaim Plant, and the Paracord were the female domains of the factories— the stitching (or "fitting") rooms. Located adjacent to the cutting rooms, usually on the upper floors of the factories, here was where the uppers of the shoe were stitched together in preparation for assembling and lasting. Usually very large and crowded, with rows upon rows of sewing machines, they were awash with the sounds of rising and falling needles.

The stitching room of a factory contained anywhere between 100 and 400 employees, almost all of them women. Male mechanics might weave their way here and there, on their way to repair a sewing machine. An occasional male might stand in the corner, operating an eyeletting machine, or on a vamping machine, which stitched the vamp around the uppers of the shoe in preparation for the Goodyear stitchers. But, in general, the stitching room was a female preserve, often ruled by "foreladies," *always* under a male superintendent.[94]

While the tanneries and the Paracord exemplified a cooperative spirit and a spirit of camaraderie, the stitching rooms were characterized by a very different atmosphere. Here, hundreds of women, from different cultures, speaking different languages, came together and competed. Work competition and petty squabbles would produce a far more segmented and individualized work culture than in the tanneries and rubber divisions. Work in the stitching rooms, as one stitcher recalled, was anything but conducive to a collective identity:

They put a time study on and then they'd check it out and set up a figure. Some of them would pay better than others, time study or not, and you got those pieces. . . . All you had to do was walk on the floor and grab your case. You'd go along the line. There might be a dozen or more cases on the floor. When you got your work done, they were on these long boxes . . . and when you got your case done and put it on the floor again, you'd go looking over the line until you found a good case you wanted to work on. You could pick anything there and you always left the poor ones on the floor so you could get a good one. That's the way the women worked. We used to call them "grabbers." . . . There was alot of rivalry between people on the same job, and you'd kinda get mad at somebody if you'd thought they had done you wrong in getting the case that you should have had yourself. There was always somebody on the job that you didn't think was very fair.[95]

Faced with the possibility of being stuck with only "poor work," stitchers kept a watchful eye out for the "good cases": "I was the last machine over, but I had a fine position because I could keep my eye out like that and find the good cases of work because you didn't always get a good case, so I'd go out and get a good case of work and bring it in."[96] Conscientious supervisors sometimes developed more equitable systems for distributing the work, but even there accusations of favoritism and arguments over work were not entirely avoided.[97]

Work competition was by no means a problem isolated to the stitching rooms and to women. It was a condition endemic in shoe factories in general. As early as 1902 the *Union Boot and Shoe Worker,* the monthly publication of the Boot and Shoe Workers' Union, commented on the problem of "grabbing" in the shoe factory:

One of the things which tends to make factory life unpleasant and unprofitable is the opportunities which hoggish workmen often have of taking more than their share of the work and picking out the best of it. Life is always unpleasant in environments where the cheekier and brassier a person is the more he gets, and very many shoe factories furnish this sort of environment. . . . These hogs are to be found in almost every factory only waiting for a loophole in the factory system to exercise their talents for "skinning."[98]

One male employee recalled how workers in the Boys and Youths Factory in Johnson City used to crawl through the windows in order to start work early.[99] Even in some cutting rooms, where the spirit of cooperation and camaraderie was relatively high, instances of work competition and "leather theft" occurred.[100] One cutter, Albert Tinney, immortalized the problems of work competition and favoritism in a poem, the "Cutters' Chorus":

Oh, the die boy is always chasing dies,
    For you and not for me.
He's always springing some surprise,
    On you and not on me.

> The die boy I can never find.
> I think he's gone to see
> If he can find a lot of dies,
> For you and not for me.
>
>   . . .
>
> They always pick the best machine
> For you and not for me.
> If there is anything serene,
> It goes to you, not me.
> They fix us some old junk to run,
> And mark it with a "T."
> It only makes a lot of fun,
> For you and not for me.[101]

Yet if work competition was present throughout the shoe factory, it reached its apex in the stitching rooms. Rare was an interviewed stitcher who did not mention the problem of "grabbing."[102] Workers did not operate in teams or in groups in the stitching rooms but as individuals. Furthermore, they were paid by piecework, a wage system that fostered individual rather than collective work behaviors. As one stitcher put it: "You'd try to grab the best tags to get the best shoes. That's all over. You'd find that no matter where you'd go. That's piecework. On timework you'd get paid whether you get the best or the worst."[103]

Ethnic divisions further intensified work tensions between the stitchers. "The Russian workers in the factories were usually fast," one employee recalled. "Boy, I'll tell you I had more arguments with the Russian girls than with any other kind . . . 'cause they were really workers, and they would get in there and maybe they'd get five or six cases to your one."[104] Another worker recited a similar story:

> It was all piecework, and they [the "foreign element"] would go in the morning at six o'clock and work right straight through. . . . Even after the eight-hour day [after 1916], some of them would go in even if they had to crawl through the window and turn the power on and start working. . . . They were brought up to work and work hard. They were a little bit grabby and very difficult at times to work with—of course, it wasn't all the foreign element either, really, but mostly that. . . . They'd hide work. Your work came by twelve or twenty-four pair lots, and if they could get a chance to hide some so that they'd have a little work when you were standing around waiting . . . [they would.][105]

Periodic bouts of short time worsened job competition, as did the absence of a strong work culture. Relatively high labor turnover rates among women, due to marriage, maternity leaves, and seasonal layoffs precipitated by the volatility of high-style women's footwear (where women were highly concentrated), decreased women's commitment to their jobs. Furthermore, the lower-skilled, lower-paid component manufacturing tasks reserved for women hardly fostered much job pride or sense of skill. Those women who were able to obtain the choice "female" jobs often reflected a self-pride that was generally lacking in their less-skilled sisters. Fancy stitchers, top stitchers, skivers, and vampers took a greater interest in their work than other women laborers. As one top stitcher boasted: "Top stitching, what I did, is probably one of the best jobs [in the stitching room]. . . . It takes, to be a good stitcher, it takes a year."[106] Generally, however, women did not define their identities by their work, which, for them, constituted either a transitional state before marriage or a strategy for family survival and betterment.

The highly competitive atmosphere of the stitching rooms did not, however, preclude all possibility of cooperation and positive social interactions. Under certain circumstances stitchers were able to transcend their differences and the individuality fostered by the system of work and payment dictated by the firm. If their work lives were characterized by competition, it was also true that "grabbers" were looked down upon. Work meant more than competition. While the women workers lived in separate neighborhoods (the "Americans" in the south side, the Italians and Slavs in the north side), attended separate churches, and shopped in different markets, their work experience created a common bond. They conversed, sometimes in broken English; they planned birthday parties, wedding and baby showers, and other social events; they played together on athletic teams. They shared their dreams, pains, joys, and frustrations. It was in work that they all came together, and it was this common bond, marred though it was by competition and ethnic tensions, that sometimes yielded a collective rather than an individual strategy for self-betterment.

Adjacent to the stitching room of a factory was the upper leather cutting department. There, dozens of workers were responsible for cutting the upper components of the shoes—the vamps and quarters—from long sheets of leather. The cutters, always males, were the elite of the shoe factories: "The workers, upper leather cutters, were among the highest paid people in the company. You could work as many hours as you wanted. Any hours that you wanted. . . . That was back when it was a trade that you could go anywhere and get a job if you were a cutter."[107] Upper leather cutters might make as much as forty or forty-five dollars a week in the 1920s and early 1930s, double the average factory wage. Their status, as the factory elite, was reflected in the pride they had in their work:

It requires a certain type of individual. Now, you take your lasting room where your shoe is lasted—a good laster has gotta be a skilled man. It takes time. It takes probably a year to make a good laster. But it takes two years to make a good cutter. And it costs the company, at that time, it cost the company $2,000 to make a cutter, because you had to know how to place your dies so as to utilize up every bit of that leather you can be—use leather was expensive.[108]

In general, cutters exhibited a very strong sense of collective identity and an equally strong work culture anchored in the traditions of their craft. They came to work in white shirts and ties, setting themselves apart from the other shoeworkers, who came in plain work clothes. Leather cutting had been the last segment of shoemaking to be mechanized, and mechanization had a relatively minor impact on the skill requirement of the craft. When the United Shoe Machinery Company first introduced the automatic cutting (or "clicking") machine—a device that forced a block on an armature down against cutting dies, thus piercing the hide and cutting out upper leather patterns—the Boot and Shoe Workers' Union journal noted that "all of the skill required in cutting shoes by hand will be required in operating this machine."[109] Indeed, since about 1908 when the machine was first introduced until well into the 1950s, the device changed little, and the skill required to cut leather remained relatively high. Only with improvements in tanning and the introduction of synthetic leathers did cutting skills begin to erode.

Lasting, like cutting, had always been a prestigious occupation (and a male one), for it was the laster who first gave shape to the shoe, wrapping the uppers around a wooden last, avoiding wrinkles, tacking them in.[110] But since the final decade of the nineteenth century, mechanical inventions of various sorts had undermined many of the skill requirements of the job and had divided lasting, once done entirely by a single worker, into various tasks—pullover, side lasting, bed lasting, and a host of additional minor operations. Yet side lasting and bed lasting still remained relatively skilled jobs and paid fairly well. Workers still needed to have manual skills and a good understanding of the complex machinery involved. It took six months to learn the more complicated job of bed lasting, somewhat shorter to learn side lasting. But it took a year to make good money on either. The length of time needed to learn such jobs discouraged many workers from entering the occupation.[111] Those who did enter it took great pride in their work and often defended their domain quite stubbornly against the encroachments of management. Lasters had always been among the more militant groups in the shoe factories.

Edge trimming, too, required a great deal of manual dexterity to master. It also paid quite well and figured very high in the factory occupational hierarchy. The job involved trimming the edge of the sole to a finished and smooth shape by placing the shoe edge against high-speed rotary cutters and moving it evenly against the cutters. It was a risky operation. Many workers lost fingers or parts of fingers in the process.[112] Several dozen men worked on edge trimming in the bottoming department of a factory. Like lasters and cutters, their common job pride was high and made for a relatively strong work culture. And, like lasting and cutting, edge trimming was a male occupation.

The outsole stitchers—the Goodyear operators and McKay stitchers—were also part of the aristocracy of the factory. They were relatively few in number, working in groups of a dozen or so. Their job was to stitch the sole to the uppers. Located in the bottoming room of the factories, where the edge trimmers were, the outsole stitchers maintained a solidarity that was characteristic of the factory aristocracy. They were, along with the cutters, lasters, and edge trimmers, among the highest paid occupational groups in the factory—a status that reflected their intimate knowledge of the complex machinery they manipulated.

The Goodyear and McKay operators, all men, rarely competed for work but developed a spirit of cooperation and fellowship partially derived from their shared craft pride and skill. Furthermore, since they were a relatively small group of workers, they came to know each other fairly well and thus were able to transcend the individualism that piecework fostered: "That's one thing. We used to work together. If I had a machine breakin' down or anything, my buddy used to work with me. So he'd get up, he'd work on my machine, maybe a half-an-hour, and he'd fix it up for me. We'd work buddy-buddy style. It worked out very good that way."[113]

The Endicott Johnson Corporation also maintained its own mechanical divisions: foundry, die shop, carpentry shops, and powerhouses. Workers employed in these departments were not shoeworkers and performed functions that were not unique to shoe factories or tanneries. The carpenters, painters, die shop workers, and mechanics employed by the firm were skilled workers who were generally paid by the hour. Like the aristocrats of the factories, they constituted distinct units, maintaining a collective identity separate from the shoeworkers—one that had important implications when the unions began to make serious attempts to organize the firm in the late 1930s.

Between the male elites of the factories—the cutters, lasters, edge trimmers, outsole stitchers, and mechanical workers—and the female stitchers, labored hundreds of other operatives throughout the plants. Floor workers, tackers, sorters, rounders, lining workers, carton makers, and packers all helped to produce and ship the final product. Few developed the sort of coherent work identities that were part of the groups described.

III

Work at Endicott Johnson, then, was anything but a collective experience. It was varied, segmented, and complex. Not only did employees labor in different physical plants, but within these structures they were divided into separate departments, each with its own unique physical and social characteristics. But they had several things in common. They *were,* after all, "E.J. Workers." They shared in the benefits of the firm's welfare system. They all felt the power of Johnson's personality. And they all, finally, confronted the "distinctions of authority" that constituted the factory caste system. As Johnson wrote, in 1920: "Inside the factories we have our distinctions of authority; outside the factories we are all fellow citizens together."[114]

It was "inside the factories" that Endicott Johnson managers hoped to reap what welfare capitalism sowed. But it was also inside the factories that the welfare ethic was often violated. As one stitcher mused: "I know everybody thinks that EJ was such a wonderful place to work. Well, it was, but in the factory, you didn't get anything for nothing."[115] If it was true that the workers "didn't get anything for nothing" in the factories, it was equally true that neither did management. The experience of work so strained the welfare ethos, which was predicated on notions of industrial partnership, collectivity, and family, that it could not help but be transformed, ignored, violated, and contradicted. Although welfarism seemed to succeed in lowering labor turnover and limiting worker militancy, in the everyday work lives of the employees, it failed in important ways. Ultimately, it was the experience of work that mediated workers' response to welfare capitalism, and it was the experience of work that limited its success.

NOTES

1. Unfortunately, nineteenth-century nativity and ethnicity data on the firm's employees are unavailable. Inferences from census data on shoeworkers residing in the county, however, suggest the conclusions above. In 1892, of the 424 enumerated shoeworkers in Binghamton and the adjacent township of Union (where the Lestershire Factory stood), 80 were foreign-born, the majority coming from Ireland (26), Germany (18), Canada (14), and England (8). New York State, Department of Labor, *Eleventh Annual Report of the Bureau of Statistics of Labor,* vol. 1, *1893* (Albany, 1894), 502–3, 644–45.

2. George F. Johnson to the editor of the *Union News Dispatch,* June 30, 1919, box 5, George F. Johnson Papers, George Arents Research Library for Special Collections, Syracuse University, Syracuse, N.Y.

3. By 1944, although the actual number of foreign-born had remained stable, the *proportion* of foreign-born workers had declined to about 27 percent of the company's entire force. The nationalities represented are shown in the table on p. 89.

4. Rose C. Feld, "An Industrial Democrat Points the Way," *New York Times Magazine,* June 3, 1934, 7. See also William Patrick Burns, "A Study of Personnel Policies, Employee Opinion and Labor Turnover (1930–1946) at the Endicott Johnson Corporation" (Master's thesis, New York State School of Industrial and Labor Relations, Cornell University, 1947), 20.

5. Imrich Mazar, ed., *Dejiny binghamtonských slovákov za dobu štyridsať rokov, 1879–1919* [Forty years of the history of Binghamton Slovaks, 1879–1919] (Binghamton, N.Y., 1919), 7–8, 60–61. For an example of one such migration, see S——, interview by Nancy Grey Osterud and Laura Kirkland, May 15, 1982, summary and partial transcription (Broome County Immigration History Project), 1 and passim. A good account of Italian and Slovak village chain migrations may be found in Josef J. Barton, *Peasants and Strangers: Italians, Rumanians, and Slovaks in an American City, 1890–1950* (Cambridge, Mass., 1975), chaps. 2 and 3.

Country of Birth	Number	Percent of Total Labor Force	Percent of Total Foreign-Born
Czechoslovakia	1,584	10%	37%
Italy	1,113	7%	26%
Poland	492	3%	11%
Austria	378	2%	9%
Lithuania	200	1%	5%
Russia	130	1%	3%
England	82	1%	2%
Turkey	46	1%	1%
Germany	43	1%	1%
Ireland	38	1%	1%
Canada	32	1%	1%
Hungary	25	1%	1%
Other	166	1%	4%
Total foreign-born	4,329	27%	
Total labor force (est.)	16,000		

SOURCE: "Endicott Johnson Foreign Born Workers," Aug. 16, 1944, box 34, ser. 1, Charles F. Johnson, Jr., Papers, George Arents Research Library for Special Collections, Syracuse University, Syracuse, N.Y. Nineteen-forty-four was a volatile year that witnessed a rapid reduction of the firm's labor force, due mainly to military conscriptions. Sixteen thousand is an approximation of the size of the labor force in early 1944—the company's "normal" contingent. The number of workers declined to a low of about 14,000 that year.

6. A fine source on the European village origins of local immigrants is the extensive oral interview collection currently being compiled and transcribed by the Broome County Immigration History Project, based in the Roberson Center for the Arts and Sciences in Binghamton, N.Y.

7. M——, interview by Nancy Grey Osterud, Feb. 24, 1982, summary and partial transcription (Broome County Immigration History Project), 1, 2, 5; *Binghamton Press*, Apr. 11, 1914; A——, interview by Nancy Grey Osterud, Apr. 23, 1982, summary and partial transcription (Broome County Immigration History Project), 9.

8. Mary Sasina Decker, interview by Nancy Grey Osterud, July 11, 1982, summary and partial transcription (Nanticoke Valley Historical Society); Mary Seversky, interview by Gerald Zahavi, with the assistance of Deborah D. Maxwell, July 22, 1982, tape recording (personal possession); Dominick Cinotti, interview by Nettie Politylo, June 8, 1978, transcript (Broome County Oral History Project); John Walikis, "An Analysis of Slovak Women in the Endicott-Johnson Shoe Corporation in the Southern Tier" (Research paper, S.U.N.Y. at Binghamton, 1974), 5 and passim; North Endicott Senior Center group, interview by Nancy Grey Osterud, Feb. 8, 1982, summary and partial transcription (Broome County Immigration History Project); Endicott Office Files, Endicott Johnson Employee Records, George Arents Research Library for Special Collections, Syracuse University, Syracuse, N.Y. Employment files contained information on length of time in the United States and in Endicott, on previous employment, on the location of wives and children ("in old country"), and on reasons for quitting ("return to old country").

9. In 1920 about 4 percent of Johnson City's enumerated residents were born outside of the United States (351 out of 8,587), compared with Endicott's 22 percent (2,073 out of 9,500) and Binghamton's 15 percent (10,368 out of 66,800). U.S. Bureau of the Census, *Fourteenth Census of the United States, 1920: Population,* vol. 1 (Washington, D.C., 1922), 690, 697–98.

10. William Inglis, *George F. Johnson and His Industrial Democracy* (New York, 1935), 88–89; *Endicott Bulletin,* Aug. 19, 1915; U.S. Bureau of the Census, *Fifteenth Census of the United States, 1930: Population,* vol. 1 (Washington, D.C., 1932), 298–99, 302–3. Restrictive clauses on deeds excluding aliens were also in force in Endicott and were partially responsible for separating the Italian and Slav neighborhoods from the "American" neighborhoods. In the mid-1920s many of these clauses became void, and a few Italian families moved "across the tracks." Jeffrey Pines, "Endicott, New York: Industry, Immigrants & Paternalism" (Honors thesis, Dept. of History, S.U.N.Y. at Binghamton, 1982), 21–23; *Endicott Bulletin,* July 18, 1924.

11. Sylvan P. Battista, interview by Gerald Zahavi, with the assistance of Deborah D. Maxwell, session 1, July 13, 1981, tape recording (personal possession); Theresa Schuttak and Fran Eckert, interview by Gerald Zahavi, with the assistance of Deborah D. Maxwell, Apr. 30, 1982, tape recording (personal possession); North Endicott Senior Center group, interview by Nancy Grey Osterud, Mar. 8, 1982, summary and partial transcription (Broome County Immigration History Project), 2–3; *Binghamton Press,* Jan. 20, Jan. 25, 1910.

12. *Binghamton Press,* Jan. 27, 1910.

13. Ibid., Jan. 6, Jan. 10, 1910.

14. Sam Salvatore emphasized Johnson's influence along these lines. Sam Salvatore, interview by Gerald Zahavi, with the assistance of Deborah D. Maxwell, July 7, 1981, tape recording (personal possession). See also Luciano J. Iorizzo and Salvatore Mondello, *The Italian-Americans* (New York, 1971), 57–58, 141. Most of the workers I interviewed who grew up in Endicott in the 1920s and 1930s acknowledged that ethnic tensions existed, but they also asserted that these were very minor in scale. They recall the rise of the Ku Klux Klan in the 1920s in amusing rather than threatening terms. This was true of both native and ethnic workers. On nativism and the Klan in the community in the 1920s, see Jay Rubin, "The Ku Klux Klan in Binghamton, New York, 1923–1928," *Bulletin of the Broome County Historical Society* 20 (Winter 1973): 1–59.

15. This was fairly typical of the boot and shoe and leather industries. Data on wage differentials by nativity can be found in U.S. Immigration Commission, *Reports,* vol. 12, pt. 9, *Immigrants in Industries, Boot and Shoe Manufacturing* (Washington, D.C., 1911), 43–46; and in idem, *Reports,* vol. 12, pt. 8, *Immigrants in Industries, Leather Manufacturing* (Washington, D.C., 1911), 334–38.

16. *Binghamton Press,* Jan. 28, 1910.

17. Endicott Office Files, Endicott Johnson Employee Records.

18. *Lestershire-Endicott Record,* Mar. 20, Mar. 27, 1915.

19. Ibid., July 15, 1915.

20. "Superintendents and Foremen," Oct. 30, 1941, box 33, ser. 1, Charles F. Johnson, Jr., Papers. About three dozen supervisors (foremen or forewomen)

had eastern or southern European surnames out of 408 listed. About a dozen of these were in the tanneries (out of 75 tannery supervisory personnel). The southern or eastern European-named supervisors in the factories were generally in charge of stitching, packing, and shipping rooms. A partial examination of employment files of supervisory personnel from the 1915–30 period further supports the above observations. A more comprehensive treatment of both employment and promotional discrimination in the corporation must await a thorough quantitative analysis of existing employment records. Endicott Office Files, Endicott Johnson Employee Records. See also Battista, interview, session 1.

21. C——, interview by Nancy Grey Osterud, Feb. 15, 1982, summary and partial transcription (Broome County Immigration History Project), 10; John Robble and Anis Robble, interview by Gerald Zahavi, June 28, 1983, tape recording (personal possession); Salvatore, interview.

22. Local 42, Boot and Shoe Workers Union Pledge Cards, Boot and Shoe Workers' Union Records (hereafter BSWU Records), State Historical Society of Wisconsin. More than 2,000 pledge cards, from the 1938–40 union campaign at Endicott Johnson, contained the names and occupations of workers. It is clear from surname and job entries that southern and eastern European ethnics had managed to make major encroachments into many of the most skillful jobs.

23. Paul Coletti [pseud.], interview by Gerald Zahavi, with the assistance of Deborah D. Maxwell, July 13, 1981, tape recording (personal possession).

24. *Endicott Bulletin,* Aug. 3, 1916.

25. Endicott Office Files, Endicott Johnson Employee Records. Hundreds of employee records listed Pennsylvania tannery towns or tanneries as places of former employment.

26. William Haight, interview by Gerald Zahavi, with the assistance of Deborah D. Maxwell, May 27, 1982, tape recording (personal possession).

27. James W. Lupole, interview by Gerald Zahavi, with the assistance of Deborah D. Maxwell, July 15, 1981, tape recording (personal possession). Segments of Lupole's account and chronology were confirmed by his father's employment record. Endicott Office Files, Endicott Johnson Employee Records. For other versions of tannery town migrations, see Paul R. Knickerbocker, interview by Gerald Zahavi, with the assistance of Deborah D. Maxwell, session 1, June 10, 1982, tape recording (personal possession); Bernice O'Connor and Roger T. O'Connor, interview by Gerald Zahavi, with the assistance of Deborah D. Maxwell, Nov. 7, 1981, tape recording (personal possession); Paul R. Eckelberger, interview by Gerald Zahavi, with the assistance of Deborah D. Maxwell, June 26, 1981, tape recording (personal possession).

28. Endicott Office Files, Endicott Johnson Employee Records.

29. H——, interview by David Nielson, June 23, 1973, transcript, 18. A similar tale of rural migration may be found in Palmer Perkins, interview by Gerald Zahavi, with the assistance of Deborah D. Maxwell, Apr. 30, 1982, tape recording (personal possession). See also Clarence Dirlam, interview by Gerald Zahavi, Dec. 12, 1979, tape recording (personal possession); Amy King, interview by Gerald Zahavi, Nov. 30, 1979, tape recording (personal possession); Kenneth

Cowan and Inez Cowan, interview by Gerald Zahavi, June 2, 1982, tape recording (personal possession); Henry Banner and Emma Banner [pseud.], interview by Gerald Zahavi, June 2, 1982, tape recording (personal possession).

30. North Endicott Senior Center group, interview by Nancy Grey Osterud, Feb. 1, 1982, summary and partial transcription (Broome County Immigration History Project), 1, 5; Endicott Office Files, Endicott Johnson Employee Records.

31. Knickerbocker, interview, session 1. Numerous variations of the above might occur. Sometimes, sons or daughters might make the initial migration and bring up parents. Stanley L. Moody, interview by Gerald Zahavi, with the assistance of Deborah D. Maxwell, June 1, 1981, tape recording (personal possession); Helen Bruno, interview by Gerald Zahavi, with the assistance of Deborah D. Maxwell, June 13, 1981, tape recording (personal possession).

32. The appearances of the same home towns on job applications (under "Last Place of Employment") further demonstrate this. Endicott Office Files, Endicott Johnson Employee Records.

33. Battista, interview, session 1; Knickerbocker, interview, session 1; Robble, interview.

34. Burns, "A Study of Personnel Policies," 53.

35. A——, interview by Nancy Grey Osterud, Apr. 23, 1982, 9. Friendship was the equivalent of kinship with respect to obtaining jobs in the firm. One rather detailed employment file, containing a long account of the work history of an Austrian worker, noted that the worker twice obtained employment in the firm by virtue of the go-between services of a friend. Employment Record of L. K., Endicott Office Files, Endicott Johnson Employee Records.

36. Margaret McGregor, interview by Diane Baker, Sept. 3, 1981, summary and partial transcription (Nanticoke Valley Historical Society), 1; Endicott Office Files, Endicott Johnson Employee Records.

37. North Endicott Senior Center group, interview by Nancy Grey Osterud, Feb. 1, 1982, 5. See also First Ward Senior Center group, interview by Nancy Grey Osterud, Mar. 2, 1982, summary and partial transcription (Broome County Immigration History Project), 2; Seversky, interview; Owen J. Ryall, interview by Gerald Zahavi, with the assistance of Deborah D. Maxwell, Apr. 30, 1982, tape recording (personal possession); Earl I. Birdsall, interview by Gerald Zahavi, May 5, 1982, tape recording (personal possession); Knickerbocker, interview, session 1.

38. See, for example, Ralph V. Russell, interview by Gerald Zahavi, with the assistance of Deborah D. Maxwell, May 27, 1982, tape recording (personal possession); Battista, interview, session 1.

39. North Endicott Senior Center group, interview by Nancy Grey Osterud, Mar. 8, 1982, 6–7.

40. Alan Dawley, *Class and Community: The Industrial Revolution in Lynn* (Cambridge, Mass., 1976), 93–94. Through the 1890s the proportion of female to male operatives in the firm had been even greater. New York State, *Report of the Factory Inspector,* 1st through 15th annual reports (Albany, 1887–1901). Nationally, between 1880 and 1900 the number of enumerated female shoeworkers (sixteen years and older) rose from 25,122 to 47,186, an increase of about 59 percent. In that same period the number of male shoeworkers (sixteen years and

older) grew from 82,547 to 91,215, an increase of only about 11 percent. Thus, between 1880 and 1900 the proportion of women in the industry labor force had risen from 23 percent to 33 percent. The relatively low proportion of women workers at Endicott Johnson (Lestershire Manufacturing Company) in 1900, compared with the national average, was probably due to the firm's specialization in heavy footwear, a sector of the industry that traditionally employed more males. U.S. Bureau of the Census, *Twelfth Census of the United States, 1900,* vol. 9, *Manufactures* (Washington, D.C., 1902), 741; Edith Abbott, *Women in Industry: A Study in American Economic History* (New York, 1910), 177–83; Frederick J. Allen, *The Shoe Industry* (New York, 1922), 262; Edgar M. Hoover, Jr., *Location Theory and the Shoe and Leather Industries* (Cambridge, Mass., 1937), 212–13.

41. "Census of Manufactures, 1919," General Schedule, Form 100, box 21, George F. Johnson Papers. This is a copy of the actual schedule filed with the Bureau of the Census.

42. "To the Workers" notice, Jan. 13, 1944, box 10, ser. 3, Frank A. Johnson Papers, George Arents Research Library for Special Collections, Syracuse University, Syracuse, N.Y.; George F. Johnson to *American Shoemaking,* Dec. 20, 1927, box 9, George F. Johnson Papers.

43. The median wage of women shoeworkers surveyed by the New York State Department of Labor in 1926 — most of whom worked for Endicott Johnson — was $18.70. New York State, Department of Labor, *Women in Binghamton Industries* (Albany, 1928), 37–38; "To the Workers" notice, Jan. 13, 1944, box 10, ser. 3, Frank A. Johnson Papers.

44. Katie Wasylysyn Chopiak, interview by Nancy Grey Osterud, session 1, Aug. 6, 1982, summary and partial transcription (Nanticoke Valley Historical Society), 4.

45. Agnes Lyon Guy, interview by Gerald Zahavi, Dec. 12, 1979, tape recording (personal possession); Mattie Drake Pitcher, interview by Gloria Comstock, summer 1981, summary and partial transcription (Nanticoke Valley Historical Society), 1; Bruno, interview; Margaret McGregor, interview by Nancy Grey Osterud, Aug. 13, 1982, summary and partial transcription (Nanticoke Valley Historical Society), 1. Endicott Office Files, Endicott Johnson Employee Records.

46. Chopiak, interview, session 1, p. 2. Boys also lied about their ages. See, for example, Thomas K. Chubbuck, interview by Gerald Zahavi, with the assistance of Deborah D. Maxwell, session 1, June 29, 1981, tape recording (personal possession). Age discrepancies on employment applications of workers who left and came back to the firm also demonstrate widespread age deceptions. Endicott Office Files, Endicott Johnson Employee Records.

47. New York State, Department of Labor, *Women in Binghamton Industries,* 37. A discussion of cultural factors that limited the working careers of Italian and other immigrant women may be found in Alice Kessler-Harris, *Out to Work: A History of Wage-Earning Women in the United States* (New York, 1982), 123–28. See also Virginia Yans-McLaughlin, *Family and Community: Italian Immigrants in Buffalo, 1880–1930* (Ithaca, 1977), chap. 7; Louise C. Odencrantz, *Italian Women in Industry: A Study of Conditions in New York City* (New York, 1919);

Thomas Kessner, *The Golden Door: Italian and Jewish Immigrant Mobility in New York City, 1880–1915* (New York, 1977), 71–77.

48. New York State, Department of Labor, *Women in Binghamton Industries,* 11, 37. George F. Johnson to *American Shoemaking,* Dec. 20, 1927, box 9, George F. Johnson Papers.

49. Frances Filip and Adaline Filip Zevan, interview by Nancy Grey Osterud, Aug. 10, 1982, summary and partial transcription (Nanticoke Valley Historical Society), 2.

50. Single women who had special medical needs also viewed the corporation as a valuable resource. One unmarried woman with a disability, for example, recalled: "So, the one thing at that time with Endicott Johnson was their medical and their doctors. You'd be taken care of. Of course, in my mind I knew that I would probably always have to have care. So I applied for a position." She was hired in spite of her medical condition. B——, interview by David Nielson, Dec. 31, 1973, transcript, 168.

51. George F. Johnson to Rev. C. John Trois, Nov. 17, 1923, box 7, George F. Johnson Papers.

52. George F. Johnson to Mrs. N. B. Snyder, Nov. 23, 1923, box 7, George F. Johnson Papers.

53. Seversky, interview.

54. George F. Johnson to Mrs. Lillian Thomas, Apr. 16, 1923, box 7, George F. Johnson Papers. He wrote Thomas that "we have never yet found it convenient or opportune to do anything of this kind, and we are not now ready." In the following year he replied to another request for day-care provisions by directing the head of the firm's Medical and Relief Department to look into the possibility of providing such services to working mothers. George F. Johnson to Zoela T. Clouse, Dec. 5, 1924, box 7, George F. Johnson Papers. Ultimately, however, Johnson decided against it. He wrote another inquiring correspondent who raised the suggestion of a day nursery: "I am not ready at this time to consider it seriously. There are many other things which we have encouraged; but this has never made any strong appeal to us." George F. Johnson to Dr. Mary A. Snowe, Oct. 24, 1925, box 8, George F. Johnson Papers.

55. Seversky, interview.

56. A preliminary summary was published in "Married Women in Industry," *Industrial Bulletin* [New York State Department of Labor] 7 (Nov. 1927): 45. A rather innocent piece (except to Johnson) based on the *Industrial Bulletin* article appeared in *American Shoemaking* 99 (Dec. 14, 1927): 30–31. See also *New York Times,* Feb. 26, 1928.

57. George F. Johnson to *American Shoemaking,* Dec. 20, 1927, box 9, George F. Johnson Papers.

58. "Endicott Johnson Workers Daily Page," *Binghamton Sun,* June 10, 1928. Emphasis in original.

59. Thomas K. Chubbuck, interview by Gerald Zahavi, session 3, June 28, 1983, tape recording (personal possession); Elmer Knowles and Audrey Knowles, interview by Gerald Zahavi, May 10, 1982, tape recording (personal possession); Jack Hobbie, interview by Gerald Zahavi, Nov. 11, 1979, tape recording (personal possession).

60. "Endicott Johnson Workers Daily Page," *Binghamton Sun*, June 2, 1928.

61. Ibid., Oct. 23, 1930.

62. For more general discussions of the issues raised by this letter and the debate that followed it, see Kessler-Harris, *Out to Work*, 250–60 and passim; Leslie Woodcock Tentler, *Wage-Earning Women: Industrial Work and Family Life in the United States, 1900–1930* (New York, 1979), chap. 6; Winifred D. Wandersee, *Women's Work and Family Values, 1920–1940* (Cambridge, Mass., 1981).

63. "Endicott Johnson Workers Daily Page," *Binghamton Sun*, Oct. 24, 1930.

64. Ibid., Oct. 27, 1930.

65. Ibid., Oct. 28, 1930.

66. Ibid., Oct. 29, 1930.

67. Ibid.

68. Ibid., Oct. 31, 1930.

69. Ibid., Nov. 3, 1930. Very went on to denounce those women who criticized married women working as "women who evidently haven't made the most of their husband's earnings, who are careless about having more babies than they can afford to care for. . . ."

70. Ibid., Nov. 5, 1930.

71. Ibid., Nov. 6, 1930. Emphasis in original. Johnson's attitude was not atypical. Few manufacturing concerns placed formal restrictions on the hiring of married women during the Depression, although informal discrimination may well have been widespread. Wandersee, *Women's Work and Family Values*, 100.

72. Some employment officers, however, either responding to or reflecting the prejudices expressed in the above debate, were less willing to hire women with young infants during the Depression. See Katie Wasylysyn Chopiak, interview by Nancy Grey Osterud, session 4, Sept. 10, 1982, summary and partial transcription (Nanticoke Valley Historical Society), 25–26.

73. Many women, while working in their early marriage years, permanently dropped out of the labor force once they became pregnant. Seversky, interview; Bruno, interview; King, interview; Schuttak and Eckert, interview; Banner [pseud.], interview; Hobbie, interview; Endicott Office Files, Endicott Johnson Employee Records.

74. On tanning processes, see the following: Endicott Johnson Corporation, photographs by Russell C. Aikens, *Partners All: A Pictorial Narrative of an Industrial Democracy* (New York, 1938); Allen, *The Shoe Industry*, chap. 5; Paul R. Knickerbocker, interview by Gerald Zahavi, with the assistance of Deborah D. Maxwell, session 3, July 22, 1982, tape recording (personal possession); Battista, interview, session 1.

75. Battista, interview, session 1.

76. It only required about two months to learn rolling, although far longer to learn to do it with speed and safety. Knickerbocker, interview, session 3.

77. "Census of Manufactures, 1919," General Schedule, Form 100, box 21, George F. Johnson Papers. A company labor relations survey appearing in 1943 noted that no women were employed in the Sole Leather Tannery, but that "several" were employed in the other tanneries. Although no accurate statistics on women employees in the tanneries in the 1940s have been found, oral interviews and company files suggest that their numbers had not appreciably

increased over the 1919 figure. Endicott Johnson Corporation, "Labor Relations Survey," p. 38, Jan. 22, 1943, box 4, ser. 2, George W. Johnson Papers, George Arents Research Library for Special Collections, Syracuse University, Syracuse, N.Y.; Knickerbocker, interview, session 3; Battista, interview, session 1. See also "What the Union Has Done for Its Members" [1947], Local 285 files, International Fur and Leather Workers Union, box 61, Joint Board of Fur, Leather and Machine Workers Records (hereafter Joint Board Records), Labor-Management Documentation Center, M. P. Catherwood Library, New York State School of Industrial and Labor Relations, Cornell University, Ithaca, N.Y.

78. Knickerbocker, interviews, sessions 1 and 3; Sylvan P. Battista, interview by Gerald Zahavi, with the assistance of Deborah D. Maxwell, session 2, Nov. 12, 1981, tape recording (personal possession); Salvatore, interview; O'Connor, interview.

79. North Endicott Senior Center group, interview, Feb. 1, 1982, 7. When the International Fur and Leather Workers' Union signed its first contract with the company in 1944, it established a minimum wage of sixty-three cents an hour, which resulted in increases for several dozen workers throughout the tanneries. In the Upper Leather Tannery a large percentage of those who were affected by this minimum were women. See "What the Union Has Done for Its Members," Local 285 files, box 61, Joint Board Records.

80. This is clear from both oral interviews and lists of tannery workers located in the Joint Board Records and National War Labor Board, Region 2 Case Files. Salvatore, interview; Knickerbocker, interview, session 3; "What the Union Has Done for Its Members," Local 285 files, box 61, Joint Board Records; Endicott Leather Workers Union, Local 285 membership list, July 25, 1945, box 15, National War Labor Board, Region 2 Case Files, Labor-Management Documentation Center, M. P. Catherwood Library, New York State School of Industrial and Labor Relations, Cornell University, Ithaca, N.Y.

81. O'Connor, interview.

82. Ibid.

83. C——, interview by David Nielson, July 26, 1973, transcript, 87.

84. Kenneth E. Compton, interview by Gerald Zahavi, May 5, 1982, tape recording (personal possession).

85. Many tanners had second jobs. Knickerbocker, interview, session 1; Battista, interview, session 2; Salvatore, interview; Haight, interview.

86. Haight, interview.

87. Salvatore, interview.

88. O'Connor, interview.

89. A fine description, with photographs, of the manufacturing processes taking place in these plants may be found in Endicott Johnson Corporation, *Partners All*, 76–83, 94–95.

90. T——, interview by David Nielson, June 1, 1973, transcript, 192. See also Eckelberger, interview, for descriptions of pressroom work.

91. Banner [pseud.], interview. Women temporarily obtained jobs in the mill during World War II.

92. T——, interview by David Nielson, June 1, 1973, 194–95.

93. Cowan, interview; Banner [pseud.], interview; T——, interview by David Nielson, June 1, 1973, 190.

94. On the sexual division of labor in shoe factories, see Allen, *The Shoe Industry,* 155, 169, and passim; Seversky, interview.

95. H——, interview by David Nielson, June 23, 1973, 22. Another stitching room worker offered a similar observation: "In the factory there is good work and there is bad work. There is cheap work, and there is more expensive work. . . . You'd clip off a coupon for every dozen. Sometimes there would be clashes. Somebody would be really fast and get all the good work." O'Connor, interview.

96. D——, interview by David Nielson, July 19, 1973, transcript, 52.

97. O'Connor, interview; Seversky, interview; Margaret Azarin [pseud.], interview by Gerald Zahavi, Nov. 15, 1983, tape recording (personal possession). Such accusations were particularly rife in the Depression. Both the Boot and Shoe Workers' Union and the United Shoe Workers of America made much of them during their organizing drives in the late 1930s and early 1940s.

98. "'Grabbing' in the Shoe Factory," *Union Boot and Shoe Worker* 3 (Mar. 1902): 18.

99. Cowan, interview.

100. John Kovak [pseud.], interview by Gerald Zahavi, with the assistance of Deborah D. Maxwell, session 1, July 15, 1981, tape recording (personal possession); Chubbuck, interview, session 1.

101. *E.-J. Workers' Review* 2 (Mar. 1920): 69.

102. Seversky, interview; King, interview; Schuttak and Eckert, interview; O'Connor, interview. Interviews by David Nielson also document the extensive work competition in the stitching rooms.

103. Schuttak and Eckert, interview. For a short discussion of the divisive impact of piece wages on women stitchers, see Osterud's essay in Ross McGuire and Nancy Grey Osterud, *Working Lives: Broome County, New York, 1800–1930, a Social History of People at Work in Our Region* (Binghamton, N.Y., 1980), 73–74.

104. O'Connor, interview.

105. King, interview.

106. Schuttak and Eckert, interview.

107. B——, interview by David Nielson, Aug. 14, 1973, transcript, 140, 156.

108. Chubbuck, interview, session 1. Chubbuck's estimate of the cost of training a good cutter appears to be a bit high. The Federated American Engineering Societies estimated the cost at about $600. See Federated American Engineering Societies, Committee on Elimination of Waste in Industry, *Waste in Industry* (New York, 1921), 14; cited in Hoover, *Location Theory,* 209.

109. *Shoe Workers' Journal* 9 (May 1908): 9. The new machine increased output and alleviated the need to sharpen knives constantly.

110. Women lasters were employed in the rubber footwear divisions in the late 1920s and early 1930s. There, the work required less skill and physical strength.

111. Richard J. Murphy, interview by Gerald Zahavi, with the assistance of Deborah D. Maxwell, July 7, 1981, tape recording (personal possession); Ryall, interview.

112. Ryall, interview. Ryall had cut every one of his fingers many times over.
113. Compton, interview. Compton worked as a Goodyear stitcher in the Fair Play Factory in West Endicott from 1928 until the early 1960s.
114. George F. Johnson, "30 Years without a Strike," *System* 37 (Jan. 1920): 45.
115. R——, interview by David Nielson, July 10, 1974, transcript, 295.

George F. Johnson (1920s). George F. Johnson Papers, George Arents Research Library for Special Collections, Syracuse University, Syracuse, N.Y.

George F. Johnson addressing factory superintendents (1937). Photograph by Russell C. Aikins, in Endicott Johnson Corporation, *Partners All: A Pictorial Narrative of an Industrial Democracy* (New York, 1938), 11.

An "informal visit" by George F. Johnson. The caption accompanying the photograph reads as follows: "George F. takes more than a conversational interest in the tannery. He regularly pays informal visits to tannery and factory. . . . George F. enjoys these shop excursions. He not only is keen to see what is going on, but he likes being with the workers." Photograph by Russell C. Aikins, in *Partners All,* 8.

Harry L. Johnson (1910s). George F. Johnson
Papers.

Charles F. Johnson, Jr. (1930s). George W.
Johnson Papers, George Arents Research Library for Special Collections, Syracuse University, Syracuse, N.Y.

George W. Johnson (1930s). George W.
Johnson Papers.

Tannery hand beamers removing fleshings and fine hair from hides (1930s). Frank Chetko Collection, Broome County Historical Society, Binghamton, N.Y.

Tannery workers rolling hides for sole leather—among the most skillful jobs in the tannery (1917). New York State Archives/Education Department, Albany, N.Y.

Sole and heel cutting (1917). New York State Archives/Education Department, Albany, N.Y.

Attaching heel to sole (1917). New York State Archives/Education Department, Albany, N.Y.

Women stitching insoles, Jigger Factory (1930). Frank Chetko Collection.

4

Negotiated Loyalty:
The Response to Welfare Capitalism

Be Loyal!

Be loyal to God and your country,
   To your innermost self be true,
But don't forget there's another debt,
   To the Boss be loyal, too!

He has paid for your time and your labors,
   You have given your promise to work;
It's up to you to be honest, true,
   And it's hardly the square thing to shirk.

It is easy to knock down the minutes,
   To clip off an hour here and there,
And none may know you are doing so,
   But ask yourself now, Is it fair?

He has taken you as his servant—
   Stenographer, bookkeeper, clerk—
He expects from you what you're paid to do—
   To be loyal to him and to work.

Would you cheat playing cards, dice, or checkers,
   Deceive any man in a game;
In a moment rash steal jewels or cash
   And think you were never to blame?

Most certainly not! You'd assure us.
   You're honest, you'd pridefully say;
Yet men like you who boast proudly, too,
   Would try to down the boss every day.

It's cowardly, despicable, yellow;
   And a man is a thief no less
Who would steal or rob when upon the job,
   And boast of his faithfulness.

> So be loyal to God and your country,
> To your innermost self be true,
> But don't forget there's another debt,
> To the Boss be loyal, too![1]

I

Glowing accounts of Endicott Johnson and its patriarchal management appeared in popular newspaper and magazine stories as well as trade publications from the mid-1910s through the 1930s. Writers typically viewed the corporation as a model of progressive business practices.[2] The loyalty of Endicott Johnson's workers was described as the product of a truly benevolent industrial endeavor and a testament to the achievement of a corporate collective identity. A 1919 *New York Times* headline noted the "Extraordinary Contentment in Shoe Manufacturing Plant Where Organizers Have Failed after Having Free Opportunity to Unionize 13,000 Workers."[3] Almost twenty years later, in the midst of a growing and militant national labor movement, a magazine writer described the Endicott Johnson workers' attitude toward the firm in these terms: "Twenty thousand loyal employees—20,000 men and women working contentedly at fair wages and considering themselves and their bosses all one big family—that is the cheering and inspiring picture presented by the Endicott-Johnson Shoe Company."[4]

While the conservative press found much to praise in Johnson's "ideal community," trade unionists and radicals did not. A concern over welfare capitalism had come to characterize much of the organized labor community and its sympathizers in the 1910s and 1920s. Strident criticism of welfare capitalism appeared in trade union papers and in many popular journals.[5] Radical and socialist critics actively joined labor leaders in assailing this "new tactic" in the social conflict of classes. Stock ownership plans were attacked as "devices or weapons in the arsenal of welfare," which, along with pension plans, health insurance, and various other corporate welfare programs, were employed in "chloroforming the group consciousness of the workers."[6] Trade union and radical publications circulated Will Herford's "Welfare Song," which, from 1913 until well into the middle of the century, summarized labor's view of corporate welfarism:

> Sing a song of "Welfare,"
> A Pocket full of tricks
> To soothe the weary worker
> When he groans and kicks.
> If he asks for shorter hours
> Or for better pay,
> Little stunts of "welfare"
> Turn his thoughts away.

Sing a song of "Welfare,"
Sound the horn and drum,
Anything to keep the mind
Fixed on Kingdom Come.
"Welfare" loots your pocket
While you dream and sing;
"Welfare" to your pay check
Doesn't do a thing.

Sing a song of "Welfare,"
Forty 'leven kinds,
Elevate your morals,
Cultivate your minds.
Kindergartens, nurses,
Bathtubs, books and flowers,
Anything but better pay,
Or shorter working hours.[7]

According to critics on the left, and organized labor as well, employer welfare programs were aimed at halting the development of a real industrial democracy by buttressing traditional exploitative relationships with minimal yet effective reforms. The socialist League for Industrial Democracy, meeting for its twelfth annual conference in 1926, extensively discussed the welfare initiatives of employers and reached a disheartening conclusion.

The net result of all these activities in some cases seems to be what the employer expects—an increased loyalty to the firm, a greater dependence upon welfare features as a part of the payment for the job. This fixation of loyalty upon the employer . . . alienates the worker from his fellow workers in the industry at large and leads him to identify his individual interests with those of the company rather than with those of his class. The result is . . . "factory solidarity" as opposed to "class solidarity."[8]

Abraham Epstein, who attended the conference, published an extensive survey of industrial welfare practices in 1926 and concluded that such reforms were indeed "sapping American trade unions." After examining the welfare programs of 1,500 firms and the general plight of organized labor, he found that "all the evidence seem[s] to indicate that the organization of wage-earners on a belligerent basis is gradually becoming a thing of the past."[9]

When critics came to write specifically about Endicott Johnson and its famed labor loyalty, they generally repeated many of the themes cited above. Depicting an authoritarian, albeit benevolent, management with a co-opted or passive work force, their hyperbolic condemnations reduced both managers and workers to caricatures. The Boot and Shoe Workers' Union, which failed in several attempts to unionize Endicott Johnson workers in the 1920s and 1930s, consistently attacked welfare capitalists in its journal. Endicott Johnson was a prime target:

> We have a few real Mussolinis in our shoe industry. One of the most prominent of these is the head of the Endicott Johnson Company. This executive exercises absolute control over the earnings and lives of several thousand employes and their families. . . . All power is exercised at the top and yet the executive seems to wish to sell the idea of a super management to his employes so as to enthuse them with greater confidence in his dictatorship.[10]

Radical critics expressed indignation over the seemingly effective dilution of class consciousness that corporate paternalism at Endicott Johnson achieved. An article from the *New York Call,* reprinted in the *E.-J. Workers' Review,* characterized the corporation's workers in these terms:

> And what a smug, contented lot I learned these thousands of wage slaves are, no more thinking of themselves as slaves than honey bees. Do they not have the most munificent wages now paid in the labor market, so that every family has its own car, dresses in the finest and is "prosperous" beyond any proletarian dream that never could come true? Do they not go to work when they please and quit when they like? One woman said to me, with a smile of the most placid satisfaction: "It's pretty nice to work as few or as many hours as you like, good pay for the work, and have a nice little bonus of $250 or more at the end of the year."[11]

Was welfare capitalism as effective in winning the hearts and minds of American workers, and specifically Endicott Johnson workers, as these critics' concerns suggest? Recent historians are not as certain. Stuart Brandes, in a survey of American welfare capitalism, asked whether workers "genuinely embraced" corporate paternalism and concluded that although some workers "appreciated" welfare programs, many more were dissatisfied and lashed out against industrial welfare practices.[12] Irving Bernstein, in his epic study of labor in the 1920s, reached a very similar conclusion. While acknowledging that new management reforms contributed to improvements in working conditions and to the enhancement of labor's long-term bargaining position, he nevertheless portrayed industrial welfarism as unstable, inherently demeaning, and temporary. "Welfare capitalism," he wrote, "stripped of the verbiage of industrial democracy, was precisely what its critics called it: paternalism. At best it could be no more than an unstable system for both employer and employee. . . ."[13]

At the root of both Brandes's and Bernstein's portrayal of the response of workers to paternalism were assumptions about the natural course of worker consciousness in America, assumptions characteristic of progressive labor historiography since the days of John R. Commons and Selig Perlman. American workers, it was held, were destined to express their interests and power in institutional forms that reflected their unique and particular needs—in other words, in trade unions.[14] Welfare capitalism was merely a temporary obstacle in their quest for power. Bernstein wrote: "The central purpose of welfare capitalism—avoidance of trade unionism—could only be achieved temporarily because paternalism failed to come to grips with the main issue: a system of shop government placed in the climate of political democracy and universal suffrage."[15]

Other scholars have been far less certain of the intrinsic failure of welfare capitalism. Daniel Nelson, for example, in his monograph on the emergence of the modern factory system, viewed the welfare movement as part of a broad effort by management to rationalize production and bring under more immediate control the factory work force—a generally successful effort.[16] David Brody argued even more forcefully for the effectiveness of corporate paternalism in generating worker loyalty. According to Brody the Great Depression had a severely crushing impact on corporate welfarism by forcing managers to take drastic cost-cutting measures that undermined workers' confidence in corporate paternalism. This in turn led to widespread worker rebellions. Unlike Brandes and Bernstein, Brody suggested that welfare capitalism did manage to win the hearts and minds of American workers. The rapid decline of union membership in the 1920s, as well as the muting of labor militancy, reinforced his conclusions. He attacked the prevailing viewpoint of progressive labor historians who were comforted by the thought that "welfare capitalism never was a success, never persuaded workingmen that they were best off as wards of the employer, and never took deep root in the American industrial order."[17] Instead, he argued:

> It is mistaken to assume, as most of us do, that American workers were not really captive to the paternalism of the 1920s, and that they would inevitably have turned to some form of independent labor organization. There is no solid evidence to support that liberal article of faith. On the contrary, I would argue that, had not the Depression shattered the prevailing assumptions of welfare capitalism, the open shop might well have remained a permanent feature of American industrialism.[18]

In asserting that paternalism may well have been acceptable to millions of American workers, Brody differentiated himself from historians who took pains to emphasize workers' instinctive rejection of welfare capitalism. Yet, while Brody came to a different conclusion over the "success" of welfarism from that reached by Brandes and Bernstein, all three historians failed to take into consideration an important dimension of corporate life. Their interpretation of welfare capitalism as either successful or unsuccessful in maintaining labor loyalty failed to come to grips with actual shop floor relations under welfarism or with how the workers felt about it. As a result they missed the complex ways in which workers translated and transformed managerial projections, in the form of welfare ideology and practices, for their own ends. A close look at the relationship between workers and managers at Endicott Johnson may suggest that our understanding of workers and welfare capitalism needs revision.

II

The 1920–21 depression hit the Endicott Johnson corporation hard. Slack business led to the stockpiling of both leather and shoes, a practice that the firm had engaged in during former recessions and depressions to sustain production and maintain employment. But the continuation of the depression forced company managers to make difficult decisions—welfare programs would have to be cut. Available surplus earnings for profit sharing declined from five million dollars in 1919 to one million dollars in 1920. The bonus checks sent out to the workers in early 1921 amounted to only one-sixth of the previous year's amount. Along with a cut in the bonus came the elimination of the firm's recreation programs. Vacations with pay and holiday pay, products of World War I, were also soon stopped. Corporate contributions to community charities and civic institutions were reduced or halted. The employee magazine ceased publication. "It was not that we lost faith in recreational activities, in the employees' magazine, in the libraries, or in the hundred and one facilities that were provided," wrote George F. Johnson in 1921, "it was a case of doing what we had to do."[19]

The firm's financial retrenchment was partially effective. Close to three million dollars a year were saved. But, apparently, it was still not enough. Strict time accounting was instituted throughout the factories, and all employees, including upper management, were required to punch time clocks.[20] Time off was docked for all workers, the work week was reduced to five days from six, and work sharing was initiated. But the most painful act was reserved for April 1921 when management cut wages by 20 percent. "There was a lot of grumblin' about that," recalled one cutter, "because a lot of 'em felt that 10 percent woulda' been enough."[21] Management tried to prepare the workers for this long in advance, in open letters appearing in the *Workers' Review,* and hoped that the reduction would be "accepted loyally by the workers."[22]

Elsewhere in the country other firms were instituting similar wage reductions. Some had done it earlier, others later, than Endicott Johnson. At the Amoskeag Manufacturing Company in Manchester, New Hampshire, another welfare firm, the 20 percent reduction came in February 1922 and precipitated a nine-month strike that destroyed that firm's "paternalistic balance."[23]

Endicott Johnson managers had never faced a real test of their corporate paternalism. Their recently adopted welfare programs, which they were now forced to curtail, had raised their workers' expectations. How would the workers react to the firm's actions? The answer was not long in coming. In mid-May, George F. Johnson wrote to a friend that the wage cut was "accepted very loyally by the Help, and we are very proud indeed, of their good will, so much in evidence."[24] The workers' loyalty held. There was no rebellion. This was neither the first nor the last test of Endicott Johnson's policies, but it was one of the more dramatic demonstrations of the "success" of welfarism at Endicott Johnson.

Throughout the 1920s Endicott Johnson managers never disguised that their labor policies were designed to maintain worker docility and to retain managerial control over the work force. They merely asserted that liberal welfare policies were a far more effective means of control than was repression. Most workers could plainly see management motives of labor control in the firm's policies, yet they could equally appreciate that employment at Endicott Johnson offered substantial benefits. The labor loyalty at Endicott Johnson, both praised and cursed, existed within the context of both real personal benefits and corporate control. The workers' recognition of these two aspects of their work lives led to a far more contradictory form of corporate loyalty than previous writers—critics and laudators, contemporaries and historians—have recognized.[25]

Welfare capitalism at Endicott Johnson existed as a compact between management and labor, one built on mutual loyalties. To maintain that compact, expectations and obligations needed to be met, particularly by management. Workers developed formal and informal strategies for extracting, sustaining, and expanding these obligations. Although they expressed loyalty to the corporation and its management, they repeatedly demonstrated that their loyalty had limits. Within the confines of two dozen shoe factories and tanneries, labor and management pulled and tugged at each other, both with and without outright coercion—each attempting to extract from the other a maximum return on its "loyalty." Ultimately, the loyalty was a negotiated allegiance, whose real meaning must be discovered in the behavior of workers, not merely in the proclamations of management.

First of all, the ideology of the "Square Deal" was transformed in the workers' minds. It became an autonomous reference point for laborers, allowing them to judge corporate policies and actions by appealing to rights and obligations that management itself had first vaguely defined. George F. Johnson recognized the transformation of the "Square Deal" from a projected corporate ideology into an independent code of just behavior, one that entrapped management. He wrote to his son in 1930: "It has come to a point where no man may without great risk to the business, change the fundamental ideas which have controlled, and which have been thoroughly accepted and adopted by the workers themselves. I should feel very sorry for the leader of E.J. who attempted to make serious changes in management and control."[26]

William Inglis, in his company-sponsored biography of Johnson, suggests something of how the "Square Deal" ideology was actually translated by the workers. Dan Sargent (actually a pseudonym) was an E.J. worker who lost his sight while in the employ of the firm. Although not eligible for compensation because the accident that led to his sight loss did not occur during working hours, he was nevertheless cared for by the company and continued to receive a regular payroll check. During the financial slump of the post–World War I period, the following conversation reportedly took place between Sargent and George F. Johnson:

> "You know, George F., these times are something awful. We go on living through force of habit." "Yes, times are bad," said Mr. Johnson, "but we've lived through worse, and we'll live through this." "True for you," said Dan. "But I've had a heavy load on my mind lately. The price of food and clothes, the price of everything, has gone up so high in the last few months that we've been pressed very hard. It's that bad, I think I ought to have a raise in my wages. What do you think, George?" "Well, to tell you the truth, Dan," said Mr. Johnson, "I haven't been thinking of it at all. But I see your point. Tell you what I'll do—I'll speak to the payroll folks about it and see what they can do." "No fear but they'll do right, with yourself jogging them," said Dan gaily.[27]

What is significant in this overstylized account is the strategy that Sargent employed in extracting benefits from the corporation. The expectation of additional compensation was an expression of the transformation of corporate-defined privileges into worker-defined obligations. Trapped within the logic of the worker's expectations, Johnson could either give in or deny him a "Square Deal." He gave in; Sargent received his raise.

While doing research in preparation for his biography, Inglis interviewed several of the company's employees. He found that older workers had been able to maintain their self-respect in Endicott Johnson's paternalistic system because, although "they were receiving help . . . they felt they were entitled to it, had worked for it."[28] For these workers as for Sargent, what mattered was more than merely maintaining self-respect; they wanted what they had earned, what they were owed. Another old-timer, an Italian worker, expressed this point quite forcefully to George F. Johnson's son, George W. Johnson, in 1934:

> Mister George, what's the matter with E.J. not have it square deal anymore. I come for this company 15 year. Every time I take it the free medicine, all family too. Every day go for the 15 cent meal. My wife now got it five kids from Mr. George F., no cost nothing. This time come from me old country three brother and wife. Powell [the employment manager] no give it job. Powell no good for E.J. Just good for tricks. Better he find the trick for give everybody job. What's matter no can. My brother he like it too for Mr. George F. be their father and he give it their wife free baby just same like me.[29]

Several months earlier, responding to similar expectations, Johnson voiced his indignation over escalating worker demands: "Given privileges that did not belong to them [the workers], they soon acquired a sense of ownership, and resent any effort to deprive them of something . . . to which they had no right."[30]

Sometimes, workers' extractive strategies could be quite ingenious. In 1935, following the printing of an open letter by George F. Johnson advocating the publication of wage scales by corporations, a worker approached his superintendent with a request for an increase in wages. He was refused and told that his wages were already quite high. "He agreed his wages were very good and indeed satisfactory, but that some other fellow was getting more. The superintendent asked how he knew this and he said he had taken pains to find out; wasn't George F. advocating 'why keep wages secret?'"[31] A frustrated George F. Johnson declared: "We have drifted into the wrong idea of treating labor, while we were seeking the right way. Everything we give them for nothing makes them a little bit lazier, and a little harder to deal with, and more prone to find fault."[32]

As the "Square Deal" ideology was transformed by workers in their assertions of corporate obligations, so, too, was it transformed on the shop floor. More than anything else, the experience of work itself limited the effectiveness of the firm's liberal welfare policies. If benevolent paternalism and the concrete benefits of the company's welfare system produced loyalty, the daily experiences of workers in the factories produced just the opposite result. The classless ideal may have been in evidence in social clubs and athletic events, in low turnover, and in an absence of militancy and trade union consciousness; on the shop floor class feelings were alive and well.

Not only did workers recall their experiences of work with a vocabulary that reflected social distance and class—their use of the term *boss* rather than *director* being an obvious example—but in their behavior on the shop floor, they demonstrated their recognition that their interests and those of the corporation diverged. While Endicott Johnson employees never achieved a generalized class consciousness, one that acknowledged common interests with an American working class, they nonetheless did exemplify a class consciousness of a more inchoate kind, one characterized by behavior and language that reflected their distance from capitalists and managers who controlled the corporation for which they worked. Furthermore, under certain circumstances groups of workers at Endicott Johnson demonstrated a proclivity to band together to challenge corporate interests. The incompleteness of the workers' attempts to unite and confront management attests to the effectiveness of welfarism, although certainly other factors were at work. But their efforts— even that they made them at all—attest to the limited success of the firm's policies.

Accessibility to top management, a central tenet of the corporation's "Square Deal" policy, gave workers leverage in shop floor negotiations. Decisions of supervisors were open to revision. In one instance, in 1927, a committee of workers approached management about the firing of a well-liked foreman by their factory superintendent. Charles F. Johnson, Jr., George F. Johnson's nephew and a general manager at the time, investigated the matter and reversed the decision; the foreman was reinstated and later replaced the superintendent who had fired him.[33]

Occasionally, workers might even overthrow supervisors. Workers in the Victory Factory in Johnson City went on strike in the winter of 1931 after appeals for the removal of a hated foreman were ignored by management. The strike began in the cutting room but soon spread to the whole factory. George W. Johnson, at this time the president of the corporation, described the events that precipitated the strike.

> The difficulty in Johnson City was all Leo Sullivan. As you know, for a long time we had been hearing that he was a tyrant with help. Last winter I had three or four anonymous letters, about which I spoke to you. This fellow warned us that we would have plenty of trouble if we did not move Sullivan. . . . He did a great many little things that the help termed underhanded, and not in accordance with the Company's policy. It made them mad. They lost confidence in him, and finally their respect, and actually demanded a change.[34]

Leo Sullivan was removed and shifted to another factory, where he worked as an upper leather cutter. The workers had effectively exercised their power.[35]

Keeping the workers satisfied was a compulsion for the corporation's management, one that continually undermined the authority of shop floor supervisors, as when firing decisions were periodically appealed and reversed. The corporation's official policy concerning discharges was outlined by George F. Johnson in 1919 in these terms:

> A position with this company is worth too much to be treated flippantly. "Hiring and firing" is played out. . . . That is why we have taken from the Directors [foremen and foreladies] the authority to discharge Workers. We have substituted simply the right of *suspension,* by Directors. There is always the right of appeal and the right to reinstatement, and the right to another chance—for those who really want it. And when they make their appeal to me, they generally get another chance.[36]

Indeed, appeals were made and, as notes appended to employment records demonstrate, decisions of employment officers were reversed. The experiences of various workers further suggest that this policy was not mere rhetoric. An appeal by a laid-off worker with several family dependents led to his reinstatement and the chastisement of the company official responsible for his firing. A seventeen-year veteran of the company, complaining about being laid off on account of his age, elicited the following curt reminder from George F. Johnson to his nephew: "Perhaps you will find that there are rights under our well advertised 'Square Deal Policy', that have been denied this Mr. Warner."[37]

"Directors" responded in a variety of ways to such limitations on their authority. Frustration was a typical reaction, as one supervisor's testimony illustrates: "If I had a worker who was disgusted and he went to Charlie, nine times out of ten, I'm the one who'd get yelled at, not the worker. He'd [Charlie] come back and bawl me out. . . ."[38] A finishing room foreman similarly recalled: "I was foreman for five years, and the company wouldn't want you to fire a man. That was one bad feature for a boss. They wanted you to get out the shoes and get the work out right. If you don't and a man don't do his work like he ought to, and you fire him, they go over and report to George F. or Charlie, whichever one was there, and they'd send them back and make a fool out of the boss."[39]

The elimination of "hiring and firing" and upper management's responsiveness to employee complaints eroded the fortresses of shop floor supervisors. Some foremen and foreladies passively accepted this erosion of authority, swallowing their frustrations and submerging their resentment of upper management. Others dug in and defended their domains quite forcefully.

> I made my mind up to one thing. And I got all my help together. I had something like twenty-five workers [and] I got 'em all together down in the stockroom. "Now," I says, "I understand that the company gave me the job of running this room." And I says, "There's one thing I want straightened out, and I want every one of ya to know it. The company tells me to run this room. *I'm gonna run it!* If anybody comes in here— Jess Jones [Leather Department manager], Charlie Johnson . . . [and] if he tells a worker in here to do somethin', and that don't—that turns out wrong, he's or she's fired. Nobody takes any orders in this room from anybody but me. . . . I've seen a lotta wishy-washy foremen around through the factories, that had these guys comin' in from the main office . . . runnin' 'em ragged and everything else." I says, "Nobody's gonna run me ragged. . . . I'm gonna run this room the way I think it oughta be run." I says, "If that ain't right, they can always fire me." So that was understood and I never had no troubles.[40]

Yet foremen who asserted their authority this vehemently might cause upper management no end of aggravation.

The uneven adherence of lower-level management to the firm's labor policies and ideology yielded a substantial amount of intramanagerial conflict. Foremen and forewomen who took the company's ideal of a corporate family seriously sometimes sided with workers against upper management, to the displeasure of the latter. Foremen like Frank Tuthill would go out of their way to satisfy their workers. Tuthill met with his men to talk out problems. If disagreements over prices occurred, he would approach the superintendent on their behalf. If that did not resolve the matter, he would recommend to his workers to get a committee together to approach upper management.[41]

Occasionally, factory supervisors identified more closely with their workers than with upper management. Foremen and superintendents might even warn workers to hold back their piece coupons or else their rates would be cut.[42] Such close identification of interests between workers and supervisors, of course, posed problems for upper management. When a particularly well-liked Victory Factory superintendent was removed in 1930, the Johnsons were faced with many angry employees circulating petitions for his reinstatement.[43] The workers' frustration at finding their petitions ignored set the stage for the 1931 strike in the Victory Factory.

Lower-level managers who protected workers' interests yielded one sort of challenge to upper management. Shop floor supervisors callously concerned about preserving their autonomy and guarding their authority, on the other hand, often violated the compact that sustained labor peace in the corporation and hence also posed problems for management. As George F. Johnson admitted to a worker:

> Several hundred hired lieutenants, who are not all infallible—in fact, many are ignorant and prejudiced, and understand, themselves, very little of the meaning of the "square deal"—presents difficulties. . . . It has been described in this way: the Head of a business desires everyone to have a "square deal," but between the "Head of the business" and "everyone," there is alot of "static"—misunderstanding, ignorance, prejudice, and innumerable difficulties.[44]

Yet whether or not supervisors took the "Square Deal" too much to heart, becoming true "partners" with the workers, or ignored it, the firm's labor policies allowed workers both to widen and exploit divisions within management that such conditions created.

The firm's reliance on labor loyalty and the expectations that its welfare policies and ideology had fostered among the workers placed company officers in a particularly vulnerable and uncomfortable position. Management found that workers sometimes bargained with their "loyalty" in order to obtain wage concessions. Such behavior suggests that the workers' understanding of loyalty may have differed strongly from management's and was predicated on management's continued willingness to compromise on important shop issues. This is vividly demonstrated in the following account of a wage negotiation:

> I'll never forget this meeting we had over prices. We voted on it three different times. The third time I voted, and I went out. "I'm not voting any more." It was a ridiculous thing, it only applied to one pattern and

they wouldn't give in and we wouldn't give in. It finally come down after I left. But before that, this man named G——, he was a really outspoken man, and he knew Charlie [Johnson] very well, and they was always talking about loyalty to the company, loyalty to the company. . . . You got this and you got to be loyal to the company. So this man . . . he said to Charlie, "Now Charlie I've worked here probably 35 years now. That's pretty damned loyal, ain't it Charlie?" and Charlie said, "Yeah, that's pretty damned loyal." "I always done good work. Ain't that pretty loyal, Charlie?" Charlie says, "Yeah, that's pretty loyal." He says, "Damn it, when you come to stick your hand in my pocket, I ain't going to be so loyal any more!"[45]

Loyalty was by no means a reflexive reaction. It required a return. Individually and collectively, workers developed strategies to extract this return.

Individuals dissatisfied with their wages could look for an opening in another department and transfer. Internal movement within and between the factories was constant and pervasive. Such movement was both a safety valve and a form of power since workers could vote on wages and personnel with their feet, without sacrificing the security of their jobs. By voting in this way, they could sometimes win concessions from management. One worker, Richard J. Murphy, recalled an instance of unfair pricing on a bed lasting job. The lasters were not able to win a price adjustment from the factory superintendent, so Murphy transferred to another department. Later approached by Charles F. Johnson, Jr., and asked why he left his position, Murphy replied that the price on the job had been unfairly set at twenty cents a dozen when it should have been more like twenty-three cents. The price was raised.[46]

Piece rates were a central shop floor concern for workers. Rates were set by the pricing departments of the company.[47] Whenever a new pattern was introduced or adjustments in old rates were to be made, factory superintendents would call in for a job timer. "He'd go around and sneak up and time you," one worker recalled. "They'd time the fastest man."[48] Workers typically slowed down when timers were present. As another worker recalled: "Even the faster worker, he'd slow down. The minute they knew they was comin' or anybody found out that there was anybody in there timing, then you'd see everybody slowin' down."[49] When it came to piece rates, the lines between workers and managers were drawn quite rigidly—hardly attesting to the existence of an industrial partnership. Corporate managers naturally sought to keep rates down, workers to maintain or increase them. The tug-of-war between the two sometimes came out in favor of the workers, sometimes in favor of management, and sometimes in Pyrrhic victories:

He had the timer sent to me. He figured well, "Mary's fast. She's a good operator." They won't have to give us much if anything. Well, when the timer came, I did a whole case of shoes; and he went back to the head boss, and he showed him how long it took me. So he says, "Give her another case." So he came with another case to see if my speed would go up on it. It didn't. So he went back. The head boss came himself and sat down at my machine because he was very good, he was a terrific operator. For a man, he was a terrific stitcher. He sat down. I don't think he did more than three shoes. Not a word, and up and away he went. We didn't get no more money. Nothing was said. That pattern never came back to our department. They gave it to another department, where they probably were doing it for the same price. . . . That's one thing that in later years we found out, that instead of giving more money for some patterns, they would try to push it on another department. And if those workers didn't complain, it stood that way.[50]

Rate variations on similar work were widespread and a cause of much resentment. Workers developed a feel for the just value of a new job. They would compare it with the effort expended on previous jobs and to piece rates available in other departments or factories. Their perceptions often differed radically from the rates set by the pricing department. Throughout the 1920s and 1930s, workers frequently organized committees to meet with foremen to settle price disputes. If unsuccessful, they might demand an audience with the superintendent or one of the Johnsons. If satisfaction was still not forthcoming, some resorted to more coercive measures. "We had no problem with that," one worker said, "cause if they wouldn't give it to us, nobody'd go to work, what the hell, we left the work right there, till we did get a result from it."[51]

The ability to affect a change in rates depended on many factors, the most important being the bargaining power that came with a particular skill. Low-skilled workers, like rack pushers, sorters, lacers, and stitchers, had less power than higher-skilled lasters, upper leather cutters, and edge trimmers. High-skilled workers were not easily replaceable and hence had far more negotiating power over wages and shop conditions than other employees. Furthermore, the common job pride and strong work culture that characterized such workers promoted collective rather than individual responses to grievances. Not surprisingly, groups of skilled and semiskilled workers were often the best organized and most militant within the shoe factories. Consistently, from the 1890s through the middle of the twentieth century, edge trimmers, Goodyear stitchers, lasters, and cutters actively resisted wage reductions and organized themselves on the shop floor to protect their interests better against encroachments by management.

In 1927, for example, a growing militancy among the edge trimmers of Endicott and Johnson City caused the Johnsons no end of consternation. In September of that year, a meeting was held between George F. Johnson and Endicott edge trimmers, in an attempt to resolve a walkout by the men over pricing policies. The proceedings of the meeting were recorded by a stenographer. In reading over the transcript, one is struck by the extremely emotional and defensive reaction that the edge stitchers' walkout elicited from Johnson. He viewed it solely as an attack on the "Square Deal":

> You are *determined* to have trouble. You don't want harmony and peace. You want to destroy the work of many lifetimes. You mean that you want to go into struggle that will mean a great deal, to a great many innocent people. . . . All this is contrary to the old E.J. spirit. I have never met with it before. I am mystified. . . . Let's keep this Valley for the world to see, as a place where friendly human relations may exist, and the best Industrial conditions be made possible, and peace and harmony prevail.[52]

Johnson's charges of disloyalty and rebellion were denied by the workers, who argued instead that the company had let them down, had betrayed the "Square Deal."

> We have no prejudice against Mr. George F. Johnson. There is no friendship broken off. He has made mistakes and we have made mistakes. Mr. Johnson, we all understand that you don't know everything. This has been going on. This thing has not arisen in a day. It has not arisen in a week or two. It has been going on for a long time. We have spoken of going to see Mr. George F. We have been told different things: "It would be all right"—"Never mind." I have said since I have been here (17 years) that we could get a square deal from Mr. George F. Johnson.[53]

The theme of the meeting became loyalty—loyalty to company, loyalty to Johnson. And there was no question in Johnson's mind that a crisis of loyalty existed among the men, that some more than emotional gesture would be needed to bring the men back into the fold. Halfway through the meeting Johnson offered a carrot to the workers: "I want to say that I believe that a better day is dawning. I think that times are not going to be so hard. We will have a better year. I believe I see possible vacations again." Further into the meeting Johnson made another peace offering to the men. "I want to say for your encouragement, that I believe, as it looks now, things will be a little better than last year. There will be a little more of that intangible thing called 'bonus.'"[54]

The meeting between Johnson and the edge trimmers seemed to have settled the matter—at least for the moment. The tensions reflected in the closing remarks, however, hinted that the final resolution was still distant. One of the worker committee leaders ended his statement by saying: "We don't want to have any trouble in the future, but would like to have things adjusted, so we will know what we are working for, and have our employers understand it that way, also." It sounded a bit too belligerent for Johnson to let it go by. He immediately took offense at the committeeman's choice of words and reminded the workers that "I want you to understand—you can't get anywhere by *demanding* a thing, when you want to discuss it."[55] The resolution of this power struggle had yet to be achieved.

When amicable settlement of important issues could not be achieved, workers took up more confrontational strategies, as the edge trimmers did in the months following the meeting with Johnson. The September session did not resolve the issues that led to the trimmers' job action. Feeling betrayed by management, they continued to organize their fellow workers. In November 1927 the Endicott edge trimmers began to organize their Johnson City counterparts. A meeting was held on November 14, 1927, with the intended purpose of forcing "certain things in connection with working hours and working conditions." Charles F. Johnson, Jr., reported to his uncle on the meeting, seemingly unperturbed by the workers' actions. "Our thought is to simply let the matter go along and see what develops. If there are any demands made we will meet those demands at that time. . . ."[56] George F. Johnson was far more concerned. No doubt still hurting from the encounter with these "rebels" back in September, he wrote his nephew:

> The question of the organization of Edge Trimmers, is one that must be faced. . . . They must be told frankly—If they are not satisfied with the present E.J. policy respecting labor, they must immediately resign—there can be but *one* organization under our plan—that's the "E.J. Workers"—All the other[s] proposed like the Edge Trimmers will be considered unfriendly to the "E.J. Workers" as a whole. . . . Call the loyal workers to stand out and the disloyal ones to get out. The best way is to discharge the "ring leaders" after you've told them what you propose to do. We have nursed these kind of people into a fairly healthy crowd, and they will soon be in shape to make us a lot of trouble—It is a good time of year to have it out—They won't like the taste of snow-balls—no work, and no bonus, so let's get at it.[57]

Two days later management began approaching individual edge trimmers in both Johnson City and Endicott. "It was explained to them that we were not willing to go along with the Edge Trimmer's Union, it was not in keeping with the Company's policy." The workers were offered an ultimatum, "either give up their organization and continue along or else get through." Most of them gave in. Three leaders, however, were fired.[58] Charles Johnson explained to his uncle that most of the men were merely misled by their leaders. Yet both uncle and nephew realized that they would have to get "closer to the people" in the future. They would have to "be more careful, and have a better knowledge of what our help are thinking and doing."[59] Plans were made to restore peace and harmony. A meeting was arranged between management and the edge trimmers: "Upon your return [I] think it would be a splendid idea for us to get together all of the edge trimmers and as many other workers as possible for a meeting in one of the diners to show our appreciation for the way the workers accepted our ultimatum, and to promote a more friendly feeling."[60] Thus ended the trimmers' organizing efforts.

In their failed attempt to build up their own shop union, the edge trimmers demonstrated that they perceived their interests to be in conflict with those of corporate officers. They were not willing to go along with the fiction of industrial partnership, and they recognized that organization for self-protection was necessary. Although the edge trimmers' behavior constituted an extreme reaction on the part of Endicott Johnson workers, albeit short of trade unionism, other workers also banded together for self-protection and, in so doing, belied the existence of a "corporate family."

Goodyear stitchers, like edge trimmers, were also highly skilled and among the best paid workers. Although they were a relatively small group in each factory, their valued skills gave them a sense of pride as well as some power over their work and remuneration. They exhibited a laudatory cooperative spirit in work, as we have seen, aiding each other if machines experienced a breakdown—often sacrificing precious pay coupons in the process. When disagreements over rates arose, they would get together and appoint a spokesman to represent their interests and to approach management. A Goodyear stitcher in the Fair Play Factory in West Endicott recalled how he and fellow stitchers typically resolved disputes:

> We always figured it like this. We probably had ten, twelve men on the job. Maybe the oldest man on the job—we'd tell him what we want and he'd represent us. We wouldn't all have to shut down. We'd keep right on working, and he'd go and see Charlie Johnson and some of those guys and—them big shots. And he'd really come back with a pretty good settlement. . . . All the years I worked there, we only had one strike, I guess. Well, you couldn't really call it a strike. We just shut down. Well, Charlie Johnson come down. We changed the shoe price, we went on a cheaper shoe, but they weren't the same quality. The boss wanted the same quality on the cheaper shoe as on the higher-priced shoe. We didn't think that was fair. So we called him down, and we said we didn't think it was fair. He said, "Naturally it ain't fair. You can't expect to make a cheaper shoe and put the same quality in it as you do on a higher-priced shoe. You boys go ahead and let your stitches out."[61]

The effectiveness of such informal grievance procedures among the Goodyear stitchers prevented a search for more formal institutions such as trade unions.

Other groups of relatively skilled factory workers also confronted management periodically. In 1932 Pioneer Factory lasters joined together and refused to accept a price reduction on their work. Unable to convince the lasters, the company transferred their work to a new factory in Binghamton. Charles Johnson wrote his uncle: "The Pioneer factory lasters, as a group, have not showed a disposition to be willing to meet the situation, show a spirit of cooperation and accept the inevitable."[62] While management's response was hardly a victory for the lasters, it did demonstrate that they were more than willing to fight management, at some cost to themselves.

Cutters were an especially well-organized group. As one former foreman recalled: "Most every cutting room had their own little group. They stuck together."[63] In the Men's McKay Factory, cutters effectively prevented the repricing and shifting of work to other factories. Pioneer Factory cutters joined the Boot and Shoe Workers' Union en masse in 1939.[64] Scout Factory cutters created a democratic shop floor organization with rotating officers that, in the late 1930s, was quite effective in negotiating adjustments of piece rates. One Scout cutter recalled their strength:

> We in the Scout Factory were the highest paid people in the industry. . . . We were organized. I don't mean union. I mean cutters. We had a lot to say. We were seventy-five–eighty cutters in that room, and we were powerful. We told them what we wanted, see, and the way we proved it to them—we had three to four men on the job and [we told them] "we will cut a new pattern and *we* will decide then what that shoe is worth." Not what *they* said! And this is what we did.[65]

When the Scout cutters felt that the price of a new eight-inch shoe was too low, and the firm made no adjustment, the men ceased work until Charles F. Johnson, Jr., the firm's vice president, arrived. They explained the reasons for their job action, and Johnson immediately adjusted the rate.[66]

The organization formed by the Scout cutters provided them with a potent force for extracting just settlements from the firm. They were not "disloyal" to Endicott Johnson, and they did not view themselves as such. Unlike the Pioneer cutters, few of them chose to join a union when the opportunity was available in the late 1930s.[67] But their loyalty did not mean accepting the corporation's definition of the term. In their organization the Scout cutters demonstrated that the corporate ideal of industrial harmony could coexist with industrial conflict.

Conflict on the shop floor could extend to more central issues than rates. At times committees might protest the very system of setting prices on jobs, as was the case when a new piece rate system was instituted in the upper leather cutting departments of the firm in the mid-1920s. The system involved crediting and debiting workers for "gained" or "lost" leather. It had a profound impact on workers, as one cutter recalled:

> A fella came into E.J.'s from Boston, and he had a system for measuring the areas of the dies to arrive at the allowances. . . . He had pluses and minuses and I don't know . . . how the dies fit, how they would lay, how close they would cut together. That was the worst time I ever had at EJ's, and it wasn't me so much, it was my sympathy for other men because your allowances were figured pretty damn accurate. . . . Then this fella topped the whole caboodle off by saying, "Now the men to gain the most

leather are the ones that are entitled to the most money, and the only way we can do that is, we will pay you at the end of each month so much a foot for every foot you've gained, or you pay so much a foot for every foot you lost." . . . It started makin' thieves out of 'em. In other words, some of the men that were inclined to be a little crooked anyway was stealing the leather off other men's jobs, see.[68]

In response to the new system, the cutters in the Pioneer Factory organized a committee and arranged a meeting with the Johnsons. Thomas Chubbuck's account of the meeting follows:

Charlie was a son-of-a-gun to meet on a committee. And . . . it turned out the committee elected me chairman. Boy, I was sittin' on the hot seat 'cause I had to produce for the men—they put me in there, and I had to be fair with the company too. Well, we had our meeting down there and we had it. . . . They were meetings! I'm telling you, everybody talked plain English, and when you wanted to emphasize it, you hit the darned desk. They were a knockdown, drag out battle . . . and old George F. come in. "What is this all"—he talked with a down east accent— "What's this all about?" So Mr. Charlie come over to us and says, tell him. So we told him. "Well, by God, he says, then throw the damned thing out!" He says, "You men always want to remember how you can get any damned thing you want if you'll only stick together." Now he told us, his workers, that.[69]

Skilled factory workers were not the only groups who could stand up to management. Tannery workers, both skilled and unskilled, exemplified a collective consciousness that often led to group resistance. In their work behaviors they demonstrated that there was no question as to whom they served. It was not the corporation, as one tannery manager discovered:

There was five people in this unit. And as the leather was finished they would put the leather on sticks and hang them up through a long, long dryer. This thing was moving slowly. We caught them cheating on their count. We had a bell inside, and as it hit the stick it would knock it over and count them. So we knew there was something wrong, and as I recall, I remember calling them together, just warning them that I know what was going on. "So if you're smart, you'd quit it!" . . . They kept it up, and up, and then I had to finally go to Mr. Johnson, George W. Johnson.[70]

Even though the workers were fired, they still stuck together. They were unwilling to confess to Johnson or to the tannery superintendent who among the group was responsible for the cheating. Ultimately, the tanners were offered their jobs back. All, except for one who had left the area, returned.[71]

Rollers, the elite of the tanneries, also showed a proclivity for self-organization comparable to cutters. While their jousts with management did not always yield successful results, their very tendency to engage in confrontations with upper management and to demand higher wages for their work demonstrated the limits of welfarism's success at Endicott Johnson. It was no wonder that when the International Fur and Leather Workers Union first began to organize tannery workers in the early 1940s, its most energetic organizers were drawn from the rollers.[72] And it was also no surprise that tannery workers, both skilled and unskilled, were among the few groups of Endicott Johnson workers ever to be unionized.[73]

Clearly, for both individuals and groups, loyalty to the corporation did not mean passive acceptance of management policies. Being "fair with the company" had its limits. Workers who were a bit too fair were disciplined by fellow workers, as was the case with one stitching room worker who had approached management with a suggestion for improving efficiency within her room. She recommended that certain "unnecessary" day workers be eliminated. Coming in the depths of the Depression, in 1932, such a proposal may have been loyal to management but hardly loyal to coworkers who would be left out in the cold, jobless. Although women stitching room workers generally showed a far lesser tendency to band together to protect their interests than the higher-skilled male workers, in this case their collective antipathy unified them. Both fellow workers and her forelady turned against the "loyal" stitcher. Even though she had been promised protection "as far as possible from getting in wrong with her forelady or fellow workers," the firm was unable to fulfill that promise. "She has had more or less of an unhappy experience since then," Charles F. Johnson, Jr., wrote his uncle.[74]

Women rarely demonstrated the sort of group resistance to management that men did. As one stitcher admitted, men had committees, "us women, we just went along day by day."[75] Yet as individuals they clearly recognized that they shared a common interest with fellow workers. Despite the competition that was so prevalent in the stitching rooms, women could rise above it:

> I had a friend who worked and she was very fast and . . . she felt as if she was so fast on the lining and she knew what the other girls were making, that she felt she'd cut their rate if she turned hers [coupons] in because then they'd expect them to bring up to it, so she'd turn in, you know, reasonable in relation to the other workers. When she left EJ, she had a large surplus of money. They didn't want to pay her, but there was a law about it, they had to pay her. She had a lot of coupons that she held back. Every week she'd turn in some of her old coupons but she couldn't turn them all in, so she had quite a lot.[76]

In hundreds of ways men and women, low-skilled workers and high, expressed their distance from the corporation. Cutters, like the stitcher above, withheld coupons or held back leather so as not to "show up the other fellows."[77] Rather than accepting wage reductions, workers might refuse certain jobs if they felt they were poorly priced. They would join together to restrict output. They criticized and isolated fast workers whose pursuit of individual gain threatened the collective interests of coworkers. They loafed on the job, gambled, talked back to supervisors, refused to work on unpleasant jobs, engaged in acts of individual sabotage, or simply walked out of the factory, never to return, for any number of reasons. If one considers the reactions of the thousands upon thousands of workers who came to work for the firm, stayed only a short time, and left Endicott Johnson, never identifying with the firm at all, then the case presented in this chapter becomes even stronger. For such workers, whose employment careers in the firm lasted only a matter of days, or weeks, or even months, the sour realities of work far outweighed the benefits of welfare capitalism. For them the "Square Deal" never did and never would exist.[78]

Workers resisted job changes, the introduction of new technology, or the institution of work arrangements that threatened them. While the firm tried to introduce new machines by first bringing in a single machine and an outside worker to familiarize employees slowly with the new device and to convince them to accept it, machine and work changes were sometimes actively fought. As individuals, workers might simply withdraw their labor. Collectively, of course, they had more power. In the Ideal Factory in Endicott, for example, workers resisted a speedup brought about by the introduction of a new system that had each bed laster operate two machines at once. The system was eventually abandoned by the firm. In the Sole Leather Tannery, a new device perfected by an employee in the Mechanical Department to replace the rolling machine met with stiff opposition from the rollers. Both its inherent flaws and worker sabotage led to its failure and rejection by management.[79] In short, anything that aided management and hurt workers would be viewed suspiciously, demonstrating that the "industrial partnership" that Endicott Johnson's corporate welfarism attempted to create was never quite realized.

And yet Endicott Johnson workers were loyal workers. Many of them stayed with the firm for years, working alongside husbands, wives, children, and other relatives. The vast majority of them repeatedly rejected unionization. Prolonged strikes were unheard of. By the criteria of unionists, radical critics, and labor historians, then, welfarism at Endicott Johnson was a success, creating and sustaining a labor loyalty to the corporation that endured even the Depression.

To ignore the price of success or its uneven manifestation, however, would be wrong. Even within this most paternalistic of industrial settings, where collective identification with the corporation was carefully cultivated, a substantial reservoir of autonomous behavior and sentiment existed and provided a source of strength in the negotiation of service and wage concessions from the corporation. Although the gulf between managers and workers was somewhat narrowed by welfarism, it was not bridged. Workers never quite viewed their loyalty in the terms that management defined it. They were never "captive" to paternalism.

NOTES

1. *E-J Workers Magazine* 1 (Dec. 1922). The poem appeared in *Forbes Magazine* and is credited to Edmund Leamy. Date and issue are not specified.

2. For example, Guy Whiting Beardsley, "He Heard Opportunity's Knock," *American Magazine* 81 (May 1916): 50–51; Frederick M. Davenport, "The Path to Industrial Peace," *Outlook* 124 (Apr. 14, 1920): 644–50; George Mortimer, "George F. Johnson and His 'Square-Deal Towns': The Story of a Big Manufacturer Who Has Interesting Ideas," *American Magazine* 91 (Jan. 1921): 36–37; Rose C. Feld, "An Industrial Democrat Points the Way," *New York Times Magazine*, June 3, 1934, 6–7; "Our Friend George F.," *Time* 32 (Dec. 5, 1938): 12.

3. *New York Times,* Nov. 9, 1919.

4. James S. Gibbons, "Has George F. Johnson Found Key to Industrial Problems?" *Manufacturers Journal* 16 (July 1937): 8.

5. The *American Federationist,* published by the AFL, constantly took aim at welfare policies of various major firms. Through the 1920s the journal came to devote more and more of its pages to criticism of welfare capitalism. See, for example, *American Federationist* 30 (Sept. 1923): 760–61; or ibid. 32 (May 1925): 355. The *Shoe Workers' Journal,* as well as other union journals, also continually criticized various welfare schemes. See *Shoe Workers' Journal* 21 (Jan. 1920): 25; ibid. 24 (Nov. 1923): 7–8; ibid. 27 (Dec. 1926): 6–8. For other critical perspectives, see Mina Weisenberg's "Labor's Defense against Employers' Welfare Tactics," *New York Times Current History Magazine* 25 (Mar. 1927): 803–8; and occasional articles that appeared in the *New Republic* during the 1920s.

6. Robert W. Dunn, "The Industrial Welfare Offensive," in *The Shaping of the American Tradition,* ed. Louis Hacker (New York, 1947), 1071. Dunn's essay originally appeared in J. B. S. Hardman, ed., *American Labor Dynamics* (New York, 1928).

7. The original appeared in *Masses* about 1913 but became part of labor's public domain soon after. The version cited above was published in *Shoe Workers' Journal* 15 (Feb. 1914): 3. A slightly different version was revived during the Endicott Johnson union campaigns of the late 1930s. See *E-J Union News,* Oct. 23, 1939, 5.

8. Harry W. Laidler and Norman Thomas, eds., *New Tactics in Social Conflict* (New York, 1926), 98. The League for Industrial Democracy, originally the Intercollegiate Socialist Society, was the intellectual arm of the Socialist party. It promoted academic discussion of socialist ideas and ideals among intellectuals and professionals.

9. Abraham Epstein, "Industrial Welfare Movement Sapping American Trade Unions," *New York Times Current History Magazine* 24 (July 1926): 516.

10. *Shoe Workers' Journal* 29 (Aug. 1928): 13. See also ibid. 21 (May 1920): 12; and ibid. 28 (June 1927): 1.

11. Nancy Dawson, "'To Laugh, That We May Not Weep,'" *E.-J. Workers' Review* 2 (Nov. 1920): 36. The article is reprinted from the *New York Call* of Sept. 18, 1920.

12. Stuart D. Brandes, *American Welfare Capitalism, 1880–1940* (Chicago, 1976), 140.

13. Irving Bernstein, *The Lean Years: A History of the American Worker, 1920–1933* (Boston, 1960), 186.

14. Selig Perlman, *A Theory of the Labor Movement* (New York, 1928), is the seminal statement of this view.

15. Bernstein, *The Lean Years,* 187.

16. Daniel Nelson, *Managers and Workers: Origins of the New Factory System in the United States, 1880–1920* (Madison, Wis., 1975), chap. 6. For a critique of Nelson, see Jeremy Brecher et al., "Uncovering the Hidden History of the American Workplace," *Review of Radical Political Economics* 10 (Winter 1978): 3. Nelson, however, also suggested that "control over the factory worker" was not as easily or as mechanically achieved, although this was hardly his emphasis, and the impression he leaves is just the opposite. Nonetheless, he acknowledged that "welfare work probably had a greater impact on the evolution of business administration than on the worker's attitude toward his supervisor, the firm, or his obligations to his employer" (p. 120).

17. David Brody, *Workers in Industrial America: Essays on the Twentieth Century Struggle* (New York, 1980), 78. On the "paralysis of the labor movement" in the 1920s, see Bernstein, *The Lean Years,* chap. 2; Brody, *Workers in Industrial America,* 63–66; Robert S. Lynd and Helen Merrell Lynd, *Middletown: A Study in Modern American Culture* (New York, 1929): sec. 1. Trade union membership in the 1920s declined from over five million in 1920 to three and a half million in 1929. Bernstein, *The Lean Years,* 84.

18. Brody, *Workers in Industrial America,* 134.

19. George F. Johnson, "What I've Learned about Business since 1920," *System* 40 (Dec. 1921): 681.

20. Ibid., 680. Of course, for upper management this was merely symbolic, as the photo in Johnson's article illustrates.

21. Thomas K. Chubbuck, interview by Gerald Zahavi, with the assistance of Deborah D. Maxwell, session 1, June 29, 1981, tape recording (personal possession).

22. See *E.-J. Workers' Review* 3 (Mar. 1921): 3; and ibid. (Apr. 1921): 3. George F. Johnson to the *Syracuse Herald,* Apr. 23, 1921, box 6, George F. Johnson Papers, George Arents Research Library for Special Collections, Syracuse University, Syracuse, N.Y.

23. Tamara K. Hareven, *Family Time and Industrial Time: The Relationship between the Family and Work in a New England Industrial Community* (New York, 1982), chaps. 11 and 12.

24. George F. Johnson to A. L. Kinsey, May 13, 1921, box 6, George F. Johnson Papers.

25. Historians who have written about Endicott Johnson and George F. Johnson, mainly in theses and dissertations, are as guilty of neglecting workers' perspectives as are the students of the more general welfare movement cited previously. See William Patrick Burns, "A Study of Personnel Policies, Employee Opinion and Labor Turnover (1930–1946) at the Endicott Johnson Corporation" (Master's thesis, New York State School of Industrial and Labor Relations, Cornell University, 1947); William Wilson Shear, "Industrial Relations in the Endicott Johnson Corporation: A Case Study of Welfare Capitalism in the 1920s" (Master's thesis,

S.U.N.Y. at Binghamton, 1978); Richard S. Saul, "An Industrial Entrepreneur: George F. Johnson" (D.S.S. diss., Syracuse University, 1966); and G. Ralph Smith, *The Endicott Johnson Corporation* (New Orleans, 1959). Although Burns surveyed employee opinion, it was a superficial survey at best.

26. George F. Johnson to George W. Johnson, Nov. 22, 1930, box 11, George F. Johnson Papers.

27. William Inglis, *George F. Johnson and His Industrial Democracy* (New York, 1935), 240–41.

28. Ibid., 245.

29. "Endicott Johnson Workers Daily Page," *Binghamton Sun*, Feb. 10, 1934.

30. George F. Johnson to James Thomson, Sept. 7, 1933, box 13, George F. Johnson Papers.

31. George W. Johnson to George F. Johnson, Mar. 5, 1935, box 13, ser. 1, Charles F. Johnson, Jr., Papers, George Arents Research Library for Special Collections, Syracuse University, Syracuse, N.Y.

32. George F. Johnson to George W. Johnson, Mar. 8, 1935, box 11, ser. 1, Charles F. Johnson, Jr., Papers.

33. Frank Tuthill, interview by Gerald Zahavi, Nov. 30, 1979, tape recording (personal possession). A conversation with Jack Hobbie on Dec. 12, 1979, confirmed Tuthill's account. See also Harry L. Gruver to George F. Johnson, Apr. 27, 1927; and George F. Johnson to Harry L. Gruver, May 2, 1927, in box 8, ser. 1, Charles F. Johnson, Jr., Papers.

34. George W. Johnson to George F. Johnson, Dec. 7, 1931, box 12, ser. 1, Charles F. Johnson, Jr., Papers.

35. Thomas K. Chubbuck, interview by Gerald Zahavi, with the assistance of Deborah D. Maxwell, session 2, July 2, 1981, tape recording (personal possession); Norman W. Councilman, interview by Gerald Zahavi, with the assistance of Deborah D. Maxwell, June 5, 1981, tape recording (personal possession). Several interviews by David Nielson further corroborate this event. See V—— and L——, interview by David Nielson, July 23, 1976, tape recording; R——, interview by David Nielson, July 10, 1974, transcript, 284; D——, interview by David Nielson, June 25, 1974, transcript, 245.

36. *E.-J. Workers' Review* 1 (Sept. 1919): 32-A. Johnson used the term "directors" because he felt it was more "democratic." Workers, however, generally stuck to "foremen" and "foreladies."

37. Endicott Office Files, Endicott Johnson Employee Records, George Arents Research Library for Special Collections, Syracuse University, Syracuse, N.Y.; George F. Johnson to Herbert C. Clarke, June 28, 1925, box 8, George F. Johnson Papers; George F. Johnson to Charles F. Johnson, Jr., July 25, 1929, box 9, ser. 1, Charles F. Johnson, Jr., Papers.

38. Paul R. Eckelberger, interview by Gerald Zahavi, with the assistance of Deborah D. Maxwell, June 26, 1981, tape recording (personal possession).

39. F——, interview by David Nielson, Aug. 3, 1973, transcript, 107. For another example, see Paul R. Knickerbocker, interview by Gerald Zahavi, with the assistance of Deborah D. Maxwell, session 1, June 10, 1982, tape recording (personal possession).

40. Chubbuck, interview, session 1. For more on the issue of shop floor authority and

the various responses of individual foremen, see Knickerbocker, interview, session 1; Richard J. Murphy, interview by Gerald Zahavi, with the assistance of Deborah D. Maxwell, July 7, 1981, tape recording (personal possession). For a general discussion of the forces eroding the authority of shop floor supervisors in the early decades of the century, see Nelson, *Managers and Workers,* chap. 3 and passim.

41. Tuthill, interview.

42. S——, interview by David Nielson, July 22, 1976, tape recording.

43. George F. Johnson to George F. Reilly, Sept. 9, Sept. 17, 1930, box 11, George F. Johnson Papers.

44. George F. Johnson to Harold R. Pettit, Nov. 4, 1933, box 13, George F. Johnson Papers.

45. C——, interview by David Nielson, July 26, 1973, transcript, 79. Unfortunately, the outcome of this exchange is not recalled in the interview.

46. Murphy, interview.

47. For a discussion of wage policies in Endicott Johnson, see Burns, "A Study of Personnel Policies," 69–74.

48. James W. Lupole, interview by Gerald Zahavi, with the assistance of Deborah D. Maxwell, July 15, 1981, tape recording (personal possession).

49. Owen J. Ryall, interview by Gerald Zahavi, with the assistance of Deborah D. Maxwell, Apr. 30, 1982, tape recording (personal possession). See also Lupole, interview; and Mary Seversky, interview by Gerald Zahavi, with the assistance of Deborah D. Maxwell, July 22, 1982, tape recording (personal possession).

50. Seversky, interview. Many workers complained about work being taken from them, repriced and shifted to other factories. Union propaganda in the late 1930s and in the 1940s (to be treated in later chapters) focused on unfair pricing methods. See also Amy King, interview by Gerald Zahavi, Nov. 30, 1979, tape recording (personal possession). The company explained away price differences on similar work as due to "varying conditions" in the different factories. Burns, "A Study of Personnel Policies," 71.

51. Murphy, interview.

52. "Report of Meeting of Edge Trimmers," Sept. 1, 1927, pp. 2–3, box 19, George F. Johnson Papers. Emphasis in original.

53. Ibid., 4.

54. Ibid., 5, 7–8. Vacations with pay had been discontinued a few years earlier, and the bonus for the previous year had amounted to only thirty-one dollars.

55. Ibid., 11–12. Emphasis in original.

56. About 40 of the approximately 100 Johnson City edge trimmers attended, according to Charles F. Johnson, Jr. Clearly, management had an informant among the 40 who attended. Charles F. Johnson, Jr., to George F. Johnson, Nov. 15, 1927, box 28, ser. 1, Charles F. Johnson, Jr., Papers.

57. George F. Johnson to Charles F. Johnson, Jr., Nov. 18, 1927, box 8, ser. 1, Charles F. Johnson, Jr., Papers. The edge trimmers' actions deeply affected George F. Johnson. See, for example, George F. Johnson to Don C. Morgan, Dec. 27, 1927, box 9; and George F. Johnson to Jewett Neiley, Mar. 14, 1928, box 9, George F. Johnson Papers.

58. Charles F. Johnson, Jr., to George F. Johnson, Nov. 22, 1927, box 28, ser. 1,

Charles F. Johnson, Jr., Papers. Two of the three leaders later asked for their jobs back and were apparently rehired. The third, Felix C. McQueen, a forty-five-year-old, self-proclaimed "roughneck," was not rehired. His employment card simply read "Q11-22-27 Dissatisfied." See Charles F. Johnson, Jr., to George F. Johnson, Nov. 23, 1927, box 28, ser. 1, Charles F. Johnson, Jr., Papers; Endicott Office Files, Endicott Johnson Employee Records.

59. George F. Johnson to Charles F. Johnson, Jr., Nov. 24, 1927, box 8, ser. 1, Charles F. Johnson, Jr., Papers.

60. Charles F. Johnson, Jr., to George F. Johnson, Nov. 23, 1927, box 28, ser. 1, Charles F. Johnson, Jr., Papers.

61. Kenneth E. Compton, interview by Gerald Zahavi, May 5, 1982, tape recording (personal possession). "Letting the stitches out" refers to the setting on the machines that determined the number of stitches per inch (a normal setting was eight stitches per inch). Fewer stitches per inch required less time to accomplish and thus increased the income of the stitchers.

62. Charles F. Johnson, Jr., to George F. Johnson, Mar. 25, 1932, box 29, ser. 1, Charles F. Johnson, Jr., Papers. See also George F. Johnson to Charles F. Johnson, Jr., Mar. 21, 1932, box 10; George W. Johnson to George F. Johnson, Mar. 21, 1932, box 13; Charles F. Johnson, Jr., to George F. Johnson, Mar. 17, 1932, box 29, ser. 1, Charles F. Johnson, Jr., Papers.

63. Ralph V. Russell, interview by Gerald Zahavi, with the assistance of Deborah D. Maxwell, May 27, 1982, tape recording (personal possession).

64. *E-J Union News,* Nov. 13, 1939, 1. An analysis of union pledge cards in the BSWU archives uncovered a disproportionate number of Pioneer Factory cutters. Local 42 Pledge Cards, BSWU Records, State Historical Society of Wisconsin.

65. John Kovak [pseud.], interview by Gerald Zahavi, with the assistance of Deborah D. Maxwell, session 1, July 15, 1981, tape recording (personal possession). A second interview with Kovak [pseud.] conducted a year later elicited more details on the cutters' organization. See John Kovak [pseud.], interview by Gerald Zahavi, session 2, Aug. 27, 1982, tape recording (personal possession).

66. Kovak [pseud.], interviews, sessions 1 and 2.

67. Only one BSWU pledge card in over 2,000 cards located in the union archive was signed by a Scout Factory cutter! Local 42 Pledge Cards, BSWU Records.

68. Chubbuck, interview, session 1.

69. Ibid. Johnson had received several complaints from workers about the system. See George F. Johnson to P. Lewington, Jan. 30, 1925, box 7, George F. Johnson Papers.

70. Knickerbocker, interview, session 1. An Upper Leather Tannery foreman confessed that one of his major duties was to watch for cheating, particularly among the lower-paid tannery workers: "There could be a lot of cheating if you didn't watch them." Russell, interview.

71. Knickerbocker, interview, session 1.

72. Knickerbocker, interviews, sessions 1 and 2.

73. Their unionization is the subject of chap. 7.

74. Charles F. Johnson, Jr., to George F. Johnson, Feb. 8, 1932, box 29, ser. 1, Charles F. Johnson, Jr., Papers.

75. Seversky, interview.

76. H——, interview by David Nielson, June 23, 1973, transcript, 20.
77. During the Depression Charles F. Johnson, Jr., learned that upper leather cutters "were making so much money that they did not dare turn it all in, but were holding back coupons so that if they went on short time, they could draw full pay for sometime in the future." He ordered the superintendents of all the factories to prevent such actions. Charles F. Johnson, Jr., "To the Superintendents of All Factories" (notice), Dec. 18, 1936, box 31, ser. 1, Charles F. Johnson, Jr., Papers. Kovak [pseud.], interview, session 1.
78. Endicott Office Files, Endicott Johnson Employee Records; Paul Coletti [pseud.], interview by Gerald Zahavi, with the assistance of Deborah D. Maxwell, July 13, 1981, tape recording (personal possession); Kovak [pseud.], interviews, sessions 1 and 2; Murphy, interview. See also David Nielson's interviews and *Labor News,* July 3, 1940, 3.
79. Endicott Office Files, Endicott Johnson Employee Records; Knickerbocker, interview, session 2.

5

The "Square Deal"
and the Depression

On October 2, 1928, George F. Johnson wrote a friend and business associate: "In the reasonably near future, we ought to have a reaction from the so-called 'great business prosperity' which is evidenced largely in automobiles and other luxuries, and the further extension of credit to the poor, who haven't anything in the shape of assets but credit, and which credit is pretty thoroughly strained at present."[1] Johnson's prediction became a reality all too soon.

The Great Depression came early to the shoe industry. Throughout the 1920s the industry had been an ailing one, characterized by boom-and-bust cycles that led to periodic layoffs and shortened work periods. Extreme competition between shoe firms made for a great deal of instability and uneven development. As one scholar, writing in 1940, noted, the shoe industry "shows overdevelopment side by side with underconsumption, efficiency in the midst of general waste and misdirection of effort, integration into large units side by side with separation into small units, monopoly and cut-throat competition, standardization side by side with breaking down of standards, organization and disorganization, order and disorder, reason and unreason at one and the same time."[2]

Endicott Johnson, among the largest shoe and leather concerns in the country, bore the endemic instability of the shoe industry relatively well. Economies of scale aided in the rationalization of production and allowed the firm to weather the cutthroat competition that came from smaller, more mobile, and more exploitative shoe firms. Yet the firm's size did not entirely insulate it from the vagaries of market capitalism. It, too, was periodically forced to curtail production and initiate layoffs. Until the late 1920s such episodes were of short duration and were generally followed by prosperous times. But 1928 brought a more serious turn of fortune. A prolonged and ominous decline in the footwear market was beginning to manifest itself, disturbing the relatively tranquil world of Endicott Johnson.

I

In May 1928 George F. Johnson found himself burdened by the unenviable responsibility of having to explain to a worker's wife why it was necessary to lay off her husband: "It has been our great good fortune, in the past, to be able to employ, and add to our army of workers. The present situation is unique and strange, and I am the most unhappy member of the family—feeling as I do, the responsibility, and the extreme necessity of reducing costs so that we may meet competition successfully."[3] Such an explanation did not satisfy the sympathetic side of Johnson. Although foremen and superintendents had been instructed to cut costs by whatever means necessary, including laying off workers, the employee in question was an older man with several children, and the act of letting go such a worker troubled Johnson's conscience. On the same day that he wrote to the man's wife, Johnson sent off the following note to the supervisor who had laid him off:

[There] are times when I would advise you to keep your best men; but these are times when I am advising you to keep the men who can least afford to be laid off—those with the greatest responsibilities; and lay off the men who would be affected the least. This is not "cold-blooded business." It is mercy. . . . Rather than lay off, there are always opportunities to curtail. Maybe you could run two or three days in the week, and not have to absolutely lay off so many people. Those with least care and responsibility could then be permitted to look elsewhere for work.[4]

A series of rapid business downturns and recoveries in the middle of 1928, causing corresponding layoffs followed by rehirings, stimulated Johnson to begin a thorough reevaluation of the firm's employment policies, all in the hope of reducing welfare expenses and providing more security for older employees and needy workers.

I do believe we should have some protection for the workers, in the employment of new Help. There should be a length of time much longer than the present [half a year], before workers can become eligible to the benefits; but we should not refuse to employ people who are able to work, but who are turned back by the Medical. There should be a list of workers not eligible to the benefits, but they should not be refused work.[5]

In August 1928 the firm began to deny medical and relief services to newly employed workers, so-called temporary workers.[6] Johnson noted that "in time, half the workers only would be beneficiaries, and that because of long service. This may be a very desirable and good way to reduce the liability and cost of the Medical service, differentiating between old and valued workers, and those younger and less responsive to kindness, and also less needing the help."[7] The firm's new employment policy was capricious and vague. "Temporary workers" remained uncertain of their status for an indefinite period of time. Truman H. Platt, head of the company's Medical and Relief Department, complained to Johnson about this vagueness and urged him to make clear to workers when and if they would become "regular" employees, eligible to receive company welfare benefits. He also cautioned that the new policy was a violation of the firm's expressed ideals: "It appears to us that carrying this plan indefinitely is a step backwards towards the old basis of 'hiring and firing only', which is quite contrary to the labor policy of our company."[8]

Business conditions in 1929 remained unstable and depressed, at least until the end of the year, when orders for the following spring began streaming in. The need to lay off a large number of employees in the spring and summer of 1929, and subsequently the abandonment of homes by laid-off workers who could not make mortgage payments, led management to consider again the firm's employment policies. Johnson recommended to his nephew that layoffs be held to a minimum and that loyal workers be allowed to retain their homes and jobs: "I am sincerely in hopes that we shall soon reach a stage when the laying off of help because of slack times, will be avoided. Therefore I would suggest it a better plan, wherever practical, that whatever work there may be, should be divided among the . . . desirables . . . until times pick up, or until they voluntarily sever their relations with the company."[9]

It was a difficult time for the firm, as Johnson noted: "We have never had such a long spell of 'bad weather,' affecting the help so severely."[10] The "Square Deal," too, was coming under extreme strain. Increasingly, the underlying assumptions forming the foundations of the firm's labor policies were being reduced to explicit contractual terms.

> Everything depends upon the worker. Judged entirely by their efforts to be *more* than a "common worker" — one who thoroughly believes in the principles of the Workers' Plan, would fight if necessary to *preserve these principles — would discourage Radicals and agitators — believes that they are building up for themselves and their children and children's children*, a great industry which is worth the best effort they have to give: *to these and only these, will come privileges beyond the wage slip.* . . .
> Lacking this idea (expressed in *action*, not in *talk*) they *never will become beneficiaries.* They will be "hired and fired." They will "quit" at their pleasure. *They can not belong to the "Royal Family", because they are not the kind of people that the "Family" want.*[11]

In short, the price of "privileges" would be loyalty. It was a message that had been expressed in the work and community lives of Endicott Johnson employees for decades, but now it was spelled out bluntly by the president of the firm. Johnson felt compelled to remind workers of the many benefits they enjoyed, something he feared they had forgotten.

But the new policy of employing workers without making an explicit commitment of benefits soon came to be perceived as too severe. Not only was Johnson coming under increasing pressure from Platt to change it, but appeals forwarded by the latter to Johnson made it clear that continuation of the new policy would only generate hardship and ill will among the workers. It was hard to ignore entreaties such as the following: "I am writing you for information about medical service. I have been an E.J. Worker since Aug. 7, 1928. I am a poor man and just trying to get started and have a baby girl that needs medical attention which I can not hardly afford."[12]

In late June 1929, finally swayed by the protests of workers and the head of the Medical and Relief Department, as well as by the additional moral and practical pressure generated by other local firms providing various medical and relief services to their workers, Johnson began to waver.

> It would seem as though we must discontinue our present "new worker" policy in regard to Medicine. New or old, they need the service, and they are learning its great value. . . . The thought of making them more appreciative by a different policy, and possibly reducing the cost, seemed to be a good one, but it does not work out, in view of the fact that our competitors—Dunn & McCarthy, Ansco, etc.—are beginning to take care of workers. . . . This is another reason why it looks as though we would have to go back to the original plan, and give the Medical service to all workers.[13]

The sheer volume of requests and appeals was making the new policy unmanageable. "It would appear," Johnson wrote Platt, "that we must find a policy respecting the use of Medicine by the workers, that will require less time, patience and investigation than the present plan requires. These persistent appeals, with the consequent necessary amount of investigation, would soon wear you and the rest of us all out."[14] A week later, at a board of directors' meeting, the employment policy was thoroughly discussed and a new one recommended. The board decided that "new workers should be hired as temporary workers for a six months' trial period and, if satisfactory, at the end of that time to be recommended by the director in charge and O.K'd by the superintendent as being entitled to become regular members of the family and entitled to medical and legal department service."[15] On July 16, 1929, the workers were notified of the new policy.[16] The new employment guidelines, although specifying a six-month duration of "temporary worker" status, retained many of the capricious qualities of the schemes they had replaced. Personal evaluations of workers would continue to be made before they could become members of the "family." Loyalty would still be the price of acceptance.

Throughout the Depression, even as the firm maintained work opportunities for its regular employees, a growing number of workers were employed under "temporary" status. If business conditions became very tight and management felt compelled to lay off workers, temporary workers inevitably were selected. Temporary workers also found that their status was open to constant redefinition whenever management saw the need to reduce labor costs. In

1932, for example, when shoe orders briefly rose and the firm required additional workers, it resorted to another revision of new worker status. Temporary workers now became "extra workers," who were not eligible for evaluation and acceptance to the "family." Charles Johnson clarified the firm's obligations to such employees:

> The Employment Departments have been permitted to add some temporary workers to help the factories take care of the unusual volume of business. . . . When these temporary workers or "Extra Workers" . . . are hired, it is understood by the worker that they are being hired temporarily with no Medical privileges and will be laid off when work lets down and we have no further need for their services. . . . These extra workers are really hired on the "Hired-and-Fired" plan.[17]

In addition to redefining the firm's obligations to new workers in order to limit the drain on welfare services and obtain flexibility in hiring and firing, Endicott Johnson managers continually reaffirmed their belief in work sharing for regular employees as a strategy for weathering the Depression.[18] In this policy they differed little from other welfare firms faced with similar dilemmas. Akron rubber factories, for example, long famed for their extensive corporate welfare systems, reduced their work days to six hours. Other firms rotated employees to distribute more equitably what work there was. United States Steel, a longtime adherent of welfare capitalism, maintained 94 percent of its regular work force in January 1931, a period in which it was operating at less than half capacity. By 1933 work sharing had spread well beyond welfare firms and characterized as many as four-fifths of the nation's industrial concerns.[19]

Work sharing was a mixed blessing for employees. While it was certainly the most democratic way of distributing what little work there was, for many of the firm's employees it constituted a threat to their livelihoods. Older workers would have preferred distribution of jobs on the basis of seniority. Others resented the shifting of workers necessitated by such an egalitarian policy as an encroachment on their job rights, "because they figured that was their job and they didn't want nobody else to come along."[20] Nonetheless, the majority recognized the justice inherent in the firm's policies and accepted them.[21]

Although marred by its policies of hiring "temporary" and "extra" workers, the corporation's employment record throughout the Depression was generally admirable. The firm retained the bulk of its pre-Depression labor force. Between January 1930 and April 1935, with a single exception in December 1933, the company did not lay off any regular workers. For the years between 1930 and 1941, layoffs at Endicott Johnson averaged 0.1 percent a month, one twenty-fourth of the average rate for the shoe industry.[22] By instituting work sharing the company was able to sustain the employment levels of the 1920s, which had hovered between 14,500 and 15,500 workers. With the recovery of the shoe and leather market after 1933, employment at Endicott Johnson rose above the 1920s levels, topping 18,000 in 1937.[23]

II

Work sharing and the redefinition of new worker status were compromises reached by corporate officers who sought to preserve as much of the "Square Deal" as possible without sacrificing the profitability of the firm. But the Depression strained far more than the firm's employment policies. Endicott Johnson profits declined precipitously in the late 1920s and early 1930s. Through the 1920s the company's net profits had ranged from 3 to 5 million dollars a year. In 1927 they amounted to about 4.3 million. In the following three years, however, profits steadily dropped, plummeting to less than 1 million in 1930. For the remainder of the Depression, profits remained at or less than 50 percent of their 1920s levels.[24]

With profits sinking it was not surprising that among the first of the corporation's welfare policies to fall prey to the Depression was the firm's profit-sharing plan. Profit sharing, as noted earlier, had been a central element in the "Square Deal," a concrete expression of partnership between capital and labor. Although little more than *deferred wages,* a term from which management did not shy away, it nonetheless maintained in the workers' minds the relationship between the company's financial success and their own personal fortunes. At least, that was what management hoped it would accomplish. In times of relative plenty, company officers invoked it as a spur to productivity and efficiency. But the Depression was hardly a time of plenty, and declining profits as well as meager profit-sharing distributions, which only served to incite workers, made the elimination of profit sharing increasingly tempting to Endicott Johnson managers.

In early 1926 the firm's profit-sharing plan had been revised, limiting qualification to workers who had spent two years with the company rather than one. Through financial manipulations (which involved the channeling of a larger portion of profits into the firm's cash reserve fund) and the institution of a "Special Bonus" for key management officials, the firm had already begun to decrease the workers' share of the "surplus profits." In 1926, despite the new two-year requirement, the profit-sharing distribution had amounted to only $30.68 for every employee. Widespread and vocal worker dissatisfaction with the low bonus payment led Johnson at first to express his regrets over management's actions of previous years:

> It seems to me, the way we divided the workers' Bonus, or computed and figured it, the first several years, was probably the way that we should divide it now. When we voted to hold up such a large amount of money before dividing, and also voted ourselves such a liberal Special Bonus,

constantly growing—we made an awful hole in the share we intended to give the workers, and I think it was a very serious error.[25]

Although the workers' share of the bonus rose in 1927 to $97.76, it dipped to its lowest level in 1928. In early 1929 the company announced that workers would receive $23.92 as their share of the profits of the previous year. Almost immediately workers again began to voice their dissatisfaction. Johnson quickly reacted by issuing a statement to employees that beseeched them to remain loyal: "If you are disappointed with the results of last year, it certainly should not be reflected in your loyalty, respect and confidence in your Management, in the coming year."[26]

The level of worker resentment and the relatively poor business performance of the previous year led management to reevaluate its commitment to profit sharing. Both George Willis Johnson and Charles F. Johnson, Jr., wanted the plan discontinued.[27] The elder Johnson was willing to change the plan, expressing his dislike of certain aspects of it. He wrote his son in February that

> the best plan is a fifty-fifty division at intervals when there is a collection of profits, and when it is timely, and in the judgement of the Directors, proper to distribute. . . . The uncertainty of the division as to size of Bonus—the fact that the workers expect it, and many of them discount it, and really spend it or gamble on the amount—are some of the unpleasant things that arise from the present plan, and are sufficient reason why we should wish to change it.[28]

In late winter and spring of 1929, company officers explored various revisions of the method of calculating bonuses and finally returned to a version of the "fifty-fifty" plan originally created in 1919. But one important change was made. Directors would pay out a bonus only if they felt that business could permit it. Some of the subterfuges that, in previous years, reduced the surplus profits were discontinued.

The new method of determining profit-sharing distributions, like the firm's new employment policies, was capricious to say the least. The corporation no longer needed to resort to various financial fictions to manipulate the workers' share of the surplus profits, since company officers determined when and if any bonus distributions were in order. Even an unpredictable bonus, management believed, could function as a "tying clause," holding workers to the firm and maintaining employee loyalty.

> It ties the working man to the Company closely, because he would scarcely be willing to quit the Company when there is a nice Bonus undivided awaiting him at the proper time. He would figure just as the stockholders figure. They would not sell their stock at a low price when they knew there was a handsome surplus yet to be divided. Neither would

a worker quit his job, under the same condition. It has, therefore, a strong tying clause. . . .[29]

Of course, during the Depression it was less necessary for management to use "tying" clauses to maintain low labor turnover. Fear of unemployment sufficed. Decreasing profits and management's preoccupation with maintaining dividend payments and a large surplus cash fund led to a decade in which company officers never deemed it appropriate to share profits.[30]

In early 1930 workers learned the bad news that there would be no bonus for the previous year. "The company have just about earned their taxes and dividends," George F. Johnson explained to the editor of the "Workers Daily Page."[31] Johnson further downgraded the place of profit sharing in the firm's labor policies. No longer did it constitute a symbol and bond of partnership, a central tenet of the "Square Deal." He wrote a friend and fellow company officer that "it is better to put the wages into weekly pay."[32] It was a conviction he continued to express through the Depression.[33]

The workers reacted predictably to the elimination of bonuses. As one employee recalled: "Everybody was sick the last year when they came out and said there was nothing, no bonus coming. Why, everybody was heartbroken, 'cause some people had spent it before. . . . A lot of people were left with debts on their hands and didn't have anything to pay them with. A lot of people started out saying they were going to join the union."[34] Had the workers known that management was still receiving a "Special Bonus" during the early years of the Depression, they might have felt themselves even more betrayed.[35]

III

The elimination of profit sharing was only one of many cost-saving mechanisms that management resorted to during the Depression. Wages, constituting the largest cost among the firm's manufacturing expenses, were also soon adjusted in response to the exigencies of the economy. Between 1922 and 1928 average weekly wages (including holiday pay and bonuses) had ranged from about twenty-five to twenty-seven dollars. But beginning with 1929, wages started to fall dramatically, dipping down to about twenty dollars a week in 1932.[36] Of course, work sharing and the reduction of available work were important factors in precipitating this decline, but so, too, were wage cuts. Not only were workers forced to accept horizontal wage reductions, in March 1931 and again in May 1932, but spot rate reductions imposed on various occupational groups, instituted throughout the Depression, further slashed employees' weekly paychecks.

Management approached the imposing of rate reductions cautiously, preferring the "democratic" method of horizontal wage cuts to selective pay cuts that only served to trigger angry reactions among workers. In February 1929, for example, just after the initiation of a round of piece rate reductions throughout the plants, George F. Johnson wrote his son: "Observe that in your effort to reduce the cost of tacking by taking off 5 to 10 percent, you created trouble immediately. Also, that there is little incentive for these people to behave on account of promised Bonuses, which they think are too small to be worth thinking about."[37] It was becoming evident to managers that selective wage reductions were arousing a great deal of ill will among the workers. Yet their determination to generate sufficient funds to maintain dividend payments to stockholders led the Johnsons to continue the practice.

In November 1930, however, company officers were having second thoughts. George W. Johnson, recently promoted to the presidency of the firm, wrote to his father, now chairman of the board, to inform him of his preference for horizontal wage reductions instead of selective pay cuts.

> It would fit with our Square Deal teachings. It would be in harmony with the partnership plan of give and take, and of treating everyone alike. It would save alot of grief. It would be very difficult to explain to one group of workmen that their rates are too high and must be reduced, while others are not. . . . It would take Charlie, the superintendents, foremen and myself a good part of the Winter conferring with different ones whose wages were reduced, and then I fear they would never feel right about it. It could even take on a serious aspect. . . .[38]

But the elder Johnson was not yet ready for a horizontal wage reduction. He encouraged his son and nephew first to reduce salaries of white-collar workers and then to approach "overpaid" workers tactfully, discussing with them the need for pay cuts.[39] However, these selective reductions were not enough to satisfy the firm's "obligations" to stockholders. In January 1931 company officers announced a 10 percent cut in the pay of salaried employees earning more than $2,000 a year. In the spring of 1932 management decreased both salaried employees' and shop workers' pay by an additional 10 percent.[40]

Through 1932, and even after horizontal wage reductions had taken place, managers continued the practice of selectively reducing wages throughout the factories. "We call this levelling down," wrote George W. Johnson to his father.[41] Whether performed with or without tact, however, the practice of "levelling down" was meeting some resistance from workers. Johnson Welt bed lasters, for example, when requested to take a pay cut, "flatly refused." West End Victory Factory workers protested such reductions. Pioneer Factory lasters were also unwilling to accept a cut in their prices. As I noted earlier, the firm was forced to transfer their work to another plant in Binghamton.[42]

Even though the majority of the workers, aware of their vulnerability during the Depression, finally accepted the wage cuts without much resistance, company officers were plagued by an ever-growing dread of a worker backlash, perhaps leading to unionization. The circulation of radical papers throughout the factories, the presence of union organizers in the area, and rising voices of discontent on the shop floor had fueled the anxieties of management.[43] As early as 1929, to gauge more accurately the level of worker discontent and to maintain a vigilant guard against union organizers and militants, the firm had employed an agent from the Pinkerton Detective Agency in Scranton. The agent was instructed to "go into some of the home[s]—possibly by seeming to try to sell something—and get some line on the talk which may be going on among the families."[44] The agent found little evidence of widespread dissatisfaction. The firm, however, was on the verge of making more extensive adjustments to the "Square Deal," adjustments that served to strain the company's already unstable consensus further.[45]

In the winter of 1929–30 conditions throughout the shoe industry worsened. Endicott Johnson officers notified the various department heads to cut expenses drastically. Throughout the 1920s, whenever the firm had hit upon a bad spell of business, George F. Johnson implored Truman Platt to cut back on his department's medical and relief work. During the time the firm began to reconsider the profit-sharing plan, Johnson repeated such sentiments to Platt: "If the Medical Department gradually works down to what it was originally— first aid, plus maternity—it would not be any great or unmixed evil for us to contemplate."[46] The limitations on access to medical services, introduced by the new employment policies of the firm, partially alleviated pressures for cutbacks, but the continued poor business showing of the corporation again led to renewed demands for curtailment of welfare services:

> We cannot guarantee the million dollar cost of Medicine and Relief. We only pay it when we can earn it, after having competed with those who do not have to pay. . . . We shall have to take it down as we put it up, piece by piece, as we are forced to, lacking money to keep up the cost. . . . We will do what we can do in the way of Medicine and Relief, and we will have to be governed entirely by business conditions.[47]

But Platt resisted Johnson's calls for retrenchment, believing in the importance of his department's work. He tried, as best he could, to limit cutbacks in welfare, and for a while it seems that he succeeded. The constant appeals by workers for medical and relief services, which Platt tactfully forwarded to George F. Johnson, as well as reports on worker sentiments, gathered by Pinkerton agents, led Johnson to recognize finally the importance of the Medical and Relief Department to the firm. "As times tighten," he wrote Platt in May 1930, "the Medical Service grows more valuable if that were possible. If it comes to a show-down, and reductions shall have to be made in operating costs, it is better that we should make a horizontal wage reduction than reduce our Medical Service." "There is no dollar we use," Johnson concluded, "that brings so much valuable return, as the Medical Service."[48]

But 1930 and 1931 were particularly tough years for the firm. Home building was temporarily discontinued. Various outside services of the Medical Department were curtailed. Much of the company's community welfare work was cut. Discretionary pensions to retired workers and widows were reduced or entirely eliminated. In all, the firm cut its welfare expenditures by about $400,000 between 1930 and 1931 (from $1,134,345 to $734,496).[49]

IV

With workers suffering from lack of work, pay cuts, and an erosion of benefits, it seems that the Johnsons could take little more from their employees without bringing down the "Square Deal" entirely. Recognizing this, they began to consider reducing dividends. "Capital should be made to understand that there must be a wider and more fair distribution of wealth," Johnson wrote to his son.[50] Yet even as the Johnsons began to explore the possibility of cutting dividends, they were coming under increasing pressure from irate stockholders and from an anxious Legal Department to eliminate all expenditures not directly related to business. "It has been mentioned by stockholders, or by people who know the habits of stockholders, that unless we can earn our dividends, they may force us to discontinue Medicine and Relief as an 'unusual proceeding', and not a proper use of stockholders' money," Johnson wrote his son in early 1931.[51] Management's fear of a stockholder's legal challenge held them back from reducing dividends for the time being.[52]

In fact, increasing pressure to maintain dividend payments finally led, in March 1931, to the transfer of support for the firm's medical programs directly to the workers, in the form of a 5 percent wage deduction. Apparently, there *was* something more that managers could take from the workers. Johnson wrote the head of the Medical and Relief Department, explaining the context and motives behind the decision to make the medical division self-supporting.

> There is unquestionably a "weakness" in our Medical plan as well as our Pensions; and that weakness is, that no one can guarantee payment of costs of Medicine or Pensions, except and when the Company make sufficient profit to justify the expense. This they have failed to do now for one, and I don't know but I might say, two years in succession. So then the inevitable result must follow.
>
> As a last resort we put the 5% tax on, which in effect means nothing more than a 5% reduction. The idea that money thus secured should be used to pay Medical charges, was simply that we might satisfy the common stockholders, who—feeling themselves without dividends— had legal redress, inasmuch as we had used money in unusual ways, which belonged to them for dividend requirements.
>
> It is unfortunate that we had to give up our "free Medicine" and liberal

policy of Pensions. But the business was more important, and had to be saved in any way we could devise. . . . I am sorry for everybody. I think I may be pardoned, however, if I am more sorry for myself than for anybody else.[53]

Everything, it appeared, would be subject to sacrifice in order to maintain dividends. "It seems to me," wrote Johnson to his son in 1931, "if things grow worse and worse, that the Medical department even today, will be a 'White Elephant.' We may have to unload it, sooner or later—*all of it*—and quit the Medical business, and attend to the shoe and leather business. All these things are possible, and may need to be done, from necessity."[54]

Yet the transfer of support of the medical division from the firm to the workers and the reduction of welfare benefits placed management in a stronger position to consider reducing dividends. Company officers, holding about 17 percent of the firm's common stock, had a great deal to lose in cutting dividends, as George F. Johnson reminded his son.[55] Nevertheless, the Johnsons finally did cut common stock dividends in the second quarter of 1931, from 10 percent to 6 percent.[56] The dividend reduction only served to provoke stockholders once again to challenge the firm's welfare policies.

While wage and benefit reductions and short-time work were straining labor-management relations on the shop floor, the corporation was establishing a reputation in the community as the most generous employer in the region. During the winters of 1930 and 1931, the firm provided free meals to needy workers and their dependents. It sent welfare workers to employees' homes, to determine their special needs. The responsibilities and activity of one such worker were recalled by his brother: "He used to go up to the North Side and he'd go into a home and he'd see where and if they was having a hard time. If they needed coal or something, he'd come back and he'd turn around and maybe send them up a half-a-ton of coal, or send them food. E.J. did that a lot during the Depression."[57] Such relief efforts were partially funded by the workers themselves from surpluses generated through meal sales in the firm's restaurants, from individual contributions made by well-off workers, and from the wage deduction that was channeled into the Medical and Relief Department. But a substantial amount of money also came from company funds.

While relief efforts financed by the firm won the accolades of local citizens, as well as generated much-needed goodwill among the firm's employees, to many of the corporation's stockholders such extraproductive ventures on the part of management seemed unjustified. Yet, ironically, the continuing protestations of stockholders about the unwarranted use of "their" money only served to stimulate management's determination to continue funding company and community relief efforts. When a stockholder wrote George F. Johnson in October 1931, complaining about the use of company funds to finance relief efforts for the needy, Johnson replied: "As a stockholder you have a perfect right to object to the use of 'company funds', but unfortunately we cannot separate 'stockholder's money' from the working men's money."[58] Confronted with the greedy demands of stockholders, Johnson's worker roots emerged.

> But as long as I am on earth to vote, I will never give the stockholders any more than I am willing to give the workers. When we took away from the common stockholders two dollars of their five dollars dividend, we took away at least two and a half from the workers, of their wages. By taking away from the workers, we were able to earn the three dollars which we now propose to give the common stockholders.[59]

When it grew clear that the firm's continuing relief work depressed the value of the corporation's stock, Johnson wrote his son: "Labor is just like raw hides, so far as they are concerned. They buy them when needed, and at the lowest possible price. . . . Labor, therefore, has no consideration, and the average buyer of stocks expressed his approval of this plan, as opposed to E.J., by paying 30 percent more for the stock [of the International Shoe Company] in the open market; and we waste sympathy, sometimes, on stockholders."[60] Although stockholder protests subsided a bit after the initial impact of the firm's dividend reduction passed, the firm's subsequent actions aroused them anew.

In 1933, after the firm donated over $200,000 to the Broome County Humane Society for relief work in the community, the objections of stockholders again grew loud and provoked one member of Johnson's board of directors to remind the chairman of the board that directors were "trustees for the stockholders" and to question Johnson's unilateral decision to use company money for community relief work.[61] At this challenge from within his ranks, Johnson's anger grew even more intense: "It probably never will occur to Mr. Bowers, that we are 'trustees' as well, to the interests of the working people, and the community at large, in which the factories operate. Isn't it quite absurd to assume that the Directors are responsible only to stockholders, and have no responsibility to the workers?"[62] Through the winter of 1933–34, Johnson's letters to his son were filled with tirades against the tyranny and selfishness of stockholders, often in language that would have made a Marxist proud.

> Can a stockholder be considered—or even a collection of stockholders— as owners of the Industry, because they have invested their cash, hoping for liberal return, and caring nothing about how these returns are earned, only that they receive them in the largest possible way? Are not stockholders willing and happy, and quite ready, to sell out their interests? And do they not do it, when it pleases them?
> How could a stockholder or group of stockholders claim to "own" the business, caring nothing about the earnings paid to the workers, or values sold and delivered to the customers? Are they not, in fact, parasites—one

and all, and every one — with selfish interest, "reaping where they have not sown" — demanding of Management, consideration of their interests, which is not their due, and which they themselves have no respect for?[63]

Although continually under pressure throughout the Depression to limit welfare and relief services — pressure that came from stockholders, his board of directors, and the firm's legal department — Johnson was able, through the use of various legal and financial subterfuges, to ward off the threat of legal challenges to his policies.

V

Stockholders were not the only outside threats to the firm's "Square Deal" policies. Activist federal and state governments, intent upon bringing the Depression to a hasty end, also came to plague the industrial order of Endicott Johnson. Economic and labor policies under Franklin D. Roosevelt and New York State Governor Herbert H. Lehman not only challenged Endicott Johnson's welfare system and the "Square Deal" but threatened private corporate welfare programs in general. They did this in three ways. First, by competing with private corporations in providing services to workers, federal and state governments undercut the bonds between workers and management that private welfare systems had cultivated in previous decades. Second, New Deal and state relief legislation created a double indemnity for private companies. Not only did progressive welfare firms need to make sufficient profits to fund their own private welfare programs, but they also had to pay new payroll taxes to fund national and state welfare, unemployment, and social programs. Last, article 7a of the National Industrial Recovery Act (NIRA) raised the specter of government-supported union drives throughout the country.

Initially, Endicott Johnson managers looked upon the NIRA, with its fair trade codes and call for increased minimum wages and reduction of working hours, with favor. While they had strong reservations about section 7a, which protected labor's right to collective bargaining, other provisions of the act more than made up for these reservations. The Johnsons advocated wage rates even higher than those set by most of the shoe manufacturers who had been called upon to draw up the shoe codes. They encouraged separate minimum wages for skilled and semiskilled workers and an end to geographic differentials. Recognizing that the major factor depressing wages and profits in the shoe industry was cutthroat competition, Endicott Johnson managers encouraged policies that limited the exploitative practices employed by the most competitive, low-wage shoe firms. As one strong critic of the firm was forced to admit: "Their policies, in comparison with those of the big shoe firms of the midwest, were superior from the point of view of labor."[64]

Although the NIRA had not gone as far as the Johnsons would have liked, with respect to rationalizing the industry, it did improve Endicott Johnson's business prospects considerably, as George F. Johnson acknowledged.

> The National Recovery Act eliminated a tremendous lot of cut-throats, so called "competitors", but who were in fact bad managers, and only lived because of exploitation of poverty which they freely practised. We certainly got rid of an army of that type, and it has helped us. Now we can cash in on some of our advantages, which we have worked so hard to create, and we shall find the going easier, so far as prices are concerned. Of this I am certain, due to the above mentioned National Recovery Act results.[65]

Yet, while many of the NIRA regulations aided the firm and were praised by company officers, other government policies came under heavy criticism. In general, management was extremely critical of government attempts to pass "social" legislation such as unemployment insurance or social security.[66] The Johnsons felt that such legislation would be debilitating to progressive employers like themselves and would indirectly aid more exploitative companies that took no responsibility for their workers' welfare.

Although the Johnsons continued to back the NIRA, the expanding economic role of government led them increasingly to question the extent to which they should support government-inspired reforms. In early 1935, for example, company officers began to consider what type of legislative replacement for the NIRA they should support. The NIRA was scheduled to expire in June 1935, although the Supreme Court would rule it unconstitutional before that date. The question faced by the Johnsons was whether to support more stringent legislation that would leave the federal government in control of wages and hours or to back a plan more in line with the self-policing policies of the NIRA. Charles F. Johnson, Jr., expressed his hesitation in backing any plan that would lead to the expansion of federal government authority: "It seems to us here if we take the position of favoring legislation as to the new NRA that would give the Federal Government the right to fix hours and wages in all industries, that it would be a serious mistake as this would be putting industry absolutely in the hands of the politicians and God only knows what might happen."[67]

Charles F. Johnson's opposition to government control of wages and hours represented not only the natural antipathy of laissez-faire businessmen to any form of government control of industry but also an emerging rift between many progressive welfare firms and federal and state governments. Beginning in June 1934, when President Roosevelt created the Committee on Economic Security, charged to investigate the prospects for implementing a national social insurance system, it was clear that the federal government was starting to chart a more radical legislative course.[68] On January 17, 1935, Roosevelt called on Congress to enact social security legislation, introducing an administration-sponsored bill on the same day.[69] In August 1935 the president signed the Social Security Act, which created a federal-state unemployment system, old-age retirement insurance, and a national welfare system. George F. Johnson, along with fellow company officers, feared that such legislation would place a double tax on the firm. "It is going to be impossible," he wrote about the anticipated payroll tax for unemployment benefits, "for us to continue to pay one-third to double as much wages, with a million and a quarter yearly for medicine, and pay double taxes because we happen to pay double wages."[70] He resented paying money to support other firms that contributed far more to unemployment than Endicott Johnson. He expressed extreme disdain for the social security program, believing that it would destroy thrift and lead to a growing federal debt.[71]

Faced with a federal government they could not control, the Johnsons also found themselves opposing state legislation equally threatening to the "Square Deal." In early 1935 the Byrne-Killgrew Bill, which sought the creation of a state unemployment insurance system supported by a pooled fund of contributions from employers, was slowly winding its way through various legislative committees, on its way to what appeared to be prompt passage. The bill constituted the most progressive unemployment compensation legislation contemplated by any state in the nation.[72] Charles F. Johnson, Jr., and George W. Johnson, along with numerous other New York State businessmen, hoping to affect a revision in the provisions of the bill by the insertion of an amendment that would allow private firms to establish their own "segregated" unemployment funds, rushed to Albany to try to persuade Governor Lehman to back this change in the bill.

> We tried to reason with him and point out how unfair this would be to companies that did not create unemployment, also tried to point out to him how unfair it would be to the liberal wage employer to be paying into a pool possibly twice as much on a percentage of payroll basis as illiberal and unfair employers of labor paying low wages, also how unfair it would be to our company if New York State did not permit companies with satisfactory financial resources to segregate their own Unemployment Insurance. . . .[73]

The Johnsons also feared that firms operating in states with less liberal unemployment provisions would benefit from the unfair advantage of paying lower payroll taxes.[74]

Although the Johnsons were unable to persuade Lehman to make major changes in the legislation, they did seem to have had some influence on its provisions. The payroll tax was reduced somewhat. But the basic policy of taxing all employers and pooling unemployment funds was retained. A month before the bill was voted upon, Charles F. Johnson, Jr., wrote his uncle: "Although we are all well pleased with the fact that Governor Lehman finally weakened as a result of our efforts together with efforts of other manufacturers in the State, who formed a group and fought the Bill as a body, we are not going to discontinue our efforts to try to get further changes made and to defeat the Bill when it comes up for a vote. . . ."[75] The bill, however, was not defeated. In April 1935 it was passed by the New York State Legislature.[76] "It is going to be interesting," George F. Johnson had written his son in February 1935, "to know how we can continue to take care of our own people, and take over the burdens of other organizations, through Government Laws, compelling us to duplicate everything we do for our own."[77] Indeed, it would be. The failure of management to halt the passage of the Byrne-Killgrew Bill, as well as the successful passage of federal social legislation, resulted in a major financial drain on the firm for the duration of the Depression.

VI

In spite of stockholder and government challenges, wage reductions, and welfare cutbacks, Endicott Johnson managers continued to demonstrate to their workers that their company would take care of them. Through public and private displays of generosity, the corporation was able to maintain the allegiance of a majority of the labor force. Workers who lived and worked through the Depression at Endicott Johnson recalled their lives in the 1930s as somewhat insulated from the harshness of the economy around them. "We never suffered during the Depression like other people did. There wasn't that much money, but we didn't seem to suffer," remembered one employee.[78] What seemed to impress employees were the many relief services provided by the company during the difficult years of the 1930s, services such as the free distribution of food and fuel, the plowing and harrowing of workers' gardens, the reduction of home mortgage payments, and the distribution of money to hard-up employees. Many workers could not recall that the firm had deducted from their wages to pay for the medical service.[79] It was not surprising.

Whatever strains might have existed between management and workers in the early 1930s due to wage and benefit cuts were greatly assuaged by actions taken by corporate officers in 1933. In June 1933 business had recovered sufficiently for the firm to initiate a 5 percent horizontal wage increase. In July the NIRA went into effect, establishing a forty-hour week and raising wages by 10 percent. In September of that year the 5 percent wage deduction for the Medical Department was eliminated, and two months later approximately $650,000 that had been "unnecessarily" collected in the previous year, when improved business conditions no longer justified the wage deduction, were returned to the workers.[80] Welfare services were also restored and even expanded. By 1934 and 1935 yearly expenditures on medical, relief, recreation, and sundry other programs had risen to $1.3 million, surpassing the levels of the 1920s.[81]

It seemed, in late 1933 and early 1934, that the worst days of the Depression were behind. One worker, expressing the heady optimism of the months that followed the restoration of many of the wage and welfare cuts, penned the following ode to the Johnsons:

> We're glad we work for the Johnson Boys
> And here's the reason why:
> They gave the depression a kick in the pants
> And a punch right in the eye.
> Working along together
> Making the shoe for everyone.[82]

Johnson acknowledged the gratitude of the workers when he wrote to one cutter: "I want you to know that there is one company or industry that sincerely desire to be fair with their working partners."[83]

But there was more than "being fair" involved in management's actions. There was also fear. The NIRA's provisions, protecting the collective bargaining rights of workers, posed a real threat to Endicott Johnson managers who had, for over four decades, enforced an open shop. That is why Pinkerton agents continued to be employed by the firm in the relatively prosperous years between 1933 and 1936.[84] That is also why management was so cautious and hesitant in instituting wage reductions.

Endicott Johnson officers were trapped by the labor management system they had created. While they could make adjustments in it, they could not abandon it, for fear of violating the explicit and implicit expectations existing under the "Square Deal." In the Depression the firm's reliance on workers' loyalty had imposed upon management an obligation that it could ignore only at its own peril. The firm's officers recognized this. A week after deducted medical charges were refunded to the workers, Johnson wrote his nephew: "I should like you to keep me posted on the Labor situation—phone, wire or write. This is your main possible difficulty. I am in hopes that what we have done will permit the people to be satisfied that they are 'collectively bargaining,' and that the government will let them alone if they are satisfied." Johnson, believing his workers to be "thoroughly wrought up by that thing called the 'Seventh Article' in the Recovery Act," warned his son and nephew to take "care of every occasion of fault-finding, no matter how trifling or small. . . ."[85] Pinkerton agent reports were read carefully by management, always on the watch for any evidence of the spread of union sentiment among the workers.[86]

By 1935 and 1936, however, it had become evident, despite the continued anxiety of corporate officers, that no major worker rebellion was forthcoming. The Johnsons had satisfied workers' expectations sufficiently to ward off such an event. The coming of the Depression had put enormous strains on the corporation's famed "Square Deal" policies, which had maintained relatively cordial labor relations for well over a decade. Battered by diminishing profits, by greedy stockholders and the imperatives of industrial capitalism, by competition with government welfare programs, and by growing discontent among their workers, Endicott Johnson managers had faced one of the most serious crises that the firm ever experienced. In the process of adjusting to both internal and external challenges, the Janus face of welfarism had been revealed. On the one hand benevolent and sincere, on the other self-interested and deceptive, the corporation's labor policies nonetheless had successfully weathered the early years of the Depression.

NOTES

1. George F. Johnson to E. H. Ellison, Oct. 2, 1928, box 9, George F. Johnson Papers, George Arents Research Library for Special Collections, Syracuse University, Syracuse, N.Y.
2. Horace B. Davis, *Shoes: The Workers and the Industry* (New York, 1940), 42.
3. George F. Johnson to Mrs. Fred C. Blesh, May 12, 1928, box 9, George F. Johnson Papers. Johnson received several letters complaining about the layoffs.
4. George F. Johnson to F. J. Stokes, May 12, 1928, box 9, George F. Johnson Papers. Johnson wrote Blesh's wife to tell her that her husband would be reinstated. See George F. Johnson to Mrs. Fred C. Blesh, May 28, 1928, box 9, George F. Johnson Papers.
5. George F. Johnson to Walter J. Riale, July 23, 1928, box 9, George F. Johnson Papers. Riale was the head of the Johnson City employment office.
6. Truman H. Platt to George F. Johnson, May 29, 1929, box 9, ser. 1, Charles F. Johnson, Jr., Papers, George Arents Research Library for Special Collections, Syracuse University, Syracuse, N.Y.
7. George F. Johnson to Truman H. Platt, May 25, 1929, box 10, George F. Johnson Papers.
8. Truman H. Platt to George F. Johnson, May 29, 1929, box 9, ser. 1, Charles F. Johnson, Jr., Papers.
9. George F. Johnson to Charles F. Johnson, Jr., May 27, 1929, box 9, ser. 1, Charles F. Johnson, Jr., Papers.
10. Ibid.
11. "To the Workers" notice, May 29, 1929, box 9, ser. 1, Charles F. Johnson, Jr., Papers. Emphasis in original.
12. E. W. Lewis to George F. Johnson, June 22, 1929, box 9, ser. 1, Charles F. Johnson, Jr., Papers. For another appeal, see Arcangelo Ciccarrelli to George F. Johnson, June 15, 1929, in the same box. Platt noted, in commenting on Ciccarrelli's appeal, that over 2,000 workers had been hired under the new policy. Truman H. Platt to George F. Johnson, June 21, 1929, box 9.
13. George F. Johnson to Charles F. Johnson, Jr., June 25, 1929, box 9, ser. 1, Charles F. Johnson, Jr., Papers.
14. George F. Johnson to Truman H. Platt, June 25, 1929, box 9, ser. 1, Charles F. Johnson, Jr., Papers.

15. Charles F. Johnson, Jr., to George F. Johnson, July 1, 1929, box 9, ser. 1, Charles F. Johnson, Jr., Papers.

16. "Endicott Johnson Workers Daily Page," *Binghamton Sun,* July 16, 1929.

17. Charles F. Johnson, Jr., to Frank Sherwood and Dick Turner, Sept. 21, 1932, box 29, ser. 1, Charles F. Johnson, Jr., Papers.

18. *Endicott Bulletin,* Dec. 3, 1929, Apr. 8, 1930.

19. David Brody, *Workers in Industrial America: Essays on the Twentieth Century Struggle* (New York, 1980), 68. On the existence and operation of internal dual labor markets during the Depression, see Sanford M. Jacoby, *Employing Bureaucracy: Managers, Unions, and the Transformation of Work in American Industry, 1900–1945* (New York, 1985), chap 7.

20. R——, interview by David Nielson, July 10, 1974, transcript, 286. See also C——, interview by David Nielson, July 26, 1973, transcript, 81; Frank Tuthill, interview by Gerald Zahavi, Nov. 30, 1979, tape recording (personal possession).

21. Tuthill, interview; James W. Lupole, interview by Gerald Zahavi, with the assistance of Deborah D. Maxwell, July 15, 1981, tape recording (personal possession); William Bertier [pseud.], interview by Gerald Zahavi, with the assistance of Deborah D. Maxwell, July 13, 1981, tape recording (personal possession); Kenneth E. Compton, interview by Gerald Zahavi, May 5, 1982, tape recording (personal possession).

22. William Patrick Burns, "A Study of Personnel Policies, Employee Opinion and Labor Turnover (1930–1946) at the Endicott Johnson Corporation" (Master's thesis, New York State School of Industrial and Labor Relations, Cornell University, 1947), 89.

23. "To the Workers" notice, Jan. 13, 1944, box 10, ser. 3, Frank A. Johnson Papers, George Arents Research Library for Special Collections, Syracuse University, Syracuse, N.Y.

24. Endicott Johnson Corporation Annual Reports, box 23, George F. Johnson Papers. For a convenient chart (although one marred by a couple of minor errors), see G. Ralph Smith, *The Endicott Johnson Corporation* (New Orleans, 1956), 24.

25. George F. Johnson to Charles F. Johnson, Jr., Feb. 19, 1927, box 8, George F. Johnson Papers. See also George F. Johnson to W. F. Dickson, Mar. 1, 1927, box 8; and George W. Johnson to George F. Johnson, Feb. 21, 1927, box 17, George F. Johnson Papers.

26. "To the Workers" notice, Feb. 7, 1929; George F. Johnson to George W. Johnson, Feb. 11, 1929, box 10, George F. Johnson Papers; Richard S. Saul, "An American Entrepreneur: George F. Johnson" (D.S.S. diss., Syracuse University, 1966), 35.

27. George W. Johnson to George F. Johnson, Jan. 28, 1929, box 17, George F. Johnson Papers.

28. George F. Johnson to George W. Johnson, Feb. 1, 1929, box 10, George F. Johnson Papers.

29. George F. Johnson to George W. Johnson, Feb. 15, 1929, box 10, George F. Johnson Papers. See also George F. Johnson to George W. Johnson, May 29, 1929, box 10, George F. Johnson Papers.

30. In 1936, however, workers received a "bonus" in the form of holiday pay. "To the Workers" notice, Nov. 24, 1936; Charles F. Johnson, Jr., to George F. Johnson, Nov. 25, 1936, box 31, ser. 1, Charles F. Johnson, Jr., Papers.

31. George F. Johnson to John W. Johnson, Jan. 12, 1930, box 10, George F. Johnson Papers.

32. George F. Johnson to Don C. Morgan, Feb. 5, 1930, box 10, George F. Johnson Papers.

33. See, for example, George F. Johnson to Senator Arthur Vandenburg, Apr. 3, 1937, box 15, George F. Johnson Papers.

34. Amy King, interview by Gerald Zahavi, Nov. 30, 1979, tape recording (personal possession).

35. George F. Johnson to George W. Johnson, Dec. 14, 1931, box 11, George F. Johnson Papers.

36. "To the Workers" notice, Jan. 13, 1944, box 34, ser. 1, Charles F. Johnson, Jr., Papers.

37. George F. Johnson to George W. Johnson, Feb. 9, 1929, box 10, George F. Johnson Papers.

38. George W. Johnson to George F. Johnson, Nov. 21, 1930, box 12, ser. 1, Charles F. Johnson, Jr., Papers.

39. George F. Johnson to George W. and Charles F. Johnson, Jr., Nov. 24, 1930, box 11, George F. Johnson Papers.

40. "Wage Increases and Decreases, March 16, 1931, to December 1, 1952," typescript, "No dates" folder, box 6, ser. 1, George W. Johnson Papers, George Arents Research Library for Special Collections, Syracuse University, Syracuse, N.Y.; Charles F. Johnson, Jr., to George F. Johnson, Feb. 9, 1933, box 29, ser. 1, Charles F. Johnson, Jr., Papers.

41. George W. Johnson to George F. Johnson, Mar. 23, 1932, box 13, ser. 1, Charles F. Johnson, Jr., Papers.

42. Charles F. Johnson, Jr., to George F. Johnson (telegram), Aug. 18, 1932; Charles F. Johnson, Jr., to George F. Johnson, Mar. 17, 1932; George W. Johnson to George F. Johnson, Mar. 21, 1932; Charles F. Johnson, Jr., to George F. Johnson, Mar. 25, 1932, box 29, ser. 1, Charles F. Johnson, Jr., Papers.

43. George F. Johnson to George W. Johnson, Feb. 11, 1929, box 10; George F. Johnson to Michael Riolo, Oct. 15, 1928, box 9; George F. Johnson to William H. Hill, Aug. 31, 1933, box 12, George F. Johnson Papers.

44. George F. Johnson to George W. Johnson, Apr. 9, 1929, box 10, George F. Johnson Papers.

45. George F. Johnson to George W. Johnson, Apr. 15, 1929, box 10, George F. Johnson Papers.

46. George F. Johnson to Truman H. Platt, Feb. 1, 1929, box 10, George F. Johnson Papers.

47. George F. Johnson to Truman H. Platt, Apr. 2, 1929, box 10, George F. Johnson Papers.

48. George F. Johnson to Truman H. Platt, May 13, 1930, box 10, George F. Johnson Papers.

49. George F. Johnson to M. E. Page, Aug. 6, 1930; George F. Johnson to Don C. Morgan, Aug. 30, 1930; George F. Johnson to G. Harry Lester, Mar. 24, 1931; George F. Johnson to Truman H. Platt, Mar. 24, 1931; George F. Johnson to George W. Johnson, Apr. 9, 1931, box 11, George F. Johnson Papers. Burns, "A Study of Personnel Policies," 51.

50. George F. Johnson to George W. Johnson, Jan. 3, 1931, box 11, George F. Johnson Papers.

51. George F. Johnson to George W. Johnson, Feb. 14, 1931, box 11, George F. Johnson Papers.

52. George F. Johnson to George W. Johnson, Feb. 23, 1931, box 11, George F. Johnson Papers.

53. George F. Johnson to Truman H. Platt, Mar. 24, 1931, box 11, George F. Johnson Papers. Johnson was very angry at Platt for resisting reductions in the medical service in previous years, and he blamed Platt for "inflating" the cost of the department to such an extent that management was forced to institute the 5 percent wage deduction. See George F. Johnson to George W. Johnson, Apr. 9, 1931, box 11, George F. Johnson Papers.

54. George F. Johnson to George W. Johnson, Apr. 16, 1931, box 11, George F. Johnson Papers. Emphasis in original.

55. George F. Johnson to George W. Johnson, Apr. 14, 1931, box 11, George F. Johnson Papers. Johnson estimated that a dividend cut would cost him alone about $100,000. Information on Johnson family common stockholdings comes from George F. Johnson to Bruce L. Babcock, July 24, 1930, box 11, George F. Johnson Papers. By 1938 the Johnsons' common stockholdings had declined to about 15 percent. See Davis, Shoes, 68.

56. George F. Johnson to Arthur B. Butman, July 21, 1931, box 11, George F. Johnson Papers.

57. Compton, interview.

58. George F. Johnson to Max Petzold, Oct. 28, 1931, box 11, George F. Johnson Papers. Petzold's letter was printed in the "Workers Daily Page." See "Endicott Johnson Workers Daily Page," Binghamton Sun, Nov. 4, 1931.

59. George F. Johnson to George W. Johnson, Dec. 10, 1931, box 11, George F. Johnson Papers.

60. George F. Johnson to George W. Johnson, Dec. 22, 1931, box 11, George F. Johnson Papers.

61. George F. Johnson to George W. Johnson, Dec. 12, Dec. 17, Dec. 25, Dec. 30, 1933, box 13, George F. Johnson Papers. Workers also grew to resent the channeling of company money into community relief work and later voted in a company referendum to direct the corporation's relief efforts to employees only.

62. George F. Johnson to George W. Johnson, Jan. 1, 1934, box 13, George F. Johnson Papers.

63. George F. Johnson to George W. Johnson, Jan. 15, 1934, box 13, George F. Johnson Papers.

64. Davis, Shoes, 148; Charles F. Johnson, Jr., to George F. Johnson, Jan. 14, 1935, box 30, ser. 1, Charles F. Johnson, Jr., Papers.

65. George F. Johnson to Arthur Eilenberger, Nov. 17, 1933, box 13, George F. Johnson Papers. See also George W. Johnson to Charles F. Johnson, Jr., Feb. 8, 1934, box 13, ser. 1, Charles F. Johnson, Jr., Papers.

66. George F. Johnson to Dr. M. S. Bloom, Nov. 28, 1931, box 11, George F. Johnson Papers.

67. Charles F. Johnson, Jr., to George F. Johnson, Feb. 6, 1935, box 30, ser. 1, Charles F. Johnson, Jr., Papers.

68. On the growing disenchantment of welfare capitalists with government social legislation, see Edward Berkowitz and Kim McQuaid, *Creating the Welfare State: The Political Economy of Twentieth-Century Reform* (New York, 1980), 78–104.

69. William E. Leuchtenburg, *Franklin D. Roosevelt and the New Deal, 1932–1940* (New York, 1963), 130–31.

70. George F. Johnson to George W. Johnson, Jan. 1, 1935, box 13, George F. Johnson Papers.

71. George F. Johnson to E. H. Ellison, Jan. 18, 1935, box 13, George F. Johnson Papers. For more on Johnson's position on government social legislation, see Jan. correspondence in box 13, ibid.

72. Robert P. Ingalls, *Herbert H. Lehman and New York's Little New Deal* (New York, 1975), 79–81.

73. Charles F. Johnson, Jr., to George F. Johnson, Feb. 6, 1935, box 30, ser. 1, Charles F. Johnson, Jr., Papers. On the battle for the passage of the Byrne-Killgrew legislation and on New York's "Little New Deal" in general, see Ingalls, *Herbert H. Lehman*, chap. 4 and passim.

74. Charles F. Johnson, Jr., to George F. Johnson, Feb. 11, 1935, box 30, ser. 1, Charles F. Johnson, Jr., Papers.

75. Charles F. Johnson, Jr., to George F. Johnson, Mar. 18, 1935, box 30, ser. 1, Charles F. Johnson, Jr., Papers.

76. Ingalls, *Herbert H. Lehman*, 82.

77. George F. Johnson to George W. Johnson, Feb. 11, 1935, box 14, George F. Johnson Papers.

78. B——, interview by David Nielson, July 1, 1974, transcript, 220.

79. Clarence Dirlam, interview by Gerald Zahavi, Dec. 12, 1979, tape recording (personal possession); Tuthill, interview; Thomas K. Chubbuck, interview by Gerald Zahavi, with the assistance of Deborah D. Maxwell, session 1, June 29, 1981, tape recording (personal possession); Earl I. Birdsall, interview by Gerald Zahavi, May 5, 1982, tape recording (personal possession); Lupole, interview; Compton, interview; William Haight, interview by Gerald Zahavi, with the assistance of Deborah D. Maxwell, May 27, 1982, tape recording (personal possession); Lucille M. Farrar, interview by Gerald Zahavi, with the assistance of Deborah D. Maxwell, July 13, 1981, tape recording (personal possession); Sam Salvatore, interview by Gerald Zahavi, with the assistance of Deborah D. Maxwell, July 7, 1981, tape recording (personal possession). Dozens of additional interviews reinforce these observations.

80. "To the Workers" notice, Sept. 11, 1933; "To the Workers" notice, Nov. 16, 1933, box 13, George F. Johnson Papers; *Endicott Bulletin*, Nov. 17, 1933.

81. Burns, "A Study of Personnel Policies," 51. George F. Johnson to W. F. Dickson, May 15, 1925, box 8, George F. Johnson Papers. In 1925 the "efficiency expense," or cost of welfare, was running about $1.25 million. Vacations with pay, which were discontinued in the early 1920s, were also revived in 1934. *Endicott Bulletin*, May 18, 1934.

82. "Endicott Johnson Workers Daily Page," *Binghamton Sun*, Apr. 30, 1934.

83. George F. Johnson to Ron Hilton, Nov. 24, 1933, box 13, George F. Johnson Papers.

84. The La Follette Committee on Education and Labor, investigating industrial espionage, cited the firm as spending close to $13,000 on espionage between 1933 and 1936. "Industrial Espionage" in House Committee on Education and Labor, *Violations of Free Speech and Rights of Labor,* 76th Cong. (Washington, D.C., 1939), 82.

85. George F. Johnson to George W. Johnson and Charles F. Johnson, Jr., Nov. 24, 1933, box 13, George F. Johnson Papers.

86. Original Pinkerton reports were not located. Summaries of such reports, however, appear in numerous letters between corporate officers. See, for example, George F. Johnson to George W. Johnson, Feb. 11, Feb. 22, Mar. 14, 1935, box 14; George F. Johnson to George W. Johnson and Charles F. Johnson, Jr., Jan. 24, Jan. 26, 1935, box 13, George F. Johnson Papers.

6

"Outsiders" and "Strangers"

For close to four decades Endicott Johnson's labor policies had been tied to a firm conviction that managers and workers could resolve their differences without the involvement of "outside" unions. The "Happy Family," the Johnsons believed, could settle its own affairs.[1] Yet in the late 1930s the corporation faced the first of a series of formidable challenges to its paternalistic, open shop regime. With the passage of the Wagner Act (National Labor Relations Act) in 1935 and the formation of the Congress of Industrial Organizations (CIO), the corporation found that to maintain an open shop would be an increasingly difficult task. That it succeeded suggests that even through the most difficult years of the Depression, corporate paternalism still remained a viable alternative to unionism for Endicott Johnson workers.

I

In April 1937, following several months of widespread sit-down strikes across the nation, George F. Johnson wrote James A. Farley, President Roosevelt's political adviser and then postmaster general, expressing his fears that Endicott Johnson's placid waters would be disturbed by sit-down strikes and labor organizers. He mentioned that he had already met with the president at Hyde Park "very early in the troublesome days between Labor and Capital" and that he wanted some assurances from the administration that Endicott Johnson would be protected from labor difficulties.

> I expect I am getting to be a damn nuisance to you, but I do want to know whom I ought to contact, so that we can do immediately, whatever is possible, to prevent any "sit downs," "sit ins," or trouble in our business.
>
> You know what we have. It has taken fifty years to build it. There must be some influence that can be brought to bear on these Labor Organizations, that will persuade them to let us entirely alone.[2]

Farley responded to Johnson's appeal by sending Edward McGrady, assistant secretary of labor, to call on him. McGrady did little more than give Johnson "encouragement to believe that perhaps" Endicott Johnson would be "unmolested." Such a vague assurance, all that was in McGrady's power to offer, apparently sufficed to give Johnson some comfort, although he continued to seek support from public officials.[3] In June 1937 he wrote to Senator Robert F. Wagner of New York, appealing for permission to use some remarks of praise for the corporation's labor policies that Wagner had made in 1931.[4]

Johnson's need for continued assurances from public officials reflected a growing siege mentality not unfounded in reality. By the summer of 1937 he had already learned that "there are plenty of followers of the C.I.O and similar Labor Organizations" among his workers, although he was not certain of exactly how many.[5] In September of that year, he wrote to a friend: "We know their organizers are in the Valley here, and creating more or less trouble with some of the manufacturers."[6]

Indeed, CIO organizers had arrived in the area in July 1937 to organize three stitchdown shoe firms in Binghamton: the Ramsey, Gotham, and Truitt shoe companies.[7] Local 141 of the United Shoe Workers of America, CIO, was established in Binghamton soon afterward, and it was only a matter of months before union officials finally approached Endicott Johnson officers. On January 6, 1938, the director of the United Shoe Workers of America, Powers Hapgood, accompanied by another union representative, paid a visit to the firm's president, George W. Johnson:

> They were very friendly, and came here in what they figured to be the interests of the whole Shoe Industry. . . . They had the bright idea that since we have handled our labor problems successfully, if we were to get our workers together and let them talk to them in a body about E.J. voluntarily accepting the C.I.O's labor policy, unionizing all of our plants, that other Shoe Industries would gladly follow our lead. Those who did not want to be identified with Labor Unions, could, through pressure they would supply with the funds received from our workers, amounting to approximately $300,000 per year, be brought into line; thereby eliminating the severe competition of numerous plants throughout the Industry that are making it hard for everyone.[8]

Johnson was not persuaded, but the two union representatives persisted, offering to go down to Daytona, Florida, to speak to his father about their proposition. George F. Johnson, however, was in hearty concurrence with his son's response and never met with them. In correspondence with his son, he responded to their visit with sarcasm.[9]

Yet sarcasm was an ineffective weapon against the conditions that were making the prospect of unionization ever more real. Business was hurting in late 1937 and early 1938, as the economy entered the second trough of the Depression. Orders at Endicott Johnson were off, and again management began cutting benefits and wages. By late March 1938 the firm completed a severe belt-tightening. It discontinued relief aid to workers. It cut back on medical services. Unnecessary hospitalization was restricted, and limits on hospital stays were imposed. On May 9, 1938, a 5 percent wage deduction for medical service was reinstituted. And then came layoffs.[10]

More significant than these measures were the wage cuts that management instituted in early 1938. Already suffering from the contraction of the work week to two or three days due to curtailed production, the workers now faced horizontal pay cuts. On February 1, 1938, full-time salaried workers were asked to accept a 20 percent salary reduction. Two weeks later the firm slashed the wages of factory workers by 10 percent. Numerous spot rate reductions throughout the plants compounded the effects of the 10 percent wage cut.[11]

Wage and welfare decreases were responses to the realities of a stagnant economy. Corporation sales and profits had begun to decline in 1936 and continued to do so in 1937. By the end of 1938, despite the firm's cost-cutting measures, the company would close the year with a net profit of only $857,191, down from the $2 million figures it generated in 1933 through 1935.[12] There was hardly any question about management's responsibilities to stockholders. This time George F. Johnson expressed few damning words about them. Wages had to be cut to sustain profits.

The presence of union organizers and management's growing anxieties about maintaining worker loyalty had helped delay such cuts. Long before February 1938, when the 10 percent wage reduction went into effect, George F. Johnson had begun encouraging his son and nephew to reduce wages to secure more orders. Their failure to do so greatly angered him: "I am giving you my honest opinion, that you are going to run into Labor troubles — not because you are not willing to pay fair wages, but because the Help are not willing to work for fair wages, and you weakly agree with them and let them run your business."[13] Indeed, the workers, while certainly not "running" the business, were limiting management's prerogatives somewhat — a state of affairs that continued to arouse the elder Johnson's ire.

Some workers, recognizing management's heightened concern over the loss of labor loyalty, exploited that anxiety to limit pay cuts. Just after the 1938 wage reduction went into effect, petitions of loyalty were circulated throughout the factories. Loyalty petitions were a regular company ritual, a public expression of the Endicott Johnson consensus, frequently used during periods of anticipated worker discontent. They were encouraged by the Johnsons and generally initiated by management go-betweens: foremen and loyal workers who identified very closely with the corporation or who had received special favors from management.[14] Most of the workers did not take these petitions very seriously. In fact, employees declaring their allegiance to management one day might join the union another.[15] But even more significant than their casual attitude was the way in which they could exploit the petition process to

extract concessions from the company. In response to the 1938 wage reduction, several groups of workers withheld their "loyalty" until rates or grievances had been adjusted. Charles F. Johnson, Jr., reporting on the status of the
petition drive, described the use of such tactics:

> There was one group in the Fibre Counter Mill that did not sign the
> petition when it first came around. They had some grievance about their
> particular job. This was straightened out and they signed their names.
>   Leonard Steed has been meeting different groups of Tabernacle factory
> workers, making adjustments that seems [*sic*] necessary. He has now
> completed his work and the total adjustments made amount to about 2
> percent. As far as he knows, all of the workers are now satisfied and we
> expect to get a renewal of loyalty from them in a day or two.[16]

Given the economic constraints under which the firm was operating and the
power that conditions of labor surplus gave management, any adjustment of
wage cuts to the workers' benefit constituted a significant victory indeed.

The severity of business retrenchment in 1938 was being borne unequally
by the firm's employees. Some factories were running full while others were
only on half time or less. The Pioneer and Binghamton Work Shoe factories
were operating as little as two and a half days a week, due to the reduced
demand for shoes manufactured in these plants; the Boys and Youths and the
Infants' factories were running full time; the Sole Leather and Upper Leather
tanneries were at less than half production.[17] By March 1938 the corporation
as a whole was operating at about 65 percent of its normal productive capacity.[18] With conditions in the factories rapidly deteriorating and the prospect of
a weakened paternalistic order increasing, it was no wonder that AFL organizers soon competed with the United Shoe Workers of America in an assault
on Endicott Johnson.

II

The history of boot and shoe industry unions since the turn of the century had
been one of extreme fragmentation and fratricide. Numerous local and regional unions, as well as several national unions, vied with one another for the
allegiance of shoeworkers.[19] By 1937, however, two unions had risen to
dominance: the AFL Boot and Shoe Workers' Union (BSWU) and the CIO
United Shoe Workers of America (USWA). The former organization had
come into existence in 1895 and had been the parent organization of the local
that Johnson destroyed in 1895 (see chap. 1). The USWA was of more recent
vintage.

In September 1933 several New York and New England unions amalgamated to form the United Shoe and Leather Workers Union (USLWU), with a
membership of approximately 60,000.[20] With the formation of the Congress

of Industrial Organizations, the USLWU went through another amalgamation in 1937. It joined with the St. Louis branch of the Shoe Workers Protective Union as well as with several other local unions to form the United Shoe Workers of America, CIO. The new union began vigorous organizing work almost immediately. Although it made good progress for a while, a failed attempt to unionize shoe factories in Auburn, Maine, in 1937, both drained its resources and demoralized its organizers.[21]

The militant activism displayed by the USWA stood in sharp contrast to the business unionism of its rival, the BSWU. The BSWU had been a relatively conservative union since 1899, when its constitution was revised to increase dues and give broader powers to the executive board. In the decades that followed the constitution's revision, the union's leadership faced continuous internal and external challenges. While the BSWU maintained support and dominance in New England, it did not, however, experience vigorous growth. By the late 1930s its membership stood at a modest 31,000.[22]

For both the USWA and the BSWU, the Endicott Johnson Corporation appeared a very desirable target for unionization in 1938. With over 16,000 workers concentrated in a relatively small area, and with a heavy commitment of capital locked into dozens of plants, it could not flee organizing efforts, as many other smaller shoe manufacturers had done in New England.[23] Furthermore, given the firm's good reputation, its management might be less willing to wage an intense battle against unionization. Like United States Steel, it might readily capitulate. For the USWA not only would the unionization of the firm's workers refill its "war" chest, it would also greatly enhance the prestige of the new union, thus aiding it in organizing other firms in New England and the Midwest. For the BSWU a triumph at Endicott Johnson would make up for the extensive losses of membership suffered during the early years of the Depression. It would also prevent the USWA from gaining overwhelming dominance in the shoe industry. With such thoughts in mind organizers from both unions began their work among Endicott Johnson workers.

On March 15, 1938, Ben Berk, a labor organizer from the BSWU, established a local headquarters in the offices of the AFL Binghamton Central Labor Union. With the aid of several other BSWU organizers and volunteers from the Binghamton Central Labor Union, Berk began to leaflet Endicott Johnson plants.[24] Soon afterward, Local 42 of the BSWU was reestablished, thus marking the return of Johnson's old nemesis. By the summer of 1938 both USWA and BSWU organizers were actively trying to unionize the factories, although the CIO union was committing far fewer resources to the effort at the time, concentrating instead on smaller shoe firms in Binghamton.

Ben Berk's initial strategy was to point out to workers the contradictions and hypocrisy inherent in the "Square Deal" that allowed dividends to continue while workers suffered wage cutbacks. A typical BSWU handout read as follows:

> The Company claims it is in no condition to give any increases as they only made a mere $1,250,000 profit last year [1937], this despite the fact they promised to return the reductions the workers so generously *GAVE* them. The workers know they can't feed their children Golf courses and swimming pools, they can't dress their kids with Dance Bands or house them in Recreation Parks. They must have more money in their envelopes to provide them with the necessities of life.[25]

The union promised to pursue wage increases, job protection, overtime pay, and equalization of work. It also vowed to establish grievance committees and to "eliminate all slave-driving, price-cutting foremen." Such messages and promises were continually repeated to workers in handbills, speeches, and radio talks.[26]

Reflecting the organizational strategy of the AFL in general, which emphasized craft units, Ben Berk concentrated his early efforts on the mechanical divisions of the company, particularly on the Johnson City and the Endicott machine shops. There, the craft consciousness of the men, Berk probably reasoned, would make them more responsive to union appeals. He was not disappointed. By October 1938 he notified George W. Johnson that he had collected pledge cards from a majority of the workers in these two units, enough to petition the National Labor Relations Board (NLRB) for certification as their bargaining agent.[27]

Yet even as Berk was actively pursuing an offensive strategy against the corporation and winning converts in the machine shops, he was facing formidable opposition from both the firm and the local community. The company was issuing constant appeals urging its workers to ignore the "strangers" in their midst and to remain loyal to the corporation. Corporate officers and company propaganda emphasized the tradition of mutuality that existed at Endicott Johnson, a tradition that outsiders were now threatening. The compact between management and labor, the "Square Deal," rested on the premise that grievances and conflict would be resolved without the involvement of intermediaries. A union presence within the corporation, managers reminded the workers, threatened the very foundations of the "Happy Family": "You may be certain IT IS NOT FOR YOUR SAKE that strangers come into the community, circulate their 'vile Propaganda,' seeking to create discontent and unhappiness and THEN DISAPPEAR, to work in SOME OTHER FIELD. Pay no attention to EVIL TEACHERS, false doctrines and UNHEALTHY PROPAGANDA."[28] George F. Johnson spent the last two weeks of April 1938 circulating through the factories and speaking to the workers on the subject of loyalty.[29] Editorials appearing in the *Binghamton Sun,* owned and controlled by Johnson and his nephew-in-law, persistently recalled to the workers their obligations to management.[30] Once again, in June 1938, loyalty petitions were circulated through the factories, "the substance of which stated that the workers were opposed to any organization."[31]

Ben Berk fought against the company's antiunion drive with all that he had, not the least of which was the National Labor Relations Act (NLRA). He filed an unfair labor practices complaint with the NLRB in late June 1938, claiming that the firm had violated section 8(1) of the NLRA, which stipulated that employers should not interfere with employees exercising their rights to organize into collective bargaining units.[32] In mid-summer of 1938 NLRB investigators arrived in the community and began to look into the accusations that Berk had made. Not surprisingly, many of his charges were corroborated: a small company union composed of maintenance workers had been initiated by a relative of the head of the firm's advertising department; management go-betweens in the machine shops had taken loyalty petitions around—they had not originated on the shop floor; threats and warnings of benefit retractions had been used to coerce workers to sign loyalty petitions; a local radio station had been pressured not to air BSWU broadcasts.[33] The NLRB finally issued a cease-and-desist order, and company officials agreed, in October 1938, to post notices throughout the plants stating that they would no longer interfere with the rights of workers to unionize.[34]

The scrutiny of NLRB investigators could not but provoke the hostile reactions of corporate officers. Meetings with investigators were delayed, and a strategy of stalling was employed by Howard Swartwood, the corporation attorney. The NLRA, as company officers recognized, was a potentially subversive piece of legislation insofar as corporate welfarism was concerned. Having more bite than section 7a of the NIRA, it threatened to interject yet one more intermediary between corporate paternalists and workers, and thus undermine the personalist bonds that helped sustain welfare capitalism. When, on October 21, 1938, Johnson, his nephew, and Swartwood finally met with the regional director of the NLRB, Henry Winters, the elder Johnson took the opportunity to express his frustration and anger to Winters. He complained about the freedoms the Wagner Act gave to labor and the limitations it placed on management. According to an NLRB memorandum, "At this meeting Mr. Johnson stated that EJ ante-dated the Wagner Act, as well as the Roosevelt Administration. He pointed out to Mr. Winters that it was entirely wrong for Berk, an outsider, to come in and tear the work of fifty years building up of relationships between the company and its employees." He further accused Berk of lying to the workers in order to get them to sign pledge cards.[35] Several days later Johnson wrote Franklin Roosevelt about the NLRB cease-and-desist order, suggesting that an earlier verbal promise by the president contradicted the present behaviors of the NLRB: "The enclosed [a copy of the NLRB order] hardly agrees with the assurance you gave me . . .

[that I would] have nothing to worry about." Roosevelt answered that he wished to reply to Johnson's statements in person.[36] If such a meeting did occur between the two men, no record remains of what transpired. Certainly, as subsequent events would prove, Roosevelt did not influence either the organizational strategy of the BSWU or the deliberations of the congressionally mandated and independent NLRB.

After the NLRB silencing of the company, antiunion efforts shifted to the community. An all-out drive, encouraged by the corporation, was begun to defend the firm from the "attacks" of the union. Loyal workers, ministers, fraternal clubs, the American Legion, and local chambers of commerce all joined together to do battle with the "strangers" in their midst. For decades local churches, clubs, and the legion had been the recipients of countless contributions by the Johnsons. Now, they had an opportunity to repay their debts. Local businessmen's committees, determined to keep the community free of industrial unions, also came out in strong support of the corporation. A Triple Cities Council had been organized by the joint efforts of the Endicott Board of Trade, the Johnson City Board of Trade, and the Binghamton Chamber of Commerce in 1937, in anticipation of a union organizing drive in the shoe plants. In November 1938, right after the NLRB ruling that limited company antiunion activities was issued, a new antiunion organization was formed, the Triple Cities Civic and Workers' Committee (TCCWC). The TCCWC was composed of workers and local business and civic leaders who identified the community's interests with a union-free Endicott Johnson Corporation. Workers active on the committee began to organize employees on a plant-by-plant basis in order to fight the BSWU.[37] In leaflets and through the local press, the TCCWC maintained a constant barrage of propaganda. A typical sample follows:

> Strangers have intruded the sacred rights of our people. They have called vile names and made false accusations against our outstanding citizens, people who have always been cherished and honored in our homes, in our churches and schools. We are asked to disbelieve these Gentlemen and to trample them under our feet. "By whom?" . . . By individuals we have never seen, have never known; and who would profit by gaining our adherence to their misleading and false promises.
> "HOLD FAST TO THAT WHICH YOU KNOW TO BE GOOD," even if strangers make you fancy promises. . . . Let every red-blooded man worthy of the name, resent the false charges made against our friends and neighbors. . . . Let us show our appreciation through our determination and efforts to preserve "The Square Deal Policy."[38]

In addition to the support of loyal workers and local businessmen, the TCCWC received the backing of community religious and ethnic associations. The St. Anthony of Padua Church, the Sons of Italy, the Holy Name Society, the St. Sebastian Club, and dozens of other associations became

involved in the committee's antiunion campaign.[39] In the months that followed the issuance of the NLRB cease-and-desist order, the community antiunion drive took on a crusading quality. As Ben Berk described it to fellow
delegates at the eighteenth convention of the BSWU:

> From October 14th to November 15th [1938] you could see the most anti-
> union fight you have ever seen. You couldn't go to church on Sunday
> without having some minister or priest get up on the pulpit and damn
> you. You couldn't have your kids go to Sunday School without having
> them hear about this terrible union that was coming in there to ruin
> Endicott Johnson. The children couldn't go to school without having the
> teachers and principals tell them this organization would ruin the cities.
> They had full page advertisements in the papers. They gave out thou-
> sands and thousands of circulars telling about Akron, the "Ghost City,"
> and what the unions did to Akron.
>   Then started a whispering campaign, and for six weeks we sat and
> listened. They had speeches, they went on the radio, and for hour after
> hour you could hear how the union would ruin Endicott Johnson. After
> six weeks the people got tired of this. It was climaxed in a series
> of meetings that were held in the City of Endicott, Johnson City and
> Binghamton.[40]

Berk was hardly exaggerating in his description of events. But there was
another significant battle shaping up in the community, not one between
company loyalists and the union but one between unionists.

Through early 1939 the BSWU was Endicott Johnson's major union antago-
nist. Although the CIO's USWA had begun organizing in some of the firm's
factories before the arrival of the BSWU (as noted earlier), the CIO's main
efforts were still being directed toward smaller shoe firms in Binghamton. By
June 1938 it had managed to obtain preferential contracts with the Gotham,
Truitt, and Ramsey shoe companies. In March and April 1939, closed shop
contracts were finally negotiated with the three firms. This accomplished,
USWA organizers were free to direct their full attention to Endicott Johnson.
With a base of 600 members gathered from the three Binghamton shops, the
USWA was in a position to utilize volunteers from the organized Binghamton
factories in its Endicott Johnson drives. An Endicott Johnson Organizing
Committee was formed soon afterward, and in the summer of 1939 the union
notified the Johnsons of its desire to establish a unit for collective bargaining
purposes.[41] Once the USWA began to pursue a more vigorous organizing
campaign at Endicott Johnson, a battle of major proportions began to take
shape between it and the AFL union.

The relationship between the BSWU and the USWA was a predictably
hostile one. Not only had the BSWU fought fratricidal wars in previous years
against the unions that amalgamated to form the USWA, but it had always,
since its birth in 1895, viewed itself as the proper representative of all shoe-

workers. In the union campaign that followed, the USWA and the BSWU cast each other in more diabolical roles than they did Endicott Johnson's management. In its journal the AFL union criticized the new CIO union as being unstable and doomed to failure. It attacked the USWA's radical militancy, displayed in the Auburn, Maine, strike, as irresponsible and detrimental to the better interest of the workers. It argued for "mutual agreement and arbitration" instead of strikes.[42]

The USWA, with a larger membership than the BSWU, viewed the latter with reciprocal contempt, believing that the BSWU behaved as little more than a company union and shirked its responsibility of organizing the unorganized. Julius Crane, an organizer of the USWA who was sent into Binghamton to take charge of the Endicott Johnson unionizing in the winter of 1938–39, addressed the second convention of the USWA in October 1939, giving this version of the rival union's motives:

> As you delegates undoubtedly know, the curse from which the Shoe Workers had been suffering all their lives whenever a militant progressive union gets into the field to organize the shoe workers, the Boot and Shoe Workers Union steps in to disrupt and split the ranks of the shoe workers. . . . It has, therefore, become the task, not only of our union, as an affiliate of the C.I.O., but of the national C.I.O. itself, to be involved in this campaign, in order to overcome the Boot and Shoe's poisonous propaganda, and to lead the Endicott Johnson shoe workers to victory for our union.[43]

Another organizer reporting on the Endicott Johnson campaign expressed similar vitriolic condemnation of the BSWU: "My opinion is, the worst enemy there is, is the Boot and Shoe and I say in conclusion that this convention if it throws all resources back of E.-J., we will lick the Boot and Shoe so damn bad they will never come up again."[44] The USWA national paper, the *CIO News* (Shoe Workers' edition), continually charged the BSWU with being a company union and with disrupting sincere organizing attempts.[45] Locally, the USWA paper, the *E-J Union News,* was filled with equally hostile charges. Letters from workers contrasted the styles of the two unions: "The CIO does not do any name calling. Instead, it talks about getting back the wage cuts while the A.F. of L. throws mud and calls E.-J. all kinds of names."[46]

Ben Berk similarly made it a point to propagandize against the CIO union, particularly harping on the theme of its association with communism. That several members of the national executive board of the USWA, as well as locally active organizers, were associated with the American Communist party provided fuel for Berk's propaganda.[47] When a delegation of BSWU workers attended a USWA meeting in Owego, New York, where Endicott Johnson operated two small shoe plants, they were surprised to find the meeting run in a democratic fashion—so thoroughly had they been convinced by Berk that the latter organization was merely a manipulated arm of the Communist party.[48] Indeed, Berk exploited the "Red" issue to his benefit on every possible occasion. He wrote John J. Mara, president of the BSWU: "I am going to have [a meeting] at the Concordia Club in Endicott. This is the Italian Club the C.I.O. was hot after but they do not want to have anything to do with those damn Communists. We will pick up alot of votes there."[49] Berk's strategy seemed to pay off. In early October 1939 he wrote to Mara: "I am pounding away at the Red issue and so far it has worked alright. We have taken several of their good men from them because of it."[50]

While the two unions kept up their internecine warfare, Endicott Johnson officers, prohibited by the NLRB from direct antiunion activities, encouraged the community antiunion drives undertaken on their behalf. The Johnsons believed that such efforts, since they were not under their direct control or initiative, would not come under the scrutiny of the NLRB. The NLRB, however, asked by Ben Berk to investigate the links between the TCCWC and the firm's management, soon decided that little distinction could be drawn between the company's antiunion activities and those of "independent" organizations. In September 1939 it ordered the corporation and the TCCWC to cease their continuing collaboration.[51]

The NLRB order put an end to the community crusade on the corporation's behalf and further restricted the firm's antiunion activities. Ironically, it proved a godsend to management since it gave the workers and the public the impression that the firm was being persecuted by the government. It cast management in the role of underdog and elicited considerable public sympathy, as this letter to the Johnsons illustrates:

> For months we have chafed and seethed at the UnAmerican muzzling of the E.J. Corporation. Weekly, vicious propaganda on printed page[s] of letters and newspapers has been thrust into our homes. We read it not because of any items of interest contained therein, but because we wanted to see how far they would go with their malicious insinuations and deliberate falsehoods. And each time we read our hearts cried out in futile rebellion "Can *this* be America—that every act of benevolence of that great company—every thotful [*sic*] deed emanating from generous hearts can be so grossly distorted, so cruelly libeled, and no one can lift their pen or voice in protest?"[52]

The antiunion campaigns of 1938 and early 1939 had recalled to the community and the workers their debt to the Endicott Johnson Corporation. For decades the corporation had built parks, paved streets, provided libraries, and funded numerous civic and charitable projects in Johnson City, Endicott, and Binghamton. For its workers the corporation had built up an elaborate welfare system, which, although somewhat scarred by the Depression, was still substantially intact. Now, "persecuted" by "outsiders"—a federal government intent on protecting the right of hostile unions to challenge what had taken "50 years to build" and by two rival unions who owed no loyalty to the community—the Johnsons sat and waited, hoping that their workers, who would ultimately make the choice, would "hold on to that which is good."[53]

III

There was no question that, by the summer of 1939, the company had won its battle against the unions—in the community. Community sentiment was overwhelmingly procompany. But the choice between the "Square Deal" and unionism was not one that the community as a whole would make. It was one left to the workers. Ultimately, the war between the company and the unions was waged on the shop floor. That was where the "Square Deal" was weakest and where the workers' sense of injustice and betrayal was strongest. That was where a victory for the unions could be won, if such a victory were possible.

The firm's wage cuts in 1938 and the continuing decline in shoe sales had reduced workers' earnings from the twenty-three to twenty-four dollars a week averages of 1935 and 1936 to about eighteen and nineteen dollars a week in 1938 and 1939.[54] Many workers were taking home less than ten dollars a week. Such meager earnings fostered a great deal of resentment among workers. Shop committees, with and without union encouragement, were established in many factory departments that had not previously shown a proclivity toward collective action. Incidents of shop floor rebellions increased: cutters in the Binghamton Busy Boys' Factory demanded the removal of a hated foreman; maintenance workers, organized by Ben Berk, threatened to strike if their pay demands were not met; cutters in the Work Shoe Factory in Binghamton sent a committee to Charles F. Johnson, Jr., to negotiate piece rate adjustments; Paracord workers struck for a pay increase.[55] Conditions in the factories had degenerated to such an extent that even the loyalty and respect that George F. Johnson normally commanded seemed to be eroding. In 1939, upon approaching striking Men's McKay Factory workers in Johnson City, who had left their jobs over a pay dispute, the aging and sickly patriarch was greeted by a mass of workers totally unresponsive to his appeals to return to work. As one CIO organizer (who would later come to regret his involvement with the union) recalled: "We was out there in the street in a body, and he went down and he parked his car in the parking lot. And he had other officials in the car with him. He tried to talk to us on the loudspeaker. Their hollerin', it was above it. It really just put him out. He drove away in tears. I really felt sorry for him that time."[56]

Both the USWA and the BSWU exploited shop floor discontent, working closely with employee committees. Ben Berk's efforts were most effective in the mechanical divisions of the firm, where he had begun his organizing work. His accounts of his relationship with shop committees suggest why, by the fall of 1939, he had managed to win over a majority of the workers in these units:

> For several weeks now the whole Die Shop has been trying to get an increase. They were tossed around and Wed. the boys just got sore and came up here for a meeting. They decided to go in the next morning and present a list of demands to the Company with the ultimatum that they get it by Thursday night or they go out on strike Friday morning. They were in the office all morning Thursday. The comm. of six men headed by [James] McCloskey made the officials sweat. They finally got Uncle George to come down and he demanded to know if Berk told them to do this. McCloskey told him I didn't tell them to do it but I did tell them the Union would back us up if they walked out and they weren't going to take anymore of his crap. He said boys for God's sake don't do anything you might be sorry for and ended up with nothing like this ever happened here before. The boys said good-bye and walked out. I went there at twelve and called a meeting in Johnson City that night. They were even more determined. The Company sent word in for the committee to have another conference Friday morning and for the men to report for work. The Comm. had another session Friday morning and when they came out without a settlement, the whole shop walked out. We had a meeting in Johnson City all Friday afternoon and while the meeting was in progress the Company sent over and asked to see the Committee. They went over about 4 o'clock and were back at 4:20 with a report that the Great E.J. had given in to their demands.[57]

While the union did not initiate this show of militancy on the part of the workers, it did lend it support. Workers who had not yet signed with the union, witnessing the success of the committee and the union, were soon won over. "There were a few men who were not signed and now we have 100%," wrote Berk to the president of the BSWU.[58] In the Johnson City Machine Shop, similar displays of militancy also surfaced.

> A committee from the J.C. machine shop under the direction of Harold Miller was pounding away at the Company for more money. They got an offer which they promptly turned down. Weds., right after work, I had a meeting with them and now there are only two men in that shop who haven't signed. All the rest did. They had their committee meet here in the office this morning and finished their counter-proposal which they will submit on Monday. They either get more money or they strike.[59]

Berk continued to "keep pushing one unit after another," while at the same time attempting to unite their disparate efforts under the umbrella of the union. He was able to convince all of his organized units to agree that "they would go out together if any one of them couldn't settle." Such an agreement undoubtedly made the company more amenable to granting concessions.[60]

By the summer of 1939 company officers, BSWU officials, and the USWA had pretty much settled the issue of an acceptable bargaining unit for a future NLRB election, an issue that had been contested and debated for months. With both the corporation and the USWA advocating a single unit, Berk gave in and abandoned his plans for either a six or a twenty-seven bargaining unit division of the corporation.[61]

From March 1938 through the summer of 1939, Berk had devoted his greatest energies toward organizing the mechanical workers. Now, faced with an election covering all 18,000 employees of the firm and with a CIO union starting to channel increasing resources to organizing the production workers, the AFL representative began to work ever harder in the factories and tanneries. He had already made some progress in these realms. In March 1939 the BSWU had opened up an office in Endicott, in order to be closer to the Endicott and Owego factory and tannery workers. Although it still drew mainly mechanical division workers to its meetings, the union was starting to make inroads into the tanneries. In fact, Berk had been attracting tannery workers, as well as Rubber Mill workers, into the union since the summer of 1938. In August of that year he filed a complaint with the United States Labor Department on behalf of both groups of workers against the company for violations of the Walsh-Healy Act, which stipulated that time-and-a-half pay should be given for overtime work on government contract jobs.[62] His efforts among the rubber and tannery workers seemed to pay off. By the summer of 1939 Berk had managed to obtain pledge cards from at least a fifth of the firm's tannery and Rubber Mill workers. In some departments such as the pressroom of the Rubber Mill, large numbers of workers had flocked into the BSWU.[63] But when Berk turned his efforts to the shoeworkers, he made far less progress. Only among small pockets of the more skilled workers, particularly cutters and lasters, was he successful—perhaps because he was able to tap their strong craft consciousness.[64]

The USWA cast a wider net than the BSWU, concentrating its organizing work mainly on the shoe factories, and waging vigorous campaigns in the firm's Owego plants, the Men's McKay and Victory factories in Johnson City, and the Endicott and West Endicott shoe factories. The union encouraged already existing worker committees and attempted to help workers create new ones. Its publication, the *E-J Union News,* contained articles in Italian, Polish, and Slovak. It brought in Italian and Slavic organizers and broadcast radio programs in various languages. Although the BSWU, in the last weeks of the union drive, followed suit and began to direct propaganda at the ethnic workers, the USWA did this as a matter of course throughout its campaign, showing a special sensitivity to the cultural obstacles that might stand in the way of organizing ethnic workers.[65]

Wherever workers rebelled against particular shop conditions or wage cuts, the USWA made it a point to step in quickly with support and publicity, a strategy also adopted by the BSWU. Numerous complaints came from the Owego plants, where the CIO union had active organizers. When lasters at the Owego No. 1 Factory demanded an increase in rates for an added operation, the *E-J Union News* publicized their demands.[66] The union also pointed out unfair practices in the cutting rooms. The following conditions were typical of those recounted in the union paper:

> During the latter part of August, two of the boys were given jobs to cut out of colored suede and it seems that they refused to cut it without first showing the foreman the condition of the stock. The condition of the stock was such that the foreman immediately took it to the superintendent. The superintendent, after looking it over, told the boys to go ahead and cut it. The boys had no alternative but to do as they were ordered. Three weeks later the foreman of the cutting room very gracefully approached the boys and sadly told them that they had some shoes to "buy"—which they had cut from this same stock.[67]

Continued difficulties in this cutting room ultimately led to a work stoppage, which the *E-J Union News* again publicized, noting the admission by Charles F. Johnson, Jr., that the factory was the "least paid factory" at Endicott Johnson.[68]

Variations in prices commonly provoked complaints throughout the factories, grievances that the USWA took pains to point out:

> The heel scourers in the Men's McKay factory get 4 cents for low heels and 5 cents for high heels. The same job in the Comfort factory pays one cent more for the same type of work, that is, 5 cents for low and 6 cents for high. In explaining to the workers this difference in prices for the same type of work, the boss over at McKay's says it is due to the difference in the grade of shoes. But the workers know that it takes the same time to scour a heel, high or low in McKay as it does in Comfort.[69]

When workers complained about low prices on jobs, the firm often transferred the work to another factory, where less resistance was expected.

> We know of the differences in prices that exist for the same shoe and the same type of work among the various factories. Work is taken from the Pioneer factory and is transferred to the Scout factory. Does the same price remain on the tags. No. Immediately without even consulting the workers, the prices are changed. The work from the Scout factory is transferred into the Workshoe factory. Again the same procedure takes place.[70]

Sometimes committees of workers successfully halted such practices. McKay Factory cutters did so in early November 1939, when an order of 1,000 cases of work was transferred to another factory. They contacted local leaders of the BSWU and the USWA, and, in a rare demonstration of unity, the two labor organizations formed a joint committee with the workers to fight this transfer. The committee confronted Charles F. Johnson, Jr., and convinced him to return the cases.[71]

Worker dissatisfaction with supervisors was the cause of a great deal of discord in the factories. In the cutting room of the Owego No. 1 Factory, tensions between workers and their foreman had reached an intense level. After a conference between the cutters and Charles F. Johnson, Jr., the latter decided to remove the hated supervisor and allow the cutters to select a foreman "of their own choosing."[72] Again and again the USWA focused on instances of shop conflict, publicized them, and encouraged the workers to unite to oppose company injustices.

Shop unity had not been a noted feature of the various stitching departments of the company, where many women were employed. The USWA understood that organizing the women shoeworkers would be a particularly difficult task. Although organizers recognized that women shoeworkers received lower wages and were "taken advantage of by the employers much more than the men workers," they found it difficult to convince many of the corporation's women of this, much less that they would be successful in getting "equal opportunities and equal pay" through organization.[73] The USWA tried hard to recruit women organizers to participate in its union drive. And indeed some women workers played active roles in the union campaign. One male organizer, working in the Men's McKay Factory in Johnson City, recalled that women and men were represented equally at USWA organizers' meetings.[74] Yet, when approached in the factory, women workers were more hostile to unionization than male workers: "Well, the women, no, they weren't quite so interested for the simple reason that the woman is not the breadwinner. . . . We got more pledge cards from the men than the women." If one looks at the number of women that the USWA's rival, the BSWU, was able to sign up, it becomes apparent that this difficulty of recruiting women characterized both unions' efforts. Of more than 2,000 surviving Local 42 pledge cards, only about 10 percent were filled out by women, although they constituted over one-third of the labor force.[75]

The USWA nevertheless did what it could. Following the same strategy it used in organizing the male departments, the USWA focused on areas of discontent and encouraged the formation of room committees, believing that a strong foundation for future union support could be built. It thus pointed out speedups in the paint-spraying department of the Sheepskin Tannery (where women were employed), unequal division of work among women employees in the treeing room of the Comfort Factory, supervisor favoritism in the fitting room of the Owego No. 1 Factory, and layoffs in the New Scout Factory.[76] The USWA brought in Frieda Casso, a member of its National Executive Board, in the hope that she might be able to appeal to the firm's women employees. In a

radio speech aired in early October 1939, she tried to address the particular
concerns that she believed were on the minds of the corporation's women
workers:

> We are the first to feel what it means not to have enough in our pay
> envelope to pay the rent, the grocery bills, to dress our families and
> ourselves. It is of first concern to us women to raise our income and the
> income of the men in our family to meet the rising cost of the necessities
> of life. . . . Only if the income of the head of the family is raised, will
> mothers and wives be able to stay at home and manage their family
> affairs. . . . Every one of us knows that we would prefer to stay at home
> and have our men folks bring enough to pay our pressing bills. How
> many working mothers would sooner remain home to take care of their
> little children, who by the way, need so badly their mother, than be
> forced to go to work in order to make ends meet. And what kind of a fair
> deal and paradise forces mothers to go to work while their children need
> them. We women work because we must help our men folks carry the
> burdens of our family.[77]

Such an appeal was clearly aimed at the women the union felt would be most
difficult to reach, married women with dependent families. These were
women who relied on and utilized most fully the corporation's welfare services—the ones who feared most the possible retraction of these services if a
union organized the corporation.

Where women organized shop committees, the union quickly stepped in
with support and publicized their courage and "spunk." When the women of
the Pioneer stitching room ceased work twice in protest over a change in shop
procedure that resulted in lower piece rates, the union heartily praised them.[78]
Effective collective protest by women stitchers in the Men's McKay Factory
received similar accolades. There, a committee formed about late October or
early November 1939 forced a change in the procedure of work distribution,
putting an end to a capricious system that fostered favoritism, jealousy, and
resentment.[79] Nonetheless, such shows of collective unity remained rare.

IV

Although both the BSWU and the USWA focused much of their attention on
shop floor grievances (the most vulnerable side of the "Square Deal"), their
ultimate enemy was the firm's paternalistic ethos itself. The USWA, more
than the BSWU, recognized that it would take time to tear down the walls of
paternalism constructed over four decades. When company and BSWU officers agreed on a speedy election in the fall of 1939, the USWA attacked the
decision:

> We are not surprised that the E.-J. Corporation wants to "get it over
> with," for every day, larger numbers of workers, slowly but surely, begin

to realize that the so-called paternalism and charitable attitude of the firm have not advanced the interests of the E.-J. workers. Every day E.-J. workers learn that the corporation's "sweet talk" and "good-will blessings" did not prevent wage cuts to follow wage cuts, while the bondholders get their dividends; do not prevent work from being transferred from one factory to another with reduction in their prices; do not prevent them from telling a worker that his services are no longer needed, regardless of how many years he or she has put in; do not prevent the medical service from being insufficient, in spite of the fact that the workers are paying a high price for it. . . . Forty-six years or more of company domination and company influence is not wiped out over night.[80]

In its conclusion the editorial was on the mark.

The days immediately preceding the union election were tense indeed. George F. Johnson, already suffering from a heart condition, had taken ill with pneumonia in late December, and daily reports on his health appeared in local papers.[81] Last-minute appeals by the CIO to delay the scheduled January 9 election, because of the probable impact of Johnson's illness on the outcome, were rejected by the NLRB.[82] Dignitaries from the BSWU and the AFL came into town to launch one last attack on their rival, the USWA. William Green, the president of the AFL, scathingly attacked the USWA on the evening of January 5, at a mass meeting attended by workers, organizers, and senior union officers. Green charged the CIO union with being a "failure, a dictatorship, and a communist-controlled group more interested in promoting a revolution and destroying American ideals than in obtaining better wages and better working conditions."[83] The CIO rebutted Green's red-baiting charges.[84] Yet the battle remained, as it had been from the first day, not essentially one between unions but one between paternalism and unionism. While the two unions got in their last-minute feuding, local clergymen preached antiunionism from their pulpits as they prayed for the health of George F. Johnson.[85]

On the evening before the election, a huge antiunion rally attended by some 8,000 workers was held in Johnson City. The *New York Times* called it a "'Strike' against Unions." Union organizers viewed it as merely another staged display of unity "encouraged by E.J. executives."[86] Whether or not the events of that night were orchestrated, on the following day the workers had an opportunity to express their true sentiments in a secret ballot. Twenty polling places in Binghamton, Johnson City, Endicott, and Owego were opened, and the "Square Deal" was put through yet another test. In the mind of one cutting room foreman, that day would always be remembered:

So the day came for the election. . . . What a time it was, oh boy. After they voted, everybody must have known what happened. I didn't know. But they all wanted to party. They went over here, and they took over the market. There was about three different factories over there in that market. And everybody got drunker than a hoot owl. That was a wild— wildest day I ever saw in my life. Women and men. Women who never took a drink in their life, they all got tight too. They had one hell of a time. There were some sorry lookin' people who came into work the next day. When it came out. They walloped the union over. . . . Well, I was surprised. I really was. I thought the best we could hope for was close, see.[87]

Of the 15,428 votes cast, the BSWU received 1,612, and the USWA received 1,079. The vote against any union representation was 12,693—80 percent of the work force.[88] In the wake of this tremendous union defeat, the workers took to the streets and celebrated.[89] The explosion of procompany sentiment seemed overwhelming indeed. Here and there, furthermore, it took on ugly features, as one pro-USWA woman worker recalled:

When we came in that day [the day after the election], this English general foreman said that I wasn't fit to work with decent people. He was talkin' right out loud, and I was gettin' scared. So then this girl came downstairs with a mob; they were comin' after me. Well, Grace—the girl that was workin' opposite me and was a friend of mine . . . her boyfriend came along and took both of us out of there ahead of the mob into his car and drove me home.[90]

The *Binghamton Sun* called the union defeat a "Victory for America" and broke its long silence over the union drives by praising the workers for their wisdom and loyalty.[91] The *Binghamton Press* claimed that the election results were a vindication of the Johnson "theory" that, "when employers go a little out of their way to aid and assist in the establishment and the maintenance of comfortable homes—to provide . . . recreation, hospitalization and medical attention at the lowest possible cost to the workman and his family—then employees in the mass and individually neither need nor desire unionization for their protection and advancement." Ultimately, concluded the *Press,* the workers were celebrating a victory of employer and employee "over doubt, cynicism, suspicion, hypothesis and formula which they demonstrated had nothing at all to do with their lives, their work and their relationships."[92]

The BSWU and the USWA failed to transform the very real discontent that existed on the shop floor into prounion sentiment. True, here and there they succeeded. In the Johnson City and Endicott machine shops, in the Foundry and Die Shop, in several tannery and Paracord divisions, and in a number of departments within the shoe factories, where shop conditions and supervisors were particularly oppressive, and where craft consciousness or work cultures were strong, the bonds between management and workers *were* severed.[93] But overall, the workers had decided that they had too much to lose in abandoning the "Square Deal," particularly when their alternatives were two unions whose motives and behavior were suspect from the start. The unions' criticism of the firm's welfarism reinforced fears, especially among the corporation's women, that company programs would be eliminated if the unions won, a possibility initially suggested by company supervisors. The feuding between the two labor organizations helped to create and sustain doubts that the unions' basic motives lay in furthering the interests of Endicott Johnson workers. It was evident, long before the election, that if the workers were losing faith in the Johnsons and the "Square Deal," they were not placing it in these two unions. According to one organizer, workers were saying, "My God, the CIO and the AF of L are both trying to get in here, and neither one of them has a good word for each other. We're rotten enough now. Why do we want to go ahead and connect ourselves with something else more rotten."[94]

But the vast majority of the workers were not losing faith in the "Square Deal." For most, the issue was a simple one: would the unions provide them with substantially more than the company? And the answer was no. Already, company officers had hinted at the restoration of wage cuts and the possibility of bonuses.[95] For those who had doubts, there was always 1933 to look back on, when the firm had indeed restored many of the wage and benefit cuts it had made in 1931 and 1932. Could they not expect management to do so again? It seemed unlikely that the unions could achieve much for the workers or that they were sincerely concerned with the workers' fate specifically. The USWA had already confessed as much in 1938 when its officers first approached the president of the firm. And John L. Lewis, in kicking off the CIO's energetic drive in the factories in the summer of 1939, had admitted in a public letter that Endicott Johnson workers were relatively well-off (yet still needed a labor union to defend them from "low-paid competitive companies").[96] Even as the unions battled on behalf of and alongside shop floor committees fighting factory abuses and price-cutting, their asserted motives and commitment to the workers continued to be questioned. The closer the date of the election came, and the louder the charges and countercharges between unions grew, the more the workers came to believe that, as Powers Hapgood admitted to delegates at the 1939 USWA convention, the real issue was which union would "be the power in the shoe industry." That was why, Hapgood declared, "this question of organizing Endicott-Johnson is the most paramount and important question that is facing the United Shoe Workers of America."[97] That was *not* the relevant question for Endicott Johnson workers.

In celebrating the defeat of the unions on the day after the election, Endicott Johnson workers demonstrated not so much their loyalty as their determination to resolve their conflicts with management outside of the context that the unions had created. The unions were and remained "outsiders" in what most workers considered a family affair. That they were useful outsiders, whose presence was exploited by the workers to extract concessions and compromises from management, is undeniable. This conclusion reemphasizes welfare capitalism's achievements and failures.

Corporate paternalism did succeed in sustaining a fundamentally personal and hermetic labor-management relationship through the Depression. Undeniably, abuses by line management and cutbacks in wages and welfare benefits eroded that relationship. The NLRB and the unions threatened to sever it. That they failed should not, however, be equated with a management "victory." As previous chapters argued, welfare capitalism entrapped both workers and managers in a relationship of mutual obligations and rights. In the depressed 1930s, to the extent that the underlying philosophy behind corporate paternalism remained alive, and it did, workers utilized external agencies — unions and federal bureaucracies — and the fear that they engendered in managers to insure that welfarism would be preserved. Where, and when, groups of workers faced major violations of the "Square Deal," mutuality was shattered and industrial conflict broke through the confines of paternalism.

Throughout the decade, but particularly in its last years, management had to walk a fine line between preserving worker loyalty and delivering profits. By invoking the legacy of the "Square Deal," and by continually branding the unions and the government as "outsiders," Endicott Johnson officers were able to preserve the idea and ideal of a "corporate family." But the price of worker "loyalty" would escalate in the 1940s, as new "outsiders" and "strangers" would pound on the walls of paternalism, and as war and a changing labor market further destabilized the corporation's paternalistic order.

NOTES

1. On George F. Johnson's view of unions and Endicott Johnson's open shop, see my dissertation, "Workers, Managers, and Welfare Capitalism: The Shoeworkers and Tanners of Endicott Johnson, 1880–1950" (Ph.D. diss., Syracuse University, 1983), 329–32.

2. George F. Johnson to Hon. James A. Farley, Apr. 24, 1937, box 15, George F. Johnson Papers, George Arents Research Library for Special Collections, Syracuse University, Syracuse, N.Y. Johnson met with Roosevelt to discuss a boycott of Italian shoe orders in response to the invasion of Ethiopia; labor matters were also brought up. *Binghamton Press*, Nov. 28, 1948.

3. George F. Johnson to Hon. James A. Farley, May 22, 1937, box 15, George F. Johnson Papers.

4. George F. Johnson to Robert F. Wagner, June 9, July 6, 1937, box 15, George F. Johnson Papers. Wagner, after some hesitation, finally agreed.

5. George F. Johnson to Rev. James W. Connerton, Aug. 18, 1937, box 15, George F. Johnson Papers.

6. George F. Johnson to E. H. Ellison, Sept. 11, 1937, box 15, George F. Johnson Papers.

7. *CIO News* (Shoe Workers' Edition), July 24, 1939.

8. George W. Johnson to George F. Johnson, Jan. 7, 1938, box 13, ser. 1, Charles F. Johnson, Jr., Papers, George Arents Research Library for Special Collections, Syracuse University, Syracuse, N.Y.

9. George F. Johnson to George W. Johnson, Jan. 10, 1938, box 15, George F. Johnson Papers.

10. Charles F. Johnson, Jr., to C. Fred Johnson, Mar. 30, 1938, box 32, ser. 1, Charles F. Johnson, Jr., Papers. "To the Workers" notice, Apr. 28, 1938, box 1, ser. 4, George W. Johnson Papers, George Arents Research Library for Special Collections, Syracuse University, Syracuse, N.Y. Welfare expenditures dropped from the $1.4 million levels of 1936 and 1937 to about $1 million in 1938. William Patrick Burns, "A Study of Personnel Policies, Employee Opinion and Labor Turnover (1930–1946) at the Endicott Johnson Corporation" (Master's thesis, New York State School of Industrial and Labor Relations, Cornell University, 1947), 51.

11. The 10 percent wage cut was made even more painful by management's decision to ask the workers to assume their share of the federal Social Security tax (amounting to another 1 percent reduction). Until then the firm had paid the workers' share. "To the Workers" notices, Jan. 31, Feb. 8, 1938, box 32, ser. 1, Charles F. Johnson, Jr., Papers.

12. Endicott Johnson Corporation Yearly Reports, 1933–38, box 23, George F. Johnson Papers.

13. George F. Johnson to Charles F. Johnson, Jr., Jan. 24, 1938, box 12, ser. 1, Charles F. Johnson, Jr., Papers.

14. In 1938 a National Labor Relations Board investigator confirmed these facts. See forthcoming discussion in text. Additional evidence on management's use of loyalty petitions may be found in Owen J. Ryall, interview by Gerald Zahavi, with the assistance of Deborah D. Maxwell, Apr. 30, 1982, tape recording (personal possession); and in "Transcript of Meeting, 1952" folder, box 2, ser. 2, Charles F. Johnson, Jr., Papers.

15. A comparison of names of workers presenting loyalty petitions in Mar. 1937 with lists of workers who filled out pledge cards for the Boot and Shoe Workers' Union in 1938 and 1939 uncovered several overlaps. Local 42 Pledge Cards, BSWU Records, State Historical Society of Wisconsin. The list of workers presenting loyalty petitions is in the printed notice "Workers Again Assure Leaders of Their Faith," in box 1, ser. 4, George W. Johnson Papers. For further evidence of the lack of seriousness with which workers viewed the petitions, see Amy King, interview by Gerald Zahavi, Nov. 30, 1979, tape recording (personal possession); and Sam Salvatore, interview by Gerald Zahavi, with the assistance of Deborah D. Maxwell, July 7, 1981, tape recording (personal possession).

16. Charles F. Johnson, Jr., to George F. Johnson, Feb. 24, 1938, box 32, ser. 1, Charles F. Johnson, Jr., Papers.

17. George F. Johnson to Charles F. Johnson, Jr., Jan. 31, 1938, box 12; Charles F. Johnson, Jr., to George F. Johnson, Feb. 7, 1938, box 32, ser. 1, Charles F. Johnson, Jr., Papers.

18. Charles F. Johnson, Jr., to George F. Johnson, Apr. 4, 1938, box 32, ser. 1, Charles F. Johnson, Jr., Papers.

19. Among the organizations were the National Assembly of Boot and Shoe Cutters (1903–13), the United Shoe Workers of America (1909–23), the Allied Shoe Workers Union (1909–23), the Amalgamated Shoe Workers of America (1923–25), the Associated Slipper Workers of New York (1928–29), the United Shoe Workers of America (1929–30), the Independent Shoe Workers Union (1929–31), the Shoe and Leather Workers Industrial Union (1929–31), the National Shoe Workers Association (1932–33), the United Shoe and Leather Workers Union (1933–37), the Brotherhood of Shoe and Allied Craftsmen (1933–). Horace B. Davis, *Shoes: The Workers and the Industry* (New York, 1940), 177.

20. Members included the National Shoe Workers Association (22,000), the Shoe Workers Protective Union (30,000), and the Shoe and Leather Workers Industrial Union (6,000). Davis, *Shoes,* 183.

21. Ibid., 183–84, 191–94.

22. Ibid., 172. On the conservatism of the union and the internal and external challenges it faced, see ibid., chap. 7; Augusta E. Galster, *The Labor Movement in the Shoe Industry, with Special Reference to Philadelphia* (New York, 1934), chaps. 7 and 9; John H. M. Laslett, *Labor and the Left: A Study of Socialist and Radical Influences in the American Labor Movement, 1881–1924* (New York, 1970), chap. 3.

23. Davis, *Shoes,* chap. 1.

24. "Calender of Important Events," NLRB Investigation folder, Local 42 files, BSWU Records. See also Maurice J. Quain, interview by Gerald Zahavi, with the assistance of Deborah D. Maxwell, June 29, 1981, tape recording (personal possession); Charles F. Johnson, Jr., to George F. Johnson, Apr. 4, 1938, box 32, ser. 1, Charles F. Johnson, Jr., Papers.

25. "George F. and His Industrial Democracy Crumbling," leaflet, [Oct. 5, 1938,] in box 4, ser. 2, George W. Johnson Papers. Another copy of the leaflet can be found in box 1, ser. 2, Charles F. Johnson, Jr., Papers.

26. A sampling of union publications and speeches can be found in box 4, ser. 2, George W. Johnson Papers; and in the Local 42 files, BSWU Records.

27. Ben Berk to George W. Johnson, telegram, Oct. 18, 1938, box 1, ser. 1, George W. Johnson Papers. Indeed, surviving pledge cards located in the BSWU Records confirm the existence of substantial support for the BSWU within the firm's mechanical divisions. Local 42 Pledge Cards, BSWU Records.

28. "Endicott Johnson Workers Daily Page," *Binghamton Sun,* Apr. 8, 1938 (capitalized in original). This statement was initially issued in May 1931, when BSWU organizers were present in the community. "Endicott Johnson Workers Daily Page," *Binghamton Sun,* May 8, 1931.

29. See, for example, *Endicott Bulletin,* Apr. 18, 1938. Johnson wrote a friend: "I have talked with all our workers now, except one factory—nearly twenty thousand people, in groups. I tell them to be cheerful and courageous, and above all things, loyal." George F. Johnson to George H. Barlow, Apr. 26, 1938, box 15, George F. Johnson Papers. For workers' recollections of his talks, see Michael P. Jerome, interview by Gerald Zahavi, May 10, 1982, tape recording (personal possession);

and Earl I. Birdsall, interview by Gerald Zahavi, May 5, 1982, tape recording (personal possession).

30. See, for example, "Loyal Hearts and Loyal Heads," *Binghamton Sun,* June 25, 1938; "Keeping the Faith," *Binghamton Sun,* July 9, 1938.

31. "Calendar of Important Events," NLRB Investigation folder, Local 42 files, BSWU Records.

32. Ibid.; Irving Bernstein, *The Turbulent Years: A History of the American Worker, 1933–1941* (Boston, 1971), 327.

33. See memoranda in NLRB Investigation folder, Local 42 files, BSWU Records.

34. Copies of the statement may be found in box 4, ser. 2, George W. Johnson Papers; and in Local 42 files, BSWU Records.

35. NLRB memorandum, "Efforts to Secure Compliance," n.d., NLRB Investigation folder, BSWU Records.

36. George F. Johnson to FDR, Nov. 1, 1938, box 15; FDR to George F. Johnson, Dec. 10, 1938, box 4, George F. Johnson Papers.

37. William Polf, "George F. Johnson and His Welfare Capitalism" (Research paper, Syracuse University, 1970), 43–44; J. Kenard Johnson to George F. Johnson, Apr. 2, 1937, box 2, George F. Johnson Papers. Information on the TCCWC can be found in box 4, ser. 2, George W. Johnson Papers. See also *Endicott Bulletin* and *Binghamton Sun* of Nov. 5, 1938, and *Endicott Bulletin,* Nov. 14, 1938, on the community antiunion campaign. A sampling of local papers from Nov. 1938 will yield the reader considerable information about the committee. See also "Warn Endicott Labor," *Business Week* 379 (Nov. 5, 1938): 35.

38. Broadside, "Are We a Bunch of Suckers?" [1938], box 3, ser. 7, George W. Johnson Papers.

39. *Binghamton Sun,* Nov. 5, Nov. 19, Nov. 28, Dec. 2, Dec. 3, Dec. 7, Dec. 12, Dec. 13, 1938; *Binghamton Press,* Dec. 2, Dec. 3, Dec. 7, Dec. 8, 1938. Just about every day, meetings and rallies were held to voice opposition to unionization of Endicott Johnson.

40. BSWU, *Proceedings of the Eighteenth Convention* (Toronto, 1939), 87–88.

41. Davis, *Shoes,* 150–51; *E-J Union News,* Sept. 9, 1939; *CIO News* (Shoe Workers' Edition), July 24, 1939; USWA, *Proceedings of the Second Convention of the United Shoe Workers of America* (Rochester, 1939), 124–25.

42. *Shoe Workers' Journal* 36 (Apr. 1937): 1; ibid. (June 1937): 2. Berk was to charge later that "there may have been some collusion . . . between representatives of the CIO group and others to defeat the aims and purposes of the Boot and Shoe Workers Union and the workers who wanted a union." *Shoe Workers' Journal* 37 (May 1941): 1. The conflicts between the BSWU and the USWA were replicated by other AFL and CIO unions. For an excellent account of these conflicts, see Walter Galenson, *The CIO Challenge to the AFL: A History of the American Labor Movement, 1935–1941* (Cambridge, Mass., 1960).

43. USWA, *Proceedings of the Second Convention,* 118

44. Ibid., 120.

45. *CIO News* (Shoe Workers' Edition), Dec. 12, 1938, May 22, Sept. 4, 1939. This is just a small sampling. Dozens of articles and editorials repeated the charge.

46. *E-J Union News,* Sept. 16, 1939. USWA officers visiting the community made it a

point to blast the AFL and the BSWU continually. Harry Sacher, chief counsel of the USWA, had this to say about the AFL and the president of the BSWU: "My experience with the American Federation of Labor has convinced me that democracy for the rank and file of workers who compose that organization is virtually dead. Government in that body does not rest upon the consent of the governed. Indeed, a handful of reactionaries in the executive council of the A.F. of L. virtually tyrannizes over the millions of workers who are to be found in the ranks of that organization. And this small handful is a source of inspiration to a number of petty tyrants who have so frequently set themselves up in the unions affiliated with the American Federation of Labor. One of these is John J. Mara, president of the Boot and Shoe Workers Union." Ibid., Oct. 2, 1939. On the BSWU response to Sacher's speech, see Ben Berk to John J. Mara, Sept. 29, 1939, Local 42 files, BSWU Records.

47. Arthur G. McDowell to Fred Shoemaker, Oct. 2, 1939, Local 42 files, BSWU Records.

48. Jerome, interview. Jerome was a laster in the Owego No. 1 Factory and was active as an organizer for the USWA between 1938 and 1940.

49. Ben Berk to John J. Mara, Sept. 29, 1939, Local 42 files, BSWU Records.

50. Ben Berk to John J. Mara, Oct. 7, 1939, Local 42 files, BSWU Records.

51. U.S. National Labor Relations Board, *Decisions and Orders of the National Labor Relations Board,* vol. 15 (Washington, D.C., 1939), 77–89. The decision was the culmination of numerous complaints brought before the NLRB by Berk. Copies of individual complaints are in Local 42 files, BSWU Records. On the ties between the Johnsons and the TCCWC, see Charles F. Johnson, Jr., to George F. Johnson, Jan. 31, 1939, box 32; George F. Johnson to Charles F. Johnson, Jr., Jan. 16, 1939, box 12, ser. 1, Charles F. Johnson, Jr., Papers.

52. Mrs. C—— et al. to George F. Johnson, George W. Johnson, Charles F. Johnson, Jr., June 10, 1940, box 4, ser. 2, George W. Johnson Papers.

53. "Hold on to that which is good" was a common expression employed by management and its supporters throughout the Depression in combatting unionization attempts. See George F. Johnson's printed speech, "I Am Willing to Work for 18,000 People, but Not for Walking Delegates" [Oct. 1934], box 1, ser. 7, George W. Johnson Papers.

54. "To the Workers" notice, Jan. 13, 1944, box 34, ser. 1, Charles F. Johnson, Jr., Papers.

55. "George F. and His Industrial Democracy Crumbling." See also various union circulars in box 32, ser. 1, Charles F. Johnson, Jr., Papers; and *Triple Cities Labor Herald,* July 29, 1938 (copy also in box 32).

56. Elmer Knowles and Audrey Knowles, interview by Gerald Zahavi, May 10, 1982, tape recording (personal possession).

57. Ben Berk to John J. Mara, Oct. 7, 1939, BSWU Records.

58. Ibid.

59. Ibid.

60. Ibid.

61. USWA, *Proceedings of the Second Convention,* 125–26. Correspondence relating to negotiations for an acceptable bargaining unit may be found in Local 42 files, BSWU Records.

62. Ben Berk to all tannery and rubber workers, Aug. 21, 1939, Local 42 files, BSWU Records; *Triple Cities Labor Herald,* Mar. 24, 1939 (in box 3, ser. 7, George W. Johnson Papers); Lee F. Springer, interview by Gerald Zahavi, with the assistance of Deborah D. Maxwell, July 15, 1981, tape recording (personal possession).

63. Local 42 Pledge Cards, BSWU Records. Information on the size of particular units came from factory lists in box 7, ser. 2, Frank A. Johnson Papers, George Arents Research Library for Special Collections, Syracuse University, Syracuse, N.Y. The 20 percent figure is a minimum, based on pledge cards located in the BSWU Records. If substantial numbers of cards were lost or missing, a real possibility, the proportion of workers who pledged for the union would have to be revised upward.

64. Local 42 Pledge Cards, BSWU Records. About 25 percent of the factory workers who filled out pledge cards were involved in cutting or lasting operations. In some cases the BSWU was able to sign up a substantial proportion of a particular department. In the Pioneer Factory cutting room, it obtained pledge cards from at least half of the cutters. See caveat in n. 63 above on the interpretation of the pledge cards.

65. Unfortunately, it is not possible to measure the relative appeal of the BSWU and the USWA to ethnic workers, since no membership data was available for the USWA as it was for the BSWU local. With respect to the BSWU, however, based on surnames appearing on BSWU pledge cards, one can tentatively conclude that ethnics with southern and eastern European surnames were as attracted or repelled by the BSWU as workers with Anglo- and northern European surnames. No significant patterns along ethnic lines were discernible. Local 42 Pledge Cards, BSWU Records.

66. *E-J Union News,* Sept. 25, 1939. Apparently, to the discouragement of the union, "the bed-lasters settled their differences and went back to the old way again." Ibid., Oct. 2, 1939.

67. Ibid., Sept. 25, 1939. The term "buy" refers to the practice of forcing workers to purchase their poorly made shoes at a wholesale price. This practice appears to have been in force only in the Owego factories and not throughout the company.

68. Ibid., Nov. 13, 1939.

69. Ibid., Oct. 23, 1939.

70. Ibid., Oct. 2, 1939. See also King, interview; and Mary Seversky, interview by Gerald Zahavi, with the assistance of Deborah D. Maxwell, July 22, 1982, tape recording (personal possession), concerning this practice.

71. *E-J Union News,* Nov. 13, 1939.

72. Ibid., Nov. 27, Dec. 4, 1939.

73. Ibid., Nov. 20, 1939.

74. Knowles, interview. Knowles acknowledged, however, that no woman organizer was active in the Men's McKay Factory.

75. Ibid.; Local 42 Pledge Cards, BSWU Records. Another USWA organizer, active in the Owego No. 1 Factory, felt that attempting to get the women to fill out pledge cards was so futile, he did not even try: "I wouldn't ask them, to tell you the truth. They knew. So if it came to a vote, they would know how to vote." Jerome, interview.

76. *E-J Union News,* Oct. 23, Oct. 30, Nov. 20, Dec. 4, 1939.

77. Ibid., Oct. 30, 1939. The address was delivered on Oct. 2, 1939.

78. Ibid., Dec. 11, Nov. 20, 1939.

79. Ibid., Nov. 13, Nov. 27, 1939. Another committee in the Fine Welt stitching room in Endicott accomplished the same change in the distribution of work. Ibid., Nov. 20, 1939.

80. Ibid., Oct. 30, 1939.

81. See *Endicott Bulletin* and the *Binghamton Sun* from Dec. 26, 1939, to Jan. 9, 1940.

82. *Binghamton Sun,* Jan. 5, 1940.

83. Ibid., Jan. 6, 1940, 1. See also *Binghamton Press,* Jan. 6, 1940.

84. *Binghamton Press,* Jan. 8, 1940.

85. H——, interview by David Nielson, June 23, 1973, transcript, 11; Springer, interview.

86. *New York Times,* Jan. 9, 1940; *Binghamton Press,* Jan. 9, 1940. One worker who took part in the march later recalled: "I remember being on a parade one day against them [the unions]. They asked us to go out and parade against it, so out we went." F——, interview by David Nielson, Aug. 3, 1973, transcript, 105.

87. Thomas K. Chubbuck, interview by Gerald Zahavi, with the assistance of Deborah D. Maxwell, session 2, July 2, 1981, tape recording (personal possession).

88. On the election, see *Endicott Bulletin,* Jan. 9, 1940; *Binghamton Sun,* Jan. 10, 1940; *Binghamton Press,* Jan. 10, 1940. The defeat of the unions was widely carried in the national press. See *New York Times,* Jan. 10, 1940; *Time,* Jan. 22, 1940.

89. *Binghamton Press,* Jan. 10, 1940. See also *New York Times,* Jan. 11, 1940.

90. Margaret Azarin [pseud.], interview by Gerald Zahavi, Nov. 15, 1983, tape recording (personal possession).

91. *Binghamton Sun,* editorial, Jan. 11, 1940. The paper, because it was partially owned by George F. Johnson, had been told to keep silent about the unions by the E.J. Legal Department after the NLRB order of 1938.

92. *Binghamton Press,* Jan. 10, 1940.

93. Local 42 Pledge Cards, BSWU Records; Springer, interview; Jerome, interview; Knowles, interview; USWA, *Proceedings of the Second Convention,* 122.

94. Knowles, interview.

95. Internal memorandum, "Workers Vote against Any Union Affiliation," Local 42 files, BSWU Records. See also interviews with workers quoted in "George F. Built Shoes and Villages," *Sun-Bulletin,* Oct. 17, 1977.

96. John L. Lewis to the Shoe Workers of the Triple Cities, c/o Local 141, USWA, June 28, 1939; copy of letter is in *CIO News* (Shoe Workers' Edition), July 24, 1939. Another copy also appears in the *E-J Union News,* Sept. 9, 1939. Powers Hapgood, director of the USWA, in a radio address delivered on July 6, 1939, reiterated Lewis's point and assured Endicott Johnson employees that the cordial relations built up between workers and management would not be disturbed by the union—that cooperation could exist between the USWA and management. See text of Hapgood's speech in above issue of *CIO News* (Shoe Workers' Edition).

97. USWA, *Proceedings of the Second Convention,* 127.

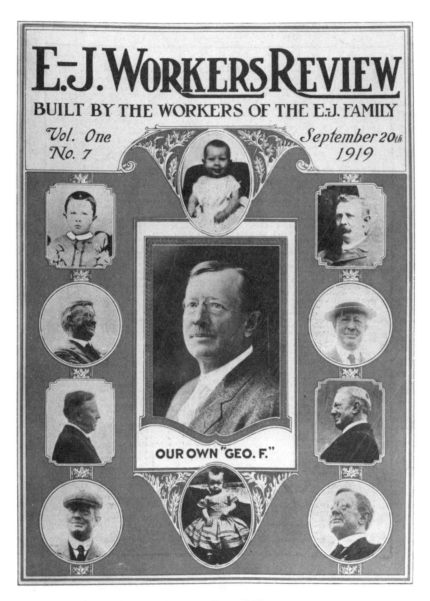

Front cover of *E.-J. Workers' Review* 1 (Sept. 1919).

Father "George F.," who lived in a shoe,
Had so many children, he didn't know what to do;
He gives them all work that they might earn their "bread"
And they have his best wishes for good luck ahead.

Back cover of *E.-J. Workers' Review* 1 (Apr. 1919).

Corporate pageantry. Workers celebrating the coming of the eight-hour day and paying tribute to George F. Johnson and Henry B. Endicott (1916). George F. Johnson Papers.

May Day celebration (1934), Endicott Johnson style—one of numerous parades sponsored by the corporation to celebrate the "Square Deal." George F. Johnson Papers.

The Endicott Johnson Workers Public Market (1937). Photograph by Russell C. Aikins, in *Partners All*, 71.

One of two arches erected just after World War I as a tribute to labor-management cooperation and in celebration of the firm's adoption of a profit-sharing plan. George F. Johnson Papers.

Company-built houses, Endicott (1937). Photograph by Russell C. Aikins, in *Partners All*, 42.

Wading pool in Ideal Park, Endicott—one of several swimming pools built by the corporation (1927). George F. Johnson Papers.

One of two recreation centers built by the Endicott Johnson Corporation in 1949. George F. Johnson Papers.

Workers celebrating the defeat of the BSWU and the USWA in the January 1940 NLRB election. Courtesy of the Binghamton Press Company.

7

Rebellion and Restoration

Welfare capitalism, Endicott Johnson style, had once again proven itself, surviving depression, prolabor government policies, and a major union threat. The "Square Deal" had always been most vulnerable where it was weakest, on the shop floor, and that is where its challengers struck most effectively. Yet the concrete walls of corporate paternalism held, demonstrating a versatility that its critics learned to take seriously, if not respect. It would be wrong, nonetheless, to ignore that Endicott Johnson's paternalistic order had also suffered erosion. An ailing and bitter patriarch less willing to defend welfarism against profit-hungry stockholders, a labor force more prone to work stoppages and strikes, a management less inhibited in its use of coercion and intimidation, as well as a new and important government role in labor-management relations were signs that the "Square Deal" was and would be transformed and diluted—from within and from without.

In the 1940s, a decade of war, escalating worker expectations, and militant unionism, outside forces would continue to undermine the strength of paternalism. The Depression, even though it had imposed strong pressure on labor-management relations at Endicott Johnson, had also reinforced the inward-turning, psychologically enveloping tendencies of the "Square Deal," characteristics that helped to define and deflect the assaults of "outsiders." But the social and economic realities of the 1940s operated in just the opposite direction and tended to open wider those fissures that emerged in paternalism in the previous decade. Only the coming of the cold war and the branding of paternalism's enemies as subversive and management's willingness to restore and expand retracted elements of the "Square Deal" were able to preserve welfare capitalism and Endicott Johnson's open shop.

I

Yes, as the January 1940 election demonstrated, the "Square Deal" had once again proven itself. But loyalty always expected a return; and this management was lax in delivering. Feeling somewhat overconfident in "their" margin of victory over the unions, Endicott Johnson managers were slow to raise wages, redress shop floor grievances, or restore the benefits that they had promised would be forthcoming if the workers only demonstrated their loyalty. In the months following the election, wages continued to stay low, and many of the factory conditions that aroused workers' ire persisted. Workers who had voted against the unions in the hope that the Johnsons would reward their loyalty were sorely disappointed. One employee, in a letter that appeared in the local USWA paper, expressed a sentiment that seemed to be spreading among fellow laborers:

> In the last campaign I was non-union, believing that the unfavorable situation that prevailed in E-J was temporary. I must admit that I was mistaken. Conditions get from bad to worse. . . . Many of my fellow workers who were promised that we would be taken care of if there was no union were insulted with a measly five cents an hour raise. It was just like throwing a dog a bone. The only reason that they gave us that was because they know there was a lot of union activity in the mechanical departments and they were afraid that we non-union workers would join the union. But they can't buy me for a lousy five cents, and I know that there are others who feel the same way.[1]

When it became clear to workers that wage and shop improvements were not forthcoming from management, many turned on the firm. In the summer of 1940 several groups went out on strike. The lasters of the West End Victory Factory initiated a work stoppage in late July 1940. At first management faced the lasters' exhibition of rebelliousness with confident inflexibility. But repeated work stoppages in August 1940 led to a compromise.[2] More surprising than this act of rebellion on the part of Victory Factory lasters (who had long held a reputation for their independence and solidarity) and a more significant barometer of growing dissatisfaction with management was the show of force by the stitchers of the Victory Factory in late August 1940. On August 22 the local USWA paper, the *Labor News,* reported that the "entire stitching room in the West End Victory Factory quit work. This action," the paper went on to note, "was the workers' protest against the firing of Forelady Pearl Riley, who, temporarily, has not been working because of illness." The workers, angry at their superintendent for Riley's firing, were conveying a message to management: it was their right to be consulted on such matters.[3]

Elsewhere, similar protests over shop conditions were taking place. Comfort Factory lasters protested the firing of fellow workers. In the Boys and Youths Factory, cutters "went to town against their foreman in a creditable show of unity." Workers in the Sunrise Factory abandoned their machines in protest over the transfer of work to another factory. One former USWA activist who had almost been attacked by a mob of fellow women workers after the January election, recalled this very different scene at the Sunrise Factory in the summer of 1940: "Then one day . . . I saw another mob comin' down. Well! I'll tell you I picked up an iron bar and thought the first one that comes near me I'm gonna kill. Because I had nobody there. My back was to the wall—I just turned my back to the wall and stood there. [Pause] They were dissatisfied with working conditions and they were walking out!! And this was just a few months later. . . . There was a walkout!"[4] Paracord workers struck in the fall of 1940, apparently over wages.[5] The Paracord strike may well have recalled to management that it had made promises to workers that it was not fulfilling, for on November 12, 1940, the company partially restored the 5 percent wage deduction it instituted in 1938 to cover the cost of the Medical Department.[6]

The partial restoration of the medical deduction was not enough to put a halt to workers' discontent. In January 1941 an "epidemic of strikes" hit Endicott Johnson, affecting the Upper Leather Tannery, the Fine Welt Factory, the Scout Factory, and the Misses' and Children's Factory.[7] Yet such displays of militancy were not being channeled into prounion sentiment, even though union challengers had finally established a united front.

In the weeks and months following the defeat of the BSWU and the USWA, a consolidation of forces was effected in the Triple Cities. The BSWU withdrew from the area, leaving only the CIO's USWA to continue organizing work. The USWA recognized that the feuding of the two unions had hardly helped matters and began to mend fences. Officers of the CIO Endicott Johnson Organizing Committee met with the former president of the BSWU local, Emlyn C. Hughes, and worked out an alliance, forming a new CIO local, Local 177. Abandoned by the national leadership of the BSWU, many of the more active members of the AFL local joined the new CIO organization.[8]

With the withdrawal of the BSWU, a spirit of unity was born. The new CIO local's paper, the *Labor News,* noted: "There is an air of quiet optimism in CIO headquarters these days when former AFL men mingle in a friendly fashion with their CIO brothers."[9] One worker wrote into the union paper: "Is it really true the two locals of the AFL and the CIO are together? It's hard to believe but it certainly warmed my heart."[10] While some AFL holdouts continued to petition the BSWU leadership to return and make a second attempt at organizing, it was all in vain. The national leadership showed little interest in expending any more of its resources on what it believed to be a losing cause.[11]

Although union organizers made slow progress in recruiting new members, continuing signs of worker dissatisfaction with management sustained their hopes that the shoeworkers would ultimately see the light and join the CIO. The *Labor News* took every opportunity to point out to employees their need for a strong, united labor organization through which they could bargain with management on a firmer foundation than the "Square Deal" permitted. But for the most part, Endicott Johnson workers seemed content to deal with managers without the unions, although they recognized that the presence of the USWA "encouraged" company officers to be attentive to worker demands. Indeed, feeling the pressure of continuing union attacks and the persistence of shop floor reaction, the corporation finally restored wage cuts in April and June 1941.[12] In late 1941 management went even further to appease the workers. It reinstituted five paid holidays and distributed lump-sum payments for the previous year's holidays.[13] The USWA, naturally enough, claimed that the firm's concessions were responses to union pressure: "The Five Paid Holidays which E-J has granted to you were given only because E-J feared the union and because E-J realizes that many workers are now joining the CIO."[14] There was a great deal of truth in their boast. But it was equally true that the coming of World War II and improved economic conditions had also made it easier for management to make such concessions.

II

Growing military expenditures and a flood of foreign orders for scarce consumer goods stimulated American industry and pulled it out of depression. Between June 1940 and the end of 1941, the number of unemployed nationwide had fallen from eight and a half million to under four million. At Endicott Johnson sales increased by 22 percent between 1940 and 1941 and continued to remain strong throughout the war years. Reflecting the national trend, employment opportunities in the shoe firm also increased. Between 1940 and 1941 the labor force grew from an average of 17,041 to an average of 18,339. But the company was careful not to take on the additional obligations associated with hiring new workers. As it had before, the corporation hired employees on a "temporary basis" with the "understanding that when there was no longer work for them to do, they would be released." Furthermore, the firm made it clear to new workers that they were not entitled to medical services or permitted to join the Sick Relief Association.[15]

With the entry of the United States into war in December 1941, the firm found it increasingly difficult both to hold on to old workers and to recruit new workers to meet its production needs. By the end of 1941 labor turnover at Endicott Johnson was rapidly increasing. It would continue to do so well into 1943. Separation rates rose from an average of less than 1 percent a month in 1940 to between 4 and 5 percent a month in 1942 and 1943. During the same period the shoe industry in general experienced comparable increases (as did numerous other industries). Yet while separation rates doubled in the 1942–46 period for the industry as a whole, at Endicott Johnson they rose more than fourfold. In the early years of the war, the upturn was even more dramatic, approximating an eight- or ninefold rise.[16] Not only did the firm face competition from higher-paying industries involved in war production that lured shoeworkers away, but with the declaration of war, military induction further depleted the company's labor force. Charles F. Johnson, Jr., noted in November 1942:

> Everything is going along as well as could be expected here, except things are tightening up a little more all the time and it is getting more difficult to take care of our customers' requirements. About 2,000 E.J. boys are already in the service and more are leaving all the time. We have also lost quite a few workers who have quit their jobs to go elsewhere to work where, at least temporarily, they can earn more money. In the total we have about 1,500 less people on the payroll now than at the beginning of the year and our production is down about 15%.[17]

Labor-shortage problems continued to plague management throughout 1942 and 1943. In a letter sent out to factory superintendents in the spring of 1943, Charles F. Johnson, Jr., reemphasized that "manpower is our major problem and will continue to get more serious as the war continues."[18] In an attempt to alleviate labor shortages, the corporation tapped kinship networks, much as it had during World War I. Managers made it known to employees that relatives of theirs could easily obtain jobs in the firm, and hoped they would pass the message along.[19]

In the Depression the workers had been dependent on the firm for relief, for work, for survival. Now, it was becoming clear that the relationship of dependency was reversed. This situation was not lost on the workers. The recollections of one cutting room foreman suggest the psychological changes that the war ushered in. He recalled an episode involving eight men in his room who were "drunks." In the prewar years he was able to scare the men effectively into abstinence on the job. But the war changed all that: "I didn't have one trouble with them until the war started. And that blew the hat off. Every damn one of the eight went all to hell cause they thought the war was on and I wouldn't fire them cause I wouldn't be able to get help."[20] The men were wrong in this case: all were replaced by cutters recruited from outside the firm. But their changed behavior, attributed by the foreman to the war's impact, probably represented a more general change in attitude taking place among the workers.

An increasing sense of power and rebelliousness was also reflected in a growing tendency of workers to join together to restrict output. Responding to speedups initiated by company managers during the labor-starved years of World War II, workers banded together and agreed among themselves to limit production in order to protect their rates and prevent overwork. So widespread had this practice become that management felt compelled to warn the workers against "stinting":

> Limiting work to a maximum amount, (commonly called "stinting"), is fundamentally wrong and could prove extremely harmful to the workers

and to the business. Straight piecework gives every man and woman not only a right, — but we think it entirely best that they do all they are willing and able to do, when there is plenty of work. This note is intended to encourage you and urge you to do exactly that.[21]

Throughout the firm, workers grew ever more stubborn and unwilling to accept the fiats of management. The same foreman who had to contend with rebellious "drunkards" soon faced obstinate cutters unwilling to cut leather on which they could not "make their rates." He was forced to accept their refusal and looked elsewhere for cutters willing to cut the leather.[22]

The war not only affected the attitudes of the workers, it also introduced institutional structures that provided workers with opportunities to bypass the firm's traditional and informal arbitration procedures that lay at the core of the "Square Deal." While it is true that, since the creation of the NLRB and the encouragement of collective bargaining by the federal government, Endicott Johnson employees had been provided with such opportunities, the war gave them greater access to machinery with which their grievances could be aired and acted upon. The National War Labor Board (NWLB), created in 1942 by executive order and designed to minimize strikes and work stoppages by providing an arbitration mechanism for both formally and informally organized workers, threatened to replace the individual and committee appeals to company supervisors. Shop floor committees had been utilized by the firm's employees in former decades and had preserved personal links between managers and workers. The NWLB, however, through related and subordinate Labor Department agencies such as the United States Conciliation Service, provided Endicott Johnson workers alternatives to direct bargaining with managers. Various groups of workers, both with and without union encouragement, took advantage of these alternatives to resolve disputes over wages in the 1940s. If management felt secure in the knowledge that the shoeworkers had rejected unionization, the willingness of various groups of workers to call upon government agencies to intercede in labor disputes must have given company officers reason to doubt their security.

Since the "Little Steel Formula" of September 1942, when wage increases were limited by the NWLB and exceptions could only be granted by appeal to the board, the volume of requests for wage increases grew tremendously. Appeals from Endicott Johnson employees who had been unable to obtain satisfactory wage adjustments from management made their way through the bureaucracy of the federal government, generally being resolved by the United States Conciliation Service under instruction by the NWLB.[23] In January 1943 a dozen "Tongue on Vamp" operators in the West End Victory Factory quit work and demanded an increase in their base pay. The workers, dissatisfied with offers made by management, sought out a lawyer and took their case to the United States Conciliation Service. The government arbitrator finally reached a compromise settlement in September of that year.[24] Similar appeals to the Conciliation Service were made by Security and Fair Play Factory lasters, by Scout Factory heel scourers, by Boys and Youths and Pioneer Factory stitchers, by Fine Welt Factory edge stitchers, by West End Victory "stitched edge" operators and vampers, by Challenge Factory Goodyear stitchers, and by Victory Factory cutters.[25] In some cases, as with the lasters of the Security and Fair Play factories, appeals to the Conciliation Service were made with union encouragement and legal support.[26]

Thus, new government bureaucracies undermined the "Square Deal" by offering alternatives to workers. Lawyers and federal investigators constituted threatening intermediaries in what had previously been "family" affairs. And yet the most serious threat to corporate paternalism remained the unions, as subsequent events would demonstrate.

III

Some time in 1941 a strategic decision was made by the USWA and its trade union ally, the International Fur and Leather Workers Union (IFLWU), of the CIO, that unionization attempts should be concentrated on certain divisions of the corporation and not on the firm as a whole, in particular on divisions that had formerly proven themselves to be somewhat sympathetic to the idea of unionization. The IFLWU, one of the more radical of the CIO unions and headed by strong and popular communist leadership, soon stepped in and began organizing in the Endicott tanneries and adjacent maintenance departments, while the USWA continued its work among the rubber- and shoeworkers in Binghamton and Johnson City.[27]

The IFLWU initiated its drive by contacting Endicott Johnson workers who were formerly employed in various Pennsylvania tanneries and who had been active in union campaigns in the past, men whom it believed would form an effective nucleus of organizers. Those in whom the IFLWU placed its hopes, men like John O'Green, Elmer Backes, and Leo Gleason, all skilled rollers and loyal unionists, would indeed prove to be successful organizers.[28]

The initial organizing work at Endicott Johnson was under the direction of Myer Klig, a Russian-born Canadian organizer who had a good track record in unionizing open shops.[29] Klig ran a careful and methodical campaign, taking on the tanneries one by one, department by department. Additional organizers were brought in from Pennsylvania to help with the work and to insure that every tannery worker was approached.[30]

As had been the case in former unionizing attempts, the corporation's management conducted a vigorous campaign against the union. Threats were exchanged on both sides, and occasional fist fights broke out in the shops. According to Klig, "Many workers were intimidated and openly threatened by foremen and company stooges. The Company violated every provision of the National Labor Relations Act."[31] But unionists were quite willing and able to fight intimidation with intimidation, as the superintendent of the Sole Leather Tannery recalled:

> There was a lot of meetings of the workers along with some of the so-called union people. . . . And then we would hold meetings after hours with some of the workers. I recall this one. . . . It was about seven-thirty in the evening. It was dark. I came back from the Upper Leather beam-house, back to my dressing room in the Sole Leather, changed my clothes and started out. This guy hollered at me, but he was in the dark. So I went back, and he said, "I consider you a friend of mine, and I want to tell you this. They're gonna get you." 'Cause I was against the unions. And I said, "That doesn't scare me. I don't know why, but it doesn't." And I was threatened.[32]

Despite the threats, violence, and intimidation that marked the organizing campaign of the union—on both sides—workers flocked into the newly formed Endicott Leather Workers Union, Local 285 of the IFLWU. After approximately a year of organizing tannery and maintenance workers in Endicott, the union had managed to obtain signed pledge cards from 1,600 of the approximately 2,200 workers employed in its targeted departments, although only 330 of these represented initiated, paying members.[33]

Facing the prospect of a union victory, management appealed to the NLRB to dismiss the proposed bargaining unit as inappropriate since the corporation was operating an integrated manufacturing enterprise of which the tanneries and maintenance departments were an important part, inseparable from the other divisions. The board, however, accepted the IFLWU's arguments that the units involved comprised a "homogeneous group" and called for a union election.[34]

The union won the December 1942 election, but just barely. Of the 1,988 votes cast, the IFLWU received 1,037, while 951 workers voted against union representation. Military induction had been partially responsible for eroding the union's support. Many of the workers who had signed pledge cards had been drafted. Others had left for more lucrative jobs in war industry plants.[35] Furthermore, some workers decided, at the last minute, that they would rather stick with the company, particularly since 1942 had been a year filled with wage increases and benefit restorations. The company seemed, to them, to be living up to the "Square Deal." Yet a majority still voted for the union, in spite of company concessions and, significantly, despite the communist affiliations of the union's leadership. As one local union officer, a practicing and devout Catholic, recalled, "They were wise enough and shy enough to keep Communism in the background."[36]

In 1942, of course, communists were not viewed with the same contempt as they had been in former years. When the Non-Aggression Pact between the Soviet Union and Germany was abruptly terminated by Barbarossa in June

1941 and the Russians joined the allies, it suddenly became less problematic to be affiliated with the Communist party (although party members continued not to publicize their party affiliation). It also became less difficult to ward off the attempts of red-baiters seeking to discredit a union by pointing to the presence of communists in its leadership or among organizers. More important, the political agenda of the union's leadership only tangentially touched local events. IFLWU organizers, like their counterparts among the United Electrical Workers (UE), another left-wing union, were first and foremost involved in the daily routine of creating a union local; they were not primarily concerned with bringing the Bolshevik revolution to Endicott.[37]

By focusing on relatively homogeneous segments of the work force, almost totally male, that were concentrated in a small area in Endicott and that had developed relatively strong and independent work cultures, the IFLWU had been able to break through the walls of paternalism. The vote, however, was not overwhelmingly prounion. The election had been a close one and indicated that the union would need to work hard to maintain and enlarge its support if it expected to survive. The election victory was only the beginning of a struggle, not the end.

Nonetheless, the IFLWU had managed to win—no small achievement. It became the first labor organization to unionize Endicott Johnson workers successfully. And while a large minority of the tannery workers remained skeptical of this "outside" intruder, it was slowly establishing its credibility among many of them. By May 1943, as Myer Klig noted in a report to the General Executive Board of the IFLWU, Local 285 had received initiation fees from 1,700 workers, "with the overwhelming majority of them paying dues regularly."[38]

The progress made by Local 285 in its early years of existence seemed to promise a bright and expansive future. The growth in membership came hand in hand with successes in collective bargaining. In agreements negotiated with the firm in 1943 and 1944, some of which were appealed and finally decided by the NWLB, the union won for its members wage increases, job security, seniority rights, a formal job bidding procedure, an enlargement of paid vacation benefits, and a guarantee that management would consult with the union before it made drastic changes in the firm's medical service—a potentially major point since it gave the union some say in the administration of corporate welfare programs. It further obtained a maintenance-of-membership clause in its contract, a standard union security provision that the NWLB offered to unions agreeing to abide by a no-strike pledge during the war.[39] To the nearly 400 members of the local who had entered employment with the firm after September 1940 and who were denied access to the firm's relief and medical services because of their status as "temporary workers," the union promised to continue pressuring the company to grant equal benefit rights. With the union publicizing this inequity, company officers soon realized that the ill will produced by continuing to define new workers as "temporary" employees and to deny them benefits would only add to the union's strength and perhaps even convince the unorganized shoeworkers that they needed union protection. In June 1943, therefore, the company announced that new workers who had been with the firm for at least six months could now join the Sick Relief Association. A year later, having lost as many as 5,000 workers to the military and to other firms, the corporation further announced that access to the Medical Department would no longer be denied to new employees as it had been since September 1940.[40] While the firm never acknowledged union pressure as a factor motivating these reversals in policy, the union took credit for the corporation's restoration of benefits. Indeed, in the minds of many workers it was clear that the presence of the union was behind these and other concessions.[41]

The growing prestige of the local through 1943 and 1944 represented the union's success in fulfilling worker expectations. Where, in the past, informal committees of workers had to confront managers directly in order to obtain concessions, a process that was limited by the small size of the groups involved, employees now challenged corporate officers with the secure knowledge that 1,600 fellow union members stood behind them. Indeed, the union's successes in 1943 and 1944 taught many workers that there were more effective ways of negotiating with management than under the aegis of the "Square Deal."

It was also true, however, that, notwithstanding the union's growing credibility, the workers' allegiance to it varied considerably. For the vast majority the union represented merely another vehicle for the airing of complaints and for extracting higher wages and benefits from management. They were not transformed into staunch unionists. Workers like Sam Salvatore, for example, joined the union with a casual attitude that hardly reflected strong prounion convictions. He recalled his reply to a union organizer who approached him after his return from service: "They came to me and said, 'Sam, you've got to join the union.' I said, 'I don't need no union. . . . What the heck a union's gonna do for me?' 'Oh, we're gonna get you pay, you know, we're gonna get you' this and that. . . . 'And besides,' he says, 'you don't have to pay nothing to get in.' 'Why not?' 'Oh, we do that for the veterans.' 'Well,' I said, 'if it don't cost me nothing, put me in then.' "[42]

For other workers, however, the union was a focus of commitment and loyalty. Some of the most active members of the local had a history of union involvement. Lee F. Springer, a mechanical department employee, for example, had been active as an organizer in Pennsylvania in the United Mine Workers. He had participated in the 1938–40 organizing drive at Endicott Johnson and served as the financial secretary of Local 42 of the BSWU. His involvement with the IFLWU, as a vice president and an executive board member of Local 285, was both predictable and natural. Similarly, Elmer

Backes, who had been fired from a tannery in Elkland, Pennsylvania, for his CIO union work in 1937, found himself once again involved in union activity and was elected chief steward of the Sole Leather Tannery. Like many of the local's officers, who had been formerly involved in unions, he brought with him from Pennsylvania a distrust of management and an equal affinity for labor organizing.[43]

Union activists were also drawn from second-generation Endicott Johnson workers and from long-time employees of the firm who felt betrayed by corporate officers and who believed that the "Square Deal" was no longer being adhered to. For them it seemed all too clear that the Johnsons who now controlled the firm, George W. Johnson and Charles F. Johnson, Jr., were cut from a different cloth than was the firm's now retired and ailing patriarch, George F. Johnson. The elder Johnson, they believed, had been a sincere benefactor, one who could balance his drive for profits with a genuine willingness to share some of those profits with his workers. But to the "younger" generation of Johnsons who now occupied the helm of the corporation (George W. Johnson was sixty-two and Charles F. Johnson, Jr., was fifty-five in 1942), generosity did not come naturally. It required the pressure of the union to prod them to live up to their obligations to the workers. As one second-generation Italian worker, who became quite active in the union, recalled:

> He [George F. Johnson] knew what your family was doing, what your family wasn't doing. But he was more lenient than George W. or Charlie or some of the other Johnsons. . . . He was the kind of guy that if you went to him and told him, "I can't live this way . . . I'll have to get out . . . ," he found a way. He'd find a different job for you, or he'd give you a raise in pay. He was that kind of a guy. He was that more generous than his son or his nephew. They were bullies, and they took a bully attitude toward you.[44]

Beyond the Johnsons' failure to respond effectively to such discontent with their regime, shop floor issues and dissatisfaction with immediate supervisors encouraged workers to join the union. One tanner, who became a union steward, felt that the greatest service the union provided him was allowing him to bid on a job he had been unfairly denied several times. "The bosses put a lot of fellows in ahead of people who was there longer," he recalled.[45] Although the corporation prided itself on its policy of internal promotions, the policy was not being applied honestly or fairly.[46] Resentment over unfair promotion decisions and job bidding procedures often precipitated shop floor reactions both before and after the union's involvement. But under a union contract, workers were afforded a clear and concise mechanism for resolving such disputes.[47]

For all of Local 285's success in enlarging its membership, however, the union remained vulnerable. During the war it had to negotiate a fine line between trade union militancy and a war-imposed conservatism. Communist IFLWU organizers like John H. Russell and Oscar Oberther, along with the national leadership of the union, often found themselves inhibiting the militancy of some of the workers. Throughout the war years the IFLWU, in following both CIO and Communist party policies, adhered to a no-strike pledge.[48] When the oil hangers in the Sole Leather Tannery quit work and forced a shutdown on August 12, 1943, for example, the union acted quickly to get the workers back on the job. The corporation's legal counsel, Howard A. Swartwood, sent a telegram to IFLWU headquarters in New York City. Two and a half hours later, Myer Klig replied stating that the workers had been ordered to return to work and that they had complied.[49] When the jack rollers of the Upper Leather Tannery struck on October 27, 1944, in violation of the no-strike provisions of the contract, the union again acted swiftly. Led by a renegade steward, ten rollers walked off the job, ignoring the collective bargaining provisions of the union contract. The union responded by ordering the men to go back to work, but they refused. When the company demanded further action on the part of the union, Rush Dunn, the local's president, pointed out that only three of the eleven men involved were union members and that the union steward who led the walkout had already been replaced. Dunn agreed to further disciplinary measures, as long as they were taken "without discrimination because of union membership."[50] Consistently during the war years, IFLWU organizers and national officers attempted to hold the line on wildcat strikes.[51] Union discipline, however, did serve to frustrate and alienate some workers.

But this was not the main source of the union's vulnerability. If the union was not militant enough for some workers, it was also true that there was no other organization to which they could turn. For better or worse they were forced to stick with the union. More problematic and a far greater threat to the continuing progress of the local was the destabilization of its leadership and membership by the high rate of labor turnover during the war. While the war brought in many prounion workers who had not developed an attachment to the firm and to the firm's managers and who had not been influenced favorably by the corporation's paternalism, it also siphoned out many activists. Some, who viewed the union mainly as a vehicle for economic self-betterment, might be lured away by more attractive jobs; if better opportunities became available in other firms, they left the corporation and the union. And, of course, the draft took its toll. It was difficult to maintain strong leadership where workers came and went. Furthermore, periodic hide shortages during the war decreased the need for tannery workers in many departments, leading to cuts in the tannery labor force. When this occurred, workers were transferred to the factories or to the Rubber Mill. Since lack of seniority was the basis of transfer decisions, and since many of the union members were recent employees of the firm, the reduction of the tannery work force eroded union strength.

Perhaps the greatest threat to the local, however, came from the IFLWU's identification with communism and the Communist party. Even formerly strong unionists, like the first president of the local, John P. Farrell, were capable of turning on the union if they felt that its commitment to communism superseded its commitment to unionism. Indeed, in the spring of 1944 Local 285 faced its first major anticommunist challenge, and even though it managed to survive, the events of that spring and the following summer foreboded an ill fate for the local.

IV

In April 1944 the *Binghamton Press* publicized that the Dies Committee had cited Ben Gold, the president of the IFLWU, and Frank R. McGrath, president of the USWA, as having close affiliations with communism and the American Communist party. The paper further charged that the unions they headed were "dominated" by communists.[52] Six weeks later the *Press* began a series entitled "Turning Red in the Triple Cities," an exposé of communist influence on local CIO unions and political organizations. The five-part series disclosed connections between USWA and IFLWU organizers and various "communist front" social and political groups.[53] In response to the articles the local CIO Executive Committee issued a statement calling the series a "smear" campaign and defended the CIO's involvement in political activities.[54] Yet the charges of communist domination of local labor unions had an impact on some of Local 285's members, for on the evening of June 4, 1944, at a meeting held at the Endicott American Legion post, twenty-two IFLWU members broke away from Local 285 and formed their own union, the Tanners Industrial Union, Independent (TIUI).

Led by John P. Farrell, Local 285's first president, the movement to form an independent union apparently was undertaken by the workers themselves, without company involvement. Certainly, however, management was served by this defection from the ranks. The new union's attorney, Paul T. Gorman of Binghamton, warned the fledgling group that it faced the "danger of becoming company dominated despite the intention of its members" and that it would have to develop solid and active rank-and-file support to avoid such domination.[55]

At its first meeting the TIUI adopted a formal resolution stating the aims of its members:

First, to save unionism for the workers; Second, to help in making unions safe for democracy; Third, to help keep democracy safe for unions.
We shall adhere to the American principle of justice to all; we reject

the alien cry of "Death to the Capitalists"; we believe that slavery to a state capitalism is as unbearable as any other form of bondage. We did not know, when we worked to organize under the International Fur and Leather banner, that its chief object was the spreading of an alien political belief. Our desire then, and our desire now, is to improve our wages and working conditions through a union controlled by ourselves.[56]

Officers of Local 285 immediately issued a response to this "treason." They claimed that the timing of the new union, coming during the course of delicate negotiations for a new contract, was deliberately intended to "create division in the ranks of the tannery workers." Essentially, the IFLWU viewed the new union as a company union—its officers motivated not by ideology but by power politics. It accused Farrell and other officers of the new union, who had been quite active in Local 285, of turning against the local because their attempts to control important union positions had been stifled in the past.[57] Farrell denied these charges, claiming that it was the IFLWU's ideological politics that led to his apostasy:

My loyalty is, and always has been, to the principle of collective bargaining. To that principle, I am still absolutely loyal. When I found that the Fur and Leather Workers had different aims and objectives, I could not sit silently by and see the union which I had helped to found perverted from its original purpose and devoted to the spreading of Communism, and I could not lend my name to what I knew was a Communist Front organization.[58]

Farrell had known that there were some communists among the leaders of the local and the international but felt that the workers could limit their influence. With time, however, his anticommunism became more virulent. He described his change of attitude to a reporter:

Within a very short time after winning the NLRB election and the installation of officers, the avalanche of Communist literature deposited on desks, chairs and window sills in the union office made one wonder if he wasn't in the headquarters of the Broome County Communist Party. . . . I am sore, after discovering the Communist control of the International, because I am gullible and egotistical enough to think I could in some way keep communism in the background, for I did not know as yet of the complete domination of the local unions by the International. But I found out to my sorrow that Communism was the main thought, word and action of the International Fur and Leather Workers Union. After being taken out to lunch by Organizer Victor Hirshfield and told by him that President Ben Gold of the International was a Communist, and that he, Victor Hirshfield, drove an ambulance on the Communist side in Spain (some call it the Loyalist side but they don't mention loyalty to what country), and that the International board was all inclined that way, I was sore.[59]

Farrell told the reporter that he had purposefully delayed expressing his real reasons for resigning from the presidency of Local 285 back in August 18, 1943, because he did not want to hurt the union case pending before the NWLB at the time.[60]

Farrell's attempts to discredit the IFLWU and Local 285 were unsuccessful. Endicott Johnson workers had witnessed red-baiting before, in the 1938–40 union campaigns and in the years that had followed. They knew its disruptive potential. Furthermore, in 1944 Russia and the United States were still allies fighting a common foe. But perhaps most important, Local 285's success in achieving substantial improvements in wages and working conditions maintained most workers' faith in the union, at least in the pre–cold war years. Like other left-wing unions, such as the UE, the IFLWU retained the loyalty of the rank and file as long as it succeeded in satisfying bread-and-butter demands.[61] And this it did. Even the vice president of the Tanners Industrial Union, Roger T. O'Connor, a former steward in Local 285, admitted that the workers were quite happy with the IFLWU at the time: "Everything worked fine when they had the union in there. Everybody was happy." He noted that there "was nobody against the union at that time. It was against the leader—Gold." When Farrell began to try to wean the workers away from the IFLWU by convincing them of its communist domination, he was met with incredulity. "They wouldn't, none of them, believe it." Local 285's leadership as well as numerous loyal union members taunted Farrell and the officers of the TIUI. They charged them with "tryin' to break the union and to get rid of it," recalled O'Connor. "They wouldn't listen to us. We'd tell them that they was dominated by the communists. They would say, 'Well, that's a good way of puttin' it so you could get rid of the union, you know.'"[62] Clearly, the majority of the union members did not believe that they were being "dominated" by communists.

The Tanners Industrial Union persisted as a minor but short-lived irritant to Local 285. It lasted for six or seven months and then "just faded away."[63] Nonetheless, the TIUI and the revelations that precipitated its rise left their legacy. Conservative community leaders, corporate officers, and noncommunist union members continued to keep a vigilant eye on the IFLWU local's leadership and direction. When Local 285 joined with the local chapter of the American Youth for Democracy (AYD), the reconstituted Young Communist League, to sponsor a "teen age canteen," local civic officials and some union members maintained a secret surveillance of the youth club's activities.[64] Sylvan P. Battista, a steward and member of the executive board of the local, recalled union members' concerns over the social organization:

> They [the CIO] were recruiting young people. . . . What they were trying to do was get a little bit more support. . . . I remember they were trying to get them interested in what the union is for—more of an educational program. . . . They had a committee set up. At first there

was a few, not a lot, maybe fifty–sixty people. It went along for awhile. We *did* decide amongst the few [of us] in secrecy that we were gonna watch very close that they didn't bring in any of their political ideas or anything like that. We had a couple of people there that kept an eye on it pretty well—went to the meetings and stuff like that. But it never got to be a big thing.[65]

But a watchful eye was all that union members felt the new club deserved. The communists, they believed, could be controlled.

As a further sign of the relative weakness of the communist issue as a disruptive force in 1944, one need only look at the progress of the USWA in Johnson City. There, the USWA-CIO began a concerted drive to organize the rubber divisions of the corporation. Through the summer of 1944, while the communist associations of the IFLWU and the USWA were being publicized by the local press, USWA petitions for an election worked their way through the NLRB bureaucracy. Hearings were held in June in Binghamton and in August in Washington, D.C. On August 21, 1944, the NLRB issued its final ruling, declaring the firm's rubber divisions appropriate units for representation by the union and calling for a speedy election. On September 12, 1944, an election was held, and by a vote of 300 to 248, the USWA won the right to represent Rubber Reclaim and Rubber Mill (Paracord) workers in Johnson City.[66] The victory that the USWA won in these plants, although not an overwhelming one, nevertheless demonstrates that the communist issue was not yet a major obstacle for the unions. Since the leadership of the USWA included numerous Communist party members and sympathizers, and since local newspapers had publicized this, the election results were a rebuff of local civic, press, and company efforts to discredit the IFLWU and the USWA.

V

With the communist issue put to rest for the time being, both the IFLWU and the USWA settled down to their normal union functions of adjusting shop floor grievances and pressuring management for further wage and benefit concessions. After the victory in Europe and Japan in the spring and summer of 1945, and the subsequent relief from the constraints of war discipline, the USWA and the IFLWU initiated new offensives. Between 1945 and 1947 the two CIO unions grew more militant. If union leadership had kept a tight rein on the workers during the war years, attempting to live up to the no-strike clause, they now let loose the reins. In October 1945 a local IFLWU organizer wrote the president of the international, Ben Gold: "Had a nice meeting— things are going well here—we got 89 new members during the month of October—and more to come—also had a couple of small work stoppages—

may be more—the fellows have decided they no longer care to work with non-union workers. I'll let you know if things get too hot to handle."[67]

In the fall of 1945 the USWA, following the completion of contract negotiations in the previous summer, began a campaign to organize the shoe factories. It set up two new locals, Local 71 and Local 72, to represent the workers in the Ideal Factory in Endicott and the Security and Security Annex factories in West Endicott. Another local was soon founded to represent Johnson City die, machine, and foundry workers; and petitions were filed with the NLRB for an election. Endicott Johnson management once again raised the issue of appropriate units but lost its appeals to the NLRB in two decisions.[68]

On May 10, 1946, the NLRB issued an order calling for an election at the Security and Security Annex factories. The election was held on June 30, 1946, and the union lost by a vote of 216 to 183. The USWA made numerous excuses for its loss, in particular, that management had bribed the workers with free beer and a day off and that "active canvassers" were sent in by company officers.[69] One USWA Local 83 officer recalled the Security Factory election and explained the union's defeat in these terms: "They had an election in Endicott in the Security Factory and they held it on company property and they lost because the bosses lined up right on the side of the paths and the sidewalks and they watched them [the workers] and they scared the shit out of the workers and they voted it down and that was the beginning of the end."[70] Most probably, the election was lost for reasons suggested by this officer's antiunion wife: "I didn't think it [the union] was any good. . . . You lost as much as you gained."[71] The union had failed to convince enough of the shoeworkers that it could offer them very much. This was not surprising. Whatever wage and benefit gains the IFLWU and the USWA had made in previous years had been passed along to the shoeworkers.

The defeat of the USWA in the Security election was not quite the "beginning of the end" for the unions. In previous elections neither the USWA nor the IFLWU had won by overwhelming majorities. Here, the USWA had not lost by much. What is noteworthy is not the union's failure in this election but the signs that the union had made important inroads among the firm's shoeworkers and that worker allegiance to the "Square Deal" had waned considerably since the early 1940s. A more concerted effort might well have turned around the thirty-three votes that had cost the union its victory. In fact, in an election held at the firm's Johnson City Foundry and Die Shop in early 1947, the USWA won.[72] Although the Foundry and Die Shop constituted a small unit of less than 100 workers, the USWA victory demonstrated that union sentiments among the workers were very much alive in early 1947. The victory in January 1947, however, marked the last one for either the USWA or the IFLWU, for in 1947 the cold war came to the Triple Cities, and it came with a vengeance.

VI

The years immediately following World War II were years of intense labor activism throughout the country. Beginning before the termination of hostilities abroad, the number of strikes and the numbers of workers involved in strikes had risen dramatically. In 1945, 4,750 strikes involving 1.34 million workers shook the nation. In 1946 the number of strikes had increased to 4,985, the largest yearly total in American history, involving close to 4 million workers. The duration of work stoppages more than tripled during the same period, as the number of "man days" idle due to strikes jumped from 38 million in 1945 to 116 million in 1946.[73] Confronted by such an overt show of force on the part of labor, both the government and the public began to demonstrate a growing mood of conservatism. For some the rise in union militancy demonstrated left-wing influence over the labor movement, a governing force that demanded ferreting out. Furthermore, the termination of hostilities in Europe and the Pacific ushered in a new war, one that would directly cripple American trade unions for years to come. The political and military exigencies that had sustained an alliance between the Soviet Union and the United States had been eliminated in 1945. The links between trade unionism and American communism, ties that had been forged back in the Depression and even earlier, now came under severe strain. This was particularly true in Endicott and Johnson City.[74]

John P. Farrell and the local press had planted the seeds of suspicion in 1944. Now the seeds grew. The communist issue had apparently not gone away; it had merely hibernated. When the president of the USWA, Frank R. McGrath, resigned in the autumn of 1946 and charged that communist executive board members were attempting to take over the union, local Binghamton papers publicized his resignation with bold headlines.[75] Through the following winter, spring, and summer of 1947, a concerted anticommunist movement gained momentum in the community.

In March 1947 John P. Farrell again surfaced and renewed his attacks on the IFLWU, issuing a sensationally worded, self-published tabloid specifically linking the IFLWU with communism and the Soviet Union.[76] This time his charges apparently reached a responsive audience. Union members who had tolerated the communist presence in previous years had grown more suspicious. Even the most loyal and active unionists, including some officers of the USWA and IFLWU locals, began to have their doubts about their unions' leadership and direction. Tensions between communists and noncommunists now emerged. In one instance Local 285 members clashed over IFLWU representatives' objections to the posting of a government-issued anticommunist notice on company bulletin boards. Sylvan P. Battista, a noncommunist union steward, recalled the event and his feelings about it:

We went over to the office, and Frank Buckingham and some of the other guys who were opposed to their politics said they had absolutely no right to do that because if the company wanted to pull something—what the company! The federal government sent them out [the posters]! And what was wrong with that? Show me what's wrong with it? If you worked in there and I know you're a communist and you're trying to do something against our company, I'll be the first one to turn you in. . . . Of course, "Red" [Oscar Oberther] didn't like it too well and Pershing [George O. Pershing, head of IFLWU, third district] didn't like it. I didn't give a damn. I had my own mind, and they weren't gonna change it for me.[77]

The revival of the communist issue swayed previously suspicious workers into taking an antiunion position. Against a communist threat generated by the local press, the government, and most of the national media, not to mention company officers, many workers came to identify the union with outside subversive elements. Anxieties over "foreign" or "outside" domination reinforced the hermetic forces that paternalism had formerly fostered and turned partially committed union members against their union.

Even strongly committed unionists split on the issue. While some stuck to the last, others abandoned what they perceived to be a sinking ship. Many union activists who had been friendly with the local's communist members and organizers grew less tolerant of their politics.[78] A few, recognizing the quickly eroding prestige of the union, tried to salvage what they could out of the situation, as Lee F. Springer did:

Four or five people in the tanneries pulled an outlaw strike, and the heads of the union were communist. . . . When they started to pull this strike, there was a group of us who didn't want to strike, and we seen that the union was gonna blow up . . . so we got in touch with the manager of the company, Charlie Johnson, and a few of us worked out . . . a deal. We worked out that they would work out some sort of a pension plan and not hold this against any of them [union members], and we would go along with the company and help get rid of the union. 'Cause we could see which way it was going—communist dominated, or one thing or another. . . . After you're in something so long and you can't see no point in continuing, you take the best way out. You gotta preserve yourself.[79]

For Springer it was not so much a personal antipathy for communism that led to his reaction but a pragmatic evaluation of its impact on the union. For other activists the risk of continued support of the union was too high, especially considering their (at best) ambivalent feelings about communism. Arthur G. Jones, a Sole Leather Tannery steward, when requested by management to sign an anticommunist/antiunion petition that was circulated in early April 1947, agreed to the request: "They called us in one at a time into the office to get us to sign against it [the union] because it was Communist. . . . I did. I guess because it was a dead issue. Everybody else had signed when they called me. . . . All I remember was that we come back from the war and they threw it at us that we had been fighting against this stuff and there was communists right in [here]."[80]

The petition came in the wake of a community-wide campaign, led by various civic organizations and business groups, to drive the "commies" out of the community. The IFLWU had been contemplating moving District 3 headquarters of the union to Endicott from Williamsport, Pennsylvania.[81] The Greater Endicott Chamber of Commerce, responding to the "threat" of "communist infiltration," initiated a local anticommunist "war."[82] The Binghamton Chamber of Commerce, the Elks, the American Legion, the Binghamton Lions Club, and numerous other local organizations soon joined with the Endicott Chamber of Commerce in its campaign to purge the community of the "red" unions.[83] Newspaper articles accused George O. Pershing, District 3 head, of being a "Blood-Red Commie, Moving in on Endicott."[84] The Binghamton Central Labor Union, wishing to assuage any doubts about *its* loyalties, quickly joined in the community condemnation of the IFLWU and in April endorsed a resolution to back an AFL attempt to organize Endicott Johnson workers.[85] The IFLWU, increasingly isolated in the community, and finding it difficult even to secure leases for offices, soon faced a major exodus of union members. When the anticommunist drive began, the IFLWU had a membership of about 1,700. In a matter of weeks the union's membership dwindled.[86]

Rather than maintain a defensive posture, both the USWA and the IFLWU went on the offensive. One worker explained a Sole Leather Tannery strike in early April as a manifestation of this, although also an act of desperation. "They saw how things were going, and they went to pull this tannery strike as a last resort. They staked everything on it."[87] The strike, however, was a dismal failure; its organizers were fired. A more significant offensive began when the USWA and the IFLWU joined in April 1947 in a concerted drive to organize the entire Endicott Johnson work force.[88] But even this proved futile, as the unions confronted numerous obstacles.

In late April the *Binghamton Press* reported that the AFL United Leather Workers Union would formally request an election in the firm's tanneries, as a challenge to the IFLWU.[89] The AFL raiding attempt distracted and partially undermined USWA and IFLWU efforts in the factories, yet it was ultimately a failure. No NLRB election was held, and the AFL Leather Workers Union soon left the area. While workers were turning their backs on the IFLWU, they were not grasping for a union alternative. In part this was due to Endicott Johnson's management.

A more formidable obstacle to the unions' offensive came from the firm itself. Within the context of community and press attempts to discredit both the IFLWU and the USWA, the corporation's own efforts proved to be quite effective in destroying the two locals. The company fought a three-front battle. First, it continued to emphasize the communist issue to undermine the unions' shop floor strength. Secondly, it fought a secret war with the aid of the National Association of Manufacturers, loyal company employees, and hired antiunion agents to purge the work force of communists and union "agitators." Finally, it tried to win over the workers with a reassertion of benevolence in the form of wage and benefit increases—in short, corporate welfarism.

The first element of the firm's strategy was carried out through anticommunist petitions and through informal conversations with workers by foremen and superintendents.[90] At the same time, the company maintained close ties with the anticommunist/antiunion campaign being waged throughout the community. The formation of the Broome County Committee for Americanism, headed by William C. Fischer, Jr., a Johnson City lawyer and ex-FBI agent with close ties to the Johnsons, marked an important link between the corporation and community efforts.[91]

While the Broome County Committee for Americanism was by no means the only organization fighting communism in the community, it was an extremely active one. The committee began its work by reasserting claims of close connections between local IFLWU and USWA officers and the American Communist party.[92] Fischer spoke before local organizations on the "menace" of communism throughout the summer of 1947 and into 1948.[93] On May 21, 1947, he went before the Binghamton Central Labor Union, which had already declared its disaffiliation with communism and communist organizations. The Central Labor Union's minutes recall his appearance in this way:

> President Smith introduced Mr. William Fischer who spoke on Communism. He outlined the purposes, aims and objectives of the Communist Party, and read excerpts from an article by J. Edgar Hoover, head of the FBI and delivered before the Un-American Committee in Washington, D.C.
>
> Delegates were asked to submit questions. After some discussion, President Smith stated that the Central Labor Union is in accord with the idea of being alert to prevent the infiltration of Communists into the organization.[94]

Fischer did more than merely spread his anticommunist message in the community; he was also involved in surveillance of suspected communists and collected information on individuals—in particular, union members and officials—that might be useful in discrediting them. Fischer's connections to the FBI and to the National Association of Manufacturers, through one Richard St. John, provided the corporation with additional resources with which to conduct its union-busting campaign.[95]

The contours of that campaign are only partially clear, hidden behind rumor and the half-remembered recollections of interviewees. Company records, however, do prove a definite connection between the firm and Fischer's efforts. Information received by the corporation from Fischer was relayed to the firm's labor relations lawyers in New York, Benjamin and Edward Seligman of the firm Seligman and Seligman. A typical sample of the type of material transmitted reads as follows:

> Attached please note further information received from Bill Fischer in regard to a conversation he and Dick St. John had with C—— G——.
> G—— worked for the company a good many years but about three years ago he started to work with the C.I.O. organizers and a few months later lost his job with the company. He is not a Communist. He has always been active in his Church at West Endicott. He was a Deacon and a Sunday School teacher. Due to his activities with the C.I.O. organizers and the fact that Endicott business men and clergymen realize that these organizers are Communistic controlled and many of them are also Communists, he was demoted in the Church and this has weighed heavily on his mind. He believes in unionization but does not favor Communism and has now decided to give the Committee for Americanism all of the inside information he can with respect to what is going on as to their activities and future plans.[96]

With Fischer's gathered information, the firm began to purge its labor force of all suspected communist activists. Charles F. Johnson, Jr., inquired of Seligman about the ramifications of firing one such worker: "H—— G—— is a Communist and has been out of step with E.J. policies for many years. The reason for sending you this affidavit is to get your opinion as to whether we would be justified in letting him out. . . ."[97]

While the firm exploited material supplied to it by Fischer and his committee to rid itself of communists and union activists, it had long ago begun to make use of loyal employees in its fight against the USWA and the IFLWU. Totally ignoring previous NLRB pronouncements and anticipating the final passage of the Taft-Hartley Labor Relations Act in the summer of 1947, corporate officers actively asserted their antiunionism through shop floor surrogates. In the Rubber Mill workers attempting to establish a future claim on company favors expressed their loyalty to the firm by relaying information to management about the union.[98] Other employees circulated petitions on the company's behalf:

> Down in the Rubber Mill, I helped out for two years, and, uh, there was a fellow by the name of Steve O——. He and I, we went around with papers [petitions] . . . and we worked to get it out. We went to everybody down the line, and we had them sign to throw the union out. And we finally got it [out]. . . . We done it through the company. . . . There was word come through, I think it probably came from Charlie—come on down through the line, but where it got to us.[99]

Support for IFLWU and the USWA was quickly eroding in April and May 1947. On May 15 the company announced the following to its workers:

> We have heretofore served notice upon the Unions representing employees in the tannery and rubber mill bargaining units that we desire to terminate the current working agreement with such Unions, as of June 1, 1947, in accordance with the provision of the contract.
>
> Since serving notice of termination on the two Unions, we have come into possession of evidence that indicated neither of said Unions represent a majority of the employees in either unit, and we have notified the Unions it would be illegal for our company to recognize them as bargaining units.[100]

The unions responded promptly. District 3 headquarters issued appeals to all locals for financial and moral support. IFLWU locals throughout the country received the following description of events in Endicott:

> Our Union is under a vicious attack in Endicott, New York. The situation is extremely serious. The Endicott Johnson Corporation has refused to bargain claiming that Local 285 does not represent a majority. We have requested the NLRB to hold a new election to prove that our local does represent the majority. The Chamber of Commerce, Police Court Justices, American Legion and many fraternal organizations have joined the Endicott Johnson Corporation to attack our union. Meeting halls have denied us use. Office space and living quarters have been denied us. The CIO Shoeworkers Local is being evicted from its office. District Director, George O. Pershing, Organizer Oscar Oberther and Business Agent John Mushock with eight others have been arrested for distributing leaflets and are out on bail. Three officers of the local have been fired. Members were tricked into signing blank postcards ostensibly against communism but now revealed to be withdrawals from the Union.[101]

The USWA and the IFLWU beseeched their members to remain loyal and to continue to pay their dues, reminding them of the many achievements that their unions had brought about during their tenure.[102]

In the weeks and months that followed the company's retraction of recognition of the two unions, petitions for certification were filed by the USWA and the IFLWU and were making their way through legal channels. Company officers, under advisement of legal counsel, stalled. They sought federal court injunctions delaying scheduled NLRB hearings and won them. During one such appeal for an injunction, the company "contended that it and 20,000 of its employees would be irreparably damaged if the hearing was conducted before August 23 when most of the provisions of the new Taft-Hartley Labor Law become effective."[103] Indeed, through most of that spring the two unions were trying to arrange for a hasty NLRB election before Taft-Hartley went into effect. But the Taft-Hartley Labor Relations Act was quickly winding its way through Congress. Management knew that it could only gain by stalling the election. Not only could it hope to win over more workers, but once section 9h of the act was implemented, union leaders would have to file noncommunist affidavits before their organizations would be offered the "protection" of the NLRB. Since many USWA and IFLWU officers were communists, the corporation recognized that both unions would lose government protection. In fact, in August 1947 the IFLWU withdrew its petition for an NLRB election because it recognized that "it could not qualify by filing the non-communist affidavits which were required by the Taft-Hartley Law."[104] The USWA soon followed suit.

The firm had apparently won the legal battle against the unions. But it also continued to wage its private war against them, utilizing Fischer, as well as several hired men from the community and outside, to do both spiritual and physical battle against the CIO unions.[105] In December 1948 John H. Russell, an IFLWU representative and union organizer, was beaten outside of an Endicott tavern and very soon afterward was arrested on a public intoxication charge. Although local police later apologized for Russell's arrest, it was clear to union leaders that the beating was a setup.[106] Indeed, even here there may have been a connection to William C. Fischer. Fischer's son recalled that his father had acted as a middleman and had made payoffs on behalf of the corporation to certain local individuals to "bust union heads."[107]

Through the next few years, the IFLWU and the USWA continued to maintain a presence in Johnson City and Endicott, forming a joint CIO Organizing Committee. Now without government "protection," both unions nonetheless decided to continue their protracted campaign to win the hearts and minds of the shoeworkers. Through the fall of 1947 and into the following year, local union members began organizing workers in numerous factories. They helped the heel scourers of the Scout Factory to obtain a settlement of a wage dispute in September 1947. They were active among the Fine Welt lasters, assisting them in their fight for a wage adjustment.[108] With the aid and encouragement of the Joint Organizing Committee, an independent Laster's Union was formed in October 1947. The IFLWU viewed the formation of this union as "conclusive proof that where workers really want to build a union they can do so without complying with the Taft-Hartley law and without using the employer-controlled N.L.R.B."[109] Yet such successes were sporadic and hardly indicative of the real plight of the locals. Two months after the firm ceased to recognize the IFLWU, the membership of Local 285 had declined to about 900. By October 1947 it stood at 390. From there it continued to drop steadily. By the end of 1948 it stood at approximately 100, and in the fall of 1949 only two or three dozen workers were paying dues.[110] The plight of Local 83 of the USWA appears to have been equally dim. Membership plummeted, and only a few brave souls remained to carry on organizing work with IFLWU activists in Endicott.[111]

By late 1948 the organizing drive in the factories was pretty much spent.

Although Local 285 hung on for another year, mainly through the financial support of the international and other locals, it was hurting badly. Minutes of executive board meetings disclose sinking morale. In a February 17, 1949, meeting, members expressed pessimism over the local's ability to organize the plants even with the much hoped for repeal of Taft-Hartley. George Pershing's and Ben Gold's association to the American Communist party (Gold had finally publicly admitted to being a member of the party in 1948) was acknowledged as being particularly harmful to the local. Although much of the talk revolved around the Taft-Hartley Labor Relations Act, the president of the local emphasized that the problem was that the majority "think they are on top of earth—no short time—not panicked."[112] The last report on the union was depressing indeed. On November 15, 1949, Raymond Davis, the secretary of the Endicott local, wrote to George O. Pershing: "In your letter you asked what the attitude of the workers was in regard to organization. From what we see and hear in the plants there is not much change in the workers. They wish they had a union when they get hurt but are not willing to do any work to get one. The workers are being chiseled on the speed up but it isn't too apparent to them that if they work and talk for a union that they can change things for themselves."[113]

VII

Thus ended the union drives of the 1940s; Endicott Johnson's open shop was restored. But the anticommunist hysteria of the early cold war years or the strong-armed tactics employed by corporate managers are not entirely sufficient to explain the defection of rank and file from the unions or the growing resistance of shoeworkers and tanners to union appeals. Although company officers continued to remind workers that both the IFLWU and the USWA were "communist organizations," and corporation agents, both hired and volunteer, continued to disrupt organizing efforts in the factories, the "stick" was ultimately not the most effective weapon in the firm's war against the unions.

Force and intimidation, as a new generation of Johnsons were coming to realize, were hardly in keeping with the corporation's long tradition of the "Square Deal." Nor would such responses to unionization help perpetuate labor's loyalty over the long term. It was thus not surprising that company officers, even as they continued their more aggressive campaign against the unions, would also attempt to woo workers away from the unions. This, of course, management had begun to do from the moment the IFLWU won its recognition election in December 1942. When the firm passed along to the shoeworkers many of the wage increases and shop floor rights that the IFLWU and the USWA had won for their members, the corporation was cultivating worker goodwill. When, just before the Johnsons declared their intention to cease negotiating with both unions, they announced a 15 percent wage increase, they were also clearly courting their workers. The wage increase, lest employees miss the point, went into effect the day after all union contracts were terminated, on June 2, 1947.[114]

Endicott Johnson managers, however, recognized that they would have to pay a higher price for loyalty than mere pay increases. And this they proceeded to do. In the summer of 1948, profit sharing, in the form of bonus payments, was revived. Although the company had legally terminated its profit-sharing plan in March 1944, to avoid possible union "vested interest" claims, it now reinstituted bonus payments on a purely discretionary basis.[115] Altogether, the firm distributed four million dollars in 1948, one million in 1949, and three million in 1950. It continued such disbursements well into the 1950s.[116] The corporation also announced to the workers its intention of adopting a formal pension plan. This had first been promised to members of Local 285 to encourage them to split with the union. After holding a referendum and receiving overwhelming worker approval, the firm put the plan into effect on January 1, 1948.[117] Also in 1948, feeling that they had lost personal touch with their workers, managers initiated the practice of holding retirement dinners, gala affairs to celebrate the loyal services of long-term employees.[118] And to further demonstrate goodwill to its workers, a year later the firm constructed two recreation centers at a cost of almost two million dollars. As a final signal to employees that management had not lost sight of its obligations under the "Square Deal," home construction for employees was also revived, after a lapse of almost a decade. In these and many other ways, corporate officers tried to persuade the workers that loyalty to the corporation was in their own best interest. The failure of the unions to recover their losses in the late 1940s and 1950s attests to their success.

Management's ultimate response to the union threat, a reassertion of welfare capitalism, was in keeping with company tradition. Whenever the "Square Deal" was seriously disrupted, and sustaining employee loyalty became problematic, the firm's managers were under strong pressure to restore it. The ideal of a "corporate family" was a central and powerful ideal that operated on several generations of Endicott Johnson workers and managers. Although war, volatile labor markets, federal agencies, and unions undermined it considerably in the 1940s, these very agents also imposed a disciplining influence on the corporation's management and, in the final analysis, forced the firm to reembrace corporate paternalism.

NOTES

1. *Labor News,* July 1, 1940.
2. Ibid., Aug. 12, 1940.
3. Ibid., Aug. 26, 1940.

4. Ibid.; Margaret Azarin [pseud.], interview by Gerald Zahavi, Nov. 15, 1983, tape recording (personal possession).
5. *Labor News*, Nov. 4, 1940.
6. "Wage Increases and Decreases, March 16, 1931, to December 1, 1952," typescript, "No dates" folder, box 6, ser. 1, George W. Johnson Papers, George Arents Research Library for Special Collections, Syracuse University, Syracuse, N.Y. For the union's damning response to how the firm calculated its "5%," see *Labor News*, Nov. 18, 1940. In reality the restoration amounted to a little more than 3 percent.
7. *Labor News*, Jan. 28, 1941.
8. Horace B. Davis, *Shoes: The Workers and the Industry* (New York, 1940), 152; *Labor News*, Apr. 8, 1940.
9. *Labor News*, Apr. 8, 1940.
10. Ibid., Apr. 22, 1940.
11. Appeals by AFL activists to reorganize the BSWU local were ignored by John J. Mara, president of the BSWU. National organizers from the BSWU—Frank Anderson, Tom Cory, and Ben Berk—gave the workers little support. A request by the president of the Binghamton Central Labor Union, addressed to Mara, asking him to return to undertake another organizing campaign, met with a negative reply. Former members of Local 42 to John J. Mara, June 8, 1940; A. B. Cleveland to John J. Mara, July 17, 1940; John J. Mara to A. B. Cleveland, July 30, 1940, Local 42 files, BSWU Records, State Historical Society of Wisconsin. On the abandonment of the workers by the BSWU, see *CIO News* (Shoe Workers' Edition), May 13, 1940. An editorial against the BSWU entitled "Black Treason" appeared in the Mar. 15, 1940, edition of the *Triple Cities Labor Herald*, the official paper of the Binghamton Central Labor Union. A reprinted copy appears in the above *CIO News* (Shoe Workers' Edition). Further information on the regrouping of union forces appears in *Labor News*. See, in particular, the Apr. 8 and July 29, 1940, issues.
12. "Wage Increases and Decreases, March 16, 1931, to December 1, 1952."
13. "To the Workers" notice, Nov. 12, 1941, box 33, ser. 1, Charles F. Johnson, Jr., Papers, George Arents Research Library for Special Collections, Syracuse University, Syracuse, N.Y.
14. USWA flyer, "To the Workers of Fine Welt," [Nov. 1941,] box 4, ser. 2, George W. Johnson Papers.
15. "To the Workers" notice, June 15, 1943, box 10, ser. 3, Frank A. Johnson Papers, George Arents Research Library for Special Collections, Syracuse University, Syracuse, N.Y.; "To the Workers" notice, Jan. 13, 1944, box 34, ser. 1, Charles F. Johnson, Jr., Papers.
16. William Patrick Burns, "A Study of Personnel Policies, Employee Opinion and Labor Turnover (1930–1946) at the Endicott Johnson Corporation" (Master's thesis, New York State School of Industrial and Labor Relations, Cornell University, 1947), 86–89. Nonetheless, turnover rates in the firm still remained below the industry average.
17. Charles F. Johnson, Jr., to Pvt. Thomas P. Guy, Nov. 4, 1942, box 33, ser. 1, Charles F. Johnson, Jr., Papers.
18. Charles F. Johnson, Jr., to Paul McIntosh et al., May 10, 1943, box 33, ser. 1,

Charles F. Johnson, Jr., Papers. Johnson noted that the firm had lost 385 workers in Apr. of that year.

19. Theresa Schuttak and Fran Eckert, interview by Gerald Zahavi, with the assistance of Deborah D. Maxwell, Apr. 30, 1982, tape recording (personal possession).

20. Thomas K. Chubbuck, interview by Gerald Zahavi, with the assistance of Deborah D. Maxwell, session 2, July 2, 1981, tape recording (personal possession).

21. "Incentive Pay vs. Piecework," notice to the workers, Mar. 20, 1944, box 5, ser. 1, George W. Johnson Papers.

22. Chubbuck, interview, session 2.

23. The NWLB generally ruled on disputes not resolvable by the Conciliation Service.

24. See "Submission to Arbitration" and "Award of Arbitrator" in "Labor Arbitration-Copeloff, Maxwell, 1942–1945" file, in box 8, ser. 3, Frank A. Johnson Papers.

25. Endicott Johnson Corporation to Maxwell Copeloff, Mar. 7, 1945; Endicott Johnson Corporation to Maxwell Copeloff, Jan. 15, 1945, box 8, ser. 3, Frank A. Johnson Papers.

26. Victor Hirshfield, a CIO International Fur and Leather Workers Union lawyer and an early organizer in the area, was selected by the lasters as their lawyer. See Ralph Albert [arbitrator, U.S. Conciliation Service] to Leo Mills and Victor Hirshfield, Sept. 17, 1943, box 4, ser. 2, George W. Johnson Papers.

27. The USWA did not pursue a vigorous campaign until 1944. It withdrew organizers soon after the IFLWU had begun its organizing work and channeled its own efforts into union drives elsewhere in the country. See USWA, *Proceedings of the Third Convention of the United Shoe Workers of America* (Worcester, 1942), 48.

28. Paul R. Knickerbocker, interviews by Gerald Zahavi, with the assistance of Deborah D. Maxwell, sessions 1 and 3, June 10, 1982, July 22, 1982, tape recordings (personal possession); James L. Backes, interview by Gerald Zahavi, May 12, 1984, tape recording (personal possession); George O. Pershing to Victor Hirshfield, Dec. 16, 1941, Local 285 files, box 61, Joint Board Papers, Labor-Management Documentation Center, M. P. Catherwood Library, New York State School of Industrial and Labor Relations, Cornell University, Ithaca, N.Y. On the Pennsylvania campaigns of the National Leather Workers Association, which merged with the International Fur Workers Union in 1939 to form the IFLWU, see Philip S. Foner, *The Fur and Leather Workers Union: A Story of Dramatic Struggles and Achievements* (Newark, 1950), chap. 46. An intimate portrait of union organizing in one Pennsylvania tannery town, identifying an organizer who played an active role in organizing Endicott Johnson's tanneries (Elmer Backes), can be found in John Bodnar, *Workers' World: Kinship, Community, and Protest in an Industrial Society, 1900–1940* (Baltimore, 1982), 160–64. Many of the workers who were "union pioneers" in Endicott were quite similar in sociological profile to male pioneers described in Ronald Schatz's "Union Pioneers: The Founders of Local Unions in General Electric and West-

inghouse, 1933–1937," *Journal of American History* 66 (Dec. 1979): 586–602. They tended to be relatively skilled workers, of Anglo-Saxon ancestry, in their late thirties or early forties, and from a union background. Unfortunately, few of them were still around for me to interview, and so this observation must remain an impressionistic one based on other workers' recollections.

29. Foner, *The Fur and Leather Workers Union,* 514–15, 598, and passim.
30. Ibid., 598–99.
31. "Report by Myer Klig" to the International Executive Board, Mar. 17 and 18, 1943, General Executive Board (GEB) Minutes, box 35, International Fur and Leather Workers Union Records (hereafter IFLWU Records), Labor-Management Documentation Center, M. P. Catherwood Library, New York State School of Industrial and Labor Relations, Cornell University, Ithaca, N.Y.
32. Knickerbocker, interview, session 1.
33. "Report by Myer Klig."
34. U.S. National Labor Relations Board, *Decisions and Orders of the National Labor Relations Board,* vol. 45 (Washington, D.C., 1942), 1092–95.
35. "Report by Myer Klig."
36. *Binghamton Press,* June 9, 1944; See also Sylvan P. Battista, interviews by Gerald Zahavi, with the assistance of Deborah D. Maxwell, sessions 1 and 2, July 13, 1981, and Nov. 12, 1981, tape recordings (personal possession).
37. On the "economism" of communist organizers, see, especially, essays by Martin Glaberman and Ronald L. Filippelli in *Political Power and Social Theory: A Research Annual,* ed. Maurice Zeitlin, vol. 4 (Greenwich, Conn., 1984). See also Ronald Schatz, *The Electrical Workers: A History of Labor at General Electric and Westinghouse, 1923–60* (Urbana, Ill., 1983).
38. "Report by Myer Klig."
39. These were only some of its achievements. See *Endicott Leather Worker* 1 (Apr. 1943): 1, 2; ibid. (Aug. 1943): 1, 2; *Fur and Leather Worker* 5 (Mar. 1943): 1, 5; ibid. (Sept. 1943): 3; Local 285 Collective Bargaining Contracts, Local 285 files, box 61, Joint Board Papers; U.S. National War Labor Board, *War Labor Reports,* vol. 16 (Washington, D.C., 1944), 17–22. On the NWLB and the issue of union security during World War II, see Joel Isaac Seidman, *American Labor from Defense to Reconversion* (Chicago, 1953), chap. 6; and Nelson Lichtenstein, *Labor's War at Home: The CIO in World War II* (New York, 1982), chap. 5. The maintenance-of-membership provision did not create a closed shop since it provided new workers with a fifteen-day "escape" period in which they could select not to affiliate with the union. Once enrolled in the union, however, they had to maintain their good standing until the next contract period.
40. "To the Workers" notice, June 15, 1943, box 10, ser. 3, Frank A. Johnson Papers; "To the Workers" notice, May 17, 1944, box 34, ser. 1, Charles F. Johnson, Jr., Papers; *Endicott Leather Worker* 1 (Aug. 1944): 3.
41. Sam Salvatore, interview by Gerald Zahavi, with the assistance of Deborah D. Maxwell, July 7, 1981, tape recording (personal possession); James W. Lupole, interview by Gerald Zahavi, with the assistance of Deborah D. Maxwell, July 15, 1981, tape recording (personal possession); Battista, interviews, sessions 1 and 2; Bernice O'Connor and Roger T. O'Connor, interview by Gerald

Zahavi, with the assistance of Deborah D. Maxwell, Nov. 7, 1981, tape recording (personal possession); Raymond Davis, interview by Gerald Zahavi, Aug. 27, 1982, notes (untaped).

42. Salvatore, interview.

43. Lee F. Springer, interview by Gerald Zahavi, with the assistance of Deborah D. Maxwell, July 15, 1981, tape recording (personal possession); Backes, interview; *Endicott Leather Worker* 2 (Feb. 1945): 3; Davis, interview; Salvatore, interview; Knickerbocker, interviews, sessions 1 and 2; O'Connor, interview; Battista, interviews, sessions 1 and 2.

44. Battista, interview, session 1.

45. William Haight, interview by Gerald Zahavi, with the assistance of Deborah D. Maxwell, May 27, 1982, tape recording (personal possession). Anger over this injustice was an important factor in convincing Haight to become a union steward.

46. A 1947 survey of Endicott Johnson workers' attitudes toward various company policies disclosed considerable displeasure with the firm's promotion practices. Burns, "A Study of Personnel Policies," 57–58, 113.

47. Wildcat strikes still occurred when workers felt management was violating the union contract. See "Russell Henneman Case," [1943,] Local 285 files, box 61, Joint Board Papers; Knickerbocker, interview, session 1.

48. On the no-strike pledge, see Nelson Lichtenstein, "Defending the No-Strike Pledge: CIO Politics during World War II," *Radical America* 9 (July-Aug. 1975): 49–75; Joshua Freeman, "Delivering the Goods: Industrial Unionism during World War II," *Labor History* 19 (Fall 1978): 570–93. See also Lichtenstein, *Labor's War at Home,* chap. 7 and passim.

49. H. A. Swartwood to Ben Gold, Aug. 12, 1943; Myer Klig to Howard Swartwood, Aug. 12, 1943 (telegrams), box 4, ser. 2, Charles F. Johnson, Jr., Papers.

50. Rush Dunn to Howard Swartwood, Nov. 14, 1944, box 4, ser. 1, George W. Johnson Papers. See other material in this box on the work stoppage.

51. Wildcat strikes in the tanneries were of very brief duration during the war years, as were strikes in USWA controlled departments in Johnson City. See "Brief for Endicott Johnson," box 14, National War Labor Board, Region 2 Case Files, Labor-Management Documentation Center, M. P. Catherwood Library, New York State School of Industrial and Labor Relations, Cornell University, Ithaca, N.Y. See also "Work Stoppage" reports, box 3, ser. 2, George W. Johnson Papers.

52. *Binghamton Press,* Apr. 15, 1944.

53. Ibid., May 31, June 1, June 2, June 4, June 5, 1944.

54. Ibid., June 5, 1944.

55. Ibid.

56. Ibid. The resolution also appeared in the *Binghamton Sun* and the *Endicott Bulletin* of June 6, 1944.

57. *Binghamton Press,* June 7, 1944. See also *Endicott Bulletin,* June 7, 1944. Local 285 established a special committee to investigate the new union and its leaders. The committee questioned the integrity of the independent's officers and recommended that the TIUI's officers be "brought before the Executive Board, to

answer the charges." On July 27, 1944, the board heard the charges and recommended expulsion. Not all of the officers were expelled, however. At least one was permitted to remain a member in Local 285 but was barred from holding office in the union. *Endicott Leather Worker* 1 (Aug. 1944): 2–3. Battista, interview, session 2. "Special Committee Report," [1944,] Local 285 files, box 61, Joint Board Papers.

58. *Binghamton Press,* June 9, 1944.
59. Ibid.
60. Ibid. For another version of Farrell's transformation, see Maurice J. Quain, interview by Gerald Zahavi, with the assistance of Deborah D. Maxwell, June 29, 1981, tape recording (personal possession).
61. Ronald L. Filippelli, "UE: An Uncertain Legacy," in *Political Power and Social Theory,* ed. Zeitlin, 4:217–52.
62. O'Connor, interview.
63. Ibid.
64. "Memorandum of Conversations regarding a CIO Sponsored Young People's Club . . . ," box 4, ser. 2, George W. Johnson Papers. Other material on the club and the AYD can be found in this box. On the AYD and its origins, see Maurice Isserman, *Which Side Were You On? The American Communist Party during the Second World War* (Middletown, Conn., 1982): 178–79. On the local AYD, see *Binghamton Press,* June 1, 1944.
65. Battista, interview, session 2.
66. U.S. National Labor Relations Board, *Decisions and Orders of the National Labor Relations Board,* vol. 57 (Washington, D.C., 1944), 1473–77; *CIO News* (Shoe Workers' Edition), Sept. 11, 1944; *Endicott Leather Worker* 1 (Sept. 1944): 3. See also Albert J. Millus, Jr., "The Shoe Company of La Mancha: Endicott Johnson Corporation" (Research paper, New York State School of Industrial and Labor Relations, Cornell University, 1977), 34–35; G. Ralph Smith, *The Endicott Johnson Corporation* (New Orleans, 1959), 53–54.
67. Oscar Oberther to Ben Gold, Oct. 31, 1945, Local 285 files, box 61, Joint Board Papers.
68. *CIO News* (Shoe Workers' Edition), Oct. 22, 1945; U.S. National Labor Relations Board, *Decisions and Orders of the National Labor Relations Board,* vol. 67 (Washington, D.C., 1946), 1342–50; ibid., vol. 71 (Washington, D.C., 1946), 1100–105. See also *CIO News* (Shoe Workers' Edition), Feb. 18, Mar. 11, 1946. The NLRB ruling recognized only the Foundry and Die Shop as an appropriate unit and excluded the fifteen Johnson City Machine Shop workers. It was nonetheless a repudiation of the company's position that called for a company-wide unit.
69. *CIO News* (Shoe Workers' Edition), July 1, 1946, 12.
70. Henry Banner and Emma Banner [pseud.], interview by Gerald Zahavi, June 2, 1982, tape recording (personal possession).
71. Ibid. Mrs. Banner [pseud.] recalled her resentment of the union because of a two-week, union-initiated strike during which her husband lost substantial income. In addition, she hated having to pay union dues.
72. This was in spite of management appeals directly to the workers not to "split up"

the company into separate bargaining units. See "A Statement of Policy," Jan. 20, 1947, box 34, ser. 1, Charles F. Johnson, Jr., Papers. The workers voted fifty-eight to seven for USWA representation. *Endicott Bulletin,* Jan. 21, 1947.

73. U.S. Bureau of the Census, *Historical Statistics of the United States: Colonial Times to 1957* (Washington, D.C., 1960), 99; James R. Green, *The World of the Worker: Labor in Twentieth-Century America* (New York, 1980), 193–94; Lichtenstein, *Labor's War at Home,* chap. 11.

74. Four essential books that trace the rise and fall of these links (from various ideological positions) are Max M. Kampelman, *The Communist Party vs. the C.I.O.: A Study in Power Politics* (New York, 1957); David J. Saposs, *Communism in American Unions* (New York, 1959); Bert Cochran, *Labor and Communism: The Conflict That Shaped American Unions* (Princeton, 1977); and Harvey A. Levenstein, *Communism, Anticommunism, and the CIO* (Westport, Conn., 1981). The article literature on the subject is immense.

75. *Binghamton Press,* Oct. 3, 1946. On McGrath's break with the union, see Kampelman, *The Communist Party,* 95–96.

76. *Endicott Bulletin,* Mar. 17, 1948. A copy of Farrell's "Low-Down on Operation Moscow!" can be found in Local 285 files, box 61, Joint Board Papers.

77. Battista, interview, session 2. "Red" was Oscar Oberther's nickname. Oberther was the head IFLWU representative in Endicott at the time. His nickname referred to the color of his hair and not to his politics, although the latter was also consistent with his nickname.

78. See Springer, interview; and Banner [pseud.], interview.

79. Springer, interview.

80. Arthur G. Jones, interview by Gerald Zahavi, June 2, 1982, tape recording (personal possession). Actually, few workers seemed to sign the petition with much conviction. Many were misled by supervisors' claims that "everyone had already signed," a ploy to get them to join the fictitious majority. See Salvatore, interview; S———, interview by Nancy Grey Osterud and Laura Kirkland, May 15, 1982, summary and partial transcription (Broome County Immigration History Project). The petition read: "We, the undersigned, do not want to be represented by a Communist-dominated union." *Binghamton Press,* Apr. 2, 1947.

81. *Binghamton Press,* Mar. 10, 1947.

82. Ibid., Mar. 29, 1947.

83. Ibid., Apr. 1, 1947. See also ibid., Apr. 3, Apr. 5, Apr. 8, Apr. 9, Apr. 11, Apr. 12, 1947. Just about every day articles chronicling the progress of the "Anti-red Campaign" appeared in local papers.

84. *Endicott Bulletin,* Mar. 28, 1947. The paper quoted from congressional hearings and distorted Pershing's past activities. Pershing circulated a reply to the *Bulletin*'s charges among union members. His reply, addressed to members of the union and dated Apr. 26, 1947, is in Local 285 files, box 61, Joint Board Papers.

85. *Endicott Bulletin,* Mar. 29, 1947; Binghamton Central Labor Union Minutes (hereafter BCLU Minutes), Apr. 16, 1947, microfilm copy, Labor-Management Documentation Center, M. P. Catherwood Library, New York State School of Industrial and Labor Relations, Cornell University, Ithaca, N.Y.

86. *Binghamton Press,* Mar. 31, Apr. 14, 1947; *Endicott Bulletin,* Mar. 31, 1947. The

number of workers in the units covered by the IFLWU contract amounted to approximately 1,900.

87. Springer, interview.

88. Knickerbocker, interview, session 1; *Endicott Leather Worker* 5 (Apr. 1947): 1, 4.

89. *Binghamton Press,* Apr. 23, 1947.

90. Memo [signed Leonard Steed], May 28, 1947, box 12, ser. 3, Frank A. Johnson Papers. The memo noted the progress of the petition drive and the number of workers who had not signed.

91. "Background of William C. Fischer," n.d., Local 285 files, box 61, Joint Board Papers. Fischer's father, a major league baseball player recruited by George F. Johnson in the 1920s to head the corporation's Athletic Association in Johnson City and Binghamton, was a close personal friend of George F. Johnson and the Johnson family. He had joined the corporation's sales department when the company found it necessary to limit its athletic programs in the late 1920s. Fischer's brother, also a lawyer, owed a great deal to the company. In the winter of 1934–35, the corporation's doctors had been instrumental in saving his life. George F. Johnson to William Fischer, Feb. 1, 1935, box 14, George F. Johnson Papers, George Arents Research Library for Special Collections, Syracuse University, Syracuse, N.Y.

92. *Endicott Bulletin,* May 17, 1947.

93. Ibid., Oct. 22, 1947.

94. BCLU Minutes, May 21, 1947. Fischer also spoke at Endicott Johnson employee gatherings. See "Endicott Johnson Workers Daily Page," *Binghamton Sun,* May 19, 1947.

95. Conversation with William C. Fischer III, June 10, 1982, notes (not taped); John O'Green to George Pershing, Dec. 1, 1948, Local 285 files, box 61, Joint Board Papers. The younger Fischer recalled the hundreds of files that his father had accumulated on local individuals. The files were ultimately destroyed. Apparently, in later life, the elder Fischer had a change of heart and regretted his earlier involvement in these matters. For more on Fischer's activities in 1947 and 1948, see *Binghamton Press,* July 30, 1948; *Fur and Leather Worker,* Sept. 1, 1948; and *Endicott Leather Worker* 5 (Aug. 1948): 1, 4.

96. Charles F. Johnson, Jr., to Benjamin Seligman, Dec. 29, 1947, box 34, ser. 1, Charles F. Johnson, Jr., Papers. I have deleted the full name of the individual involved to protect his privacy.

97. Charles F. Johnson, Jr., to Benjamin Seligman, Dec. 23, 1947, box 34, ser. 1, Charles F. Johnson, Jr., Papers. More letters on the communist issue can be found in this box and in box 35.

98. M. to Mr. Johnson, Aug. 4, 1947; M. and A. to Leonard Steed, Jan. 21, 1949, box 13, ser. 3, Frank A. Johnson Papers.

99. Owen J. Ryall, interview by Gerald Zahavi, with the assistance of Deborah D. Maxwell, Apr. 30, 1982, tape recording (personal possession).

100. "To the Workers" notice, May 15, 1947, box 34, ser. 1, Charles F. Johnson, Jr., Papers.

101. George O. Pershing, "To All Staff Members," May 19, 1947, Local 285 files, box 61, Joint Board Papers.

102. See, for example, the numerous leaflets in the Local 285 files, box 61, Joint Board Papers. See also "United Shoe Workers of America" file in box 331, Union Files Collection, Labor-Management Documentation Center, M. P. Catherwood Library, New York State School of Industrial and Labor Relations, Cornell University, Ithaca, N.Y.

103. *Binghamton Press,* Aug. 11, 1947.

104. Edward F. Seligman to Charles F. Johnson, Jr., May 27, 1948, box 19, ser. 1, Charles F. Johnson, Jr., Papers [enclosure of company reply brief to NLRB petition]. See also Foner, *The Fur and Leather Workers Union,* 646–48.

105. John O'Green to George O. Pershing, Dec. 1, 1948, Local 285 files, box 61, Joint Board Papers.

106. *Binghamton Press,* Dec. 29, 1948, Jan. 7, 1949. See also Local 285 files on the Russell beating.

107. Conversation with William C. Fischer III.

108. John Russell to Abe Feinglass, Sept. 27, 1947, Local 285 files, box 61, Joint Board Papers. See also leaflets circulated by the unions in Local 285 files.

109. *Endicott Leather Worker* 5 (Nov. 1947): 1.

110. The membership figures are based on financial statements of the local, Local 285 files, box 61, Joint Board Papers.

111. Kenneth Cowan and Inez Cowan, interview by Gerald Zahavi, June 2, 1982, tape recording (personal possession); Banner [pseud.], interview.

112. Minutes of Local 285, Feb. 17, 1949 (handwritten), Local 285 files, box 61, Joint Board Papers.

113. Raymond Davis to George O. Pershing, Nov. 15, 1949, Local 285 files, box 61, Joint Board Papers.

114. *Binghamton Sun,* May 9, 1947.

115. Howard A. Swartwood to Charles F. Johnson, Jr., July 21, 1948, box 23, ser. 1, Charles F. Johnson, Jr., Papers.

116. "Wage Increases and Decreases, March 16, 1931, to December 1, 1952." Between 1951 and 1955, over nine million dollars in bonus payments were distributed to Endicott Johnson workers—equivalent to about two or three weeks' wages a year for every worker. "Charles F. Johnson Biographical Sketch," n.d., box 1, ser. 1, Charles F. Johnson, Jr., Papers.

117. Smith, *The Endicott Johnson Corporation,* 63–64; "To the Workers" notice, Oct. 24, 1947, box 34, ser. 1, Charles F. Johnson, Jr., Papers.

118. The corporation published retirement dinner booklets giving short profiles of retiring workers and celebrating their long years of service to the corporation. See box 13, ser. 3, Frank A. Johnson Papers, for some examples.

Conclusion

On Sunday evening, November 28, 1948, at 10:20 P.M., George F. Johnson died. Binghamton, Endicott, and Johnson City papers mourned his passing by devoting substantial coverage to his achievements and to his many contributions to the local community. Tens of thousands attended his funeral. In his death Johnson took with him much of the spirit that had sustained the corporation's labor policies. That is not to say that welfarism died abruptly in 1948, for as we have seen, it did not. Like Johnson's end, which had been drawn out for eight years of illness and partial consciousness, corporate paternalism at Endicott Johnson was destined to suffer an equally lingering death.

The defeat of the IFLWU and the USWA in the late 1940s did not spell the end of challenges to corporate hegemony. Union drives continued through the next two decades. The United Rubber Workers, the International Association of Machinists, the Textile Workers Union of America, the Amalgamated Meat Cutters and Butcher Workmen of North America, as well as the United Shoe Workers all tried to organize various departments of Endicott Johnson in the 1950s and 1960s. All failed. The Amalgamated Meat Cutters, which had absorbed the IFLWU in early 1955 after a purge of its communist leaders, waged the longest and most serious campaign in 1956–59. By that time, however, the NLRB had grown quite conservative and was no longer willing to accept segmented bargaining units as appropriate for union representation. The Amalgamated's petition for an election to represent the firm's tannery workers was thus rejected and its organizing drive foiled.[1] But a conservative NLRB was not what held back the unions. It was evident, from the repeated failures of numerous unions to organize the firm's employees, that the workers were remaining loyal to the company, to the extent, at least, of rejecting unionization.

In the years that followed the defeat of the IFLWU and the USWA, the corporation had reasserted its commitment to its employees, restoring and expanding many of the concrete ingredients of the "Square Deal" that had sustained labor loyalty in former decades. Corporate officers even attempted to mimic George F. Johnson's ineffable personal quality, which constituted the less tangible, nevertheless very important, facet of corporate welfarism at Endicott Johnson. The corporation persisted in celebrating and advertising the corporate bonds that united workers and managers. Officers continued to reside among the workers and commingled with them to some extent. Appeals from workers still made their way to the president of the firm. Charles F. Johnson, Jr., who was elected to the presidency of the firm upon the death of his uncle and the promotion of George W. Johnson to chairman of the board, made it a point to involve himself continually in shop floor matters, helping to resolve conflicts between workers and low-level managers. He periodically circulated through the factories, attended clambakes and employee parties, sent flowers to grieving widows of Endicott Johnson workers, and in numerous other ways tried to live up to the reputation of his dead uncle. Among many workers, he succeeded. But for others, those who had come into the firm in the 1920s and earlier, there would be no one like George F. Johnson, whose death marked for them the beginning of the company's decline.

In fact, George F. Johnson's passing *did* mark a rough turning point in the firm's history, although not necessarily one related to his demise. Already, despite its reassertion of certain aspects of the "Square Deal," the corporation was exhibiting evidence of its weakened commitment to many of the ideals that had ruled it in former years.

Financially, while not doing badly, the firm was hardly showing exceptional profits. It had rebounded during World War II from the depths of the Depression, but its profitability had declined drastically. The firm had to double its dollar sales volume to match profit levels of the 1920s. In 1948 it made a net profit of $3.6 million on sales of $149 million; in 1928 its net profit of $3.6 million came on sales amounting to $69 million.[2] Facing rising foreign competition and higher labor costs, as well as the additional labor expenses associated with its welfare policies, the firm found itself increasingly in a precarious financial position, one that ultimately undermined its ability to sustain corporate welfarism.

Central aspects of Endicott Johnson's welfare ethos had been questioned in earlier years, particularly during the Depression. Then, faced with growing federal and state taxation designed to finance and create a state welfare system, the corporation began to reevaluate its traditional labor policies. In early 1935 George F. Johnson even considered fleeing New York and opening factories in Pennsylvania to escape anticipated state "social" taxes.[3] It was, at the time, merely an expression of frustration, and there is little evidence that the firm seriously began to consider corporate flight as a viable option for evading increasing taxation or rising labor costs. For years Johnson had criticized the blackmail of communities and workers by firms that moved from one place to another, fleeing from unions or attempting to extract tax and property concessions from towns in need of industry and jobs.[4]

Yet in 1945, after receiving a pledge of monetary support from several communities, Endicott Johnson began operations in Pennsylvania. A community nonprofit corporation was established to help finance the construction of a factory in Archbald, Pennsylvania. A similar corporation was also organized in Forest City. With the incorporation of the Keystone State Shoe Company, Endicott Johnson's subsidiary in Pennsylvania, the firm continued opening up factories—in Scranton, Tunkhannock, and Mildred.[5] The expansion of the corporation into depressed economic communities in Pennsylvania in the mid-1940s was a response to union encroachments at home and to the relatively high wages management was forced to maintain to keep the unions out of the factories. The "Square Deal" was becoming too expensive. A company memorandum, evaluating prospects in Pennsylvania, made that quite clear:

It should also be considered with Mr. Prins what he thinks about the possibilities of union organizations being successful in organizing the workers and if such organization should develop, what in his opinion would be the attitude of the union with respect to securing additional wages and benefits for the workers. Would they expect to get for Tunkhannock workers approximately the same earnings as workers are now getting, doing similar work in Johnson City? Tunkhannock is not too far away from Johnson City—approximately 45 miles—and if we started a factory and later found ourselves in a position where organized labor will expect to get the same earnings and benefits as our workers in Johnson City we, of course, would find that our purpose in starting the factory would have been defeated.[6]

In expanding the sphere of their corporate community and becoming absentee proprietors, Endicott Johnson managers found themselves betraying some of the central tenets of the corporation's "Square Deal" ethos. New managers for plants in Pennsylvania would not come from those communities but from without: from Endicott, Johnson City, and Binghamton.[7] Subsequent decisions regarding plant expansion further undermined the company's professed ideals, as the firm continued to invest its profits in ventures outside the Triple Cities. In the late 1950s the corporation opened up a factory in Mississippi.[8] And in the fall of 1966 the firm announced plans to expand operations into Puerto Rico. By then the company's commitment to close corporate and community ties had been severely eroded. Faced with ever-growing pressure from corporations operating in cheap labor markets, the firm had been forced to sacrifice the ideals of the past. Its Puerto Rican employees would not be brought into the "corporate family." The company's obligation to them and to its Puerto Rican venture as a whole would be minimal. The Puerto Rico Industrial Development Company had agreed to supply the firm with a factory and equipment; the Puerto Rican government agreed "to assume the cost of training personnel."[9]

The geographic expansion of the firm, at least when it began, did not signal a decline in production in the Triple Cities area. In fact, through the early 1950s the firm's work force remained quite large, numbering about 17,000 to 18,000. But a transformed economy would soon change all that. The Korean War had maintained the profitability of the company, but it also had given the firm a false sense of security. Because of its concentration on the production of work shoes and other heavy-duty footwear, Endicott Johnson had limited its share of a far more profitable and quickly expanding segment of the American consumer market, composed of lighter and more stylish shoes.[10] This only compounded existing financial woes caused by managerial failures and keen competition from more exploitative firms. As a result, in the latter years of the 1950s and into the 1960s, the corporation experienced severe business crises. Profits declined drastically. In 1960 the firm suffered a loss of $1.5 million. Management changes were made, and Frank A. Johnson, who had taken the place of Charles F. Johnson, Jr., in 1957, after the latter had suffered a stroke, was replaced as president of the company by Pasquale J. Casella, a former executive of the Radio Corporation of America (RCA). Continuing losses led to another change in management. In 1963 Eli White, recruited earlier from the General Shoe Company, took over as president of the firm.[11] No longer was management recruited "from the ranks."

Two years earlier, in 1961, a year in which the firm suffered a staggering $12 million loss, the last manifestation of worker and community loyalty to the corporation was demonstrated. A community-wide movement successfully kept an "outside" holding company from acquiring a controlling interest in the corporation. Old men and children, workers and nonworkers alike, banded together to purchase 63,000 shares of Endicott Johnson stock and prevent the takeover of the corporation.[12] But even as the antitakeover movement was gaining momentum, workers were expressing their doubts about the management of the firm. "The Johnsons are not doing the job they should do," said one worker in commenting on the takeover attempt. Another was in favor of "a change. It might be better. Things seem to be getting worse." And a third felt that "management doesn't care about the workers, just about themselves."[13] Despite the public show of support, the workers' attitudes toward the firm had changed considerably in the previous decade. No longer were they sending their children to work at "EJs," but to IBM, whose corporate welfare policies far exceeded the offerings of Endicott Johnson.[14]

The demonstration of fealty in 1961 would not be repeated. The corporation could no longer live up to the expectations of either its workers or local citizens. Continuing to suffer from the twin ills of foreign competition and poor management, Endicott Johnson began to streamline its operations. It closed down factories in Binghamton, Johnson City, Endicott, and Owego; it leased out its recreation centers, originally built for the workers; it ceased its home building program and sold off remaining homes; its medical departments were finally shut down in 1969, replaced by a Blue Cross and Blue Shield plan.[15] Local papers noted nostalgically the "passing era of EJ" and the decline of its policies of corporate and community paternalism. "It was perhaps the furthest reach of a reign of industrial paternalism that many feel was unmatched in 20th Century America," wrote one reporter.[16] It was a fitting epitaph.

Thus was the "Square Deal" put to rest. For over five decades the Endicott Johnson Corporation had sustained an industrial order, which, not unlike the society around it, managed to maintain a balance between consensus and conflict. Through benevolence and occasionally repression, the corporation was able to weather the numerous challenges that threatened to destroy the relationship between managers and workers that corporate paternalism had carefully cultivated. In the end, however, Endicott Johnson's paternalistic order fell prey to the realities of modern multinational capitalism, where the pressures of competition and the quest for quick profits outweighed both the economic and the humane motives that gave rise to and maintained corporate welfarism.

And yet important components of industrial paternalism at Endicott Johnson did not die. They were partially transformed into bureaucratic forms that now constitute part of the wage bargain between many corporate institutions and their employees. The legacy of Endicott Johnson still survives, even as the patriarchs who pioneered in its development lie buried. It survives not only in company health plans, pensions, profit sharing, and a host of other employment benefits that many workers in certain sectors of the economy now take for granted but also in the rhetoric, attitudes, and behavior of modern-day corporate managers. Surviving, too, however, are the contradictions and limits of welfare capitalism.

Welfare capitalism celebrated a partnership between capital and labor, but it cultivated a blatantly unequal one. That was obvious to thousands of Endicott Johnson workers who daily experienced the Janus face of welfarism. The contradictions inherent in their working lives yielded a mixed loyalty, one that continues to characterize millions of America's workers. Union or nonunion, they extract whatever security they may from the nation's corporations and in return defer to the dictates of management. To the extent that welfare capitalism *can* continue to provide security to workers, management may expect continuing "cooperation." But the incompleteness of that cooperation—measured in productivity, shop floor behavior, and morale—suggests that even security cannot buy total loyalty. Although a common interest in the prosperity of their industries weds managers and workers, they remain adversaries on questions of how to distribute prosperity and how to achieve it. Where industrial hierarchies exist and domination of the many by the few remains a fact of everyday life, cooperation and partnership will always be elusive goals.

NOTES

1. I have not gone into the details of these unionization attempts since they generally followed the contours of events narrated in the previous chapter. For those interested in pursuing the subject, information on attempts to unionize Endicott Johnson workers in the 1950s and 1960s can be found in box 13, ser. 3, Frank A. Johnson Papers; in boxes 35–40, ser. 1, Charles F. Johnson, Jr., Papers; in box 4, ser. 2 of the George W. Johnson Papers, George Arents Research Library for Special Collections, Syracuse University, Syracuse, N.Y. The records of the Amalgamated Meat Cutters and Butcher Workmen of North America, located at the State Historical Society of Wisconsin, also contain several files on its 1956–59 tannery organizing drive at Endicott Johnson. Letters, leaflets, and clippings relating to the Amalgamated's and several other organizing campaigns in the 1950s can be found in the files of the Broome County Federation of Labor, located in Johnson City. I would like to thank Leo Heavy, president of the federation, for allowing me access to the files. The minutes of the Binghamton Central Labor Union from 1950 through 1960 also provide valuable information on the coordination of union forces in the various unionization drives at Endicott Johnson. Maurice J. Quain, an ex-officer in the Binghamton Central Labor Union and a labor activist since the 1930s, was an invaluable source on the local labor movement in the 1940s and 1950s. See Maurice J. Quain, interview by Gerald Zahavi, with the assistance of Deborah D. Maxwell, June 29, 1981, tape recording (personal possession).

2. Endicott Johnson Financial Reports, box 23, George F. Johnson Papers, George Arents Research Library for Special Collections, Syracuse University, Syracuse, N.Y.

3. George F. Johnson to George W. Johnson and Charles F. Johnson, Jr., Mar. 18, 1935, box 14, George F. Johnson Papers.

4. See, for example, George F. Johnson to Walter Moore, Nov. 4, 1924, box 7, George F. Johnson Papers.

5. Charles F. Johnson, Jr., to Albert F. Hess, June 6, 1946, box 34, ser. 1, Charles F. Johnson, Jr., Papers. See also box 6, ser. 2, and box 1, ser. 1, in the same collection for more on the firm's Pennsylvania subsidiaries. Boxes 10 and 12, ser. 4, in the Frank A. Johnson Papers also contain information on operations in Pennsylvania.

6. "Tunkhannock Factory" memo, Apr. 5, 1945, box 12, ser. 4, Frank A. Johnson Papers. The corporation planned mainly to employ women in the new plants, anticipating that they would accept lower wages and would be less likely to join unions than men. In the Tunkhannock factory, for example, management hoped to establish a labor force composed of 90 percent women and girls. Charles F. Johnson, Jr., memo, Apr. 11, 1945, box 12, ser. 4, Frank A. Johnson Papers.

7. Charles F. Johnson, Jr., to Bill Sullivan, Aug. 21, 1946, box 12, ser. 4, Frank A. Johnson Papers.

8. See Annual Financial Reports, 1959–61, in box 23, George F. Johnson Papers.

9. *Binghamton Evening Press,* Oct. 18, 1966.

10. Stephen Mahoney, "What Happened at Endicott Johnson after the Band Stopped

Playing," *Fortune* 66 (Sept. 1962): 130. Mahoney's article is an excellent discussion of the decline of Endicott Johnson.

11. Eli G. White, *The Awakening of a Company: The Story of Endicott Johnson Corporation* (New York, 1967), 10–19. This short, reprinted Newcomen Society speech by the president of Endicott Johnson is a fine summary of corporate changes in the 1950s and 1960s.

12. Mahoney, "What Happened at Endicott Johnson," 127. See also Jan. and Feb. issues of the *Binghamton Evening Press* on the takeover attempt and community response.

13. *Binghamton Sunday Press,* Jan. 8, 1961.

14. Numerous interviewees made this clear. See, especially, James W. Lupole, interview by Gerald Zahavi, with the assistance of Deborah D. Maxwell, July 15, 1981, tape recording (personal possession).

15. *Binghamton Evening Press,* Jan. 18, Jan. 21, Jan. 24, Mar. 6, June 25, 1962, Jan. 23, 1963, Mar. 23, 1964, June 14, Oct. 7, 1966, Dec. 3, 1969; *Binghamton Sunday Press,* Mar. 4, 1962.

16. *Binghamton Sunday Press,* Mar. 4, 1962.

Appendix

TABLE A

Endicott Johnson Employment and Wage Data, 1887–1966

Year	Average Number of Workers	Average Weekly Wages (dollars)	Average Yearly Wages (dollars)
1887	281	NA	NA
1888	285	NA	NA
1889	425	NA	NA
1890	475	NA	NA
1891	425	NA	NA
1892	425	NA	202.00
1893	400	NA	414.00
1894	420	NA	440.00
1895	640	NA	490.00
1896	700	NA	NA
1897	1,000	NA	NA
1898	1,250	NA	NA
1899	1,300	NA	NA
1900	1,800	NA	NA
1901	1,900	NA	NA
1902	2,010	NA	NA
1903	2,709	NA	NA
1904	NA	NA	NA
1905	2,442[a]	NA	NA
1906	2,733[a]	NA	NA

NOTES:

Average weekly earnings include bonus and pay for vacations and holidays.

[a]Number of workers at time of inspection by New York State factory inspectors.

[b]Rough estimate pieced together from newspapers and New York State inspectors' averages for individual factories.

[c]Years with extreme variations in number employed. Estimates, not averages.

SOURCES: New York State Factory Inspector's reports; New York State Bureau of Statistics of Labor; "To the Workers" notice, Jan. 13, 1944, box 34, ser. 1, Charles F. Johnson, Jr., Papers; Burns, "A Study of Personnel Policies"; *Binghamton Press*.

TABLE A (*continued*)

Year	Average Number of Workers	Average Weekly Wages (dollars)	Average Yearly Wages (dollars)
1907	3,500[a]	NA	NA
1908	NA	NA	NA
1909	2,400[b]	NA	NA
1910	4,000	NA	NA
1911	NA	NA	NA
1912	NA	NA	NA
1913	6,009	10.81	562.12
1914	6,489	11.76	611.52
1915	7,630	13.79	706.68
1916	10,632	14.76	767.52
1917	12,078	16.96	881.92
1918	11,327	20.90	1,086.80
1919	12,082	29.30	1,523.60
1920	13,265	29.42	1,529.84
1921	11,905	28.37	1,475.24
1922	14,210	28.75	1,495.00
1923	15,458	25.92	1,347.84
1924	14,367	26.05	1,354.60
1925	15,716	27.01	1,404.52
1926	14,396	25.68	1,335.36
1927	15,539	27.64	1,437.28
1928	14,478	25.52	1,327.04
1929	14,698	24.94	1,296.88
1930	14,551	22.05	1,146.60
1931	14,985	23.08	1,200.00
1932	15,069	20.55	1,068.60
1933	15,833	22.27	1,158.04
1934	17,723	23.02	1,197.04
1935	17,908	23.68	1,231.36
1936	17,858	23.24	1,208.48
1937	18,588	23.91	1,243.32
1938	17,788	18.13	942.76
1939	17,748	19.24	1,000.48
1940	17,041	20.24	1,052.48
1941	18,339	27.98	1,454.96
1942	18,929	33.16	1,724.32
1943	16,651	35.91	1,867.32
1944	14,000[c]	39.92	NA
1945	15,000[c]	43.94	NA
1946	NA	41.74	NA
1947	18,076	NA	NA
1948	17,800	NA	NA
1949	NA	NA	NA
1950	NA	NA	NA
1951	20,909	NA	NA

TABLE A (*continued*)

Year	Average Number of Workers	Average Weekly Wages (dollars)	Average Yearly Wages (dollars)
1952	20,608	NA	NA
1953	20,738	NA	NA
1954	20,182	NA	NA
1955	20,307	NA	NA
1956	19,731	NA	NA
1957	19,069	NA	NA
1958	17,800	NA	NA
1959	17,427	NA	NA
1960	16,775	NA	NA
1961	15,269	NA	NA
1962	13,562	NA	NA
1963	11,832	NA	NA
1964	12,410	NA	NA
1965	11,751	NA	NA
1966	10,159	NA	NA

TABLE B
Endicott Johnson Gross Sales and Net Profits, 1914–1966

Year	Gross Sales (dollars)	Net Profits (dollars)
1914	20,422,013	1,940,148
1915	26,070,404	2,170,430
1916	34,515,400	3,669,797
1917	44,144,673	4,630,471
1918	52,896,275	4,398,187
1919	62,713,039	4,955,286
1920	74,970,102	3,150,441
1921	58,892,347	4,642,888
1922	63,659,075	5,617,530
1923	66,565,812	4,154,278
1924	66,378,176	4,175,644
1925	32,651,325[a]	4,312,064
1926	70,661,674	3,697,878
1927	73,078,800	4,332,685
1928	69,333,401	3,601,263
1929	68,415,057	2,771,563
1930	54,499,477	765,267
1931	48,203,352[b]	2,580,566[b]
1932	43,599,145	1,188,240
1933	49,818,140	2,154,941
1934	56,248,313	2,167,677
1935	58,328,338	2,117,403
1936	61,570,963	1,974,833
1937	67,134,962	1,520,714
1938	51,734,973	857,191
1939	58,525,022	1,611,367
1940	57,635,909	1,664,315
1941	80,852,388	2,351,110
1942	103,875,698	2,343,766
1943	95,779,269	2,310,148
1944	95,566,262	1,663,448
1945	102,093,259	2,266,872
1946	105,888,544	2,337,349
1947	142,029,121	2,753,870
1948	148,650,282	3,623,162
1949	131,677,018	2,297,825
1950	133,330,507	1,391,683
1951	157,317,152	2,319,302
1952	142,923,701	2,572,161
1953	140,096,792	2,095,120

NOTES:
[a]Sales between Jan. 1 and July.
[b]Jan. 1–Nov. 30. New fiscal year calendar initiated.

SOURCES: Burns, "A Study of Personnel Policies"; Saul, "An American Entrepreneur"; Endicott Johnson Corporation yearly financial reports.

TABLE B (*continued*)

Year	Gross Sales (dollars)	Net Profits (dollars)
1954	133,316,999	2,135,249
1955	143,057,526	2,843,956
1956	151,359,762	2,771,158
1957	146,016,168	2,693,739
1958	134,553,027	1,895,109
1959	146,099,113	1,504,500
1960	141,467,778	− 1,506,273
1961	132,977,631	− 12,215,748
1962	129,333,744	621,135
1963	118,405,437	− 4,266,568
1964	127,082,970	1,066,278
1965	129,519,513	1,110,285
1966	145,416,362	2,211,098

TABLE C

Endicott Johnson Factories, Tanneries, and Other Physical Plants,
including Dates of Construction and Locations, 1890–1950

Year	Facility	Location
1890	Lestershire Factory (also known as "Corliss Ave." and later Pioneer Factory)	Lestershire (Johnson City)
1901–2	Fine Welt Factory (later Ideal Factory)	Endicott
1902	Sole Leather Tannery	Endicott
1903	Fine Welt Annex	Endicott
1905	Upper Leather Tannery	Endicott
1905–6	Sales Department [building and warehouse] (expanded in 1914)	Endicott
1908	New York City Distribution Warehouse	New York City
1908	Calfskin Tannery	Endicott
1910	Upper Leather Tannery Annex	Endicott
1912	Scout Factory (later Misses' and Children's Factory)	Lestershire (Johnson City)
1913	Charles F. Johnson Factory (housed Boys and Youths Factory and Men's McKay Factory)	Lestershire (Johnson City)
1913	Heeling Factory (later Jigger Warehouse)	Lestershire (Johnson City)
1913	Charles F. Johnson Powerhouse	Lestershire (Johnson City)
1914	Box Toe Factory	Lestershire (Johnson City)
1914	Chrome Leather Tannery	Endicott
1916	Foundry and Die Shop	Johnson City
1916	New Scout Factory	Johnson City
1916	Pioneer Annex	Johnson City
1916–17	Hidehouse	Endicott
1917	Fibreboard Mill	Johnson City
1917	Carton Factory	Johnson City
1917	Mechanical Department [building]	Endicott
1918	Service Department [building]	Johnson City
1921	Victory Factory (housed Women's Fine McKay Factory and Victory Factory)	Johnson City
1921	Charles F. Johnson Annex (Heeling and Trimming departments)	Johnson City
1921	Infants' Factory (in Pioneer Annex)	Johnson City
1921	New Chrome Sole Tannery	Endicott
1922	Paracord (or Rubber Mill)	Johnson City
1922	Binghamton Busy Boys' Factory	Binghamton
1923	Every Day Factory (later Security Factory)	Endicott
1923	South End Factory (later All Sports Factory)	Johnson City
1923	Fair Play Factory (and Fair Play Annex)	West Endicott
1925	Owego Factory	Owego
1925	St. Louis Sales and Distribution Center	St. Louis

SOURCES: *Binghamton Sun;* Inglis, *George F. Johnson; Binghamton Press; Endicott Bulletin;* George F. Johnson Papers.

TABLE C (*continued*)

Year	Facility	Location
1926	George F. Johnson Factory (also known as the Old Tabernacle Factory)	Binghamton
1926	Jigger Factory	Johnson City
1926	George F. Improved Factory	West Endicott
1927	Rubber Reclaiming (or Reclaim) Plant	Johnson City
1928	Owego Factory Annex	Owego
1929	Chemical Department [building]	Endicott
1929	Sheepskin Tannery	Endicott
1929	Split Leather Tannery	Endicott
1929	Sunrise Factory	Johnson City
1931	Challenge Factory	Johnson City
1932	Binghamton Work Shoe Factory	Binghamton
1944–45	New Rubber Mill	Johnson City
1945	Keystone Shoe Company factories; Scranton, Tunkhanock, Forest City, Archbold, and Mildred	Pennsylvania

Bibliography

I. MANUSCRIPT COLLECTIONS

Amalgamated Meat Cutters and Butcher Workmen of North America. Records. State Historical Society of Wisconsin, Madison, Wis.

Binghamton Central Labor Union. Minutes. Broome County Federation of Labor, AFL-CIO. Johnson City, N.Y.; and Labor-Management Documentation Center, M. P. Catherwood Library, New York State School of Industrial and Labor Relations, Cornell University, Ithaca, N.Y.

Binghamton Typographical Union. Local 232, International Typographical Union. Minutes. Labor-Management Documentation Center, M. P. Catherwood Library, New York State School of Industrial and Labor Relations, Cornell University, Ithaca, N.Y.

Boot and Shoe Workers' Union [BSWU]. Records. State Historical Society of Wisconsin, Madison, Wis.

Endicott Johnson Corporation Employee Records, Endicott Office Files. George Arents Research Library for Special Collections, Syracuse University, Syracuse, N.Y.

International Fur and Leather Workers Union [IFLWU]. Records. Labor-Management Documentation Center, M. P. Catherwood Library, New York State School of Industrial and Labor Relations, Cornell University, Ithaca, N.Y.

Johnson, Charles F., Jr. Papers. George Arents Research Library for Special Collections, Syracuse University, Syracuse, N.Y.

Johnson, Frank A. Papers. George Arents Research Library for Special Collections, Syracuse University, Syracuse, N.Y.

Johnson, George F. Papers. George Arents Research Library for Special Collections, Syracuse University, Syracuse, N.Y.

Johnson, George W. Papers. George Arents Research Library for Special Collections, Syracuse University, Syracuse, N.Y.

Joint Board of Fur, Leather and Machine Workers. Papers. Labor-Management Documentation Center, M. P. Catherwood Library, New York State School of Industrial and Labor Relations, Cornell University, Ithaca, N.Y.

Local History Files. Broome County Historical Society Library, Roberson Center for the Arts and Sciences, Binghamton, N.Y.

National War Labor Board [NWLB]. Region 2 Case Files. Labor-Management Documentation Center, M. P. Catherwood Library, New York State School of Industrial and Labor Relations, Cornell University, Ithaca, N.Y.

New York State Joint Legislative Committee to Investigate Seditious Activities (Lusk Committee). Papers. Manuscript Division, New York State Library, Albany, N.Y.

Plymouth Cordage Company. Records. Baker Library, Harvard University Graduate School of Business Administration, Boston, Mass.

Putnam, Frederick Wallace. Document Collection. Binghamton Public Library Special Collections, Binghamton, N.Y.

Union Files Collection. Labor-Management Documentation Center, M. P. Catherwood Library, New York State School of Industrial and Labor Relations, Cornell University, Ithaca, N.Y.

II. Oral Sources

[Location of public, oral-history archives given in brackets following first citation.]

A———. Interview by Nancy Grey Osterud, Apr. 23, 1982. Summary and partial transcription, Broome County Immigration History Project. [Roberson Center for the Arts and Sciences, Binghamton, N.Y.]

Azarin, Margaret [pseud.]. Taped interview by Gerald Zahavi, Nov. 15, 1983. Personal possession.

B———. Interview by David Nielson, session 1, Dec. 31, 1973. Transcript, pp. 167–83, in Nielson's possession.

———. Interview by David Nielson, session 2, July 1, 1974. Transcript, pp. 214–29, in Nielson's possession.

B———. Interview by David Nielson, Aug. 14, 1973. Transcript, pp. 139–66, in Nielson's possession.

B———. Interview by David Nielson, July 9, 1974. Transcript, pp. 248–76, in Nielson's possession.

Backes, James L. Taped interview by Gerald Zahavi, May 12, 1984. Personal possession.

Banner, Henry, and Emma Banner [pseud.]. Taped interview by Gerald Zahavi, June 2, 1982. Personal possession.

Battista, Sylvan P. Taped interview by Gerald Zahavi, with the assistance of Deborah D. Maxwell, session 1, July 13, 1981. Personal possession.

———. Taped interview by Gerald Zahavi, with the assistance of Deborah D. Maxwell, session 2, Nov. 12, 1981. Personal possession.

Bertier, William [pseud.]. Taped interview by Gerald Zahavi, with the assistance of Deborah D. Maxwell, July 13, 1981. Personal possession.

Bilek, Josephine Apalovich. Interview by Nancy Grey Osterud, Nov. 8, 1981. Transcript, pp. 1–39, Broome County Immigration History Project.

Birdsall, Earl I. Taped interview by Gerald Zahavi, May 5, 1982. Personal possession.

Bruno, Helen. Taped interview by Gerald Zahavi, with the assistance of Deborah D. Maxwell, July 13, 1981. Personal possession.

C———. Interview by David Nielson, July 26, 1973. Transcript, pp. 76–97, in Nielson's possession.

C——. Interview by Nancy Grey Osterud, Feb. 15, 1982. Summary and partial transcription, Broome County Immigration History Project.

Chopiak, Katie Wasylysyn. Interview by Nancy Grey Osterud, session 1, Aug. 6, 1982. Summary and partial transcription, Nanticoke Valley Historical Society. [Maine, N.Y., and in Osterud's possession]

——. Interview by Nancy Grey Osterud, session 2, Aug. 10, 1982. Summary and partial transcription, Nanticoke Valley Historical Society.

——. Interview by Nancy Grey Osterud, session 3, Aug. 14, 1982. Summary and partial transcription, Nanticoke Valley Historical Society.

——. Interview by Nancy Grey Osterud, session 4, Sept. 10, 1982. Summary and partial transcription, Nanticoke Valley Historical Society.

Chubbuck, Thomas K. Taped interview by Gerald Zahavi, with the assistance of Deborah D. Maxwell, session 1, June 29, 1981. Personal possession.

——. Taped interview by Gerald Zahavi, with the assistance of Deborah D. Maxwell, session 2, July 2, 1981. Personal possession.

——. Taped interview by Gerald Zahavi, session 3, June 28, 1983. Personal possession.

Cinotti, Angelina. Interview by Nettie Politylo, May 26, 1978. Transcript, pp. 1–6, Broome County Oral History Project. [Broome County Historical Society Library, Roberson Center for the Arts and Sciences, Binghamton, N.Y.]

Cinotti, Dominick. Interview by Nettie Politylo, June 8, 1978. Transcript, pp. 1–12, Broome County Oral History Project.

Coletti, Paul [pseud.]. Taped interview by Gerald Zahavi, with the assistance of Deborah D. Maxwell, July 13, 1981. Personal possession.

Compton, Kenneth E. Taped interview by Gerald Zahavi, May 5, 1982. Personal possession.

Councilman, Norman W. Taped interview by Gerald Zahavi, with the assistance of Deborah D. Maxwell, June 5, 1981. Personal possession.

Cowan, Kenneth, and Inez Cowan. Taped interview by Gerald Zahavi, June 2, 1982. Personal possession.

D——. Interview by David Nielson, July 19, 1973. Transcript, pp. 27–53, in Nielson's possession.

D——. Interview by David Nielson, June 25, 1974. Transcript, pp. 230–47, in Nielson's possession.

Davis, Raymond. Interview by Gerald Zahavi, Aug. 27, 1982. Notes, personal possession.

Decker, Mary Sasina. Interview by Nancy Grey Osterud, July 11, 1982. Summary and partial transcription, Nanticoke Valley Historical Society.

Dirlam, Clarence. Taped interview by Gerald Zahavi, Dec. 12, 1979. Personal possession.

Eastman, Harold. Interview by Gerald Zahavi, with the assistance of Deborah D. Maxwell, June 5, 1981. Notes, personal possession.

Eckelberger, Paul R. Taped interview by Gerald Zahavi, with the assistance of Deborah D. Maxwell, June 26, 1981. Personal possession.

F——. Interview by David Nielson, Aug. 3, 1973. Transcript, pp. 98–138, in Nielson's possession.

Farrar, Lucille M. Taped interview by Gerald Zahavi, with the assistance of Deborah D. Maxwell, July 13, 1981. Personal possession.

Filip, Frances, and Adaline Filip Zevan. Interview by Nancy Grey Osterud, Aug. 10, 1982. Summary and partial transcription, Nanticoke Valley Historical Society.

First Ward Senior Center. Group interviews by Nancy Grey Osterud, Mar. 2, Mar. 9, Mar. 16, Mar. 23, 1982; Apr. 1, Apr. 13, Apr. 20, Apr. 26, 1982; May 18, 1982; July 1, 1982; Sept. 21, 1982; Jan. 25, 1983; Feb. 23, 1983; Mar. 1, Mar. 15, 1983; Apr. 5, Apr. 12, 1983. Summaries and partial transcriptions, Broome County Immigration History Project.

Fischer, William C., III. Conversation with Gerald Zahavi, June 10, 1982. Notes, personal possession.

Freeman, Fred. Interview by Nancy Grey Osterud, Mar. 16, 1982. Summary and partial transcription, pp. 1–3, Broome County Immigration History Project.

Gimmie, John, and Anna Makis. Interview by Michele Morrisson, Sept. 30, 1982. Transcript, pp. 1–22, Broome County Immigration History Project.

Goida, Andrew. Interview by Nettie Politylo, Jan. 2, 1978. Transcript, pp. 1–27, Broome County Oral History Project.

Gruss, Michael. Interview by Anna Caganek, Jan. 5, 1978. Transcript, pp. 1–17, Broome County Oral History Project.

Guy, Agnes. Taped interview by Gerald Zahavi, Dec. 12, 1979. Personal possession.

H——. Interview by David Nielson, June 23, 1973. Transcript, pp. 1–26, in Nielson's possession.

H——. Interview by David Nielson, July 24, 1974. Transcript, pp. 317–28, in Nielson's possession.

H——. Interview by Nancy Grey Osterud, Feb. 14, 1982. Summary and partial transcription, Broome County Immigration History Project.

Haight, William. Taped interview by Gerald Zahavi, with the assistance of Deborah D. Maxwell, May 27, 1982. Personal possession.

Heavy, Leo. Conversation with Gerald Zahavi, June 29, 1981. Notes, personal possession.

Hobbie, Jack. Taped interview by Gerald Zahavi, Nov. 17, 1979. Personal possession.

——. Conversation with Gerald Zahavi, Dec. 12, 1979. Notes, personal possession.

J——. Interview by David Nielson, July 15, 1974. Transcript, pp. 200–213, in Nielson's possession.

Jerome, Michael P. Taped interview by Gerald Zahavi, May 10, 1982. Personal possession.

Jones, Arthur G. Taped interview by Gerald Zahavi, June 2, 1982. Personal possession.

Joseph, Edward [pseud.]. Taped interview by Gerald Zahavi, Nov. 17, 1979. Personal possession.

Ketcham, Rodney K. Conversation with Gerald Zahavi, Dec. 8, 1980. Notes, personal possession.

King, Amy. Taped interview by Gerald Zahavi, Nov. 30, 1979. Personal possession.

Knickerbocker, Paul R. Taped interview by Gerald Zahavi, with the assistance of Deborah D. Maxwell, session 1, June 10, 1982. Personal possession.

——. Taped interview by Gerald Zahavi, with the assistance of Deborah D. Maxwell, session 2, June 18, 1982. Personal possession.

————. Taped interview by Gerald Zahavi, with the assistance of Deborah D. Maxwell, session 3, July 22, 1982. Personal possession.

Knowles, Elmer, and Audrey Knowles. Taped interview by Gerald Zahavi, May 10, 1982. Personal possession.

Kolb, Donald C., and Gladys A. Kolb. Taped interview by Gerald Zahavi, with the assistance of Deborah D. Maxwell, June 5, 1981. Personal possession.

Kovak, John [pseud.]. Taped interview by Gerald Zahavi, with the assistance of Deborah D. Maxwell, session 1, July 15, 1981. Personal possession.

————. Taped interview by Gerald Zahavi, session 2, Aug. 27, 1982. Personal possession.

Levine, Herbert. Interview by Nettie Polityo, Sept. 15, 1978. Transcript, pp. 1–27, Broome County Oral History Project.

Lupole, James W. Taped interview by Gerald Zahavi, with the assistance of Deborah D. Maxwell, July 15, 1981. Personal possession.

McGregor, Margaret. Interview by Diane Baker, Sept. 3, 1981. Summary and partial transcription, Nanticoke Valley Historical Society.

————. Interview by Nancy Grey Osterud, Aug. 13, 1982. Summary and partial transcription, Nanticoke Valley Historical Society.

Marca, Carl. Taped interview by Nancy Grey Osterud, Feb. 24, 1982. Broome County Immigration History Project.

Moody, Stanley L. Taped interview by Gerald Zahavi, with the assistance of Deborah D. Maxwell, June 1, 1981. Personal possession.

Murphy, Richard J. Taped interview by Gerald Zahavi, with the assistance of Deborah D. Maxwell, July 7, 1981. Personal possession.

N————. Interview by David Nielson, July 26, 1974. Transcript, pp. 329–51, in Nielson's possession.

N————. Interview by David Nielson, summer 1974. Transcript, pp. 298–316, in Nielson's possession.

North Endicott Senior Center. Group interviews by Nancy Grey Osterud, Feb. 1, Feb. 8, Feb. 16, 1982; Mar. 8, 1982. Summaries and partial transcriptions, Broome County Immigration History Project.

O'Connor, Bernice, and Roger T. O'Connor. Taped interview by Gerald Zahavi, with the assistance of Deborah D. Maxwell, Nov. 7, 1981. Personal possession.

Olsofsky, Eva Brhel. Interview by Nancy Grey Osterud, Aug. 8, 1982. Summary and partial transcription, Nanticoke Valley Historical Society.

P————. Interview by David Nielson, June 26, 1973. Transcript, pp. 54–75, in Nielson's possession.

P————. Interview by Michele Morrisson and Frank Sacco, Sept. 20, 1982. Summary and partial transcription, Broome County Immigration History Project.

Pembridge, Mary. Taped interview by Gerald Zahavi, Dec. 7, 1979. Personal possession.

Perkins, Palmer. Taped interview by Gerald Zahavi, with the assistance of Deborah D. Maxwell, Apr. 30, 1982. Personal possession.

Pitcher, Mattie Drake. Interview by Gloria Comstock, summer 1981. Summary and partial transcription, Nanticoke Valley Historical Society.

Quain, Maurice J. Taped interview by Gerald Zahavi, with the assistance of Deborah D. Maxwell, June 29, 1981. Personal possession.

R——. Interview by David Nielson, July 10, 1974. Transcript, pp. 277–97, in Nielson's possession.

Robble, John, and Anis Robble. Taped interview by Gerald Zahavi, June 28, 1983. Personal possession.

Russell, Ralph V. Taped interview by Gerald Zahavi, with the assistance of Deborah D. Maxwell, May 27, 1982. Personal possession.

Ryall, Owen J. Taped interview by Gerald Zahavi, with the assistance of Deborah D. Maxwell, Apr. 30, 1982. Personal possession.

S——. Interview by David Nielson, May 1973. Transcript, pp. 197–99, in Nielson's possession.

S——. Interview by Nancy Grey Osterud and Laura Kirkland, May 15, 1982. Summary and partial transcription, Broome County Immigration History Project.

S——. Taped interview by David Nielson, July 22, 1976. In Nielson's possession.

Sacco, Antoinette Santodonato, and Anthony Sacco. Interview by Leora Ornstein, Apr. 25, 1983. Transcript, pp. 1–27, Broome County Immigration History Project.

Salvatore, Sam. Taped interview by Gerald Zahavi, with the assistance of Deborah D. Maxwell, July 7, 1981. Personal possession.

Schuttak, Theresa, and Fran Eckert. Taped interview by Gerald Zahavi, with the assistance of Deborah D. Maxwell, Apr. 30, 1982. Personal possession.

Sedlak, John. Interview by Nettie Politylo, Feb. 8, 1978. Transcript, pp. 1–18, Broome County Oral History Project.

Sepelak, Irene. Interview by Nancy Grey Osterud, July 8, 1982. Summary and partial transcription, Nanticoke Valley Historical Society.

Seversky, Mary. Taped interview by Gerald Zahavi, with the assistance of Deborah D. Maxwell, July 22, 1982. Personal possession.

Sovik, Mary. Interview by Anna Caganek, Apr. 10, 1978. Transcript, pp. 1–8, Broome County Oral History Project.

Spisak, Anne. Interview by Nettie Politylo, Dec. 29, 1977. Transcript, pp. 1–23, Broome County Oral History Project.

Springer, Lee F. Taped interview by Gerald Zahavi, with the assistance of Deborah D. Maxwell, July 15, 1981. Personal possession.

T——. Interview by David Nielson, June 1, 1973. Transcript, pp. 184–96, in Nielson's possession.

Tuthill, Frank. Taped interview by Gerald Zahavi, Nov. 30, 1979. Personal possession.

V—— and L——. Taped interview by David Nielson, July, 23, 1976. In Nielson's possession.

Valenta, Alfred. Taped interview by Gerald Zahavi, with the assistance of Deborah D. Maxwell, June 26, 1981. Personal possession.

Warski, John, Sr. Interview by Nettie Politylo, Nov. 16, 1977. Transcript, pp. 1–17, Broome County Oral History Project.

Wasyliw, Maria. Interview, edited and translated by Zenon Wasyliw, 1977. Transcript, pp. 1–8, personal possession.

Wright, Ernest, and Bessie Bahler. Interview by Nancy Grey Osterud, Aug. 14, 1982. Summary and partial transcription, Nanticoke Valley Historical Society.

Zobkiw, William. Taped interview by Gerald Zahavi, Nov. 7, 1983. Personal possession.

III. Newspapers and Journals

American Federationist.

American Shoemaking.

Binghamton Advocate. [Labor-Management Documentation Center, M. P. Catherwood Library, New York State School of Industrial and Labor Relations, Cornell University, Ithaca, N.Y.]

Binghamton Daily Democrat. [Binghamton Public Library, Binghamton, N.Y.]

Binghamton Daily Republican. [Binghamton Public Library]

Binghamton Evening Herald. [Binghamton Public Library]

Binghamton Evening Press. [Binghamton Public Library]

Binghamton Press. [Binghamton Public Library]

Binghamton Republican. [Binghamton Public Library]

Binghamton Sun. [Binghamton Public Library]

Binghamton Sunday Press. [Binghamton Public Library]

Broome Republican. [Binghamton Public Library]

CIO News (Shoe Workers' Edition). [State Historical Society of Wisconsin, Madison, Wis.]

Democratic Daily Leader. [Binghamton Public Library]

Democratic Weekly Leader. [Binghamton Public Library]

E-J Union News (E.-J. Workers' Organizing Committee). [United States Department of Labor Library, Washington, D.C.]

E-J Workers Magazine. [George F. Johnson Memorial Library, Endicott, N.Y.; and in George W. Johnson Papers]

E.-J. Workers' Review. [Broome County Historical Society Library, Roberson Center for the Arts and Sciences, Binghamton, N.Y.; George F. Johnson Papers; and in various other local depositories]

Endicott Bulletin. [George F. Johnson Memorial Library]

Endicott Leather Worker. [Joint Board of Fur, Leather and Machine Workers Papers, Labor-Management Documentation Center]

Endicott Times. [George F. Johnson Memorial Library]

Fur and Leather Worker. [State Historical Society of Wisconsin]

Johnson City-Endicott Record. [George F. Johnson Memorial Library]

Labor News (United Shoe Workers of America). [United States Department of Labor Library]

Lestershire-Endicott Record. [George F. Johnson Memorial Library]

Lester-Shire News. [Broome County Historical Society Library]

Lestershire Record. [Broome County Historical Society Library; Olin Library, Cornell University]

Magazine. [Broome County Historical Society Library; and in George F. Johnson Papers]

Morning Sun. [Binghamton Public Library]

News-Dispatch. [George F. Johnson Memorial Library]

New York Herald.

New York Times.

Record (Johnson City, Endicott, Union). [George F. Johnson Memorial Library]

Shoe Workers' Journal. [State Historical Society of Wisconsin; and in various other depositories]

Sun-Bulletin. [Binghamton Public Library]

Triple Cities Labor Herald. [George W. Johnson Papers]

Union Boot and Shoe Worker. [State Historical Society of Wisconsin]

IV. Public and Union Documents

Binghamton. *City Directory.* 1888–1900, 1905, 1910, 1915, 1925, 1939–41.

Boot and Shoe Workers' Union [BSWU]. *Proceedings of the Eighteenth Convention.* Toronto: BSWU, 1939.

———. *Report of Proceedings of the Joint Convention of Boot and Shoe Workers.* Boston: BSWU, 1895.

———. *Report of Proceedings of the Second Convention of the Boot and Shoe Workers' Union.* Boston: BSWU, 1896.

Endicott. *City Directory.* 1910, 1915, 1925, 1939–41.

International Fur and Leather Workers Union [IFLWU]. *Proceedings of the Fifteenth Biennial Convention of the International Fur and Leather Workers Union.* Atlantic City, N.J.: IFLWU, 1944.

———. *Proceedings of the Ninth Annual Convention, Leather Division, International Fur and Leather Workers Union.* Detroit: IFLWU, 1942.

———. *Proceedings of the Seventeenth Biennial Convention of the International Fur and Leather Workers Union.* Atlantic City, N.J.: IFLWU, 1948.

———. *Proceedings of the Sixteenth Biennial Convention of the International Fur and Leather Workers Union.* Atlantic City, N.J.: IFLWU, 1946.

Johnson City. *City Directory.* 1925, 1939–41.

Lestershire. *City Directory.* 1892–1900, 1905, 1910.

New Jersey. Bureau of Statistics of Labor and Industries. *Twenty-seventh Annual Report.* Trenton: State Printers, 1904.

New York State. Annual *Report of the Board of Mediation and Arbitration.* 1st through 8th. Albany: State Printers, 1888–95.

———. Annual *Report of the Factory Inspector.* 1st through 15th. Albany: State Printers, 1887–1901.

———. "Census of Population: 1892." For Broome County, N.Y. Manuscript.

———. "Census of Population: 1925." For Broome County, N.Y. Manuscript.

———. Department of Labor. Annual *Report of the Bureau of Statistics of Labor.* 7th through 18th. Albany: State Printers, 1890–1901.

———. Department of Labor. *Special Bulletin: Women in Binghamton Industries.* Albany: New York State Department of Labor, 1928.

———. Department of Labor. *Third Annual Report of the Commissioner of Labor.* Albany: State Printers, 1904.

———. Department of Labor. *Trend of Employment in New York State Factories from 1914 to 1939.* Albany: New York State Department of Labor, 1940.

United Shoe Workers of America [USWA]. *Proceedings of the Second Convention of the United Shoe Workers of America.* Rochester, N.Y.: USWA, 1939.

———. *Proceedings of the Third Convention of the United Shoe Workers of America.* Worcester, Mass.: USWA, 1942.

U.S. Bureau of Labor Statistics. *The Betterment of Industrial Conditions*. Prepared by Victor H. Olmstead. Bulletin, 31. Washington, D.C.: Government Printing Office, 1900.

———. *Employers' Welfare Work*. Prepared by Elizabeth Lewis Otey. Bulletin, 123. Washington, D.C.: Government Printing Office, 1913.

———. *Welfare Work for Employees in Industrial Establishments in the United States*. Bulletin, 250. Washington, D.C.: Government Printing Office, 1919.

U.S. Bureau of the Census. Eighth Census, 1860. "Census of Manufactures." For Broome County, N.Y. Manuscript.

———. Eighth Census, 1860. *Population of the United States in 1860*. Washington, D.C.: Government Printing Office, 1864.

———. *Eleventh Census of the United States, 1890*. Vol. 1, *Population*. Pt. 1. Washington, D.C.: Government Printing Office, 1892.

———. *Fifteenth Census of the United States, 1930: Population*. Vol. 1. Washington, D.C.: Government Printing Office, 1932.

———. *Fourteenth Census of the United States, 1920: Population*. Vol. 1. Washington, D.C.: Government Printing Office, 1922.

———. *Historical Statistics of the United States: Colonial Times to 1957*. Washington, D.C.: Government Printing Office, 1960.

———. Tenth Census, 1880. "Census of Manufactures." For Broome County, N.Y. Manuscript.

———. Tenth Census, 1880. "Population of the United States in 1880." For Broome County, N.Y. Manuscript.

———. Twelfth Census, 1900. "Population of the United States in 1900." For Broome County, N.Y. Manuscript.

———. *Twelfth Census of the United States, 1900*. Vol. 9, *Manufactures*. Washington, D.C.: Government Printing Office, 1902.

U.S. Congress. House. Committee on Education and Labor. *Violations of Free Speech and Rights of Labor.* "Industrial Espionage." 76th Cong. Washington, D.C.: Government Printing Office, 1939.

U.S. Department of Labor. *Thirteenth Annual Report of the Commissioner of Labor.* Vol. 1. Washington, D.C.: Government Printing Office, 1899.

U.S. Immigration Commission. *Reports*. Vol. 12, pts. 8–9, *Immigrants in Industries, Boot and Shoe Manufacturing*. Washington, D.C.: Government Printing Office, 1911.

U.S. National Labor Relations Board. *Decisions and Orders of the National Labor Relations Board*. Vols. 15–117. Washington, D.C.: Government Printing Office, 1939–57.

U.S. National War Labor Board. *War Labor Reports*. Vols. 16–28. Washington, D.C.: Bureau of National Affairs, 1942–46.

V. Published Works by George F. Johnson

Johnson, George F. "Fewer Bosses, More Thinkers—Our Management Plan." *System: The Magazine of Business* 49 (May 1926): 633–36, 693.

———. "A President's Letters to His Workers." [Part 1.] Edited by Samuel Crowther. *System: The Magazine of Business* 46 (Sept. 1924): 270–74, 350.

————. "A President's Letters to His Workers." [Part 2.] Edited by Samuel Crowther. *System: The Magazine of Business* 46 (Oct. 1924): 441–45, 495–98.

————. "A President's Letters to His Workers: Some Common Sense about Wages." [Part 3.] Edited by Samuel Crowther. *System: The Magazine of Business* 46 (Nov. 1924): 583–87, 646–47.

————. "A President's Letters to His Workers: How Should Profits Be Divided?" [Part 4.] Edited by Samuel Crowther. *System: The Magazine of Business* 46 (Dec. 1924): 724–28, 789–91.

————. "A President's Letters to His Workers." [Part 5.] Edited by Samuel Crowther. *System: The Magazine of Business* 47 (Jan. 1925): 46–50, 96–97.

————. "A President's Letters to His Workers." [Part 6.] Edited by Samuel Crowther. *System: The Magazine of Business* 47 (Feb. 1925): 164–68, 235–37.

————. "A President's Letters to His Workers." [Part 7.] Edited by Samuel Crowther. *System: The Magazine of Business* 47 (Mar. 1925): 320–24, 364–68.

————. "30 Years without a Strike." *System: The Magazine of Business* 37 (Jan. 1920): 45–48, 164–65.

————. "What I've Learned about Business since 1920." *System: The Magazine of Business* 40 (Dec. 1921): 679–83, 728, 730.

Johnson, George F., et al. *The Management and the Worker.* Chicago: A. W. Shaw Co., 1920.

VI. MONOGRAPHS AND ARTICLES

Abbott, Edith. *Women in Industry: A Study in American Economic History.* New York: D. Appleton and Co., 1910.

Allen, Frederick J. *The Shoe Industry.* New York: Henry Holt and Co., 1922.

Allen, James B. *The Company Town in the American West.* Norman: University of Oklahoma Press, 1966.

Auerbach, Jerold S. *Labor and Liberty: The La Follette Committee and the New Deal.* Indianapolis: Bobbs-Merrill Co., 1966.

Balch, Emily Greene. *Our Slavic Fellow Citizens.* New York: Charities Publication Committee, 1910.

Ballou, Adin. *History of the Town of Milford.* Boston: Franklin Press, 1882.

Barton, Josef J. *Peasants and Strangers: Italians, Rumanians, and Slovaks in an American City, 1890–1950.* Cambridge: Harvard University Press, 1975.

Beardsley, Guy Whiting. "He Heard Opportunity's Knock." *American Magazine* 81 (May 1916): 50–51.

Bedford, Henry F. *Socialism and the Workers in Massachusetts, 1886–1912.* Amherst: University of Massachusetts Press, 1966.

Belden, Thomas, and Marva Belden. *The Lengthening Shadow: The Life of Thomas J. Watson.* Boston: Little, Brown and Co., 1962.

Bendix, Reinhard. *Work and Authority in Industry: Ideologies of Management in the Course of Industrialization.* New York: Harper and Row, 1956.

Berkowitz, Edward, and Kim McQuaid. "Businessman and Bureaucrat: The Evolution of the American Social Welfare System, 1900–1940." *Journal of Economic History* 38 (Mar. 1978): 120–41.

————. *Creating the Welfare State: The Political Economy of Twentieth-Century Reform.* New York: Praeger Publishers, 1980.

Bernstein, Irving. *The Lean Years: A History of the American Worker, 1920–1933.* Boston: Houghton Mifflin Co., 1960.

————. *The Turbulent Years: A History of the American Worker, 1933–1941.* Boston: Houghton Mifflin Co., 1971.

Binghamton Board of Trade. *Board of Trade Review of Binghamton, New York.* Binghamton, N.Y.: James P. McKinney, 1892.

Binghamton Chamber of Commerce. *The Valley of Opportunity Year Book 1920.* Binghamton, N.Y.: Charles W. Baldwin, 1920.

Biographical Review [Binghamton]. Boston: Biographical Review Publishing Co., 1894.

Blackford, Mansel G. "Scientific Management and Welfare Work in Early Twentieth Century American Business: The Buckeye Steel Castings Company." *Ohio History* 90 (Summer 1981): 238–58.

Blewett, Mary H. "The Union of Sex and Craft in the Haverhill Shoe Strike of 1895." *Labor History* 20 (Summer 1979): 352–75.

————. "Work, Gender and the Artisan Tradition in New England Shoemaking, 1780–1860." *Journal of Social History* 17 (Winter 1983): 221–48.

Bodnar, John. *Workers' World: Kinship, Community, and Protest in an Industrial Society, 1900–1940.* Baltimore: Johns Hopkins University Press, 1982.

Boettiger, Louis A. *Employee Welfare Work: A Critical and Historical Study.* New York: Ronald Press Co., 1923.

Boon, Gerard Karel. *Technology and Employment in Footwear Manufacturing.* Maryland: Sijthoff and Noordhoff, 1980.

Boot and Shoe Recorder. *The Shoe and Leather Lexicon.* 5th ed. Boston: Boot and Shoe Recorder Publishing Co., 1926.

Bragg, Ernest A. *The Origin and Growth of the Boot and Shoe Industry in Holliston Where It Began in 1793 and in Milford Massachusetts Where It Continued in 1795 and Remained into 1950.* Boston: Recording and Statistical Corp., 1950.

Brandes, Stuart D. *American Welfare Capitalism, 1880–1940.* Chicago: University of Chicago Press, 1976.

Braverman, Harry. *Labor and Monopoly Capital: The Degradation of Work in the Twentieth Century.* New York: Monthly Review Press, 1974.

Brecher, Jeremy. *Strike!* San Francisco: Straight Arrow Books, 1972.

Brecher, Jeremy, et al. "Uncovering the Hidden History of the American Workplace." *Review of Radical Political Economics* 10 (Winter 1978): 1–23.

Brissenden, Paul Frederick, and Emil Frankel. *Labor Turnover in Industry: A Statistical Analysis.* New York: Macmillan, 1922.

Brody, David. *The Butcher Workmen: A Study of Unionization.* Cambridge: Harvard University Press, 1964.

————. *Steelworkers in America: The Nonunion Era.* Cambridge: Harvard University Press, 1960.

————. *Workers in Industrial America: Essays on the Twentieth Century Struggle.* New York: Oxford University Press, 1980.

Broome County Chamber of Commerce. *Site Selection Information for Business and Industry.* Binghamton, N.Y.: Broome County Chamber of Commerce, [1978].

Broun, Heywood. "After Its Fashion." *Nation* 140 (July 10, 1935): 47–48.

Brown, Leo Cyril. *Union Policies in the Leather Industry.* Cambridge: Harvard University Press, 1947.

Buder, Stanley. *Pullman: An Experiment in Industrial Order and Community Planning, 1880–1930.* New York: Oxford University Press, 1967.

Buroway, Michael. *Manufacturing Consent: Changes in the Labor Process under Monopoly Capitalism.* Chicago: University of Chicago Press, 1979.

Burt, Edward Williard. *The Shoe-Craft: Its Organization.* Boston: Everett Press, 1917.

Carpenter, Niles. *Medical Care for 15,000 Workers and Their Families: A Survey of the Endicott Johnson Workers Medical Service, 1928.* Washington, D.C.: Committee on the Costs of Medical Care, 1930.

Catchings, Waddill. "Our Common Enterprise: A Way Out for Labor and Capital." *Atlantic Monthly* 129 (Feb. 1922): 218–29.

Chandler, Alfred D. *The Visible Hand: The Managerial Revolution in American Business.* Cambridge: Harvard University Press, 1977.

Cochran, Bert. *Labor and Communism: The Conflict That Shaped American Unions.* Princeton, N.J.: Princeton University Press, 1977.

Commons, John R. "American Shoemakers, 1648–1895: A Sketch of Industrial Evolution." *Quarterly Journal of Economics* 24 (Nov. 1909): 39–83.

Cumbler, John T. *Working-Class Community in Industrial America: Work, Leisure, and Struggle in Two Industrial Cities, 1880–1930.* Westport, Conn.: Greenwood Press, 1979.

Davenport, Frederick M. "The Path to Industrial Peace." *Outlook* 124 (Apr. 14, 1920): 644–50.

Davis, Horace B. *Shoes: The Workers and the Industry.* New York: International Publishers, 1940.

Dawley, Alan. *Class and Community: The Industrial Revolution in Lynn.* Cambridge: Harvard University Press, 1976.

Dawson, Nancy. " 'To Laugh, That We May Not Weep.' " *E.-J. Workers' Review* 2 (Nov. 1920): 36.

Derber, Milton. *The American Idea of Industrial Democracy, 1865–1965.* Urbana: University of Illinois Press, 1970.

Destler, Chester McArthur. *American Radicalism, 1865–1901.* Chicago: Quadrangle Books, 1966.

Douglas, Paul H. *Real Wages in the United States 1890–1926.* Boston: Houghton Mifflin Co., 1930.

Dubofsky, Melvyn. *Industrialism and the American Worker, 1865–1920.* Arlington Heights, Ill.: AHM Publishing Corp., 1975.

———. "Not So 'Turbulent Years': Another Look at the American 1930's." *Amerikastudien* 24 (1979): 5–20.

Duchaine, William J. "Industrial Recreation Here Embraces the Entire City." *Industrial Sports* 12 (Aug. 15, 1952): 27–28, 31.

Dulles, Foster Rhea. *Labor in America: A History.* New York: Thomas Y. Crowell Co., 1949.

Edwards, Richard. *Contested Terrain: The Transformation of the Workplace in the Twentieth Century.* New York: Basic Books, 1979.

Eilbert, Henry. "The Development of Personnel Management in the United States." *Business History Review* 33 (Autumn 1959): 345–64.

Endicott, Wendell. *Henry B. Endicott: A Brief Memoir of His Life and His Services to the State and Nation.* Boston: McGrath-Sherrill Press, 1921.

Endicott Johnson Corporation. *Partners All: A Pictorial Narrative of an Industrial Democracy.* Photographs by Russell C. Aikins. New York: Huntington Corp., 1938.

Epstein, Abraham. "Industrial Welfare Movement Sapping American Trade Unions." *New York Times Current History Magazine* 24 (July 1926): 516–22.

Essex Institute. *Life and Times in Shoe City: The Shoe Workers of Lynn, a Special Exhibition, 14 Sept. 1979–27 Jan. 1980.* Salem, Mass.: Essex Institute, 1979.

Faler, Paul G. *Mechanics and Manufacturers in the Early Industrial Revolution: Lynn, Massachusetts, 1780–1860.* Albany: State University of New York Press, 1981.

Feld, Rose C. "An Industrial Democrat Points the Way." *New York Times Magazine,* June 3, 1934, 6–7.

———. "Keep Close to Your Men!" *Trained Men* 5 (Nov.-Dec. 1925): 171–73, 191.

Fine, Sidney. *Laissez Faire and the General-Welfare State: A Study of Conflict in American Thought, 1865–1901.* Ann Arbor: University of Michigan Press, 1956.

Flexner, Jean Atherton. "Selling the Company." *New Republic* 38 (Apr. 9, 1924): 171–74.

Foner, Philip S. *The Fur and Leather Workers Union: A Story of Dramatic Struggles and Achievements.* Newark, N.J.: Nordan Press, 1950.

———. *History of the Labor Movement in the United States.* Vol. 2, *From the Founding of the A.F. of L. to the Emergence of American Imperialism.* 2d ed. New York: International Publishers, 1975.

"For George F." *Time* 35 (Jan. 22, 1940): 19.

Frail, Jennie A. *Historical Background of Johnson City.* N.p.: Privately printed, [1955].

Freeman, Joshua. "Delivering the Goods: Industrial Unionism during World War II." *Labor History* 19 (Fall 1978): 570–93.

Friedlander, Peter. *The Emergence of a UAW Local, 1936–1939: A Study in Class and Culture.* Pittsburgh: University of Pittsburgh Press, 1975.

Galenson, Walter. *The CIO Challenge to the AFL: A History of the American Labor Movement, 1935–1941.* Cambridge: Harvard University Press, 1960.

Galster, Augusta E. *The Labor Movement in the Shoe Industry, with Special Reference to Philadelphia.* New York: Ronald Press Co., 1934.

Garraty, John A. "The United States Steel Corporation versus Labor: The Early Years." *Labor History* 1 (Winter 1960): 3–38.

Gelber, Steven M. "Working at Playing: The Culture of the Workplace and the Rise of Baseball." *Journal of Social History* 16 (Summer 1983): 3–22.

Genovese, Eugene D. *Roll, Jordan, Roll: The World the Slaves Made.* New York: Pantheon, 1974.

Gibbons, James S. "Has George F. Johnson Found Key to Industrial Problems?" *Manufacturers' Journal* 16 (July 1937): 8–10.

Gilman, Nicholas Paine. *Profit Sharing between Employer and Employee: A Study in the Evolution of the Wages System.* Boston: Houghton, Mifflin and Co., 1893.

Gladden, Washington. *Working People and Their Employees*. Boston: Lockwood, Brooks, and Co., 1876.

Goodwyn, Lawrence. *The Democratic Promise: The Populist Moment in America*. New York: Oxford University Press, 1976.

Goodyear Tire and Rubber Company. *The Work of the Labor Division*. Akron, Ohio: Goodyear Tire and Rubber Co., 1920.

Gordon, David M., Richard Edwards, and Michael Reich. *Segmented Work, Divided Workers: The Historical Transformation of Labor in the United States*. New York: Cambridge University Press, 1982.

Green, James R. *The World of the Worker: Labor in Twentieth-Century America*. New York: Hill and Wang, 1980.

Grob, Gerald N. *Workers and Utopia: A Study of Ideological Conflict in the American Labor Movement, 1865–1900*. New York: Quadrangle Books, 1969.

Gutman, Herbert G. *Work, Culture & Society in Industrializing America*. New York: Random House, Vintage Books, 1977.

Haber, Samuel. *Efficiency and Uplift: Scientific Management in the Progressive Era, 1890–1920*. Chicago: University of Chicago Press, 1964.

Hacker, Louis, ed. *The Shaping of the American Tradition*. New York: Columbia University Press, 1947.

Hagedorn, Homer J. "A Note on the Motivation of Personnel Management: Industrial Welfare, 1885–1910." *Explorations in Entrepreneurial History* 10 (Apr. 1958): 134–39.

Hall, John P. "The Knights of St. Crispin in Massachusetts, 1869–1878." *Journal of Economic History* 18 (June 1958): 161–75.

Hansen, Harry L. *A Study of Competition and Management in the Shoe Manufacturing Industry*. N.p.: National Shoe Manufacturers Association, 1959.

Hareven, Tamara K. *Family Time and Industrial Time: The Relationship between the Family and Work in a New England Industrial Community*. New York: Cambridge University Press, 1982.

———, ed. *Family and Kin in Urban Communities, 1700–1930*. New York: New Viewpoints, 1977.

Hareven, Tamara K., and Randolph Langenbach. *Amoskeag: Life and Work in an American Factory-City*. New York: Pantheon Books, 1978.

Harris, Howell John. *The Right to Manage: Industrial Relations Policies of American Business in the 1940s*. Madison: University of Wisconsin Press, 1982.

Hawley, Ellis W. "The Discovery and Study of a 'Corporate Liberalism.'" *Business History Review* 52 (Autumn 1978): 309–20.

Hazard, Blanche Evans. *The Organization of the Boot and Shoe Industry in Massachusetts before 1875*. Cambridge: Harvard University Press, 1921.

Heald, Morrell. *The Social Responsibilities of Business: Company and Community, 1900–1960*. Cleveland: Press of Case Western Reserve University, 1970.

Helburn, I. B. "Trade Union Response to Profit-Sharing Plans: 1886–1966." *Labor History* 12 (Winter 1971): 68–80.

Henderson, Charles Richard. *Citizens in Industry*. New York: D. Appleton and Co., 1915.

Hobsbawm, E. J., and Joan Wallach Scott. "Political Shoemakers." *Past and Present* 89 (Nov. 1980): 86–114.

Hoopes, James. *Oral History: An Introduction for Students*. Chapel Hill: University of North Carolina Press, 1979.

Hoover, Edgar M., Jr. *Location Theory and the Shoe and Leather Industries*. Cambridge: Harvard University Press, 1937.

Hopkins, Charles Howard. *The Rise of the Social Gospel in American Protestantism, 1865–1915*. New Haven: Yale University Press, 1940.

Houser, J. David. *What the Employer Thinks: Executives' Attitudes toward Employees*. Cambridge: Harvard University Press, 1927.

Hurd, D. Hamilton, comp. *History of Middlesex County, Massachusetts*. Vol. 3. Philadelphia: J. W. Lewis and Co., 1890.

Ingalls, Robert P. *Herbert H. Lehman and New York's Little New Deal*. Foreword by George Meany. New York: New York University Press, 1975.

Inglis, William. *George F. Johnson and His Industrial Democracy*. New York: Huntington Press, 1935.

Iorizzo, Luciano J., and Salvatore Mondello. *The Italian-Americans*. New York: Twayne Publishers, 1971.

Isserman, Maurice. *Which Side Were You On? The American Communist Party during the Second World War*. Middletown, Conn.: Wesleyan University Press, 1982.

Ives, Edward D. *The Tape-Recorded Interview: A Manual for Field Workers in Folklore and Oral History*. Rev. and enlarged ed. Knoxville: University of Tennessee Press, 1980.

Jacoby, Sanford M. *Employing Bureaucracy: Managers, Unions, and the Transformation of Work in American Industry, 1900–1945*. New York: Columbia University Press, 1985.

Johnson, David N. *Sketches of Lynn; or, The Changes of Fifty Years*. Lynn, Mass.: Thos. P. Nichols, 1880.

Johnson City Sixtieth Anniversary Committee. *Frontiers: Johnson City's Sixtieth Anniversary, 1892–1952*. Johnson City, N.Y., 1952.

Kahler, Gerald E., and Alton C. Johnson. *The Development of Personnel Administration, 1923–1945*. Madison: Bureau of Business Research and Service, Graduate School of Business, University of Wisconsin, 1971.

Kampelman, Max M. *The Communist Party vs. the C.I.O.: A Study in Power Politics*. New York: Frederick A. Praeger, 1957.

Kasson, John F. *Civilizing the Machine: Technology and Republican Values in America, 1776–1900*. New York: Grossman, 1976.

Kaysen, Carl. *United States v. United Shoe Machinery Corporation: An Economic Analysis of an Anti-Trust Case*. Cambridge: Harvard University Press, 1956.

Kennedy, David H. *The Art of Tanning Leather*. New York: Baker and Godwin, 1857.

Kennedy, Susan Estabrook. *If All We Did Was to Weep at Home: A History of White Working-Class Women in America*. Bloomington: Indiana University Press, 1979.

Kessler-Harris, Alice. *Out to Work: A History of Wage-Earning Women in the United States*. New York: Oxford University Press, 1982.

Kessner, Thomas. *The Golden Door: Italian and Jewish Immigrant Mobility in New York City, 1880–1915*. New York: Oxford University Press, 1977.

King, Sheldon S. *Trolleys of the Triple Cities*. Elmira Heights, N.Y.: Author, 1977.

Kirkland, Edward Chase. *Dream and Thought in the Business Community, 1860–1900*. Chicago: Quadrangle Books, 1964.

————. *Industry Comes of Age: Business, Labor and Public Policy, 1860–1897.* Chicago: Quadrangle Books, 1961.

Korman, Gerd. *Industrialization, Immigrants, and Americanizers: A View from Milwaukee, 1866–1921.* Madison: University of Wisconsin Press, 1967.

Laidler, Harry W., and Norman Thomas, eds. League for Industrial Democracy Symposium on *New Tactics in Social Conflict.* New York: Vanguard Press, League for Industrial Democracy, 1926.

Laslett, John H. M. *Labor and the Left: A Study of Socialist and Radical Influences in the American Labor Movement, 1881–1924.* New York: Basic Books, 1970.

Lauck, W. Jett. *Political and Industrial Democracy, 1776–1926.* New York: Funk and Wagnalls Co., 1926.

Lawyer, William S., ed. *Binghamton: Its Settlement, Growth and Development and the Factors in Its History, 1880–1900.* Binghamton, N.Y.: Century Memorial Publishing Co., 1900.

Lescohier, Don D. *The Knights of St. Crispin, 1867–1874.* Bulletin of the University of Wisconsin, no. 355. Madison: University of Wisconsin, 1910.

Leuchtenburg, William E. *Franklin D. Roosevelt and the New Deal, 1932–1940.* New York: Harper and Row, 1963.

Levenstein, Harvey A. *Communism, Anticommunism, and the CIO.* Westport, Conn.: Greenwood Press, 1981.

Lewis, L. L. "Playing Fair with Employees." *Rotarian* 49 (Dec. 1936): 48–50.

Lichtenstein, Nelson. "Defending the No-Strike Pledge: CIO Politics during World War II." *Radical America* 9 (July-Aug. 1975): 49–75.

————. *Labor's War at Home: The CIO in World War II.* New York: Cambridge University Press, 1982.

Lindsey, Almont. *The Pullman Strike: The Story of a Unique Experiment and of a Great Labor Upheaval.* Chicago: University of Chicago Press, 1942.

Litchfield, Paul W. *The Industrial Republic: Reflections of an Industrial Lieutenant.* Cleveland: Corday and Gross Co., 1946.

Lubove, Roy. "Workmen's Compensation and the Prerogatives of Voluntarism." *Labor History* 8 (Fall 1967): 254–79.

Lynd, Alice, and Staughton Lynd, eds. *Rank and File: Personal Histories by Working-Class Organizers.* Princeton, N.J.: Princeton University Press, 1973.

Lynd, Robert S., and Helen Merrell Lynd. *Middletown: A Study in Modern American Culture.* New York: Harcourt, Brace and World, 1929.

————. *Middletown in Transition: A Study in Cultural Conflicts.* New York: Harcourt, Brace and World, 1937.

MacAlpine, Rev. William. *A Brief Memoir of Harry Leonard Johnson.* Johnson City, N.Y.: Privately printed, [1922].

McDonnell, Lawrence T. "'You Are Too Sentimental': Problems and Suggestions for a New Labor History." *Journal of Social History* 17 (Summer 1984): 629–54.

McGuire, Ross, and Nancy Grey Osterud. *Working Lives: Broome County, New York, 1800–1930, a Social History of People at Work in Our Region.* Binghamton, N.Y.: Roberson Center for the Arts and Sciences, 1980.

Mack, Ruth Prince. *Consumption and Business Fluctuations: A Case Study of the Shoe, Leather, Hide Sequence.* New York: National Bureau of Economic Research, 1956.

McKelvey, Blake. "A History of the Rochester Shoe Industry." *Rochester History* 15 (Apr. 1953): 1–28.

McQuaid, Kim. "Corporate Liberalism in the American Business Community." *Business History Review* 52 (Autumn 1978): 342–68.

Mahoney, Stephen. "What Happened at Endicott Johnson after the Band Stopped Playing." *Fortune* 66 (Sept. 1962): 127–31, 160, 170, 175–78.

Malone, Dumas, ed. *Dictionary of American Biography*. Vols. 6, 10, 14, 20. New York: Charles Scribner's Sons, 1933.

"Married Women in Industry." *Industrial Bulletin* [New York State Department of Labor] 7 (Nov. 1927): 45.

Marx, Leo. *The Machine in the Garden: Technology and the Pastoral Ideal in America*. New York: Oxford University Press, 1964.

Mathewson, Stanley B. *Restriction of Output among Unorganized Workers*. Carbondale: Southern Illinois University Press, 1931, 1969.

Mazar, Imrich, ed. *Dejiny binghamtonských slovákov za dobu štyridsat' rokov, 1879–1919*. [Forty years of the history of Binghamton Slovaks, 1879–1919]. Binghamton, N.Y.: Sbor 104, Slovenskej Ligy, 1919.

Meno, John Bedford. *The Art of Boot and Shoemaking: A Practical Handbook*. London: Crosby Lockwood and Co., 1887.

Meyer, Stephen, III. *The Five Dollar Day: Labor Management and Social Control in the Ford Motor Company, 1908–1921*. Albany: State University of New York Press, 1981.

Milford Historical Commission. *A History of Milford, Massachusetts, 1780–1980*. Milford, Mass.: Milford Historical Commission, 1980.

Montgomery, David. *Workers' Control in America: Studies in the History of Work, Technology, and Labor Struggles*. New York: Cambridge University Press, 1979.

Morgan, H. Wayne, ed. *The Gilded Age*. Rev. ed. Syracuse, N.Y.: Syracuse University Press, 1970.

Mortimer, George. "George F. Johnson and His 'Square-Deal Towns': The Story of a Big Manufacturer Who Has Interesting Ideas." *American Magazine* 91 (Jan. 1921): 36–37.

Mulligan, William H., Jr. "Mechanization of Work in the American Shoe Industry: Lynn, Massachusetts, 1852–1883." *Journal of Economic History* 41 (Mar. 1981): 59–63.

National Civic Federation. *Profit Sharing by American Employers*. New York: E. P. Dutton and Co., 1921.

National Industrial Conference Board. *Effect of the Depression on Industrial Relations Programs*. New York: National Industrial Conference Board, 1934.

———. *Industrial Relations: Administration of Policies and Programs*. New York: National Industrial Conference Board, 1931.

———. *Practical Experience with Profit Sharing in Industrial Establishments*. New York: National Industrial Conference Board, 1920.

———. *What Employers Are Doing for Employees: A Survey of Voluntary Activities for Improvement of Working Conditions in American Business Concerns*. New York: National Industrial Conference Board, 1936.

———. *The Workmen's Compensation Problem in New York State*. New York: National Industrial Conference Board, 1927.

Nelson, Daniel. *Frederick W. Taylor and the Rise of Scientific Management*. Madison: University of Wisconsin Press, 1980.

———. *Managers and Workers: Origins of the New Factory System in the United States, 1880–1920*. Madison: University of Wisconsin Press, 1975.

Nelson, Daniel, and Stuart Campbell. "Taylorism versus Welfare Work in American Industry: H. L. Gantt and the Bancrofts." *Business History Review* 46 (Spring 1972): 1–16.

Nevins, Allan. *Herbert H. Lehman and His Times*. New York: Charles Scribner's Sons, 1963.

"New Men to Match a New Line: Endicott Johnson Puts Best Foot Forward after Restyling Management, Merchandizing." *Business Week* 1681 (Nov. 18, 1961): 93–97.

Noble, David F. *America by Design: Science, Technology, and the Rise of Corporate Capitalism*. New York: Oxford University Press, 1979.

Norton, Thomas L. *Trade-Union Policies in the Massachusetts Shoe Industry, 1919–1929*. New York: Columbia University Press, 1932.

Odencrantz, Louise C. *Italian Women in Industry: A Study of Conditions in New York City*. New York: Russell Sage Foundation, 1919.

O'Neil, Daniel C. "The Endicott Johnson Medical Service." *Industrial Doctor* 1 (Oct. 1923): 167–70.

———. "A Plan of Medical Service for the Industrial Worker and His Family." *Journal of the American Medical Association* 91 (Nov. 17, 1928): 1516–19.

———. "Where Industrial Service Becomes Community Service." *Nation's Health* 6 (Jan. 15, 1924): 1–3, 60.

"Our Friend George F." *Time* 32 (Dec. 5, 1938): 12.

Ozanne, Robert. *A Century of Labor-Management Relations at McCormick and International Harvester*. Madison: University of Wisconsin Press, 1967.

"A Pair of Shoes." *Harper's New Monthly Magazine* 70 (Jan. 1885): 273–89.

Perlman, Selig. *A Theory of the Labor Movement*. New York: Macmillan, 1928.

Pollard, Sidney. "Factory Discipline in the Industrial Revolution." *Economic History Review* 16 (Dec. 1963): 254–71.

Portelli, Allessandro. "The Peculiarities of Oral History." *History Workshop* 12 (Autumn 1981): 96–107.

Powderly, Terence V. *Thirty Years of Labor, 1869 to 1889*. Columbus, Ohio: Excelsior Publishing House, 1890.

Price, Richard. "Theories of Labour Process Formation." *Journal of Social History* 18 (Fall 1984): 91–110.

Ramirez, Bruno. *When Workers Fight: The Politics of Industrial Relations in the Progressive Era, 1898–1916*. Westport, Conn.: Greenwood Press, 1978.

Raucher, Alan R. *Public Relations and Business, 1900–1929*. Baltimore: Johns Hopkins University Press, 1968.

Rayback, Joseph G. *A History of American Labor*. New York: Free Press, 1959.

Rich, George A. "Leather-Making." *Popular Science Monthly* 41 (July 1892): 339–64.

———. "Manufacture of Boots and Shoes." *Popular Science Monthly* 41 (Aug. 1892): 496–515.

Ripley, Charles M. *Life in a Large Manufacturing Plant*. Schenectady, N.Y.: General Electric Co. Publications Bureau, 1919.

Robinson, Charles Mulford. *Better Binghamton: A Report to the Mercantile-Press Club of Binghamton, N.Y.* Cleveland: J. B. Savage Co., 1911.

Rodgers, William. *Think: A Biography of the Watsons and IBM.* New York: Stein and Day, 1969.

Roethlisberger, Fritz J. "The Foreman: Master and Victim of Double Talk." *Harvard Business Review* 23 (Spring 1945): 283–98.

Rosenzweig, Roy. *Eight Hours for What We Will: Workers and Leisure in an Industrial City, 1870–1920.* New York: Cambridge University Press, 1983.

Roy, Donald. "Efficiency and 'The Fix': Informal Intergroup Relations in a Piecework Machine Shop." *American Journal of Sociology* 60 (Nov. 1954): 255–66.

Rubin, Jay. "The Ku Klux Klan in Binghamton, New York, 1923–1928." *Bulletin of the Broome County Historical Society* 20 (Winter 1973): 1–59.

Saposs, David J. *Communism in American Unions.* New York: McGraw-Hill, 1959.

Schatz, Ronald. *The Electrical Workers: A History of Labor at General Electric and Westinghouse, 1923–60.* Urbana: University of Illinois Press, 1983.

———. "Union Pioneers: The Founders of Local Unions in General Electric and Westinghouse, 1933–1937." *Journal of American History* 66 (Dec. 1979): 586–602.

Schleppi, John R. "'It Pays': John H. Patterson and Industrial Recreation at the National Cash Register Company." *Journal of Sport History* 6 (Winter 1979): 20–28.

Scott, Joan Wallach. *The Glassworkers of Carmaux: French Craftsmen and Political Action in a Nineteenth-Century City.* Cambridge: Harvard University Press, 1974.

Scranton, Philip. "Varieties of Paternalism: Industrial Structures and the Social Relations of Production in American Textiles." *American Quarterly* 36 (Summer 1984): 235–57.

Seidman, Joel Isaac. *American Labor from Defense to Reconversion.* Chicago: University of Chicago Press, 1953.

Sennett, Richard. *Authority.* New York: Alfred A. Knopf, 1980.

Seward, William Foote, ed. *Binghamton and Broome County New York: A History.* 3 vols. New York: Lewis Historical Publishing Co., 1924.

Shultz, George P. *Pressures on Wage Decisions: A Case Study in the Shoe Industry.* New York: Technology Press of MIT, John Wiley and Sons, 1951.

Slichter, Sumner H. "The Current Labor Policies of American Industries." *Quarterly Journal of Economics* 43 (May 1929): 393–435.

———. *The Turnover of Factory Labor.* New York: D. Appleton and Co., 1921.

Smith, G. Ralph. *The Endicott Johnson Corporation.* New Orleans: Faculty Committee on Research, College of Business Administration, Loyola University, 1956.

Smith, H. P., ed. *History of Broome County.* Syracuse, N.Y.: D. Mason and Co., 1885.

"The 'Square Deal': Johnson's Labor Principles Rout A.F.L. and C.I.O." *Newsweek* 15 (Jan. 22, 1940): 48.

Stolarik, M. Mark. "From Field to Factory: The Historiography of Slovak Immigration to the United States." *Slovakia* 28 (1978–79): 66–89.

Stone, Katherine. "The Origins of Job Structures in the Steel Industry." *Review of Radical Political Economics* 6 (Summer 1974): 113–73.

Tarbell, Ida M. *New Ideals in Business: An Account of Their Practice and Their Effects upon Men and Profits.* New York: Macmillan, 1917.

Tentler, Leslie Woodcock. *Wage-Earning Women: Industrial Work and Family Life in the United States, 1900–1930*. New York: Oxford University Press, 1979.

Thernstrom, Stephan. *Poverty and Progress: Social Mobility in a Nineteenth Century City*. Cambridge: Harvard University Press, 1964.

Thompson, Edward P. "Time, Work-Discipline, and Industrial Capitalism." *Past and Present* 38 (Dec. 1967): 56–97.

Thompson, Paul Richard. *The Voice of the Past: Oral History*. New York: Oxford University Press, 1978.

Tolman, William H. *Social Engineering: A Record of Things Done by American Industrialists Employing Upwards of One and One-Half Million of People*. New York: McGraw-Hill, 1909.

Tracy, Lena Harvey. *How My Heart Sang: The Story of Pioneer Industrial Welfare Work*. New York: Richard R. Smith, 1950.

United Shoe Machinery Company. *The Story of Three Partners*. Beverly, Mass.: United Shoe Machinery Co., [1912].

Veblen, Thorstein. *The Theory of the Leisure Class: An Economic Study of Institutions*. New York: New American Library, Mentor Editions, 1953.

Wall, Joseph Frazier. *Andrew Carnegie*. New York: Oxford University Press, 1970.

Wandersee, Winifred D. *Women's Work and Family Values, 1920–1940*. Cambridge: Harvard University Press, 1981.

Ware, Norman J. *The Industrial Worker, 1840–1860: The Reaction of American Industrial Society to the Advance of the Industrial Revolution*. Boston: Houghton Mifflin Co., 1924.

———. *The Labor Movement in the United States, 1860–1895: A Study in Democracy*. New York: D. Appleton and Co., 1929.

"Warn Endicott Labor." *Business Week* 479 (Nov. 5, 1938): 35.

Warner, W. Lloyd, and Josiah O. Low. *The Social System of the Modern Factory, the Strike: A Social Analysis*. Vol. 4, *Yankee City Series*. 1947. Reprint. Westport, Conn.: Greenwood Press, 1976.

Weinstein, James. *The Corporate Ideal in the Liberal State, 1900–1918*. Boston: Beacon Press, 1968.

Weisenberg, Mina. "Labor's Defense against Employers' Welfare Tactics." *New York Times Current History Magazine* 25 (Mar. 1927): 803–8.

Wesser, Robert F. "Conflict and Compromise: The Workmen's Compensation Movement in New York, 1890s–1913." *Labor History* 12 (Summer 1971): 345–72.

White, Eli G. *The Awakening of a Company: The Story of Endicott Johnson Corporation*. New York: Newcomen Society of North America, 1967.

Wood, Norman J. "Industrial Relations Policies of American Management, 1900–1933." *Business History Review* 34 (Winter 1960): 403–20.

Wray, Donald E. "Marginal Men of Industry: The Foremen." *American Journal of Sociology* 54 (Jan. 1949): 298–301.

Wyllie, Irvin G. *The Self-Made Man in America: The Myth of Rags to Riches*. New York: Free Press, 1966.

Yans-McLaughlin, Virginia. *Family and Community: Italian Immigrants in Buffalo, 1880–1930*. Ithaca, N.Y.: Cornell University Press, 1977.

Yellowitz, Irwin. *Industrialization and the American Labor Movement, 1850–1900*. Port Washington, N.Y.: Kennikat Press, 1977.

————. "Skilled Workers and Mechanization: The Lasters in the 1890s." *Labor History* 18 (Spring 1977): 197–213.

Young, Doreen. "Henry Bradford Endicott." *Courier Magazine* 2 (Dec. 1953): 16–18, 33.

Zeitlin, Maurice, ed. *Political Power and Social Theory: A Research Annual.* Vol. 4. Greenwich, Conn.: JAI Press, 1984.

VII. Dissertations, Theses, and Unpublished Works

Bley, Barry H. "The Endicott Johnson Corporation." Research paper, Columbia University, [1963]. [On file at the George F. Johnson Memorial Library, Endicott, N.Y.]

Burns, William Patrick. "A Study of Personnel Policies, Employee Opinion and Labor Turnover (1930–1946) at the Endicott Johnson Corporation." Master's thesis, New York State School of Industrial and Labor Relations, Cornell University, 1947.

Hall, John Philip. "The Gentle Craft: A Narrative of Yankee Shoemakers." Ph.D. diss., Columbia University, 1954.

Kelly, Dennis P. "The Contrasting Industrial Structures of Johnstown, Pa., and Binghamton, N.Y., 1850–1880." Ph.D. diss., University of Pittsburgh, 1977.

Lieberman, Steve. "IBM and E-J: How through Liberal Benefits and a Prudent Use of the Local Newspapers They Kept the Unions Out." Research paper, State University of New York at Binghamton, 1972. [On file at the Broome County Historical Society Library]

Miller, Alice. "Binghamton's Good Women—1890 to 1917." Research paper, State University of New York at Binghamton, 1980. [In possession of Prof. Sarah Elbert, State University of New York at Binghamton]

Millus, Albert J., Jr. "The Shoe Company of La Mancha: Endicott Johnson Corporation." Research paper, New York State School of Industrial and Labor Relations, Cornell University, 1977. [On file at the Broome County Historical Society Library, Roberson Center for the Arts and Sciences, Binghamton, N.Y.]

Pines, Jeffrey. "Endicott, New York: Industry, Immigrants & Paternalism." Honors thesis, Department of History, State University of New York at Binghamton, 1982.

Polf, William. "George F. Johnson and His Welfare Capitalism." Research paper, Syracuse University, 1970. [On file in box 36, George F. Johnson Papers, George Arents Research Library]

Saul, Richard S. "An American Entrepreneur: George F. Johnson." D.S.S. diss., Syracuse University, 1966.

Scheinberg, Stephen J. "The Development of Corporation Labor Policy, 1900–1940." Ph.D. diss., University of Wisconsin, 1967.

Shear, William Wilson. "Industrial Relations in the Endicott Johnson Corporation: A Case Study of Welfare Capitalism in the 1920s." Master's thesis, State University of New York at Binghamton, 1978.

Smith, G. Ralph. "Aspects of Economic Development of Broome County, New York, 1900–1951." Ph.D. diss., Syracuse University, 1954.

Walikis, John. "An Analysis of Slovak Women in the Endicott-Johnson Shoe Corporation in the Southern Tier." Research paper, State University of New York at Binghamton, 1974. [Broome County Historical Society Library]

Zahavi, Gerald. "Workers, Managers, and Welfare Capitalism: The Shoeworkers and Tanners of Endicott Johnson, 1880–1950." Ph.D. diss., Syracuse University, 1983.

Index

Books in the Series
The Working Class in American History

Worker City, Company Town:
Iron and Cotton-Worker Protest in Troy
and Cohoes, New York, 1855-84
Daniel J. Walkowitz

Life, Work, and Rebellion in the Coal Fields:
The Southern West Virginia Miners, 1880-1922
David Alan Corbin

Women and American Socialism, 1870-1920
Mari Jo Buhle

Lives of Their Own:
Blacks, Italians, and Poles in Pittsburgh, 1900-1960
John Bodnar, Roger Simon, and Michael P. Weber

Working-Class America:
Essays on Labor, Community, and American Society
Edited by Michael H. Frisch and Daniel J. Walkowitz

Eugene V. Debs: Citizen and Socialist
Nick Salvatore

American Labor and Immigration History, 1877-1920s:
Recent European Research
Edited by Dirk Hoerder

Workingmen's Democracy:
The Knights of Labor and American Politics
Leon Fink

The Electrical Workers:
A History of Labor at General Electric
and Westinghouse, 1923-60
Ronald W. Schatz

The Mechanics of Baltimore:
Workers and Politics in the Age of Revolution, 1763-1812
Charles G. Steffen

The Practice of Solidarity:
American Hat Finishers in the Nineteenth Century
David Bensman

The Labor History Reader
Edited by Daniel J. Leab

Solidarity and Fragmentation:
Working People and Class Consciousness in Detroit, 1875-1900
Richard Oestreicher

Heritage University Library
3240 Fort Road
Toppenish, WA 98948